The Garth Countryside

part of
CARDIFF'S GREEN MANTLE

A Natural History

by MARY E. GILLHAM

A Stop Gap in an old Pleached Hedge

OTHER WORKS BY THE AUTHOR:

INSTRUCTIONS TO YOUNG ORNITHOLOGISTS, IV. SEA BIRDS
Brompton Library Series, Museum Press, London, 1963

•

A NATURALIST IN NEW ZEALAND
Museum Press, London, and Reeds, New Zealand, 1966

•

SUB-ANTARCTIC SANCTUARY: SUMMERTIME ON MACQUARIE ISLAND
Victor Gollancx, London and Reeds, New Zealand, 1967

•

THE NATURAL HISTORY OF GOWER. First and second editions
D. Brown & Sons, Cowbridge, Glamorgan, 1977 and 1979

•

SWANSEA BAY'S GREEN MANTLE
D. Brown & Sons, Cowbridge, Glamorgan, 1982

•

THE GLAMORGAN HERITAGE COAST WILDLIFE SERIES:

Volume 1. SAND DUNES, Heritage Coast Committee, Bridgend, 1987

Volume 2. RIVERS. Heritage Coast Committee, Bridgend, 1989

Volume 3. LIMESTONE DOWNS. Glamorgan Wildlife Trust, Bridgend, 1991

Volume 4. COASTAL DOWNS. Glamorgan Wildlife Trust, Bridgend, 1993

Volume 5, CLIFFS AND BEACHES. Glamorgan Wildlife Trust, Bridgend, 1994

•

TOWN BRED, COUNTRY NURTURED. A Naturalist looks back fifty years
Gillham, Cardiff, 1998

•

ISLANDS OF THE TRADE WINDS. An Indian Ocean Odyssey
Minerva, Press Ltd., London, 2000

WITH OTHER AUTHORS

THE FLORA OF A CHANGING BRITAIN
Botanical Society of the British Isles, Middlesex, 1970

•

EVERYMAN'S MATURE RESERVE: IDEAS FOR ACTION
Devon Trust for Nature Conservation, David and Charles, Devon, 1972

•

A GUIDE TO THE HISTORIC TAFF VALLEY: SOUTH WALES, Volumes 1, 2 and 3
Merthyr Tydfil & District Naturalists' Society, 1979, 1982 and 1986

•

MERTHYR TYDFIL: A VALLEY COMMUNITY
Merthyr Teachers' Centre Group, D, Brown & Son, Cowbridge, 1982

•

DISCOVERING THE COUNTRYSIDE WITH DAVID BELLAMY: COASTAL WALKS
Hamlyn, London, 1982

CONTENTS
Page

LIST OF ILLUSTRATIONS & PHOTOGRAPHS	vi
PREFACE	xiii
INTRODUCTION	xiv
THE SETTING	1

1. THE GREAT GARTH: UPLAND HEATH AND ACID WOOD

Introductory	5
1. Panorama from the Mountain Top	7
2. Old Drift Mines	12
3. Water Supply and Shifting Population	14
4. Open Commonlands, Fields and Quagmires	16
5. Regenerating Oakwoods of the Mountain Skirts	19
6. Conifers on old Woodland Sites	23

2. COED-Y-BEDW NATURE RESERVE: HISTORY, VEGETATION AND STREAM LIFE

Introductory	27
1. Status, Geology, Mining and Myths	28
2. Woodland History and Management	32
3. Flowers and Fungi	35
4. Tufa Streams and smaller Water Life	38
5. Fish and Frogs	43

3. COED-Y-BEDW NATURE RESERVE: MORE ANIMAL LIFE

1. Mammals	46
2. Birds	48
3. Nest Boxes and Ringing Recoveries	50
4. Insects: the more obvious Species	54
5. Beetles, Bugs and Others	56

4. THE UNDERGROUND WORLD OF THE LITTLE GARTH

Introductory	60
1. Rock Formations and Cave Dwellers	62
2. Cave Formations and Invertebrate Life	64
3. Early Iron Mining	72
4. The Iron Mines in Modern Times	76

	Page
5. THE DAYLIGHT WORLD OF THE LITTLE GARTH	
1. Modern Quarrying	80
2. Nature moves back into the Working Quarry	85
3. Rehabilitation of the old Ty Nant Quarry	89
4. Plants of the Little Garth Beechwood	93
5. Fauna of the Little Garth Beechwood	98
6. CREIGIAU: DISUSED MINES AND RAILWAYS OF THE WEST	
Introductory	104
1. From Mines to Mammals in the Tyn-y-Coed Woods	105
2. Railway Routes and Creigiau Station	109
3. Old Passenger Line to the North	113
4. Old Mineral Line to the North	116
5. Old Passenger Line to the South	119
6. The Swallowing up of the Old Mineral Line to the South	123
7. CREIGIAU FARMS, PONDS AND QUARRY	
Introductory	129
1. Craig-yr-arfau: Cromlech, Farm and Pond	130
2. Castell-y-Mynach Frog Pond	135
3. The Playing Field Complex	139
4. Creigiau Quarry: History and Working	141
5. Creigiau Quarry: A Decade of Reprieve	145
8. PENTYRCH'S SOUTHERN SLOPES	
Introductory	149
1. Craig-y-Parc Woods	150
2, Old Pack Horse Road and the Llwynda-ddu Iron Age Fort	156
3. Coed Cae and Pant-tawel Woods	161
4. Permanent and Seasonal Pools	165
5. Loop Walk South of Garth Woods	168

	Page

9. GWAELOD-Y-GARTH ON THE WESTERN FLANK OF THE TAFF VALLEY

Introductory	175
1. The River Flats Downstream	177
2. The Greening of the Old Iron Works	189
3. Woodland swallows the Riverside Drift Mines	198
4. Power Station Fly Ash on Ynys Gau Farm	204
5. North to Gedrys Wood and Rhyd-yr-Helig Colliery at Maesbach	210

10. THE RIVER TAFF

Introductory	220
1. Physical Features of the River: Ferries, Fords and Spa	222
2. Flash Floods on the River Taff	229
3. Water Quality: Fisheries and Other River Life	237
4. Otters, Mink and Riverside Birds	244
5. Plant Colonisation of Boulder Revetments and Coal Dust Beaches	254

11. ANIMAL LIFE AT GWAELOD-Y-GARTH

Introductory	264
1. Mammals	264
2. Reptiles and Amphibians	271
3. Garden Birds	276
4. Other Birds	284
5. Invertebrate Life	296

12. SEASONAL WILDSCAPE VIEWING

1. Winter Wildlife	308
2. The Flavour of Winters in the Nineteen nineties	316
3. From Verdant Spring to Summer Drought	323
4. The Last of the Summer Wine	326
5. Weather Patterns for the New Millennium	331

APPENDIX LIST OF PLANTS. ALPHABETICALLY UNDER ENGLISH NAMES 335

ACKNOWLEDGEMENTS 347

Illustrations and Monochrome photographs

ILLUSTRATIONS   Page

Frontis. Stop gap in old pleached hedge
          Administrative areas around the Taff Gorge, 1974-1994 xvi
          Solid Geology around the Taff Gorge   3
          Drift Geology around the Taff Gorge   4

Chap.1.   Contour Map of land west of the Taff Gorge   6
          The Great Garth Common: Geology and Vegetation   9
          Painted Lady and Red Admiral Butterflies   10
          Skylark and Sheep's-bit   12
          Yellow Archangel and Green Alkanet   15
          Ivy-leaved Bellflower   17
          Cornish Moneywort   17
          Acid Titbits: Wood Sorrel, Common Sorrel and Sheep's Sorrel   20
          Sitka Spruce, Norway Spruce and Lodgepole Pine   24

Ch.2.   Geology of Coed-y-Bedw Valley   29
          Map of Coed-y-Bedw Nature Reserve   31
          Small Woodland Fungi   32
          Large Woodland Fungi   36
          Frogspawn Alga   39
          Parasitic Wasp   41
          Net-spinning Caddis, Tube-building Caddis
          parasitised by Ichneumon Wasp, and Flatworm   42
          Apparatus for Electric Fishing   43
          Brook Trout   44

Ch.3.   Pied Flycatchers   48
          Redstart   51
          Giant Lacewings   55
          Thick-legged Flower Beetle   57
          Leaf Hoppers   58
          Rare Wood Louse   59

Ch.4.   Wild Arum   61
          Cave Cranefly   65
          White Cave Spider and Rounded Snail   67
          Two Meta Cave Spiders   68
          Herald Moth and Tissue Moth   69
          Dozy Dung Fly   70
          Web-spinning Gnat   71

Ch.5.   Tufa deposited on Stream bed   83
          Beech Catkins and Nuts   85
          Soil Lichens   89
          Tremiscus Jelly Fungus   90
          Sweet Chestnut Burrs   91
          Columbine, Sweet Woodruff, Yellow Bird's-nest and Bistort   94
          Broad-leaved Helleborine and Bird's-nest Orchid   97
          Guelder Rose, Spindle and Dog Rose Fruits   100

Ch.6   Creigiau: Solid Geology Map   106
          Creigiau: Contours and Railway Map   107
          Red Bartsia and Wild Basil   111
          Common Blue Butterfly on Bird's-foot Trefoil   114
          Spotted Flycatchers   117

	Willow Warblers and Sloes	121
	Galled Jointed Rush	124
	Pond Skater	125
	Water Vole	127
	Neolithic Cromlech, Caer-yr-arfau	131
	Caer-yr-arfau Farmhouse, now demolished	131
	Mare's tail at Caer-yr-arfau	132
Ch.7.	Tripartite and Nodding Bur Marigold	134
	Castell-y-Mynach Farmhouse	135
	Great Pond Snails in Creigiau Pond	136
	Broad-leaved Pondweed	138
	Rue-leaved Saxifrage	144
	Spring Whitlow grass	145
	Bristol Fach, now demolished	147
Ch.8.	Field Maple	152
	Hornbeam. in March, May and August	153
	Wood Anemone and Goldilocks Buttercup	155
	Reed Bunting and Grey Sallow	158
	Geology Map of the Southern Slopes	160
	Shaggy Inkcaps	162
	Foxes by old pleached Hedgerow Tree	165
	Foxglove	167
Ch.9.	Contour Map of the Taff Valley at Gwaelod-y-Garth	178
	A Hawkweed: *Hieracium exotericum. f. grandidens*	182
	Japanese Larch, Hybrid Larch and Western Hemlock	186
	Short-tailed Field Voles	190
	Map of Old Mines and Railways at Gwaelod-y-Garth	192
	Grey Squirrel on a Reconstruction of the old Pentyrch Light Railway	196
	Lesser Spearwort and Creeping Buttercup	199
	Ynys Gau Railway Bridge	200
	Evening Primrose and Rosebay Willow Herb	202
	Moles in Clover	207
	Rabbits, Dandelion and Ribwort	208
	Engine House and Coke Ovens, Rhyd-yr-Helig, Maesbach	213
	Engine House, Rhyd-yr-Helig Colliery	215
	Wormwood and Mugwort	216
Ch.10.		
	Hemlock Water Dropwort ripped out by Floods	231
	Life History of the Eel	238
	Chaetagaster and Tubificid Warms, Helobdella Leech and	
	Chironomid Midge Larvae	239
	Cock Salmon	241
	Stream Crowfoot	244
	Otter	245
	Mink	247
	Goosanders	248
	Moorhens	249
	Dippers	251
	Coal Measure Fossils in Pennant Sandstone Revetments	254
	Knot Grass, Water Pepper, Pale Persicaria and Black Bindweed	256
	Mallard 261	
Ch.11.	Hedgehogs	266
	Pipistrelle Bats, Stoat and Weasel	268
	Young Grass Snake and Toad	271

	Frog and Winter Leaves of Lesser Spearwort	274
	Blue Tit Family and Dog Rose Hips	280
	Sun-bathing Blackbird and Hop Trefoil	278
	Grey Wagtail and Moorland Water Crowfoot	289
	Ash Keys and Autumn Influx of Fieldfares	293
	Peacock Butterfly with Buddleja	296
	Red Admiral and Comma Butterflies with Gwaelod Strawberry Tree	297
	Willow Beauty and Little Emerald Moth Caterpillars on Birch	300
	Solomon's Seal Sawfly Caterpillars	300
	Greater Bee Fly	303
	Cockchafers or Maybugs	304
	Water Cricket and Mayfly	305
Ch.12.	Winter Heliotrope in December and March	313
	Stinkhorn and 'egg', Norway Spruce Cones nibbled by Squirrels	315
	White Poplar Catkins	316
	Ground Ivy, Coltsfoot and Wild Arum	317
	Spring Hares and Daffodils	318
	Lesser Cudweed	324
	Wall Speedwell	327
	Edible Morel, Caterpillar Club, Coral Fungus and Field Mushroom	330
	Clitocybe nebularis, *Galerinia rubiginosa* and *Mycena galericulata*	331
	Candle Snuff, Gum Drops and Dead Man's Fingers	335

MONOCHROME PHOTOGRAPHS

Ch.1	A corner of the plaque erected on the Garth summit by Pentyrch History Society in 1999.	26
Ch.2	Paths through the Coed-y-Bedw Nature Reserve were much improved by the end of the millennium.	45
	"Coed y Bedw" means "Wood of Birches", Patriarches become mossy with age.	45
Ch.4	View to the north through the Taff Gorge showing the river, road, and rail routes, and the old viaduct spanning the gorge with Little Garth	73
	Some fine calcite crystals on a chunk of dolomite found in Nant Llwydrew.	79
Ch.5.	A corner of Walnut Tree Quarry in December 1984, with view over coastal plain.	82
	Wild Solomon's Seal in the beechwood east of the Taff Gorge.	86
	Hedgerow Honeysuckle	103
Ch.7.	Castell-y-Mynach old farmhouse (front)	139
	Castell-y-Mynach old farmhouse (rear)	139
	The old railway lines through Creigiau now serving as footpaths.	142

Ch.8.	Looking down on Pentyrch village from west end of the Great Garth.	150
	View east to Castell Coch from Cwm Farm, Morganstown.	170
	Western gorse branches freely when not constantly nibbled by sheep.	172
	Ruins of Ysgubor Fawr on morainic mounds south of the Little Garth.	174
Ch.9.	Pen and wash drawing of Gelynys farm.	180
	Old Station House, under the old Ty Nant quarry.	184
	Excavating new sewer on the west bank of the Taff at Gelynys.	188
	Iron Bridge where Pentyrch line crossed the Taff, south of the Gorge.	197
	Tongwynlais Village drowses beneath Castell Coch. View north	219
Ch.10.	Last of the Pentyrch Iron Works. The old Engine Shed.	221
	Construction of the covered reservoir above Tongwynlais. View north through Taff Gorge	228
	New & old Ynys Bridges from the crushing plant on the Little Garth.	224
	The Taff returns to rural tranquillity below the Gorge.	257
Ch.11.	Baled Hay on glacial mounds north of Gwaelod-y-Garth	284
	Ynys Gau hay barn with Mynydd Meio behind.	287
	Cattle by the Ynys Gau farm bridge over the Taff Vale railway.	307
	Renovations at Ynys Gau farmyard. July 1999.	307
Ch.12.	The Ynys Gau toboggan slope in the late 1970s.	310
	Frozen Aquifers in the Taff Gorge. February 1998	312
	Orange Fairy Club, *Clavaria helvola*.	322
	Yellow Waxcaps, *Hygrocybe chlorophanus*.	323
	Board Walk constructed by the Welsh Guards. Coed-y-Bedw reserve	334

The author and the publishers are indebted to the National Museums & Galleries of Wales, Department of Industry, for permission to reproduce the aerial view of the old viaduct spanning Taff Gorge (from the Tempest collection), see Ch. 4, p.73

Colour Photographs

1. Bronze Age Tumulus with Trig Point on the summit of the Great Garth. 1999
2. Eastern flank of the Great Garth from the Taff Flood Plain. 1999.
3. Garth Mountain from the east. Pentyrch on left flank, Gwaelod on right flank, and Taffs Well in front.
4. Garth Mountain, east flank after felling of conifers in the 1990s.
5. Foxgloves, Garth east flank after tree felling. View north to Gedrys.
6. Rushy 'unimproved' paddock in the Coed-y-Bedw Valley, August 1999
7. Giant Horsetail
8. Pheasant Chick
9. Improved ryegrass paddock in the Coed-y-Bedw Valley, June 1982. The wooded hollow is an old mine entrance.
10. Lesser Celandine
11. Wood Sorrel
12. Wild apple trees as well as crabapples spring up on the hillsides
13. Damsons on suckered sapling from a derelict cottage garden on the east flank of the Garth
14. Footbridge in the north-west of the Coed-y-Bedw Nature Reserve. April 1995
15. Swallowtail Moth
16. Hedgehog
17. Dry Hedgehog skin showing white knobs at inner edge of spines holding them in place
18. Walnut Tree Quarry in the Little Garth, December 1984. Trees on left brink mark the narrow ridge between this and the old Ty Nant Quarry.
19. Wood Spurge on quarry brink
20. Walnut Tree Quarry: lime-burning plant and western pillars of the Barry Railway viaduct. May 1971.
21. Ramsons or Wild Garlic
22. Maytime sward of Ramsons under Beeches on the limestone of the South Border Ridge
23. Sylvan path through the Little Garth Beechwood
24. Wild Arum, Cuckoo-pint, Lords-and-ladies or Jack-in-the-pulpit
25. *Cepaea* Hedge Snails by the rock 'anvil' of a Song Thrush, showing the predominance of shells matching the red soil of the Little Garth Dolomite
26. Red Cardinal Beetle
27. Green Tiger Beetle
28. Greater Bee-fly

PLANTS OF THE BEECHWOOD RIDES AUGUST 1999
29. Rosebay Willow-herb and Hemp Agrimony
30. Greater Willow-herb or Codlins-and-cream
31. Creigiau Farm from Quarry entrance. View to Caerau Hill near Llantrisant
32. Creeping St. John's Wort
33. Bistort
34. Creigiau Tennis Courts and Allotments on the newer, softer Lias Limestone rocks beside the Carboniferous Limestone quarry
CREIGIAU FROG POND
35. Yellow Iris flowers
36. Yellow Iris fruits flopped onto massed, submerged Curled Pondweed
37. Five Moorhens and Greater Spearwort, July 1999
38. Saprophytic Bird's-nest Orchid
39. A splendid burl on a Creigiau Elm, September 1962. Valuable for veneers
40. Broad Helleborine Orchid
41. Old Ton Mawr Quarry to the west of Walnut Tree Quarry which can be seen on the skyline. 1998
42. View from Pentyrch (the top of Heol Goch) to Garth Mountain (left) and Graig yr Allt. May 1969
43. View north from Garth summit. Efail Isaf left, Church Village right. August 1999
44, 45, 46 and 47. Four of the ponds on the undulating Glacial Drift between the Little Garth and Morganstown, December, 1982. Tree-bordered ones are permanent. The others drain away in summer. Note the drowned fence and hedge
48. Gelynys Barn and the old Ty Nant Quarry on Little Garth. August 1999
9. Gelynys Barn and working Walnut Tree Quarry on the Little Garth. August 1999
50. Taffs Well Viaduct from Castell. Coch in the 1960s. Walnut Tree Quarry left, Garth Mountain right
51. Iron Bridge and Castell Coch from the Motorway Bridge over the Taff. January 1985
ROAD WORKS IN THE TAFF GORGE. 1971
52. The new Ynys Bridge under Little Garth Quarry, February
53. The new Roundabout and A 470 under Castell Coch, November
54. View south through the Taff Gorge over Taffs Well from Graig-yr-Allt. February 1971
55. View south through the Taff Gorge over Heol Beri and the Pig Farm. October 1971 before the building of the River Glade and South Glade housing estates

56. Taff Vale Railway Bridge over the Taff from the Ffygis Frog Spawning Pond, February 1984

57. T V R Bridge over the Taff from the Pont Sion Phillips Footbridge in the July 1999 drought

58. The old main road, Cardiff to Merthyr, winds north from Gwaelod under the east face of the Garth Mountain, 1999

THE ROLLING COUNTRY OF THE END MORAINES WHERE THE TAFF GLACIER MELTED AND DUMPED ITS LOAD ON YNYS GAU UNDER THE GARTH MOUNTAIN

59. Winter snow fall, January 1982, looking towards Graig-yr-Allt

60. Summer haytime, July 1999, looking towards the Little Garth

61. Gwaelod Main Road passes north through Ynys Gau Farm towards Mynydd Meio, April 1995

62. Young burrs on 430 year old Sweet Chestnut Tree at Gelynys Farm. August 1999

63. Yellow Toadflax and Rosebay Willow-herb by the T V R line over Ynys Gau. July 1965

64. Common Toad

65. Hart's Tongue Fern, anomalously forked

66. Yew Seeds nibbled by small Rodent or Grey Squirrel

67. Short-tailed Field Vole

68. Greater Bird's-foot Trefoil

69. Soapwort on the Taff revetments

70. Tall Centaury in long grass

71. Tormentil on acid grass heath

72. The walk to Ynys Gau cow byre for milk, when Gwaelod was 'cut off. January 1982

73. Near the bottom of Mountain Road, Gwaelod-y-Garth. December 1967

PREFACE

This book aims to suit the tastes of both layman and. expert. It embraces something of human history, as far as this can be traced on the ground, as well as the main theme - of natural history, set in its geographical context of hill and valley, with special reference to the main artery of the.River Taff.

It is a countryside study, written in the relaxed style of traditional naturalists such as Kenneth Alsopp, to whom the Steepholm Island Nature Reserve is dedicated, without detracting from scientific accuracy.

Regions are dealt with on a factual basis, laced with anecdotal material where appropriate, and tinged with the pleasure that can be derived from spells of quiet watching.

Scientific names are not used for mammals, birds or common plants except where confusion could arise with more obscure species or because of a duplication of popular names, and for Invertebrates other than butterflies, Flowering plants and ferns mentioned in the text are listed alphabetically under common names in an appendix, with scientific nomenclature for clarification.

This is an attempt to lead the reader through some of the lesser known corners of a representative part of Cardiff's green backdrop, indicating how much there is to to seen for those with eyes to see. For historical facts the author has had to rely an the written or spoken ward. - There may be errors here, but, hopefully, fewer on the scientific side.

MARY E. GILLHAM
Cardiff

INTRODUCTION

A Natural History of the Garth Countryside
Part of
CARDIFF'S GREEN MANTLE
by Mary E.Gillham

Cardiff, capital of the now emancipated principality of Wales, is a growing city which has not sacrificed its surroundings irrevocably to bricks and concrete. The magnificent line of green hills backing the coastal plain is visible from all parts of the city. Some is wooded, some grassed, all forms the perfect adjunct to the busy metropolis for airing overworked people and underworked dogs.

What better way to celebrate the Millennium than to consider this precious environment in its entirety, from the rocks which dictate its shape and provided its past wealth, through the green mantle of vegetation and the animal life which this sustains?

During this millennium the land has run full circle, from pristine countryside, through the clamorous winning of minerals - from well before the onset of the industrial revolution - and back again to woods and fields.

These no longer serve a community of farmers and woodsmen, but provide recreation and refreshment for the vast population residing in the new housing estates that have mushroomed up throughout.

Our region embraces Coalfield hill land with shallow soils suited only to sheep, a fertile limestone ridge supporting Britain's most westerly native beechwoods, and valley wetlands unsuited to building development. The IN word at the end of the twentieth century is BIODIVERSITY. We have it now, will it be sustained?

Not least remarkable are the healed scars of old industrial sites, the forges and furnaces, iron and coal mines, limestone quarries and charcoal producing woodlands on which past prosperity depended. The hub of all this was Gwaelod-y-Garth, now a conservation area and the author's home for 37 years. Forge, furnace and brickworks were aggregated where the Taff Valley narrows to squeeze through the Taff Gorge.

Water power to keep the wheels turning came from the Taff along Forge Dyke and from the western hills along Nant Llywdrew. Iron ore and limestone were trundled down from the Little Garth, charcoal and coal from the Great Garth and the western riverside.

This, the nucleus of so much endeavour during the second half of the millennium, along with the other two villages in this Community Council area, Pentyrch and Creigiau, is the part of Cardiff's green backdrop that concerns us here. Our story spills over the boundaries a little, but does not probe the splendid wooded uplands east of the Taff, from Castell Coch and Fforest Ganol to Graig Llanishen and Graig Lisvane.

The entire ridge is a treasure beyond price, saved from despoliation by far-sighted Local Authorities and the untiring efforts of the Caerphilly Mountain Countryside Project. This is the heritage that our conservation-conscious age leaves to our successors in the third millennium, the background for the new Assembly and the building blocks that they will have to work with.

Writers and historians of the future will know how it was at the end of the twentieth century. Will populations of plants and animals be as healthy in their day as in ours? Will numbers of species have increased and natural habitats enlarged, or will urban sprawl have pushed all the others back? It is up to them.

Mary E.Gillham
Cardiff. 1999

Portobello Weir on the RiverTaff under Gwaelod-y-Garth, showing Pont Sion Phillip footbridge. Note the row of miner's cottages along the Mountain Road, the absence of woodland above, and the building on the right of the skyline. (Reproduced from an early postcard)

PENTYRCH ADMINISTRATIVE BOUNDARIES

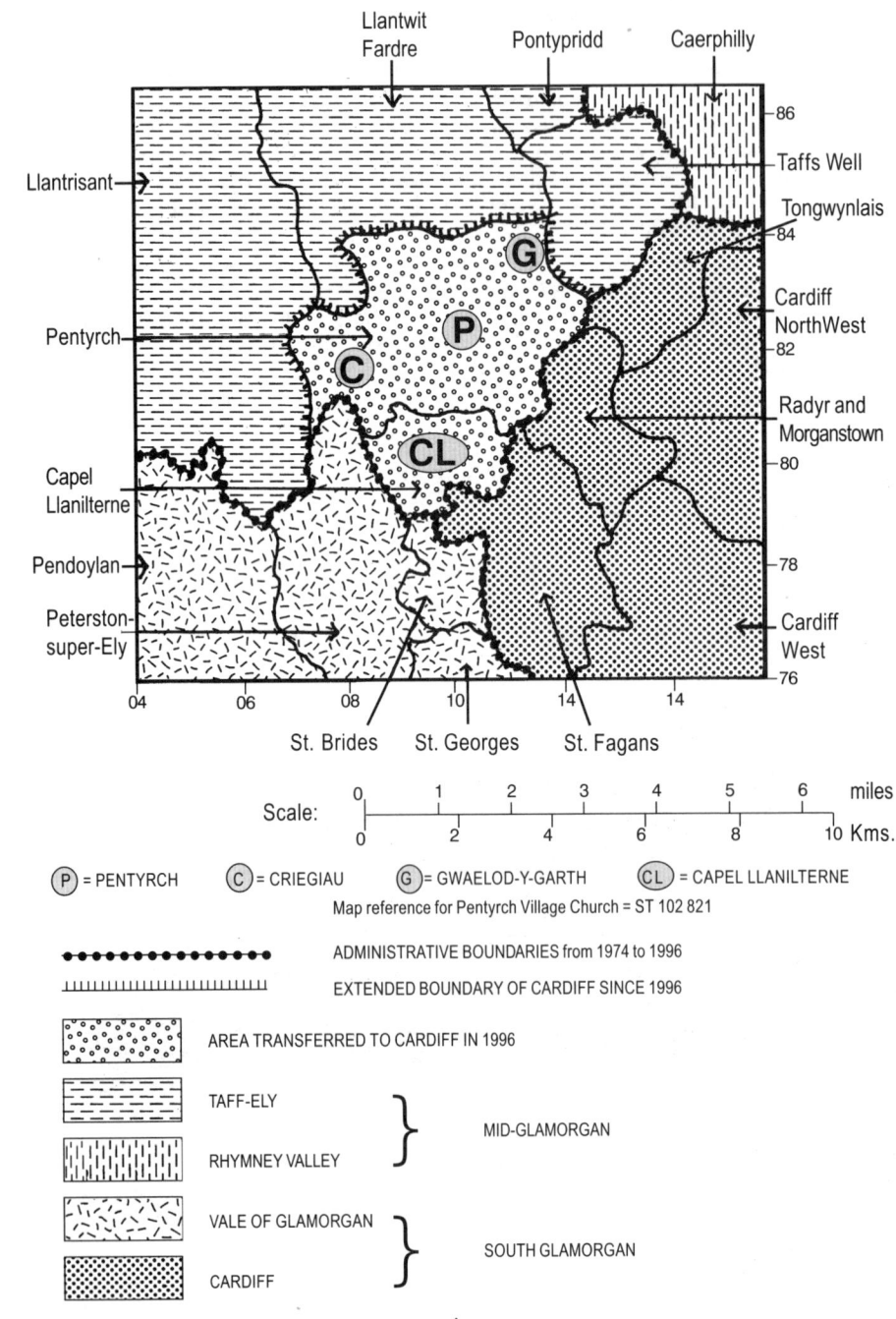

Llantwit Fardre Pontypridd Caerphilly

Llantrisant
Taffs Well
Tongwynlais
Pentyrch
Cardiff NorthWest
Radyr and Morganstown
Capel Llanilterne
Pendoylan
Peterston-super-Ely
Cardiff West

St. Brides St. Georges St. Fagans

Scale: 0 1 2 3 4 5 6 miles
       0 2 4 6 8 10 Kms.

(P) = PENTYRCH (C) = CRIEGIAU (G) = GWAELOD-Y-GARTH (CL) = CAPEL LLANILTERNE

Map reference for Pentyrch Village Church = ST 102 821

●●●●●●●●●●●●●● ADMINISTRATIVE BOUNDARIES from 1974 to 1996
⊥⊥⊥⊥⊥⊥⊥⊥⊥⊥⊥⊥ EXTENDED BOUNDARY OF CARDIFF SINCE 1996

AREA TRANSFERRED TO CARDIFF IN 1996

TAFF-ELY
RHYMNEY VALLEY } MID-GLAMORGAN

VALE OF GLAMORGAN
CARDIFF } SOUTH GLAMORGAN

THE SETTING

Cardiff, the capital of Wales, is among the most fortunate of cities in possessing a wealth of green places where citizens may refresh themselves. There is the sea in front, albeit narrowed into the 10-11 mile wide Bristol Channel, the hills behind and two green corridors penetrating the heart of the built-up area. The main parkland, garden and playing field complex reaches invitingly inland alongside the River Taff, from Cardiff Castle to the Forest Farm Country Park and Glamorganshire Canal Nature Reserve at Whitchurch. The lesser leafy belt follows the lake-dominated streamsides, flower beds and play areas of Roath.

It is the green backdrop of hills that concerns us here, the uplands to the west of the Taff Gorge, where the biggest of Cardiff's three rivers has broken through the triple ridge that bounds the southern flank of the South Wales Coalfield. This is part of the land set aside by the local authorities for amenity use, under the auspices of the Caerphilly Mountain Countryside Project. It is the part that formed the hub of the south-based industry in past centuries, revolving around the winning of iron and coal from the rocks, with the grimy bustle of tin-plate works, brick-yards and muddy dramroads taking haematite and other products up-valley to the northern ironworks around Merthyr Tydfil, as well as down-valley for shipment from the growing port of Cardiff.

First it yielded up its forests to the charcoal-burners, then its coal to keep the furnaces stoked. Now charcoal-burners, foundry-workers and coal miners have gone and the trees have grown again, the brick-yard is a riverside housing estate and the dramroads are rural walkways.

Three rivers reach the sea at Cardiff, the Taff the only one mighty enough to lower itself down through the ridges delimiting the Coalfield. It achieved this by following a geological fault, recognisable in the non-alignment of the hills to either side of Taff's Well and the Taff Gorge, and was helped in its mammoth task by the great weight of ice scraping its way down from the Brecon Beacons and Central Wales during past Ice Ages.

The River Rhymney made it from a more easterly part of the Coalfield into the Caerphilly Basin, but was unable to tackle the barrier ahead and made an ignominious detour around its eastern end to Machen and back west to Cardiff along the lowland now used by the M4 motorway and Eastern Avenue trunk road.

The Ely, Cardiff's third river, sneaks in past Tonyrefail, avoiding the more formidable obstacles by passing west of Llantrisant and letting itself down to the Vale of Glamorgan more gently through Pontyclun, Miskin and Peterston to weave its way sinuously across the Penarth flats to the Taff-Ely Roads, these meanders now eliminated by water engineers.

All the lesser streams are tributaries of these three main waterways. Springs are plentiful - as aquifers in the Coal Measures, underground rivers in the limestones, deep-seated reservoirs under the sandstones and fluctuating water tables in the river gravels. Their distribution dictated where people might live and sink their garden wells or congregate at the village pumps.

Most famous of the rises is at Taff's Well in the township which takes its name. Although hard against the river bank since the Taff moved eastwards after the building of the Portobello Weir, the water is quite separate and was used from ancient times as a healing well. In the slump of the 1930s it supplied an open-air swimming pool, built by the unemployed, but destroyed by high river floods in the 1950s. The superstructure enclosing it awaits a face-lift when the money is available to make it into the littlest British spa that it once was.

The region proposed in the early 1970s as the Caerphilly Mountain Country Park became re-scheduled eventually as the Caerphilly Mountain Countryside Project. It stretches for eleven miles along the multiple upland running W S W to E N E across Cardiff's hinterland, a leafy green belt backing the 7 mile wide coastal plain. Only a quarter of the designated zone lies west of the Taff Gorge, but this is arguably the most interesting. It includes the same Devonian and Carboniferous rocks as the rest, acid and alkaline, and encroaches in addition onto the newer Triassic and Liassic strata to the south and west. More recent deposits include glacial clays and gravels and the swathe of river alluvium along the Taff's flood plain.

The area is dominated by the highest point on the range, the Great Garth, which just makes it to mountain status of a thousand feet above ordnance datum. This is part of the uptilted edge of the Coal Measures. To its south lie the similarly uptilted beds of the older Carboniferous Limestones, manifested mainly as the dolomitised rock of the Little Garth and containing two big working quarries, one here and the other at Creigiau. The more ancient Devonian Old Red Sandstones to the south lie unconformably against the Triassic New Red Sandstones, which were formerly extracted as conglomeritic 'Radyr Stone' in the Radyr Quarry towards the cathedral city of Llandaff.

Appreciation of the region's mineral wealth started long before the establishment of the mighty Pentyrch Iron Forge at Gwaelod-y-Garth. Iron Age men, whose artefacts have been found in the cave system under the Little Garth, are likely to have found the iron for their weapons and implements in the haematite vein outcropping closeby. Archeologists have suggested that metals were first discovered when melted from the rocks by cooking fires. Could that have happened here? However they were discovered, the iron-bearing rocks were first chipped from the surface of

1. Solid Geology around the Taff Gorge

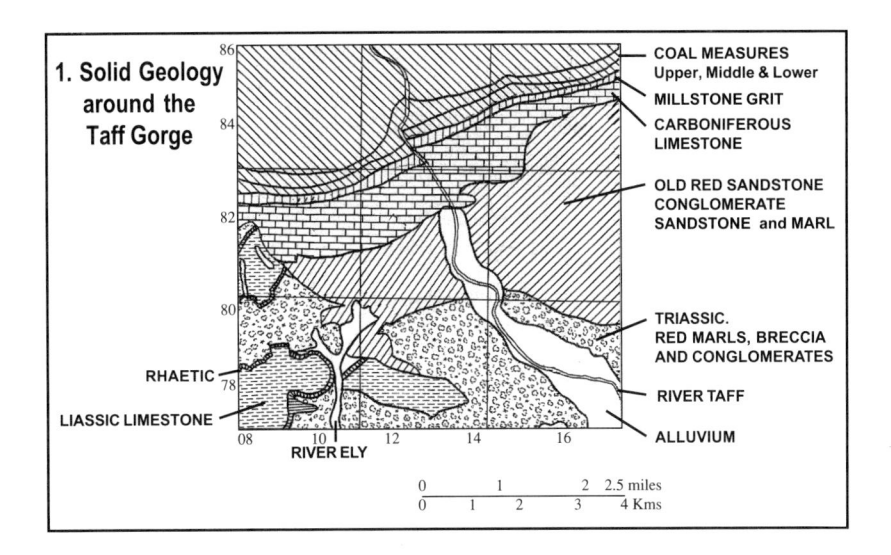

- COAL MEASURES Upper, Middle & Lower
- MILLSTONE GRIT
- CARBONIFEROUS LIMESTONE
- OLD RED SANDSTONE CONGLOMERATE SANDSTONE and MARL
- TRIASSIC. RED MARLS, BRECCIA AND CONGLOMERATES
- RHAETIC
- LIASSIC LIMESTONE
- RIVER TAFF
- RIVER ELY
- ALLUVIUM

the Dolomite, then quarried and then mined, ever deeper over the centuries. Archeology is upside down here, with the oldest remains on top and the youngest deep down in the 'iron soul' of the hill.

The industrial era has passed, although quarrying continues, and Nature is reclaiming her own, with upstanding beechwoods on the limestone slopes, grass:bracken heaths on the higher hills, and oak:alder woods in the moister valleys. Citizens lightheartedly walk the old dramroads where horses pulled their wearisome loads, and take refreshment at the picnic sites erected for their pleasure. Today's horses carry riders along hoof-pocked bridleways and more exotic sports, such as hang-gliding, are sometimes practised when the wind is right.

The long distance, west to east Ridgeway Walk, from Bridgend via Llantrisant to Caerphilly, follows the northerly ridge, to cross the long distance south to north Taff Trail on the other side of the river. Sheep exploit the hill grazings and dairy cows feed over the glacial mounds and alluvial river terraces of the flood plain. Coed-y-Bedw, along the recessed Millstone Grit valley between the Coal Measures and the Dolomite, is designated as a nature reserve, managed by the Glamorgan Wildlife Trust since 1968, and other parts have been accorded the status of S S S I s (Sites of special scientific interest).

Most of our area falls within the rural community of Pentyrch, which embraces the other two villages of Creigiau and Gwaelod-y-Garth, this last a conservation area, but it spills over into Llantwit Fardre in the north and Morganstown in the south. Traditionally part of the administrative district of Taff-Ely, Pentyrch has recently been transferred to the jurisdiction of Cardiff City, now Cardiff County, hopefully not to become merged into the urban sprawl as just another suburb. Most of us had hoped that the impressive barrier breached only by the Taff Gorge would have been sufficient of a demarcation to link us with the countryside beyond and spare us this take-over.

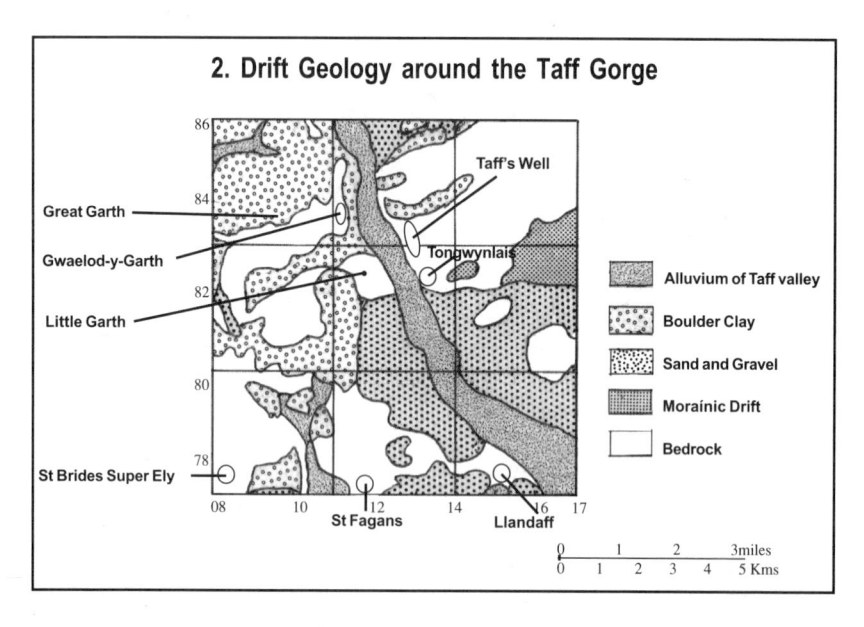

2. Drift Geology around the Taff Gorge

One of the "Valleys' sprinter trains" follows the Taff flood plain.
View south through the Taff Gorge from Gwaelod-y-Garth.

4

Chapter 1

THE GREAT GARTH: UPLAND HEATH AND ACID WOOD

Introductory

Some maps show the Great Garth as just over 1,000 feet (308 metres) high, others show it as falling slightly short of this, depending on whether measurement is made from the original pre-historic land surface or the top of the tumulus with which Bronze Age man crowned its summit and which now holds the triangulation point. Whichever is correct, it is the highest point along the ridges bounding this part of the Coalfield and is referred to locally as "The Mountain". It is central to this north-western quarter of the Caerphilly Mountain Countryside Project area, so it seems logical that we should start our survey of the Pentyrch parish here.

Garth Mountain was the obvious location for the beacon fire celebrating King George V's accession to the throne in 1911. In 1985 an 82 year-old recalled his memories of that occasion. It was the year when Edward Llewellyn took over "The Colliers' Arms", these premises part and parcel of the celebrations. People came from all around for the free teas and refreshments and there was dancing in the Long Room to the strains of a piano. The octogenarian remembered the horse and cart loaded with fruit - oranges to be bought at six a penny and apples at tuppence a pound! The Boy Scouts camped on the mountain summit and children played 'fox and hounds' among the bracken.

Another beacon on the mountain top commemorated Queen Elizabeth II's silver jubilee in 1977, this being lighted when flames were sighted at the next to the east and triggering the lighting of that next to the west. That was in the days when locals were still free to enjoy themselves, untrammelled by the tangled red tape which curtails and mollie-coddles us in this modern, spoon-fed age. The Community Council's enterprising scheme to have another beacon fire in January 1993, to celebrate the new European unity and advent of a single European market, as part of the 'Beacon Europe' celebrations, was squashed *"because of problems with access, safety and possible bad weather!"* Can we no longer walk uphill, or watch a bonfire without setting ourselves alight, and are today's anoraks and gumboots less weather-worthy than the simpler garments of our forebears? Similarly, could two hundred of today's much enlarged population be mustered to scale the Garth on a cold morning to view the eclipse of the sun, as in 1927? Fortuitously, the total eclipse of the sun on 11th August 1999 occurred on a summery mid-morning, so many of us made it to the top.

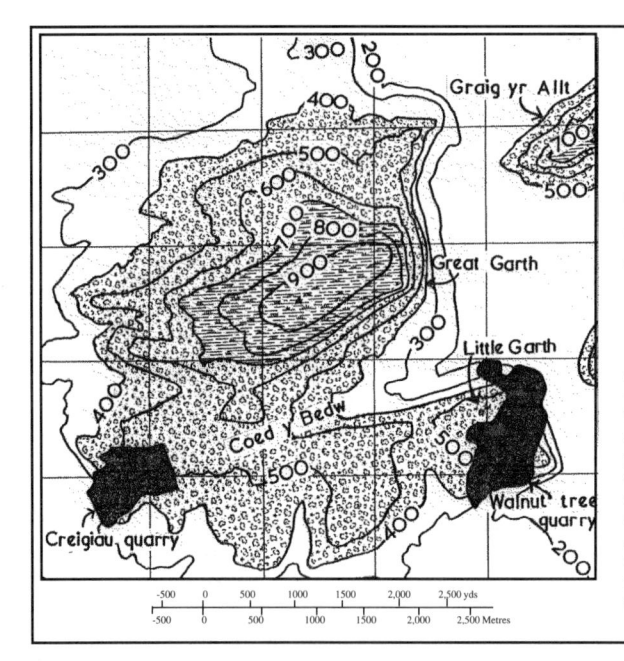

Contour Map of land west of the Taff Gorge

Showing land over 400ft (123m), the two working quarries in Pentyrch parish, Creigiau and Gwaelod-y- Garth, the essentially acid Great Garth, and the calcareous Little Garth, with Coed-y-Bedw Nature Reserve between.

    The strata of the South Wales Coalfield and the older layers which support it, can be visualised as a pile of giant saucers, slashed across by the rivers. The Great Garth is part of the southernmost rim of the coal-bearing rocks, a rim known as 'The South Crop'.

    The layer immediately below is of Millstone Grit - not the unyielding grits of which millstones were made, but of the softer shales associated with them. Being more vulnerable to weathering, the edge of this saucer has been worn down to form a valley, leaving the rim of the harder one below to protrude well above it to the south. That is the dolomitised Carboniferous Limestone and its east to west outcrop is known as 'The Southern Border Ridge', represented here by the Little Garth.

    South of this again, the lowest and oldest of the rock saucers is the Old Red Sandstone, in somewhat more modified form than in the Graigs towards Caerphilly. Nestled along the foot of the triple ridge, like a frozen sea congealed against the base of its bounding shore, are the flatter, lower lying rocks of the coastal plain, which were laid down subsequently.

    We are exhorted by the bible to "Lift up our eyes unto the hills". When conditions are propitious, it is good to lift more than the eyes, for there is a great deal to see from the top

1. Panorama from the Mountain top

The easiest way to tackle the 850 feet ascent from the Taffside village of Gwaelod-y-Garth to the Garth summit is south by west along the single track mountain road and back across the gentler contours of the western slope, past Garth Uchaf. As I toiled the last few steps to the top of the southern tumulus, I had the whole of South Glamorgan at my feet - along with parts of Mid Glamorgan and Gwent, while the outline of Somerset and Devon dissolved into the mists across the water.

It was midsummer day, 1993, with the westering sun glinting on the clustered buildings of the Welsh capital, transforming uncompromising high-rise blocks into a jig-sawed backdrop for the spires and chimneys. This is a bi-nucleated city, divided by "Cardiff's Green Corridor" along the River Taff and dappled with a rich endowment of open spaces. I settled on the grass at the foot of the triangulation obelisk with my binoculars to suss out the land and seascape.

From my point of vantage the horizon described a complete circle, as from a ship at sea, its outline smoothest to the west where the rolling contours of Exmoor and the North Devon coast melted into the Bristol Channel haze. Mynydd Margam dipped steeply seaward behind the Port Talbot levels and the edge of the land rose again east of the two great dune systems of Kenfig and Merthyr Mawr - to the twelve mile stretch of the Heritage Coast cliffs.

The new British Airways building at Rhoose Airport rose grey and blocky, like a mediaeval castle to the left of the Aberthaw Power Stations and Cement Works, the cliff line etched sharply against the silvered strip of sea to Penarth Head. Boats and houses of the new 1980s Penarth Marina, fronted by the River Ely, caught the sun's rays at its foot and buildings climbed from dock to clifftop church.

I was looking due south now, with the sturdy outline of Steepholm looming in mid channel behind Penarth. The parent headland of Brean Down, from which the island had become separated in the geological past, was clearly visible, but I failed to pick out Brent Knoll. Steepholm is part of England. Flatholm to its left, surmounted by the whitewashed lighthouse, has belonged to the parish of St. Mary's in Cardiff since 1066.

Left again were the Taff-Ely Roads biting into the coast between Grangetown and Butetown - a fine stretch of tidal estuary destined soon to fall victim to the modern mania for building tidal barrages. It was bounded to the east by the oil storage tanks in what remains of the once busy Cardiff Docks, with the white blur of Burnham-on-Sea behind.

Gradually the houses thinned, from city through suburb, until the coastal plain was green again beneath the south-facing scarp of Graig Llanishen and Graig Lisvane beyond the upstanding radio mast of the Wenallt.

The distant orange scar at the far end of the Caerphilly Basin must have been Machen Quarry. Behind it rose the irregular profile of the Gwent Hills, below it flowed the deflected River Rhymney, unable to break through the line of hills as the mightier Taff has done. Sweeping round to the north, the rolling outline of the Coalfield was overtopped by the glowering mass of the Brecon Beacons: the unmistakable flat top of Corn Du with the slightly higher Pen-y-Fan peaking to its right at 2,880 feet (886 m).

Setting my sights lower I took in the closer scene, withdrawing to the spreadeagled housing of Efail Isaf and Church Village where the Coalfield dips to the west of Pontypridd. The Vale of Glamorgan was predominantly green still; the patchwork of fields dissected by the dark lines of hedges and spinneys. Radyr Quarry was swallowed up by tall trees but the red Dolomite scar of Walnut Tree Quarry lying athwart the South Glamorgan/Mid Glamorgan county boundary at Morganstown and, although invisible from the foot of the mountain, was huge in plan view, with newly opened workings west of the clustered buildings, conveyor belts and stone crushers.

Two other Dolomite quarries further east along the ridge showed as blatant gashes in the earth's surface, the Cefn Garw Quarry lying directly behind the stately outline of Castell Coch, and beyond it the bigger Blaengwynlais Quarry. Taffs Well, with its broad factory roofs, was portrayed like a town plan on the eastern flood plain, where the Taff looped across to the western side of its valley, gnawing its way into the steep face below Gwaelod-y-Garth.

Closer, to the south and east, the tree-clad dip of Coed-y-Bedw and the Little Garth beechwood surged against the mountain's foot and continued beyond the orange scar of the Taff Gorge as the Forestry Commission lands about Castell Coch and so to Cardiff City's woodlands on Rhiwbina Hill, the Wenallt and the Graigs beyond: all part of the delectable green hills of the Caerphilly Mountain Countryside Project.

It was a sobering thought that the long dead residents who had raised the tumulus on which I sat and had already begun on the tree clearance, must have looked out over much the same countryside from their mountain eyrie at the dawn of history as I did now. The changelessness of our ever-changing world is reassuring. The years between had brought more land to the Cardiff foreshore, imprisoned behind 'sea walls' of rubble, had seen the walling around of docks, filched from the edge of the tidal Channel, and the straightening of the lower Taff, but these were as surface scratches when viewed in

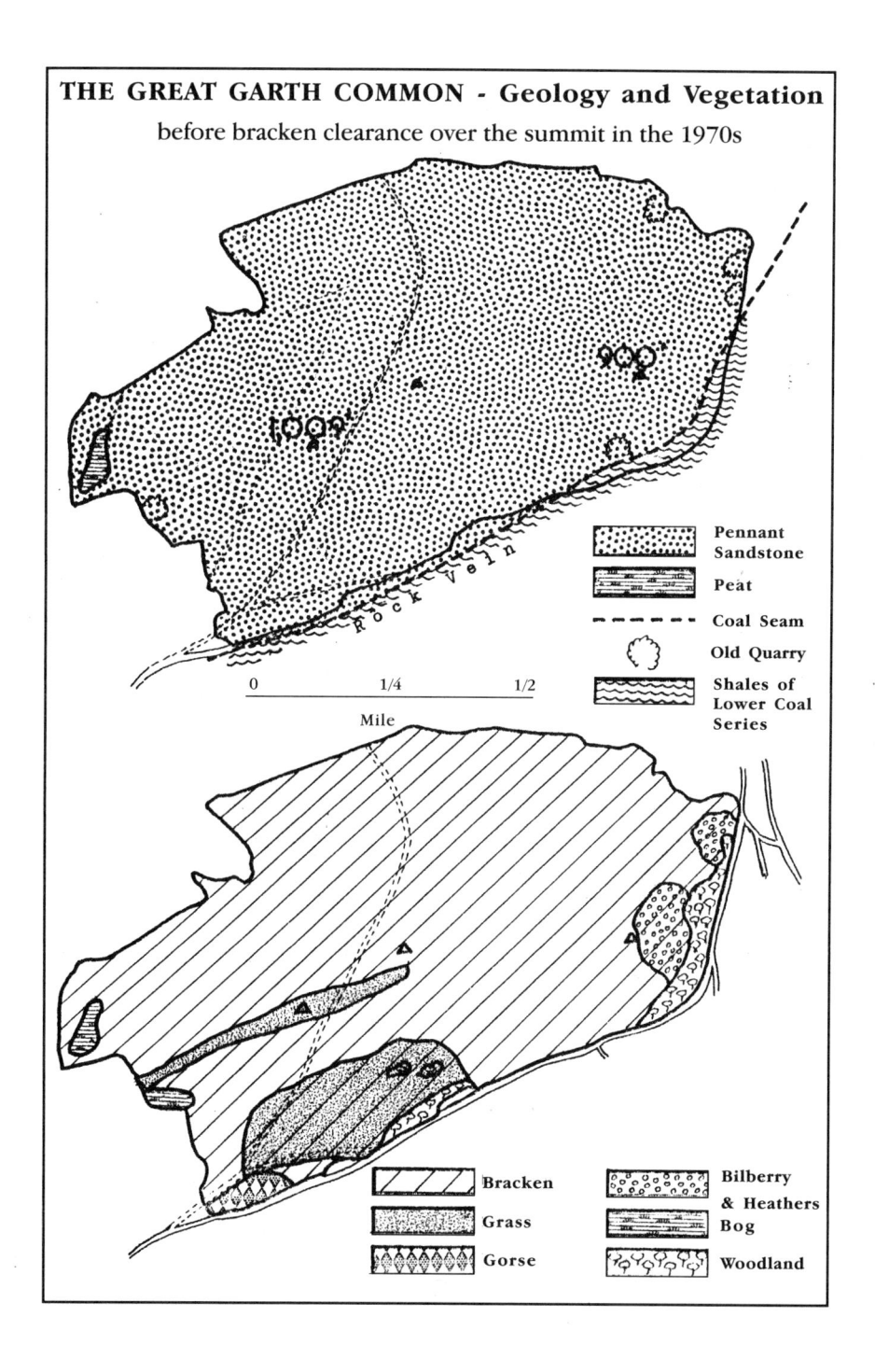

THE GREAT GARTH COMMON - Geology and Vegetation
before bracken clearance over the summit in the 1970s

Pennant Sandstone
Peat
Coal Seam
Old Quarry
Shales of Lower Coal Series

Bracken
Grass
Gorse
Bilberry & Heathers
Bog
Woodland

perspective from their vantage point and mine.

It was a sunny sunday afternoon and I was not alone on my breezy hill.

"Never been up here before: I've always meant to" quoth one young man. *"I've lived here all my life"* said another, older, *"and not once have I climbed to the top."*

A group of long distance walkers enquired the way to the Wenallt: a goodly step over hill and valley, although seemingly so close. They would have to leave the ridge to cross the Taff Valley, with its teeming A 470 trunk road to reach their goal. The late David Jenkins, one of the older Caerphilly voluntary wardens, remembered when groups of village girls used to yodel to each other across the valley 70 years ago in the early 30s. One lot stood atop the Garth, the other on Graig-yr-Allt on the further side. It is likely that their girlish trebles would be drowned by the roar of traffic today. In my own youth we used morse and semaphore signalling flags for long-distance communication. Today's wardens are furnished with personalised telephones!

Only the energetic can attempt the entire "Ridgeway Walk", but the scaling of the Garth is well worth the effort for the less ambitious. And not only for the panoramic spread: there are other diversions close at hand.

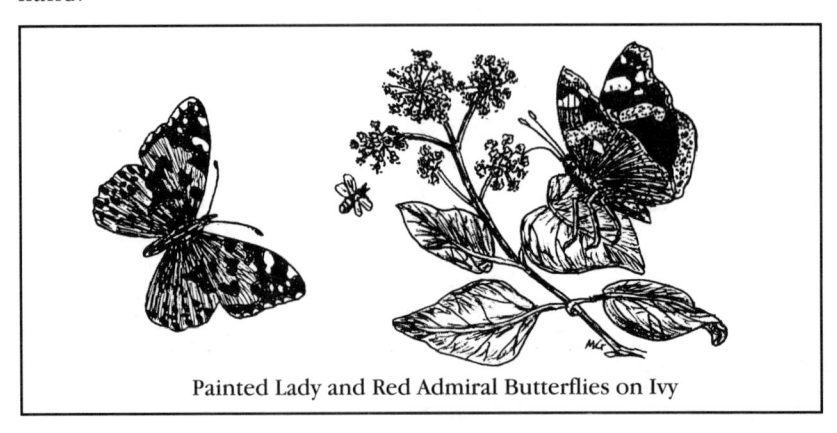

Painted Lady and Red Admiral Butterflies on Ivy

Throughout my sojourn at the trig point, I had been fascinated with the handsome red admiral butterfly that wished only to sun itself on a particular rock, but was constantly buzzed by a restive painted lady. Perhaps the 'lady' was male and the 'admiral' female, but he-she-it persisted and the aerial chases were many and intricate .

These two butterflies are powerful fliers; migrants from Mediterranean shores, the painted lady from the North African side: an unbelievable achievement for those fragile wings. It was too early for the British-bred generation to be on the wing, so these two must have made the long journey, but had obviously not exhausted their capabilities. Their business now was to raise a family, as quickly as possible and, as there seemed to be only one of each kind, this was leading to certain frustration. These are the two species most likely to be found on windy summits and I saw no others up here today, although there were whites, browns and skippers down by the mountain road.

Other masters of the air were the swifts, swooping back and forth over the three tumuli, sieving breeze-borne insects from the sky. Some of the lower-flying swallows seemed to have tired and were resting rather incongruously on bracken fronds. Skylarks never let up in their singing: as one dropped to earth another rose to continue the carolling that was a delightful accompaniment to my viewing so close to the urban hub. Forty carrion crows, which may have learned their comparatively new habit of flocking from the ever present jackdaws, were cavorting over the more easterly tumulus, where the mountain sheep had gathered, those which had eluded the shearers shedding tufts of wool as they walked.

A buzzard mewed its way across the valley and I flushed a meadow pipit on the scramble down to the steep path across the sparkling runnel from an eastern declivity. This path, heading obliquely down from summit to lane, was a mere thread of rock and soil when I first walked it in the early 60s. With increasing use, it became badly eroded and teams from the Caerphilly Project have given it a face-lift, fashioning timber-edged steps above the new stone-flagged stream-crossing and a more durable stone staircase below.

A handsome golden-ringed dragonfly *(Cordulegaster boltoni)* zoomed along the stream course, leading my gaze to a blue eggshell from a dunnock's nest. Further down I spotted another blue eggshell, of a song thrush this time, and watched a bird of the first brood poking for goodies in the leaf mould. A white-rumped jay shot between the trees to the accompaniment of irate chatter, as smaller nest owners saw it off.

The top of a fence post materialised into the back view of a little owl. In response to my whistle the bird turned its head through 180 degrees to stare my way, then twisted it back through 360 degrees to stare again under frowning brows, in no hurry to take off. Blue tits and great tits, contrary to their usual practice, had been foraging with the pipits among the bracken above, but the gossipping family of long-tailed tits newly released from the confines of their spherical nest, remained true to their natal terrain and enlivened my walk back down the lane to the village.

2. Old Drift Mines

From summit to base the south-facing scarp of the Great Garth changes from Upper Coal Measures through Middle and Lower Coal Measures to the narrow band of soft Millstone Grit Shales, which has eroded to form the valley between here and the Little Garth. Hard Pennant Sandstone stands out at intervals along the crest, but is overlain by ice-transported Boulder Clay where the land falls away in the north into the parish of Llantwit Fardre, and this material also blankets the southern valley.

Skylark and Sheep's-bit

Because the strata - coal seams interbedded with shales and sandstones - dip northwards into the hillside, their edges crop out along the south face, allowing miners to follow the seams obliquely into the mountain, winning "black gold" from square one. Geologists have identified no less than 20 coal seams here, some large, some medium and some little more than a smudge of coal in a bed of shale. The main seams to surface are the closely parallel Rhondda No.1 and Rhondda No.2 and the old addits or drift mines leading into these and lesser veins can still be seen above and below the Mountain Road. This narrow lane climbs steeply from the village of Gwaelod-y-Garth, and then follows approximately along the 650 foot contour line, where the steep upper slope changes to a gentler lower one, providing the highest convenient gradient on which to build a road.

Most of the addits above this are now mere hollows overgrown with bracken, bramble or gorse, but locals in their seventies can recall crawling right down to the coal face when they were young. One mine opening just above the water storage tanks, burrowed under the lane and was known as Rocks Level, because of the tenacity of the sandstone beds which it penetrated - hard on picks and shovels and harder on the men who wielded them. Outside another is an old rotary iron shaft and turntable, where two patient horses walked round and round, drawing tramloads of coal obliquely out from underground. This is still intact and is kept clear for viewing, although gorse was encroaching from the uphill side by 1994. Children of the 1930s and 40s used the iron turntable and levelled horse circuit as a stage for amateur dramatics

The private taking of coal was illegal, even freeholders owning their land only to a depth of 3 feet. Mineral rights belonged to the coal barons, but several cottagers had private mines in their back yards and the woodland on the lower slopes is full of humps and hollows from old coal-winning enterprises. Some of these are bell pits, where miners dug down to a seam a few yards below the surface and then burrowed sideways at this level to exploit it. Such bell pits are well seen today on the south-facing slope of Rudry Common near Caerphilly.

There is a lovely story of two brothers who rented a cottage called Maes-yr-Aer (Sunny Field) at the foot of the field below the kissing gate onto the mountain road. Neither could read or write, but they were not stupid, and worked a mine under their kitchen floor, using the winder from the laundry mangle to winch a bucket up from 10 feet below the stone flags. Coal was the standard fuel and the coal merchant became suspicious when they bought none - and some of their closer neighbours very little. He reported them and the brothers' premises were inspected and the mine sealed. Rumour has it that they opened another in the wood nearby! The site of their cottage is in the top of the wood, the foundation an unsuitable rooting medium for trees, so the Forestry Commission left this unplanted when they stocked the slope with conifers.

The deeply incised track leading past it to the village street below, is an old pack-horse trail, down which coal was brought from the mines above the now ruined "Colliers' Arms" public house. It is very much an ancient 'hollow way', the more hollow because it got so muddy that the horses foundered and the men who led them had to dig the sludge out with shovels and pile it alongside. This accounts for the height of the banks, well above the level of the wood behind. Today's walkers in the upper wood have formed a new path along the top of the firm southern ridge, using sturdy saplings to steady themselves, as water flowing down the deeply trodden incision still fails to remove all the mud from underfoot.

When coal was coming down, two big red iron doors, like level crossing gates, are said to have halted road traffic. The pack horses continued down the wooded scarp below the village to the top of the high stone wall which persists above the riverside path downstream of the Zig-zag and footbridge. This broad path was an ancient tramroad from the Rock Vein or Sandrigg Colliery at Ffygis, and the panniers were tipped from the top of the now fern-clad wall into waiting trucks for transport down valley to iron foundry and tin works.

Two other mines opened at this level, the Pentyrch Drift or Llan Mine, worked until an explosion on December 5th, 1875, which killed 12 miners outright and another 5 of their injuries later, and the Cwm Dous Mine, closed around 1913. Later, during the first world war and the 1930's depression, miners re-opened several of the hidden holes, going in with pick and shovel for domestic fuel, but some, like the Rock Drift Mine, were too wet once pumping ceased and became the sources of streams bounding down to the Taff. Water seeps more gently from others, nurturing annual crops of frogspawn between the rocky walls. One such cleft, an airway ventilating a tunnel within, has held frogspawn unfailingly every February over the 37 years that I have known it, although the puddle at its entrance is only a few inches deep, a foot or so across and a few yards long. No water lingers in the run-off, which is almost vertical below the path, so the frogs must have travelled far overland to remain so faithful to this ancestral breeding site. Mine effluents from the Garth Rhondda seam below the mountain road are rusty with ferric iron leached from the mine walls and rendered gelatinous by aquatic bacteria, and these support little or no life apart from the iron-consuming micro-organisms.

3. Water Supply and Shifting Population

The spring water emerging to fill the Welsh Water Board's black iron tanks below the lane above Gwaelod is unsullied and unquenchable. When everyone else's water was turned off for part of the day in the rationing of the 1975 and 1976 droughts, residents of Gwaelod enjoyed a constant supply. Blocking of the domestic input merely caused the irrepressible flow to spill over into the River Taff, so the taps were quickly opened again. This supply was blocked off again in the 1990s, and the tanks were removed in 1998. I wonder why?

The next stream south of this was dammed as a swimming pool by boys of the early 1930s. By the 1950s the pool was silting up but tadpoles were still collected there to take to school. By the 1970s the erstwhile 'spa' was no more than a boggy hollow, drying out in summer. Now, in the 1990s, the leaf mould has built up and there is nary a trace.

The Coalfield rocks are well supplied with aquifers, impermeable shales providing the main water-bearing strata and nurturing little patches of upland bog where they surface, or carving steep-sided runnels down to the Taff. The cast iron water pump which stood at the south end of the village 'square' (which is by no means square) has gone, but springs gurgle up in sundry gardens and go bounding off to assuage the thirst of kingcups and moorhens on the wooded river terraces below the houses.

The local population has been moving steadily downhill since the heyday of the mining era - physically rather than metaphorically, I hasten to add. Miners' cottages were built along the east side of the mountain from locally hewn sandstone at various levels, some near Pentyrch, others clustering about the old "Colliers' Arms" public house. Most are now ruins, with ash and sycamore trees astride their sturdy walls, ivy and honeysuckle draping the open hearths.

All that remains of the "Colliers' Arms" is the arched stone cellar and the stream from the armchair-shaped hollow directly above, tumbling down alongside, this no doubt the old pub's water supply. The Caerphilly Mountain wardens have cleared a picnic site closeby, but it is a matter of 'bring your own' nowadays. Blackbirds cough up crop pellets of hawthorn stones on the wooden tables and song thrushes smash their snail shells on the benches.

Garden plants have proved more tenacious than gardeners. There is still a harvest of red cherries, rosy apples and blue-bloomed damsons to be gleaned by those willing to tackle the thickets which surround them. Gooseberry, raspberry and currant pips have been spread around by the birds which have taken over and these have germinated to succour more nestlings. Garden privet, feral lilac, snowberry and Japanese honeysuckle have held their own against the indigenous species which are making a come back. The attractive ground cover of yellow archangel with variegated

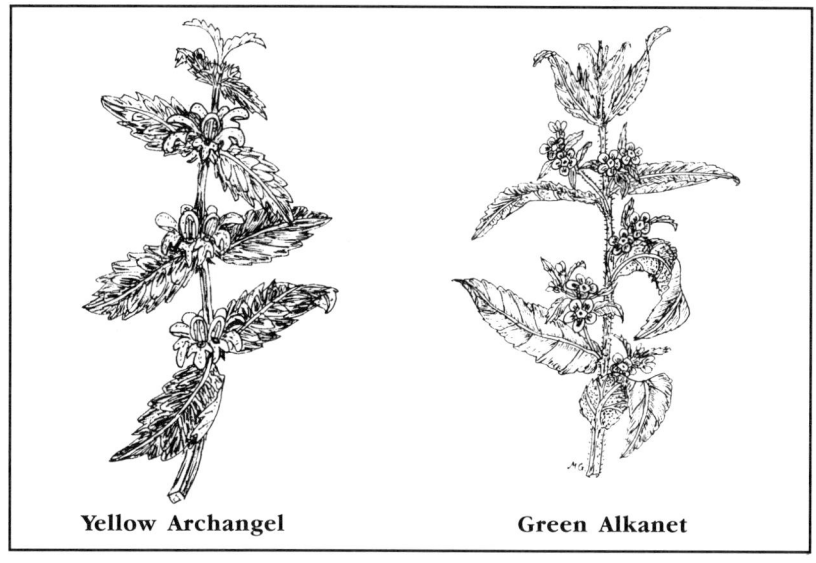

Yellow Archangel   Green Alkanet

leaves is probably of garden origin and is now commoner than the native green leaved kind and is resplendent with pale yellow flowers in April and May. The gentian blue flowers of green alkanet put in a first appearance in 1983.

Pied wagtails build their nests in crumbling masonry, stock doves in a hole which housed the end of a beam and wrens have taken over niches choked by creepers. Robins bring up broods of speckled chicks in discarded household utensils and tawny owls perch atop old chimney stacks to call their warning to the night-time world. Bats occupy summer roosts in those same chimneys. Slow worms (legless lizards) wriggle into cracks where the mortar has disintegrated and grass snakes are sometimes spotted. Beetles hide under paving slabs and cross spiders *(Araneus diadematus)* spin their orb webs in kitchen cupboards, unmolested by house-proud housewives, while funnel-web spiders *(Agelena labyrinthica)* lurk in silken tunnels opening onto webbing sheets furnished with a labyrinth of trip wires for the unwary.

Present day Gwaelod, a designated "Conservation Area", grew up in past centuries along the eastern skirt of the Mountain, well above river level. Residents of the mining settlement at the highest level were re-housed in the Garth Olwg Estate, which spills down below the village post-office half way to the river flood plain at Ffygis. Next came the houses at Heol Beri further downstream on the site of the old brick works and holding ponds, where the chimneys survived until the 1950s. They were above most floods on terraced fluvio-glacial gravels. The latest additions, spreading estates of desirable residences at River Glade and Souh Glade, are built on 'made land' and protected from the rush of water from the Brecon Beacons by stout flood banks. Physically Gwaelod can go no lower and still keep its head above water.

4. Open Commonland; Fields and Quagmires

The Great Garth is commonland, criss-crossed by paths, and it remained agriculturally unimproved until recent years. It is typical of the southern Coalfield hills in being clad in bent:fescue grass heath with bracken instead of purple moor - grass moor with mat grass as in the higher, rainier north. The turf contains sweet vernal and crested dogstail grass and is sprinkled with the modest flowers of tormentil, heath bedstraw and the blues of sheep's-bit scabious, heath milkwort, heath speedwell and heath violet. Needle-leaved wavy hair grass cushions some of the many anthills, and their peppery-flowered sheep's sorrel.

Bracken had advanced to cover almost the entire grass sward by the summer of 1968, when Extra Mural students from Cardiff University

1. Bronze Age Tumulus with Trig. Point on the summit of the Great Garth. 1999

2. Eastern flank of the Great Garth viewed from the Taff Flood Plain. 1999

3. Garth Mountain from the East.
Pentyrch on left flank, Gwaelod on right flank, and Taff's Well in front.

4. Garth Mountain
East flank, after the felling of the
conifers in the 1990s

5. Foxgloves,
Garth East flank, after tree felling.
View North to Gedrys.

mapped the vegetation as part of the national 'Commons' Survey' prior to the registration of commons. Most of the summit has been cleared now and is back to a year-long grass sward interrupted only by tumps of rushes, with almost unbroken bracken cover on the steeper slopes.

The bracken spread was helped by the former practice of burning to get rid of the dead fronds, which hindered the pushing through of the 'early bite' needed by the commonland sheep in spring. Unlike bracken in many parts of the world, ours is not winter-green, a point brought home to me when I took two Australian foresters along the top in April 1994 and they assumed that the fronds had been killed by herbicide.

The brittle winter trash is inevitably very fire-prone, and burning always gives the bracken a boost, because it causes no harm to the underground stems from which the new fronds will sprout, but damages all the more superficially rooted plants like grasses and heather which compete with it for space. Grazing animals dislike bracken (and can be poisoned by it) so the leaves are not kept in check by grazing as others are and herbicides are usually necessary to eliminate them.

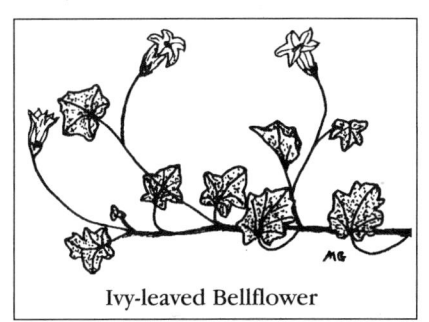

Ivy-leaved Bellflower

Damp patches support lesser spearwort, pink lousewort, lady's smock and the rare ivy-leaved bellflower. Where water stands for part of the year mosses, including the acid-loving *Sphagnum,* build up. Lesser skullcap and marsh bedstraw huddle among rushes, sedges and marsh thistle. There are two wetland areas on deep peat where the rare Cornish moneywort *(Sibthorpia europaea)* creeps among the similar but more robust marsh pennywort. Associated with it are the leafy liverwort, *Calypogeia fissa*, and the elegant pink bog pimpernel and New Zealand willow-herb. Smooth-stalked sedge *(Carex laevigata)* reaches to 45 inches (112 cm). Other sedges are oval, yellow, star and remote *(Carex ovalis, C. demissa, C. echinata* and *C. remota).* Vegetation can be pulled away from the clifflet at the back of this armchair-shaped depression to reveal a 12-18 inch wide coal seam. The water seeping into the hollow comes from the clay shales immediately below this seam

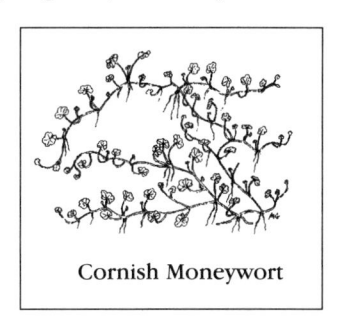

Cornish Moneywort

Damp rushy pastures in the north-west beyond Lan Farmhouse bear fine crops of kingcups and marsh violets in spring, then bogbean, ragged robin and heath spotted orchids in June, although the former globe flowers are but a memory. Brooklime, water blinks and silverweed survive in trampled gateways.

These enclosed fields show a greater diversity of plants than the common, which has been almost a free-for-all as grazing land over the years and hence over-exploited. Herbaceous cow-wheat *(Melampyrum pratense)* and spiky petty whin *(Genista anglica)* survive in the paddocks, with residual woodland species such as pig-nut and wood anemone. Damper patches hold bugle and greater bird's-foot trefoil, with water mint and red rattle. The high acidity resembles that of moorland, as shown by the bilberry, many-headed cotton-grass, deer sedge *(Trichophorum caespitosum)* and the patches of *Sphagnum* and *Polytrichum commune* moss. Tall bosses of tussock sedge *(Carex caespitosa)* rise from the wet soil by the Lan stream.

Among the beef cattle that have been reared on the Lan Farm fields are belted Galloways, a black and white breed from Scotland seldom seen in these parts but better able to thrive on this type of land than most. The continental beef breeds took over in the 90s, as they have from the now seldom-seen Shorthorns and even many of the more popular Herefords.

Splendid displays of white-flecked scarlet fly agaric toadstools, sufficient for an active community of gnomes, sprout through the autumnal sward where birches are invading the drier parts of these fields. Fungi of the open commonland are smaller but some are just as bright. Scarlet wax cap *(Hygrophorus coccineus)* is bright red, *H. conicus* more conical in shape and orange. *H. citrinus* is a buttery yellow, as is *H. psittacinus*, but that has surprising green patches on stipe and cap. *H. pratensis* is biscuit coloured, *H. laetus* a sticky toffee colour and *H. niveus* a snowy white. This group can be distinguished by the widely spaced gills under the cap and has now been re-named *Hygrocybe*. *Rhodophyllus sericellus, Panaeolus rickenii* and the slender-stalked *Stropharia semiglobata* with semi-globose cap grow on sheep dung and there are many more to be found as autumn advances.

The open, often windy, heights are the haunt of wheatear and linnet as well as skylark and meadow pipit , some of the pipits ill-used by cuckoos. Curlew and lapwing are seldom seen now, although not uncommon in the 1960s and 70s, but buzzards are often about, sometimes five at a time. Kestrels hover, searching for voles, and peregrines have been hunting over the mountain in recent years, since their recovery from the pesticide setback. Ravens tumble overhead in courtship flight and there are usually carrion crows and magpies about - as well as the inevitable flocks of jackdaws that crowd all the valleys, nesting in chimney stacks and making a general nuisance of themselves. Rabbits and hares are less plentiful than in past years, but foxes are probably more so, their twisted scats to be found everywhere, and the Pentyrch Hunt comes across at intervals through the winter. Most of the common small mammals have been observed here during my 37 years of residence in the village below, but none frequently. There are stoat and weasel, hedgehog and mole, mice and voles, shrews and bats.

Meadow brown and small heath butterflies fly freely on less windy days, with small coppers, common blues, large and small skippers and wall browns in season. Brown silverlines moths *(Lithina chlorosata)* are among the few whose caterpillars eat bracken and the sward is alive with little white grass moths *(Crambus hortuellus)* in summer.

Grasshoppers set up a fine chorus on sultry summer days when the gorse pods are popping and squirting their ripe 'peas' off to conquer new acres. September sees plagues of craneflies, with spiders everywhere: wolf spiders with egg cases, garden spiders with orb webs and spiderlings spinning silken parachutes to drift away on the breeze.

Craggy slopes facing onto the river suffer little grazing and there is residual heather and bilberry here, with tall stands of foxgloves, golden rod and wood sage and little pockets of cotton-grass. Only here can trees seed themselves without being nipped off in their youth and there is spontaneous regeneration of rowan, birch, sallow, hawthorn and oak, as the indigenous woodland reclaims lost ground.

The mountain top is classified as Grade 5 agricultural land, the poorest of all. In 1968 simple soil analyses were carried out during the Commons' Survey. Soil acidity was found to fluctuate between pH 4.5 and 5.5, rising closer to neutral (to pH 6.2) at the laneside where road making materials altered the reaction.

The boulder clay valley to the south is Grade 4. Until 1974 it was run-down farmland, ill-drained, with swards of rushes and shaly tumps crowned with haw, sloe and bramble. In the mid seventies much was fenced and fertilised. Ploughing for a turnip crop in the field between the kissing gate onto the lane and the woodland path down to lower road level uncovered some George IV coins! The root crop was eaten off without lifting, in March 1975, a flock of fieldfares and redwings mingling with the munching sheep on the partially flooded ground. Subsequently a new grass crop was sown here and it has been ploughed spasmodically since, but constant vigilance is necessary and bracken, rushes and nettles were advancing again by the 1990s.

5. Regenerating Oakwoods of the Mountain's Skirts

The woodland clothing the lower south and east slopes of the Great Garth contains some fine big beeches and oaks, but is mostly of post-industrial re-growth. The ground is pocked with the irregularities of former mining projects and the old addits spread almost down to river level where the Taff has cut through the Lower Coal Measure seams at right angles to their natural outcrop on the south scarp.

Mossy remnants of engine houses and kilns associated with the old coal mines cower in the undergrowth. A big arched opening below Gwaelod-y-Garth Main Road gives access to a tunnel which I am told was used as an air raid shelter during the second world war. Methane gas was generated within and it was later walled off to keep children out, but they got in anyway, through a hole in the roof - to smoke in private! - so the wall was removed. Every now and again gas escapes into somebody's kitchen up the mountain, generated in the Cwm Dous mine opening below the zig-zag path.

The woodland was well on the way to maturity 50 years ago and the local children gathered sundry titbits from it. *"It was bread and cheese at home: we probably craved the fresh greenstuff."* "Granny gruncheons" were a favourite, these the leaves and scaly stem bases of the wood sorrel, with their sharp acid taste.*"But you need a good handful."*

The unrelated sheep's sorrel and common sorrel leaves were also gathered for their acid zing and it is interesting to note that the scientific names of these three plants are *Oxalis acetosella, Rumex acetosella* and *Rumex acetosa* in deference to this culinary quality. Then there were the crunchy underground corms of pignut, their hideaways advertised by tufts of wispy foliage. The substance of the corms is used in producing the lacy white carrot flowers and seeds, new stores developing as the season advances.

Young beech leaves were munched, just as the buds were opening. *"We'd eat a whole branch full, but they had to be young. Leave 'em a week and they'd be like leather."*

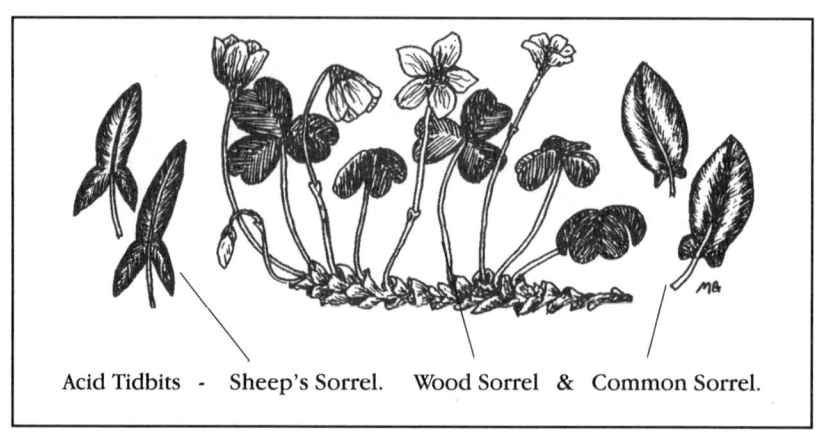

Acid Tidbits - Sheep's Sorrel. Wood Sorrel & Common Sorrel.

Caterpillars know this too, and concentrate on the young leaves. Older ones are not only tougher, but imbued with a bitter tannin, unpalatable enough to protect them from attack by nibbling insects and browsing children. Young hawthorn leaves were also chewed in spring, these known as 'bread and cheese, as they were in South-east England. Haws were plucked in autumn, the cheesy yellow flesh sucked off and the stones ejected, possibly to germinate into new 'quicks' which could be used to plug gaps in hedges.

Nature's almost complete takeover from the smoky, clanking past is remarkable. The woodland, although not rich in species, is superficially as rural now as woodlands anywhere - suggesting that the natural world may triumph in the end however much we abuse it with no thought for the consequences. A helping hand has been given by the villagers in the 1990s with the planting of roadside daffodils.

We are at the junction here of the lowland pedunculate oakwoods which predominate in the Vale of Glamorgan and the upland sessile or durmast oakwoods of the hills, so many of the local trees are hybrids, with characters of both. Strictly the pedunculate has stalked acorns and sessile leaves (seated directly on the twig with no stalk) and the sessile has sessile acorns and stalked leaves, but there is every excuse here for not knowing t'other from which.

First comers when grazing lets up are the birches, whose featherweight, wind-borne seeds waft everywhere. These are downy birch rather than the more gracefully pendant silver birch. Others follow: ash, rowan, sycamore, beech, crabapple and aspen, with the odd pine and yew and a shrub layer of hazel, holly, hawthorn, sloe, guelder rose and cherry laurel.

Much is a sea of bluebells in May, this spilling out into the open where late winter bracken fires do no more harm than scorching the leaf tips, leaving the safely buried bulbs intact. There are a few patches of anemones - relics of ancient woodland, which often outlive the trees. Other flowers are unremarkable, violet, speedwell, yellow pimpernel, enchanter's nightshade and wood avens, with honeysuckle and ivy. Some, like wood sorrel and hard fern, are as common outside the wood as in and there are plenty of other ferns, with fine feathery stands of giant horsetail, growing even in the foulest of the iron-stained mine seepages.

Autumn is the time for woodland fungi, birch bracket or razor strop *(Piptoporus betulinus)* the commonest but *Laetiporus (Grifola) sulphureus* the most eye-catching with its yellow flanges, apricot above and sulphur below. A smaller bracket, a type of oyster-of-the-woods, is *Pleurotus dryinus*, another *Trametes confragas*. Big old beeches are likely to nurture perennial white shelves of *Trametes gibbosa* or cinnamon-coloured ones of *Ganoderma applanatum*.

Sticky *Oudmansiella mucida* toadstools push up among the copper coinage of fallen beech leaves. Others are *Pluteus cervinus*, butterscotch-sheened 'penny-tops' *(Collybia dryophila)*, white 'milky mycenas' *(Mycena galopus)* and alkali-scented *Mycena alcalina*. Eruptions of the ubiquitous yellow 'sulphur-tuft' *(Hypholoma fasciculare)* cluster around tree boles with the more reprehensible honey fungus *(Armillaria mellea)* which is an insidious tree killer.

Warted 'earth balls' *(Scleroderma aurantium)*, patterned like oversized, browned-off golf balls, are unusually abundant in the leaf mould. Orange blobs of *Dacrymyces deliquescens* ooze across sodden wood after rain and little pea-sized mounds of *Lycogala epidendron* change from soft coral pink to brittle fawn on ageing fence posts.

Sparrow hawks hunt among the trees and woodpeckers can be heard hammering away while feeding, home-building or just communicating with a fellow. Nuthatches and tree-creepers also scour the trunks for insects, while goldcrests join the roving bands of tits in the colder months. Woodcock occasionally winter here, but are very hard to see with their cryptic colouration. Some of the noisiest residents are the jays and 1993 was a particularly good year for these.

Early 1994 was remarkable for the huge numbers of bramblings feeding on beech-nuts in Gwaelod and across the river around Castell Coch. Several hundreds of these colourful finches from Northern Europe, with orange breasts and shoulder patches and eye-catching white rumps, were sifting through the fallen leaves in the steep beech hanger between Gwaelod Main Road and the Taff on 14th February. An overnight snowfall hid the beech-nuts under a 4 inch deep blanket of white. Next day the bramblings, unable to scratch for their food as blackbirds do, were forced out onto the pavement and adjacent bank, where the snow cover was broken.

Flocks of up to 40 siskins with a few redpolls also visit here from the North in February and March, hanging upside down to feed on the alder cones, like the coal tits which tweak seeds from the cones of larches. Theirs is a success story, siskin numbers having been on the up and up during the past few decades. Bright green ring-necked parakeets, which have been breeding successfully in the wild for many years now, have been seen shooting between the tree trunks.

Speckled woods are the only essentially woodland butterflies but various white species, particularly green-veined and orange-tip, are associated with damp patches, while brimstone caterpillars feed on the leaves of alder-buckthorn.

Conspicuous at dusk are white wave moths *(Deilinia pusaria)* and satin waves *(Acidalia subsericeata)*. Chestnut moths *(Conistra vaccinii)* are on the wing in September and October, their caterpillars munching away at the tree leaves from April to June. Angleshades *(Phlogophora meticulosa)*, although highly ornamental with their triangular wing pattern, can merge invisibly with drying leaves until they take wing, which they are most likely to do after dark.

Ginger-winged maybugs or cockchafers *(Melolontha melolontha)* no longer come blundering into car windscreens as habitually as they used to, but they are still around for a few weeks in May and June, making crash landings or falling into pools. Their root-chewing grubs live for 4 years in the ground and are no friends of the farmer.

On the whole, insects appreciate sunshine and one of the best times to see them is when the sun emerges after a protracted spell of rain which has prevented them from feeding. Sunny sites like the little open ragwort paddock by the cattery at Georgetown can be alive with them in July and August.

Glistening green thick-legged flower beetles *(Oedemera nobilis)* feed on St. John's wort and knapweed here; soldier beetles *(Rhagonycha fulva)* on angelica and hogweed, whilst hover flies and drone flies suspend themselves over centaury and corn mint, but not all get away with it. Crab spiders lie in wait for them, their colour often exactly matching that of the flower in which they lurk.

The stripy black and yellow caterpillars which sometimes strip the ragwort of its leaves are those of the black and red cinnabar moths *(Tyria (Callimorpha) jacobaea)*, which may fly in profusion in midsummer, along with the black and red five-spot and six-spot burnet moths *(Zygaena trifolii* and *Zygaena filipendulae)*.

6. Conifers on Old Woodland Sites

Plots to north and south of the broad-leaved woodland backing Gwaelod-y-Garth were planted with conifers in 1965. The northern plantation lies below the path which leads up valley from the hairpin bend behind the Gwaelod-y-Garth Inn, where indigenous broad-leaves persist above, producing a fine deep leaf mould. This ancient track crosses Owl Gully, a rift which gashes obliquely across the slope past Eddy Phillip's house on the Mountain Road and marks the subsidence above the modern Nant Garw Mine, which was finally closed in the 1980s. When the collapse occurred doors and windows at Garth Olwg and Ffygis split away from walls and plaster could be heard cracking behind the wallpaper.

The shallower Ffygis mine subsided towards the deeper tunnel far below, its roof caving in, and a fine watercress stream disappeared into the bowells of the earth. Such are the hazards of life in ex-mining villages! The Tyn-y-Darren Quarry close to the rift is the one which supplied building stone for most of the village houses, the tooled blocks reputed to have been brought down in donkey carts. Kestrels often nest there now and badgers have a sett in this same cliff further up the valley.

A new Forestry Commission track cut in the 1980s leads off this older one and traverses the lower wood to emerge onto the valley road at Gedrys, where timber was being extracted in the early 1990s. This bridged the North Sea Gas Main and had a broad swathe taken out for a pipeline in 1993.

Thirty-five year old western hemlock trees predominated in the planted area before felling in the late 1990s, but there were spruce, fir, pine and cypress mixed in - as in the southern plantation above Georgetown, which extends to the fringes of the Coed-y-Bedw Nature Reserve below the road up the valley to Pentyrch. This wood covers 63 acres, but is an awkward shape, involving a length of fencing more usual for 100 acres. Fencing is essential in the early stages, to save the young trees from the sheep, but both fences and stiles have collapsed long since, the trees well able to look after themselves by the time the posts rot and collapse.

The land was in private ownership prior to 1965, with the useful timber contracted out to a firm which was slow to remove it. The Forestry Commission had to lend a hand, but planting was, nevertheless, delayed until May when the trees were sprouting green. Foresters worked up and down the slope, spade in hand and apron pocket full of young trees, which had spent two years in the nursery seedbed and one in transplanted lines. They dug out the clay clods by hand and stamped the saplings in with well practised heels. Most of the little trees took, any gaps spontaneously filled by self sown birches. Plenty of nurse trees were left as protection - oak, ash, sycamore, birch and alder - these likely to be shaded out as the 'nurselings' grew up.

Norway Spruce

Lodgepole Pine

Sitka Spruce

92,000 Norway spruces went in: *"Rather more than will be needed, to allow for those which will be nicked as Christmas trees".* (This wry comment from the head forester on the ground). Western hemlock, one of the most graceful of conifers, with pendulous branches, was planted at the top of the wood (still well out of the wind on this leeward face). Japanese larch occupied a strip along the bottom and up the northern fenceline, as a fire belt half a chain wide where there was most fire hazard near village and road, this being less inflammable than the others. Larches also score in growing faster than the rest on these deeper soils, while their yellowing foliage in autumn and fresh green in spring give them a high amenity value.

Another concession to appearance was the planting of beech alongside the old hollow way up to the mountain road. Poplars *(Populus serotina)*, which are not subject to cankering of the trunk as some poplars are, were planted in a damp patch at the bottom - 20 feet apart. Closer planting of the conifers ensured straight stems and the early death of side branches to prevent the enlargement of knots in the timber. Dead twigs were knocked off prior to thinning and the brashings left to rot, the increased fire hazard which these posed offset by their contribution to the formation of a good forest soil.

The first harvest of thinnings was scheduled to come out when the trees were 15-20 years old - cut into longer poles than those formerly used as pit props in the mines. This would reduce the trees from about 17,000 an acre to 800, the survivors due to mature at about 80 years old but likely to be felled long before this, as we saw in 1993. Growth rate slows after the earlier years, as it does with fattening livestock, and waiting for the final years' input is not an economic proposition. Early fellings in the Gedrys woodland in 1989 opened the way for a splendid crop of biennial foxgloves flowering in 1990. An equally fine spread of foxgloves occurred in 1993-4, 2 years after the clear felling of the western hemlock in the northern plantation on the lower slope up-valley from the famous hairpin bend.

The water table is high over much of the planted area, with old mine workings often brimful, and this inhibits the growth of hardwoods, which have deeply penetrating taproots, all the bigger trees being on the better drained slopes. The superficial spread of roots produced by the conifers is above most of the water and consequent oxygen deficiency, but give a less firm anchorage and often fails to hold in a gale, as seen in the upturned root slabs of those suffering wind-blow.

Little trees can be ring-barked at the base by field voles or rabbits (there are no ponies to do this at a higher level). Grey squirrels, the chief de-barkers and de-budders, prefer sycamore. They do no harm stripping the cones for the winged seeds as no seed crop is required.

In the native woodland these spritely little animals have a bonanza when the hazel nuts ripen and the surface of the mountain road can be littered with the split shells left over from their feastings.

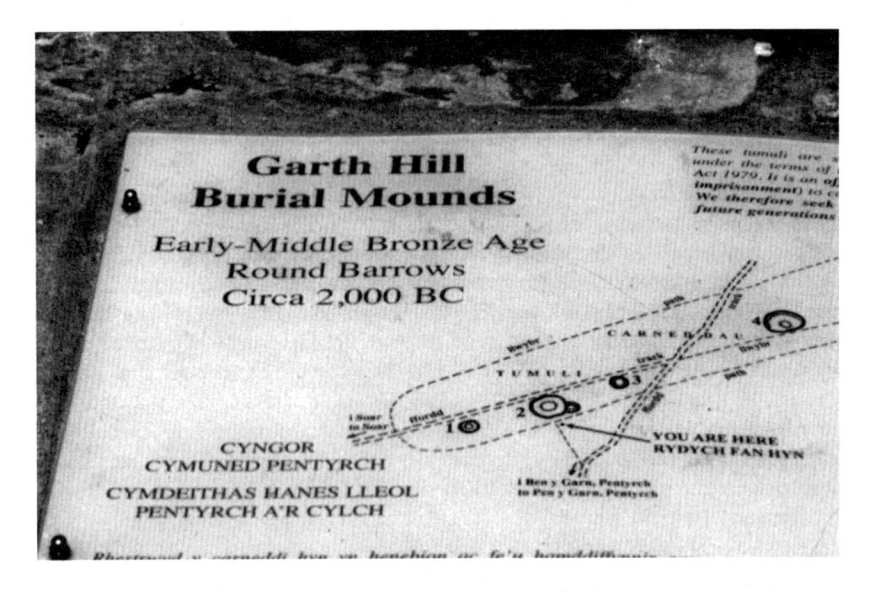

A corner of the plaque erected on the Garth summit by the Pentyrch History Society in 1999

Chapter 2

COED-Y-BEDW NATURE RESERVE, HISTORY, VEGETATION AND STREAM LIFE

Introductory

Coed-y-Bedw, is a strip of woodland east of Pentyrch, occupying the valley between the Great Garth and the Little Garth, and is of especial interest on many counts. It is rich in human history, having been part of the 16th to 19th century industrial complex, yet a sufficiently diverse flora and fauna has survived to merit its designation by the Nature Conservancy Council as an S S S I (Site of Special Scientific Interest).

41 acres (16.6 hectares), rising from 70 m to 150 m below the Heol Goch road, which climbs from Lower Gwaelod to Pentyrch, have been managed as a nature reserve by the Glamorgan Wildlife Trust since 1968 and the site has been well used in the training of zoology students from the University of Wales at Cardiff and for special studies, such as that of Dr. Michael Claridge on leaf-hoppers and of Dr. John Edington on caddis insects.

History tells us that the valley was part of the estates of the Castell-y-Mynach family until 1720, when it passed by marriage to Lord Talbot of Hensol and from him to Lord Dynevor. This worthy handed it to Colonel Wingfield of Barrington Park, Gloucester with one of his daughters as a marriage dowrie and the Colonel sold it to the Forestry Commission in 1959.

The County Wildlife Trust held it on a 14 year licence from the Commission until 1983, when it bought the site outright for £10,000, £1,000 of this contributed by the local Community Council, which valued the opportunity to keep the area as a rural asset in perpetuity. The Commission retained 5 acres in the east to give access to the 62 acres of their adjacent Rhiw'r Ceiliog conifer plantation. The steep tumble of mossy rocks along the north-east was not included in the Forestry Commisssion transactions. This is part of the reserve by default, having been 'fenced out' by Messrs. Browen and Williams, owner and occupant of Garth Uchaf Farm alongside.

Over the years the reserve has prospered under the able management of the volunteer wardens, first Dave Duckett and then Brian Stiles, helped and succeeded by Alan Lock, and since 1998 by Cliff Woodhead. Many hundreds of voluntary man hours have been put in erecting fences, repairing and making paths, constructing more than a dozen foot bridges and laying boardwalks over wet ground, clearing obstructive tree casualties, chopping out the noxious Japanese knotweed, deepening one pond and making another, putting up nest boxes for birds and other routine management tasks.

1. Status, Geology, Mining and Myths

Coed-y-Bedw's diversity arises largely from its borderline position geologically, between the South Crop of the Coalfield and the South Border Ridge of Limestone. Occupying the valley of the east flowing Nant Cwmllwydrew, a tributary of the Taff, it lies mostly on the limey side of the stream, at the foot of the Little Garth, so most has a shady northerly aspect.

The belt of soft Millstone Grit which forms its heart is only 60 feet (19 m) wide and is partly sandstone and partly shale, which has worn away to form the valley. This is the miners' 'Farewell Rock', where these hewers of stone bade farewell to the coal.

It has little effect on the vegetation, being covered, except in the west by ice-borne deposits: Boulder Clay in the mid-west and Glacial Sand and Gravel in the east. Surface soil has slid into it from the south face of the Great Garth in the process of sollifluction, engendered by freeze and thaw and consequent slumping after the last Ice Age.

The central stream has cut down into the boulder clay to form a mini gorge through the upper valley. Lower down it winds more gently through rich black leaf mould and alluvium which never fully dries out, so that gumboots were a 'must' for any visit prior to the construction of paths.

Before emptying into the Taff the stream waters were dammed back into a reservoir on the gravel river terrace now occupied by Heol Beri green. The substantial head of water was discharged over two wheels to power the old Pentyrch Iron Furnace with the tail race driving the Forge. Because of the steep gradient and cutting power of the stream, the reservoir suffered silting and around 1790 it was replaced as a source of water power for the forge by the Gwaelod Canal, which led water off the Taff from behind the Portobello Weir upstream to supply the tin-rolling mills beyond.

An ancient iron mine, much older than this, was sited within the reserve and is marked by a heap of burned iron ore and limey slag, less massive and more pulverised than that from the Brass Vein outside the Cwm Dous Coal Mine by the River Taff. T.W.Booker wrote of this ancient Cwmllwydrew furnace in 1843, when it was already in ruins.

This 16th century blast furnace was built of stone set into the hillside, to facilitate loading iron ore and charcoal fuel from the local woods into the top. Molten iron was run off at the bottom into a bed of sand, but was brittle, due to its high content of carbon. Edgar L. Chappell, in his "Historic Melingriffith" (1940), records that iron guns were made here at Pentyrch in 1574. For a period of over a century little is known of the works until they were revived again around 1740. During rebuilding an old plate dated 1643 was unearthed.

One of the clay pipes found by Alan Lock in 1980 and 1981 was dated at the National Museum of Wales at between 1680 and 1720. The initials 'M D' on its base indicated that it had been made by Morris Decon of Broseley, Salop.

The tramway system transporting this material, and later coal, is marked on the 1841 tithe map and the 1876 Ordnance Survey map. An iron tram wheel was found in 1979 by the late John Tyler, author of "Iron in the Soul", the story of iron mining on the Little Garth. Wheels were of cast iron and without flanges, like the pit wheels then in use. They ran along the L shaped iron rails which were bolted directly to stone blocks, without recourse to wooden sleepers. Lengths of rails sometimes surface: two appeared in stream beds in 1980: and one of the stone sleepers perforated with bolt holes has been lodged in the National Museum of Wales. Use of a metal detector by Martin John has brought to light various relics of the old mining days - a pick, an axe, rock drills and wedges, these last from the Little Garth Iron Mine.

The main extraction of haematite ore started one and a half centuries later - on the Little Garth. It affected the reserve only in the dumping of limestone spoil in the south-east, some of this from the production of red and yellow ochre from limonite ore, which was used in the manufacture of paint in the late 19th century. Some was removed in the

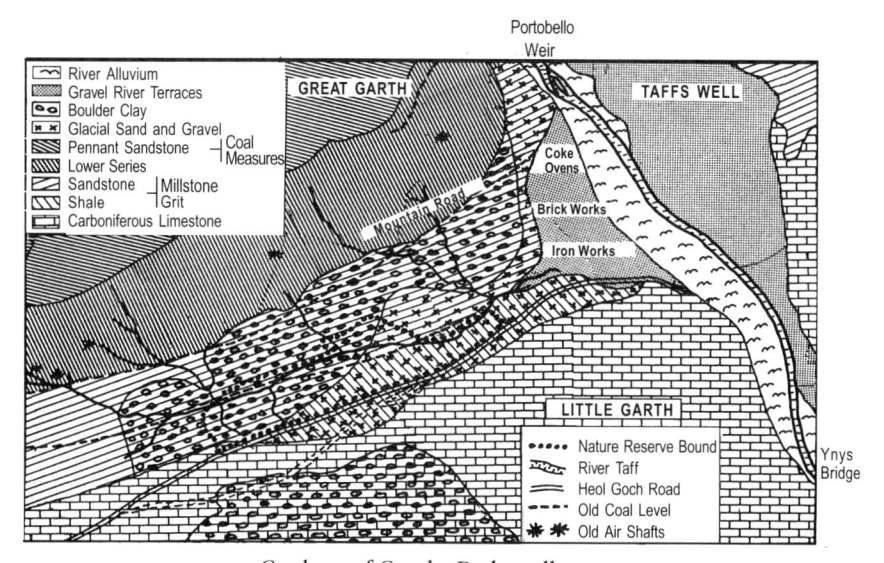

Geology of Coed y Bedw valley

1930s to building sites in Gwent by a local contractor, and the mighty concrete blocks on which his diesel-powered crusher stood are still witness to these past endeavours. Much limey rubble remains, however, to nurture a calcicolous (lime-loving) flora.

Another of Coed-y-Bedw's associations with mining was the taking of coal from the Coidy Beddw level in the north-west of the reserve. This colliery was opened in 1827 by Morgan Thomas (born 1781), who was poet as well as mine owner. He lived in the now ruinous Maes yr Houl House alongside - a two-storey building with stables attached. Later the windows were bricked up and it was used as kennels for the hounds of the Pentyrch Hunt.

The coal level was said to be 860 yards long with an air shaft for ventilation and its stone arched entrance is still very obvious, but too dangerous to enter. The tunnel roof has subsided uphill to the north to form a big depression, now full of trees, with the planted perennial rye-grass and cocksfoot leys lapping up to its margins - an involuntary 'setaside'. Chappell (1940) records that around 1832 Blakemore and Co., who employed 200 people, opened a Coed-y-Bedw Colliery.

Some of the coal went via the Glamorgan Canal to Cardiff to be off-loaded at Albert Wharf - some to power steamships plying from Cardiff and some for export. More was used locally, the method of fusing ironstone with coal instead of charcoal having been perfected by 1763 and the Melingriffith Forge being in existence down river from 1750, the tin-plate factory there from 1790. T.W.Booker, one time part owner of Pentyrch Ironworks, acquired the mine for a time and the coal was used in iron smelting at Heol Beri, but no more coal came from here after 1913.

The large amount of spoil removed from underground accumulated as a long ridge above the western boulder clay and supports today's only grassy clearings in the woodland. The friable grey material, apparently unsuitable for spontaneous tree growth, is beloved by yellow field ants *(Lasius flavus)* whose mounds dot the surface. These become pocked with the narrow incisions made by the beaks of geen woodpeckers, which have a passion for ants. The birds' white-ended, walking stick shaped droppings are full of the undigested yellow exo-skeletons of the ants, their abundance indicative of the vast number needed to sustain a bird the size of a woodpecker.

Vegetation and glacial deposits mask most of the fossil-bearing rocks, but some have been brought to light by mining operations. Dolomitisation destroys fossils, so none are found in the red Dolomite, but grey limestone exposures have yielded the two corals, *Syringopora* and massed tubular growths of *Lithostrotion*, also the twinned halves of *Brachiopod* lamp shells in limestone fragments, whilst fossil fish scales were found in 1981. Others are coal measure plants, to be picked up in the spoil heaps. Commonest are forebears of our modern horsetails and club-mosses, *Calamites, Sigillaria, Lepidodendron* and *Stigmaria*, which last are tree roots. Much rarer are the climbing *Sphenophyllum* and *Asterophyllites*. Ancient fern-allies include *Sphenopteris, Mariopteris, Alethopteris, Neuropteris, Cyclopteris* and *Orricularis*. (*Pteris* implies fern, as in *Pteridium*, the bracken). Unfortunately none of these early plants have easily remembered vernacular names.

With so large a population living so close, myths and legends have inevitably grown up around the valley. Edgar Chappell, in his book, "Old Whitchurch", tells us that the Bendith y Manau (fairies) dance through Cwmllwydrew Woods on allhallows eve and the Ladi Wen (white witch) is also about on occasion. Y Brennin Llwydd (King of the Mist) haunts the old iron mine on the Little Garth. The one-armed ghost reputed to haunt the Cwmllwydrew Cottage is likely to be the local school attendance officer or 'whipper in' who is reputed to have committed suicide there in 1930.

Man's impact on the area during the 20th century has been in the realms of forestry, farming and conservation, rather than mineral extraction.

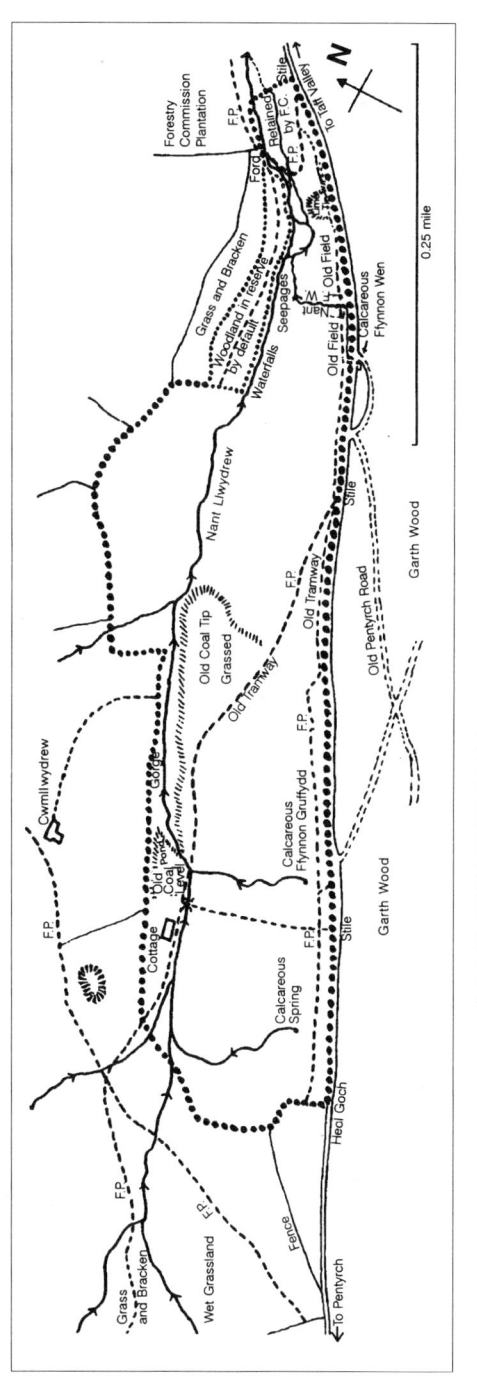

2. Woodland History and Management

The translation of 'Coed-y-Bedw' is 'Wood of Birches', suggesting that the name was given after some initial disturbance such as charcoal making. Birchwoods are normally temporary, as birch is a successional phase on the way to something more permanent, such as beech, oak or pinewood.

The tiny winged seeds, set free from crumbling birch catkins, are wafted everywhere on the wind and germinate wherever there is space, the chief enemy of the resulting seedlings being sheep. Acorns and beech mast arrive later, but are able to germinate in the light shade cast by birch trees. Birch seed is unable to germinate under the denser shade of beech or oak, so recruitment dwindles and the wood changes in character, with birch relegated to clearings.

Because of the long history of exploitation, there must have been boosts to the birch all along the line and a lot remains into the present conservation epoch. First there were the charcoal burners: the 'corders' who cut and bundled the small timber, and the 'colliers' who fired it under the oxygen-excluding soil cover. One acre of forest was necessary to supply the charcoal to make three tons of iron and charcoal continued to be used for a time alongside coal. Throughout the periods of iron mining and coal mining many uses would have been found for timber, both industrial and domestic, with almost every cottager needing bean poles and pea sticks, hen houses and sheds, as well as fuel and fencing.

Conifer planting is not a new phenomenon and there were conifers on both sides of the Heol Goch Road after the first world war. These were clear-felled in 1930 and the logs dragged out by Sonny, a big shire horse, who was fondly remembered by the late David Jenkins. A few oaks and birches were left standing, but brambles grew into a dense

Small woodland fungi: *Galerina hypnorum*, Caterpillar Club *(Cordiceps militaris)*, *Crepidotus variabilis*, *Lycoperdon pyriforme* puffball, Stump *Lycogala epidendron* and *Mycena galopus*.

7. Giant Horsetail

6. Rushy 'unimproved' paddock in the Coed-y-Bedw valley. August 1999.

8. Pheasant Chick

9. 'Improved' Ryegrass paddock in the Coed-y-Bedw valley, June 1982.
The wooded hollow is an old mine entrance.

10. Lesser Celandine

11. Wood Sorrel

12. Wild Apples as well as native Crabapples spring up on the hillsides.

13. Damsons on suckered sapling from a derelict cottage garden on the east flank of the Garth mountain.

tangle with the ingress of light, excluding both small boys and the Pentyrch fox-hounds, but not the hounds' quarry. Foxes have always resided in the wood during living memory and could easily give their pursuers the slip here.

The name Coed-y-Bedw is not entirely inappropriate, even in the now, more settled, phase. Apart from a few small trees in the lower valley, all today's birches are downy birch *(Betula pubescens)*, the true silver birch *(Betula pendula verrucosa)* with pendant branches being rarer in the district generally. They tend to be tall and vulnerable to wind-blow and a whole birch spinney by the Heol Goch road was devastated in the winter gales of 1990, the trunks falling more or less parallel and blocking the southern path. (Three old established public footpaths traverse the wood and more have been constructed to facilitate the taking of circular walks.)

It is likely that the wet alderwood along the valley bottom has suffered little or no disturbance. Currently the drier slopes in the west are occupied by beechwood similar to that on the Little Garth and the moister eastern slopes by mixed oakwood with birch, ash and sycamore, like that on the lower slopes of the Great Garth. Hazel occurs throughout, its roots supporting parasitic toothwort near the ford. One of the crab apple trees is unusually large and there is wych elm, guelder-rose, holly, hawthorn and alder buckthorn. The limey side is characterised by field maple, dogwood and wild clematis, but only one spindle bush is known to survive. Bullace *(Prunus institia)* is here as well as sloe, and six Scots pines.

Something of the vegetational history can be gleaned from a study of the old maps. The 1841 tithe map refers to a time when the Coidy-Beddw Colliery was being worked and shows most of the slopes between the reserve and the Mountain Road along the Great Garth to have been wooded. A narrow field occupied the south-eastern strip of reserve as far uphill as the track onto the Little Garth, where woodland changed to fields on the western heights.

The 1876 map shows the main stream to have been culverted under the area known today as 'the waterfalls', to enable spoil to be transported across it. The water surfaced at the east near the main ford by the Glamorgan Wildlife Trusts' stone cairn. The pasture persisted along the south-east but was subject to spoil dumping.

The map shows the original industrial tramway extending beyond the reserve in the north-west and three other tramways, which have now been incorporated into footpaths, but with stone sleepers remaining alongside the foundations of one of the mine buildings. A tramway bridge spanned the Pentyrch Road (Heol Goch), this made of 24 inch blocks of timber supported on stone pillars with tooled coping stones.

It was used to bring spoil across from the Little Garth for dumping.

The bridge is omitted from the 1900 Ordnance Survey map and trees appear for the first time on the western spoil tip. The present Heol Goch road is marked, replacing the former one which remains as the muddy track along the foot of the Little Garth.

The 1920 map shows loss of woodland on the slopes to the north, with grass fields encroaching right to the edge of the reserve, and the spoil tip still marked in the east. Bramble and scrub are cut annually to prevent the grassy clearing from being absorbed into the treescape as woodland advances towards the summit. The margins are currently occupied by woodland herbs: a dense sward of enchanter's nightshade and six foot high foxgloves.

Felling is known to have been carried out until 1919, the logs taken by horse and cart to Creigiau railway station for shipment. Coppicing is thought to have been done until about 1940, with standards cut on a 24 year cycle and bushes every 7 to 8 years - these mostly hazel for hedge stakes, although hedge laying ceased long since hereabouts, with most field boundaries now of post and wire.

Some coppicing was carried out in the 1980s, but is unlikely to be repeated, as there is no outlet for the timber and the canopy is sufficiently open for a good flowery understorey. Trees were still being bulldozed outside the reserve and piled in awkward heaps around the woodland edges in 1982, some burned and some left to rot.

Tree planting was carried out in the 1930s, but the Forestry Commission introduced no conifers durings its tenure (1959-1983), so fences fell into disrepair and sheep wandered indiscriminately through the woodland. Access was later controlled and there is officially no sheep grazing in the reserve at present, but Welsh Mountain ewes have an uncanny knack of finding their way into places where they are not supposed to be.

The little group of ewes present in July 1993 seemed to be keeping to the paths, nipping off the bramble leaves quite selectively and leaving the tall grass virtually untouched. (Two grass species exclude almost all others, these the bristly-leaved tufted hair grass and the paler wood false brome, which are evidently unpalatable.) Bramble encroachment is not a problem at present, despite the good penetration of sunlight, and it looks as though light sheep grazing might help to keep it that way.

The 1983 summer drought was regarded as an emergency and cattle from the desiccated fields above had to be allowed down to the stream to drink. There was inevitable physical damage. Already a flight of steps had had to be rebuilt after their depredations the previous August. Steep slopes, soft ground and heavy-footed kine do not mix well in nature reserves.

(I am grateful to the wardens, Brian Stiles and Alan Lock for the foregoing historical and management information and much else appearing in this chapter.)

3. Flowers and Fungi

Spring is the most colourful time in Coed-y-Bedw, as in woodlands everywhere, and the visitor can enjoy three different sequences of flowering here, the wet, the limey and the acid.

First to open in the boggy valley bottom is the golden saxifrage, lightening dark quagmires with its lacey greenish-yellow flowers - these overtaken in late March by a blaze of golden kingcups. Others are more muted: the pale mauve of marsh violet and pink of marsh valerian, followed by the taller cat's valerian, with hemp agrimony and meadowsweet from the end of June. Much of the marsh remains green throughout, however, some dominated by feathery stands of giant horsetail and some in the west by a thick cover of great pond sedge. Parts are sufficiently acid to support pale mats of *Sphagnum* moss with darker mounds of *Polytrichum*.

Drier areas bear celandines at first, almost as bright as the kingcups and opening even earlier, with dog's mercury on the limey side. Then come wood anemones and a sprinkling of primroses, after which the calcareous slopes disappear under an aromatic white sheet of ramsons or wild garlic, while most of the rest is awash with bluebells, the blue interrupted here and there by a clump of whitebells. Midsummer brings a few wild rose and honeysuckle flowers.

Peeping out among the dominants are heath violet, wood sorrel, pignut and red campion. Yellow pimpernel, lady's mantle and herb Robert persist through the summer, alongside wood avens and enchanter's nightshade and the muted background of wood sedge, remote sedge and woodland grasses. Plants to be sought on limey rather than acid soils are moschatel and sanicle in the shade, pearly everlasting on the yellow ochre tip and creeping cinquefoil in clearings. Most notable are the handsome pink spikes of the rare bistort or snake-root *(Polygonum bistorta)*.

In early winter, when the flowers fade, the fungi come into their own. Slabby fawn *Clitocybe nebularis* toadstools come bursting through the carpets of fallen leaves and dark india rubber blobs of black bulgar or black stud fungus *(Bulgaria inquinans)* appear on rotting logs, alongside purple sploshes of *Coryne sarcoides*. Brightest are the scarlet elf cups *(Sarcoscypha (Peziza) coccinea)*, on partially buried sticks, outshining the rubbery brown cups of *Peziza badia*.

Crumple-topped, saddle-shaped false morels *(Helvella crispa)* assume weird shapes among the more orthodox gingery deceivers *(Laccaria laccata)* and bright mauve amethyst deceivers *(Laccaria amethystea)*. One of the most bizarre is the wood hedgehog *(Hypnum repandum)*, the spore-bearing underside of the cap covered with dangling teeth instead of radiating gills or massed pores.

Fungi are fleeting, their above ground lives are short and they break surface at infrequent intervals, or stay permanently hidden in moist soil or rotting wood. Each season reveals something different and no less than 119 species have been recorded in the reserve on casual visits over the years - too numerous to mention all by name.

A fungus foray here led by Roy Perry, mycologist at the National Museum of Wales, yielded 46 different toadstools, brackets, fairy clubs, stinkhorns, puffballs and slime fungi. This sortie was on 28th October, a peak period for this group, falling earlier or later depending on seasonal rainfall and temperature.

The toadstool form of a disc-shaped cap elevated on a stipe or stalk is commonest. Among the smallest were delicate gingery parasols of *Galerina hypnorum* growing among mosses on tree branches, the mosses themselves sometimes associated with the lichen, *Cetraria glauca*. Among the largest were pink blushers *(Amanita rubescens)* and brittle yellowish russules *(Russula xanthochlora)*.

White-spored milk-caps were similarly chunky and notable for the exudations of white milky sap when broken. The mild or oak milk-cap

Large Woodland Fungi: Red -cracked Bolete *(Boletus chrysenteron)*, Dog Stinkhorn *(Mutinus caninus)* with longitudinally cut volva or egg, and Brown Roll-rim *(Paxillus involutus)*.

(*Lactarius quietus*) emitted a sweet oily smell and left a mildly bitter taste on the tip of the tongue. *Lactarius vietus*, growing by the stream, had a fiercely hot peppery taste. The milky mycena (*Mycena galopus*) was another producing a milky juice.

Cystoderma amianthemum was recognisable by the scaly base to the stipe, brown roll-rim (*Paxillus involutus*) by the soft, suedelike edge to the inrolled cap and the extension of the gills down the stipe. Winners on the culinary front were the fleshy mauve wood blewits (*Lepista nuda*, better known as *Tricholoma nudum*), but one of the most unusual finds was a *Merulius* related to the dry rot fungus.

Many woodland fungi have a close mycorhizal association with forest trees which is of benefit to both, the underground filaments of the fungi wrapping themselves round or penetrating into the tree roots. They pass dissolved soil minerals to the trees and receive sugars in return. Few trees can grow without them and it is likely that their tardiness in colonising the old spoil heap was due to the absence of the necessary soil fungi. Red-cracked bolete (*Boletus chrysenteron*) was one here having a close partnership with beech. The underside of the warted brown cap where the spores are produced consisted of a spongy mass of vertical yellow pores instead of radiating gills.

Biggest of the brackets found on that late October day were rather mushy giant polypores (*Meripulus giganticus*, better known as *Grifola gigantea*) clusted round the base of a beech. Individual shelves were up to 30 cm across and the clump spanned a metre. Much commoner were the firm flanges of artists' fungus (*Ganoderma applanatum*), also on beech and shedding cinnamon coloured spores like cayenne pepper over all and sundry. This causes eventual heart rot in its host and continues to live on the dead wood as a saprophyte.

A pink bracket, turning pinker when bruised, was *Trametes rubescens*, growing on sallow and other soft-barked trees. One of the smallest, found on sticks among the grass, was the kidney-shaped *Crepidotus variabilis*, with gills rather than pores, like a little oyster-of-the-woods. The true 'oyster' (*Pleurotus ostreatus*) is here too. Not a true bracket, but forming curved upside-down shelves on elder trunks, were the rubbery, flesh-coloured flaps of Jew's ear fungus (*Auricularia auricula*).

The scarlet caterpillar fungus (*Cordyceps militaris*) manifests itself as crimson and orange truncheons a few centimetres high. This is a parasite, growing on and killing moth chrysalids, whose caterpillar stage sought refuge underground in vain. Another truncheon shape, larger and less often found, was the dog stinkhorn (*Mutinus caninus*) growing by the ford. Like the commoner white stinkhorn (*Phallus impudicus*), this sprouts from a jelly-filled egg or volva at the soil surface. The orange thimble-shaped tip becomes coated with black mucous which smells of dung and serves to attract flies which will carry the spores away.

Pear-shaped stump puffballs *(Lycoperdon pyriforme)* occurred, these the only true puffballs to grow on wood instead of soil. The so-called bark 'puffball' *(Reticularia lycoperdon)*, resembling half a golf ball protruding from a tree trunk, is actually the solid phase of one of the slime moulds .

The reserve is poor in lichens but rich in bryophytes (mosses and liverworts), these seeming to have appropriated most available surfaces in the high humidity. Roy Perry recorded 69 different mosses and 20 liverworts between 1976 and 1983. Midwinter, before the tree leaves expand, is a good time to see these small plants. Spore capsules are appearing then on the abundant *Mnium hornum* and *Polytrichum formosum*, while banks are shaggy with lopsided *Dicranum majus* and pale fronds of *Thuidium tamariscinum*. The moss *Hookeria lucens*, which is rare in Glamorgan, has leaves in two rows, resembling the liverwort, *Plagiochila asplenioides*, which is named after the little fern with a similar leaf arrangement. There are two species of *Fissidens* mosses with two-rowed leaves.

Dog lichen *(Peltigera)* is one of the few locally common lichens, seen mainly round the old cottage and in damp grass. *Cladonia* species have been found on an old ash as well as the ground, but the main tree dwellers are old man's beard lichen *(Usnea subfloridana)* and *Parmelia perlata*.

4. Tufa Streams and Smaller Water Life

The name "Cwmllwydrew" translates into "Valley of the Hoar Frost" and there is no doubt that this valley between the Great and Little Garths acts as a frost pocket. Regular winter commuters crossing the stream by Heol Beri Green are familiar with the swish of icy slush under their wheels and sparkling ice crystals on the grass alongside when there is no visible sign of frost to north or south

The valley can produce strange ice formations, as well as clear cut animal tracks in the snow. February 1977 yielded a fascinating collection of vertical ice rods, like closely packed, oversized acupuncture needles, splaying slightly from molehill sized mounds formed on frozen peat. It seemed as though water was being forced relentlessly up from underground by expansion of that below, freezing as it surfaced and pushed out too gently to break the square-cornered millimetre wide rods, which welled up, thousands together among the flopped remains of giant horsetail stems.

Ice had sealed in only the quieter sections of the stream, but a slight drop in level had left a series of horizontally aligned ice discs the size of half crowns, suspended just above the water on the ends of ice-sheathed grass blades.

Nant Llwydrew rises on acidic coal measures in the west, near the hamlet of Pen-y-Garn. Two acid tributaries join it from the north, one from the scarp above the Great Garth Mountain Road, the other from the mine in the reserve. This leaves along the tramroad which gave access to the mine, the rich orange staining by precipitated iron hydroxide not inhibiting the fine bed of water mint.

Two calcareous springs bubble from the limestone where this abuts onto the Millstone Grit, depositing a thin film of tufa or calcite on their way to join the main stream. A third spring supplying an old horse trough above the Heol Goch Road is piped under the road into the reserve. This is the Ffynnon Wen or White Spring, possibly because of a former white coating of tufa.

During the early years of the 1990s Ffynnon Wen cut a narrow, 2 metre deep gorge just below one of the footbridges, the mini chasm spanned by a mesh of beech roots the thickness of a man's leg. Not all the water disappeared underground, into what looked a bit like the collapsed roof of a hidden cave, some tumbling on downhill in a very modest channel.

The central limestone spring, Ffynnon Gruffydd, was reputed to have healing properties, like those of the opposite bank of the Taff which gave its name to Taff's Well. Folk are reputed to have come from far and wide in the hope of curing eye complaints.

The springs are more permanent than the main source and it is these that maintain the flow during droughts. The stream course is constantly changing as it meanders back and forth, cutting into steep wooded banks and undermining a boundary fence which had to be relocated.

Vacated channels may fill again during subsequent spates. When water continues to flow in both, islands are formed, a considerable sized one lying south of the ford, its end bunded off when the south-east entrance track was made. The south channel flows along the stony track to join the other at the ford, eroding both track (now unused and overgrown)

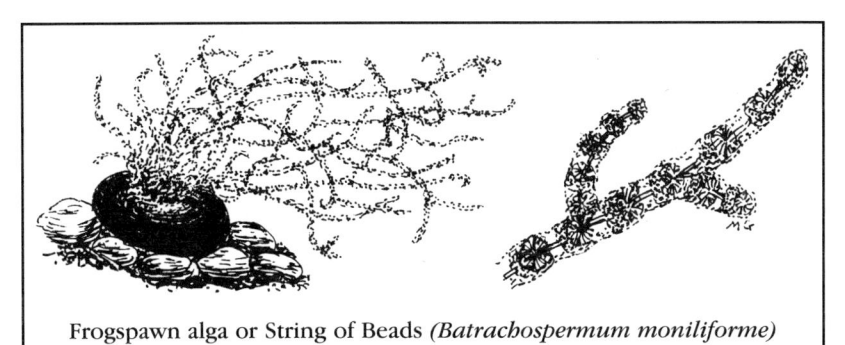

Frogspawn alga or String of Beads *(Batrachospermum moniliforme)*

and the path by the cairn, where it has excavated a fine exposure of glacial gravel

Most water plants are tolerant of acidity and the iron fouling which often goes with it, but animals are not. A plant sharing the faunal dislike of acidity and pollution and occurring only in the third, unnamed limey spring source, is the frogspawn alga *(Batrachospermum moniliforme)*. Red algae are mostly seaweeds and this is one of the very few to grow in fresh water. It appears brownish-green against the clean-washed shingle where the water emerges and it takes two forms.

The adult phase, present in spring and summer, is irregularly branched and encased in transparent jelly. The juvenile form, or *Chantransia* stage is filamentous and undistinguished, coating pebbles with a shiny red paint-like growth equivalent to the early filamentous growth of mosses, the protonema. Branched adults are budded off from *Chantransia* threads as the familiar mosses are budded off from protonema.

Adult fronds consist of a central axis beset with numerous dense whorls of tiny branches bearing the reproductive organs, these placed like a series of sweeps' brushes along its length. They are easily seen with a hand lens and supply the other name of "string of beads". The cylinders of jelly in which they are embedded make them as difficult to hold as eels and impossible to pull from a pebble or float onto a piece of paper for drying, as they glug off with the water. It is this character which gives the names of "frogspawn alga" and *Batrachospermum*, frogs being Batrachians, but a better name, in view of the linear alignment, would be "toadspawn alga".

The only plant associate in the crystal clear water is the rare liverwort *Solenostoma tristis*, formerly *Jungermannia tristis*. Another, *Pellia fabbroniana*, occurs just downstream, bearing sex organs in early spring. Fragile spore capsules like attenuated drumsticks appear on the related *Pellia epiphylla* at the end of winter, but this species, like the larger *Conocephalum conicum*, is not confined to limey sites, coating vertical as well as horizontal surfaces wherever moisture and space allow.

Psectrocladius midge larvae jack-knife out from the jellied fronds and medium sized *Dytiscid* beetles shelter among them. Freshwater shrimps *(Gammarus pulex)* scud everywhere in the gushing water which swirls less active animals round and round, although some, like the cone-shaped *Ancylus* river limpets, are firmly fixed. Most numerous of the sedentary animals are the *Agapetis* caddis larvae and pupae in their cemented tubes of tiny pebbles. *Tinodes unicolor* caddis build sinuous galleries of silt grains glued to stones or tufa lumps.

John Edington's studies of *Psychomyiid* caddis larvae in the early 1970s showed that this species, common here, occurred in 19 of the 98 streams examined and in all of these the calcium content of the water exceeded 60 miligrams per litre, with calcite usually being precipitated out on the bed. *Tinodes rostocki* was not so demanding of lime and seemed to be the southern lowland counterpart of *Tinodes dives*, which typified upland, moorland streams in the Brecon Beacons. *Lype reducta*, which is rare in Britain as a whole, proved to be common in tributaries of the Rivers Ely and Rhymney as well as the Taff.

Tinodes and others graze on the blue-green algae, *Phormidium* and *Microphormidium*, which are associated with the lime thrown out of solution. Chunks of tufa broken across show concentric rings of algal growth inside. These inner layers were peripheral when the lump was smaller and the algae helped the tufa to grow by actively absorbing carbon dioxide from the soluble calcium bicarbonate so that the insoluble calcium carbonate or limestone was left behind in a limey deposit. As this natural cement increased the algae grew outwards to stay in the light. *Tinodes* can feed on the buried algae by secreting an acid fluid to dissolve away the lime. A moss associated with this growth here is *Cratoneuron commutatum*.

Tinodes larvae live in tubular galleries, 4-6 times their own length, which they cement onto the surface of the food-bearing calcite. These are of sand grains lined with silt, but are sufficiently transparent to allow light to filter through, so that the algae can grow inside them. The whole operation is slightly suggestive of the 'farming' of fungus gardens in ants' nests. The larva is slender enough to turn round inside the tunnel and it emerges wholly or partly at either end to graze the algae within easy reach. Having exhausted this, it detaches the end of the tube and swings it round to an adjacent feeding patch, allowing more to grow on the grazed area - and in a shorter time than with rotational cattle grazing!

Another caddis, *Silo pallipes* is the particular victim of a parasitic ichneumon wasp, *Agriotypus armatus*, which is able to walk on and under the water. The adult wasp ambles around on the surface film, like a pond-skater, then crawls under water in a very unwasplike manner, looking for a Silo larva to victimise, although apparently not adapted to underwater breathing in any way. It lays an egg in the caddis larva and the wasp grub, when it hatches, consumes its host economically, sparing all the vital parts until after it has pupated, when the unwilling host finally dies.

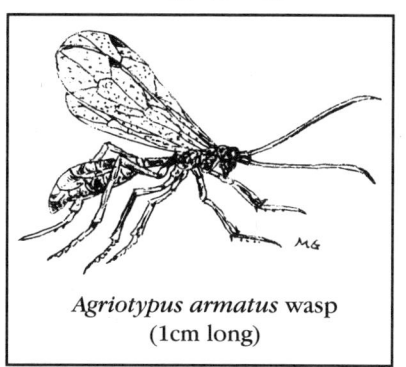

Agriotypus armatus wasp
(1cm long)

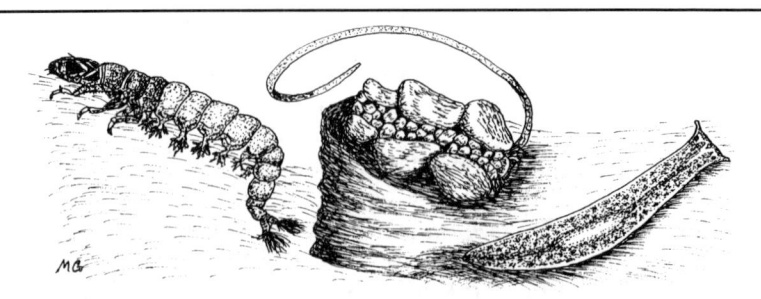

(left) Net-spinning *Hydropsyche* caddis larva, (centre) Tube-building *Silo* caddis pupa parasitised by *Agriotypus* ichneumon wasp, (right) *Polycelis felina* flatworm.

Infected caddis tubes can be recognised by the ribbon of silk 1-5 cm long and 2 mm wide which the wasp pushes out of the stony cocoon. This may help it to breathe. Whatever its function, it is a vital one, for the wasp dies if it is removed. If not, it is likely to emerge as an adult wasp during summer, to overwinter, then mate and lay its own eggs, to continue the cycle at the expense of another hapless victim.

At first the caddis case of healthy animals is little more than a tube of elasticised silk, extruded by the spinning glands and fashioned into shape with forelegs and mouth-parts. The placement of the masonry comes later, the case increasing in diameter as the larva grows and vacates the narrower hind end, which it usually bites off. Not for these are the flimsy tubes of plant material made by caddis inhabiting quieter waters. In as brisk a current as this the house must be built on rock, and of rock.

Other tube-forming caddis and net-building ones are common in both acid and basic waters and four types of caddis cases can be found here. Commonest are those made of sand grains and tiny pebbles, rarest are those of cut leaf segments. Caddis food-catching nets become quite conspicuous when they begin to silt up with orange iron bacteria, but they can be torn assunder in spates.

Mayflies, the anglers' 'green drake' *(Ephemera danica)* and *Ecdyonurus*, are an integral part of summer, as are the *Nemura* stoneflies, but have been observed on the wing in March, when their natal waters are crusted with ice around the edges. There are a few dragonflies and damselflies in season and crowds of *Simulium* blackflies gyrating low over the stream in May and June. Pond skaters and water crickets skitter across pools, their feet dimpling the surface film to give sextets of round shadows on the streambed in a bubble ballet fantasy.

Flatworms, leeches and *Chironomid* midge larvae live on stream and pond beds, with wandering and dwarf pond snails *(Lymnaea peregra* and *Lymnaea truncatula)* and Jenkin's spire shells *(Potamopyrgus jenkinsi)*. Horse hair worms *(Gordius)* resemble horse hairs quite closely and grow to a foot or more long in the main stream, appearing also in a test hole dug for the new pond.

There is lesser life, invisible to the naked eye. Roy Perry collected some of the spume where the stream churned through mini rapids in February 1979. After a week under sterile conditions in the laboratory, six species of *Fungi imperfecti* had appeared. Cultures of rotting oak and alder leaves yielded minute animal life akin to the well known *Amoeba* of elementary biology classes.

5. Fish and Frogs

There are plenty of brook trout in the stream, little brown trout *(Salmo trutta fario)*, from 4 to 9 inches long, but apparently no other kinds and the trout are seldom visible. They lurk under stones in the deeper pools awaiting the arrival of prey rather than doing battle with the current and expending valuable calories.

In the 1988 drought the upper stream ceased to flow and 20 or so trout, including some nine-inchers, were found stranded in pools on 2nd August. Three were dead and a few evaded capture, but the warden caught 14 and relocated them further down, where permanent tributaries ensured a more dependable flow.

The stream seemed empty of life when I visited with Piers Langhelt of the National Museum of Wales on an electric fishing survey in 1973, but little fish fairly leapt into his net as he moved upstream. He set the pulse unit on the bank with the small petrol motor that powered the

Electric Fishing with 'wandering' anode and net.

Honda generator (a 220 v 280 watt unit,) and threw a metal grid cathode into the stream - this subsequently replaced by cathodes on the soles of the operator's very necessary gumboots. He then stepped into the water with a wooden handled 'wandering anode' in one hand and a soft nylon net in the other, working slowly upstream, while I followed with a bucket to hold the catch.

The fish received a negative charge proportional to their surface area, so the bigger ones remained stunned for longest - facilitating the routine weighing and measuring that was the object of the excercise. Little ones and the many invertebrates apprehended had mostly regained their equilibrium by the time they surfaced. The fish were surprisingly varied as regards the pattern of red spots on the lateral white 'fingerprints'.

Brook Trout

The stream was worked in hundred yard stretches and the catch replaced to return to their home territories, which were estimated to consist of a 40 yard linear stretch. This survey method gives a reliable index to the number and size of fish in small brooks such as this, but is necessarily more approximate on larger rivers where whole shoals can be missed.

No frogs were caught. These prefer the woodland pools and swamps, the velocity of stream flow being too great for comfort. The main pool in the south was 30 inches deep when full, until deepened in the 1980s but dries out as early as April some years. It did so in 1978, stranding great slabs of frogspawn, only some of which were collected by village children.

On 17th April a drake mallard was on site, not exactly licking his lips, but evidently 'loitering with intent'. He had not been attracted for a swim. (Mallard occasionally nest in the reserve, leading their ducklings downstream and across Heol Beri Green to the River Taff to join the families based near the Taffs Well station footbridge).

Frogs gathering in the waterfall area downstream to spawn at the end of February 1982 found their usual 'Iron Bacteria Pool' full of dead leaves, but had no qualms about moving to a nearby flood channel left by the stream. Spawn also appeared in a subsidiary pool near the South Pond that year, so it seems that frogs are not irrevocably tied to ancestral sites. It is interesting to note in connection with the local name of Hoar

Frost Valley that spawn is likely to appear later here than on the hills round about and that tadpoles are slower to develop. On 22nd May 1990 Coed-y-Bedw tadpoles showed no signs of leg formation, whereas those in Pisgodlyn Mawr at Welsh St. Donats had four legs apiece and almost no tails and were walking ashore the next day like hordes of glistening bluebottles.

Paths through Coed-y-Bedw Nature Reserve were much enhanced by the end of the millennium.

Those that make it to adulthood in Coed-y-Bedw may help to sustain a few grasssnakes, but there is only one known sighting of this snake, which was swimming in the waterfall area. Toads, too, are rare, skulking in damp undergrowth and tempting few predators because of their noxious skin exudations. Newts have not been recorded.

A fine new pond excavated in a hollow clearing near the mine entrance in 1988, its clear waters invaded early by water starwort and meadowsweet, should increase the range of aquatic life as it 'grows in.'

"Coed y Bedw" means 'Wood of Birches'. Patriarchs become mossy with age.

45

Chapter 3

COED-Y-BEDW NATURE RESERVE. MORE ANIMAL LIFE

1. Mammals

Mammals are always difficult to detect, their survival depending on secrecy, and evidence is often indirect - and sometimes surprising in the numbers revealed. Thus, although foxes were seldom seen in the 70s and 80s, the neighbouring farmer killed 34 in 1978, catching them in wire loop snares set in their runs under fences, in the belief that they were "getting at the lambs". They are less molested now and much bolder, but are not thought to breed in the reserve. In winter, however, foxes habitually occupy part of the big old badger sett in the wood centre, leaving the remains of their meals outside.

There are no badgers there now, but well over a dozen holes, kept open by the foxes, show that the sett once held a big family group. This is likely to have died out, by unknown means, in the mid 1940s, but fragments of the plank platform erected in a nearby tree for badger watching, remain into 1993. Badgers breed nearby, two badger diggers having been aprehended on the Little Garth in 1987, and given fines totalling £374, but there have been no attempts by surplus animals to recolonise what seems to be a highly desirable residence.

There are a few records of polecats from the 1960s and 70s, but none since. Both stoats and weasels are rare and there are no records to date of mink moving upstream from the Taff, where a healthy population has been established since the end of the 1980s.

Hedgehogs are usually encountered as road casualties or their passing indicated by dung pellets glistening with beetle remains, their favourite earthworms leaving little trace. Moles burrow actively throughout the coldest winters, throwing up mounds of subsoil through the lightly frozen crust beneath heavy undergrowth.

Winter is a good time to assess the mammal population as revealed by tracks in the snow and hares could often be flushed under these conditions, especially in summer, but are rare now. Rabbits are seldom seen. Grey squirrels are also active at such times, seeking buried treasure. Pipistrelle and long-eared bats emerge only in mild spells.

Miss E.M.Jones of Cardiff University Zoology Department made a study of small mammals in Coed y Bedw as part of her honours degree in 1966. She set 24 Longworth Live Traps in 4 different environments to gain some indication of the habitat preferences of different species. These were in bramble-grown stone ruins with little ground cover, a dense bracken/bramble thicket, a closely grazed grass sward and an open grassy bank under hawthorn and beech.

Traps were baited with cheese and apple and provisioned with rat cubes, with dry hay as bedding material. They were left open for the first few days, to enable the animals to come and go freely, then set and examined after 24 hours over 6 separate periods during November and December. Animals caught were marked with a number, using a dye made from I C I Durefor black flakes dissolved in boiling water and hydrogen peroxide, so that they could be excluded from future counts if recaught after release.

Only wood mice or long-tailed field mice and bank voles were captured, although short-tailed field voles might have been expected in the grassy habitats, their superficial runs being particularly noticeable through grass after snow melt. Nothing at all turned up in the short grass during the trapping programme and only mice on the grassy bank, where 22 were caught - as compared with 20 in the ruin and 10 in the bracken - suggesting their preference for medium to open cover.

Bank voles preferred the dense bracken/bramble, where 17 were caught as against 13 in the ruin and none in either of the grassy habitats. Their liking for dense cover is probably related to the fact that they are active by day as well as night. Diurnal:nocturnal comparisons revealed 12 night-going and 8 day-going voles, 16 nocturnal wood mice and none at all by day. Both species feed on seeds, fruits and insects (as opposed to the mainly grass and root diet of field voles) and the diurnal outings of the bank vole may reduce the competition to some extent.

Throughout the winter caches of discarded food remains can be seen outside their burrows, these including the shells of hazel nuts, acorns and beech mast and 'bored' stones of hawthorn and wild cherry, also the discarded scales of oak buds, the tender centres of which have been eaten. In autumn mice often leave a litter of nibbled rose hips in vacated hedgerow birds' nests where they take up sleeping quarters.

Another, less orthodox, investigation of the small mammal population was carried out by Steve Howe of the National Museum of Wales, as part of a litter picking sortie in October 1978. Many one pint milk bottles had been discarded by users of the Heol Goch road and these are effective traps, for both small mammals and insects such as ground beetles. These enter for shelter, food or drink and are unable to climb out up the slippery glass slope and die a lingering death in their glass prison.

Nine bottles were taken for examination, two of these each containing the remains of six mammals - one 4 short-tailed field voles and 2 common shrews, the other 4 common shrews, 1 field vole and 1 bank vole. The average number of mammals in the 9 bottles was 3.6. Thirty three individuals had died, over an unknown period, identifications being made from skeletal remains, principally skulls.

Most numerous were short-tailed field voles at 14, with common shrews not far behind, at 12. There were 8 wood mice and 2 bank voles. All bottles were found within 10 yards of the road, so they record only the 'woodland edge' animals. The scarcity of discarded bottles elsewhere, thank goodness, precludes comparison with other types of habitat.

Other unorthodox ways of assessing the small mammal population is by the dissection of owl pellets and the study of what the cat brings home.

All three species of shrew are known to be present in the reserve, the velvety black and white water shrew and the tiny pygmy shrew, as well as the common species so often encountered dead on paths. Yellow-necked mice have not been found closer than Brecon. Their skeletons are almost identical with those of wood mice, so intact animals, alive or dead, are needed for identification.

2. Birds

As a bird habitat, Coed-y-Bedw has many features in common with the woods of Central Wales. Tinkling streams, black quagmires and shaded grass under mossy trees makes an ideal environment for the three 'indicator species' of Western, Northern and Mid Wales oakwoods: pied flycatchers, redstarts and wood warblers. Numbers of the first have

Pied Flycatchers

been given a boost by the erection of nest boxes to compensate for the lack of big old trees with suitable holes.

The more widespread spotted flycatchers are probably the last of the migrants to return in spring, their rather squeaky songs helping to alleviate the monotonous bisyllabic calls of chiff chaffs and cuckoos, but

14. Footbridge in the north-west of the Coed-y-Bedw Nature Reserve, April 1995

15. Swallow-tail Moth

16. Hedgehog

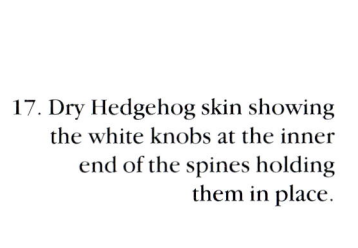

17. Dry Hedgehog skin showing the white knobs at the inner end of the spines holding them in place.

18. Walnut Tree Quarry in the Little Garth, December 1984. Trees on the left brink mark the narrow ridge between this and the old Ty Nant Quarry.

19. Wood Spurge on quarry brink.

20. Walnut Tree Quarry. Lime-burning plant and western pillars of the Barry Railway viaduct. May 1971

cuckoos were seldom heard calling over the Garth in the latter half of the 1990s. Willow warblers find accommodation in the damp scrub and whitethroats in nettlebeds. Blackcaps are notable in that they started overwintering in 1971-72 and the odd few have been doing so quite regularly since.

The diminution in thrush numbers nationally in the early 1990s has not affected this locality. Both song thrush and missel thrush add their melodious notes to those of blackbird, robin and dunnock and a few redwings may drop in during cold spells. Red and yellow-capped goldcrests sneak through the branches and tits are always in evidence, the winter flocks building up progressively as more fledgelings leave the nests. In 1990 big family parties of long-tailed tits were chattering through the trees as early as 22nd May.

Chaffinches are as common as tits. Bullfinches flash white rumps in gloomy thickets and greenfinches churr contentedly from high branches. Redpolls and siskins can be spotted in summer as well as more noticeably in winter flocks, but goldfinches, linnets and yellow hammers prefer the woodland edge, where they can range out over open fields. Reed buntings have nested spasmodically during the last three decades under brambles, 1971 being a particularly good year for them. They are usually spotted perching within a few feet of the ground - a height matching that of the reeds and sedges of their more traditional sites.

Sparrow hawks gain a living among these small birds, the open tree canopy offering few obstacles to their deft hunting flights. Four separate plucking posts were found during January 1977. Buzzards and kestrels hunt better in the open, the domain of raven, carrion crow and jackdaw, but both can be disturbed from taller trees in the reserve.

Tawny owls are quite regular, their eerie night calls carrying long distances. Several were watched slipping silently between the trees on an evening visit at the end of May in 1991. Little owls seldom enter the wood, but in 1971 an orphaned little owl was being brought up by Mollie Patmore, long-term clerk of the Community Council, who lives just below the reserve. During mid July the youngster was learning to fly - up and down the hall!

Tree pipits nest in the smaller spinneys on the slopes to the north, where they have plenty of open space for their musical song flights, visiting the woodland only briefly. These spinneys have been retained as game bird (and probably fox) coverts, but the roofed bird rearing pens had fallen into disrepair by the beginning of the 1980s.

According to Mr. Fisher, the gamekeeper, 200 pheasants, 50 red-legged partridges and 50 grey partridges were released in 1979, some finding their way into the reserve, and at least one batch of pheasant's eggs was laid in 1981 by an escapee. Woodcock are quite frequently flushed in winter, the wet soil well suited to the probing of their long soft bills.

Shooting is not allowed on the reserve, but the Forestry Commission retains the right to control wood pigeons in its plantation alongside, these, like magpies, sometimes damaging the tree leaders. They are one of the chief exploiters of the ivy berries, which fill the hungry gap after most of the autumn fruits have disappeared, persisting into May and even June. No other pigeons or doves have been recorded, not even the collared dove, which recently moved into the village.

Thrushes and blackbirds also enjoy ivy berries, almost overbalancing, with wings aflutter, in reaching out to sprays unable to support them. Jays, too, exploit all soft fruits. 1993 was a good year for these usually shy birds, which became much bolder, and Coed-y-Bedw saw some of the big influx of continental jays which occurred a decade earlier in the autumn of 1983.

Kingfishers bred on the lower stream in 1968 and have tried to do so since, but have been thwarted by children taking the eggs and have retreated to more inaccessible sites along the banks of the Taff. Grey and pied wagtails work their way along the gravel shoals all year, sometimes joined by white wagtails in winter. Yellow wagtails have been observed on spring passage and a dipper has been spotted, but only as a traveller. A heron flew up from the stream on one occasion, startling the wardens who flushed it, but these prefer the Taff, with its more spacious take-off facilities.

3. Nest Boxes and Ringing Recoveries

With good ground cover and rich insect life, it was evident that the chief factor limiting the numbers of hole-nesting birds was the lack of sufficient ancient trees to provide adequate nesting holes. Even those master carpenters, the woodpeckers, go for the more yielding timbers: most others need ready made holes. The deficiency has been remedied by the erection of nest boxes.

A modest start was made in 1985 with 9 boxes. All were taken up, the 9 broods housed producing 68 fledgelings from the 70 eggs laid. Not all were tits: there was a significant number of that most coveted bird, the pied flycatcher.

1984 had been a particularly good year for these in woods to the north and west, the supply of caterpillars poor at first, when the tits were seeking them, but plentiful later on when the pied flycatchers returned from migration. More young were heading north in 1985 and seeking homes. Some spotted the new supply of desirable residences and elected to go no further. Twenty two young pied flycatchers were added to the previously meagre population in 1985, along with 28 great tits and 18 blue tits.

More boxes were put up and in 1986 these provided homes producing 55 young pied flycatchers, 76 great tits and 141 blue tits. The number of flycatcher fledgelings dropped to 28 in 1987 but was up to 79 the following year. Part of the reason for the drop was that the nest boxes were taken over by tits before the flycatchers returned from their winter quarters. The cure was not to open up the boxes until after 20th April, when most of the tits were already housed. This has worked, the number of breeding pairs being 14, 22 and 19 in 1989, 1990 and 1991, with an average brood size of 7 and few of the eggs laid failing to hatch.

This was not at the expense of the tits. Seventy two boxes were in place by 1988, when 122 great tits and 235 blue tits were brought off, with numbers continuing to rise as the number of nest boxes was increased. Fortunately for the pockets of the parishioners who supply peanuts through the winter, by no means all the fledgelings survive, natural mortality during the first year bringing the population down to a realistic replacement level. (Even one brood of blue or great tits consisting of 10 birds would increase the population fivefold if all lived). Cruel Nature decrees that there shall be sufficient for the predators and carrion feeders, so that the little blue and yellow feathered balls shall not jostle too thickly along the village window sills.

By 1993 some 120 bird boxes had been positioned, along linear spinneys and hedgerows beyond the bounds of the reserve as well as within. Great tits have nested in crevices appearing behind boxes: marsh tits, willow tits and coal tits are not interested and long-tailed tits prefer to create their own hanging baskets in the bushes.

Redstart

The equally delightful redstarts have been tempted, although these were breeding in natural holes before the coming of the boxes. Redstarts took up residence in three of the new style homes in 1988, 2 pairs producing 9 fledgelings from 10 eggs, but none of the 3 eggs laid in the third box hatched. In 1991 there were 6 pairs breeding, but only two in artificial holes. These pairs had chosen the boxes with side entrances against the tree trunk, erected for tree creepers, which normally edge in under slabs of loose bark to build.

Nuthatches have taken up residence on a regular basis since 1987. They plaster round the entrance hole with mud, as with natural tree crevices, which are likely to be of less accommodating shape. In 1991 a female, finding little need of her labours around the nicely contoured opening, plastered over the lid as well, so that the wardens had to break in to monitor the eggs and chicks. Seven young were successfully reared by this diligent pair, which continued popping in and out of the nest at frequent intervals during the May time visit of a large party of bird watchers.

It has been found necessary to circle the entrances of boxes to prevent vandalism by grey squirrels and woodpeckers, which have a taste for eggs and chicks, not with mud, but with copper bands. Larger boxes have been erected for woodpeckers to use legitimately, but these got taken over by starlings before the woodpeckers appreciated the new opportunity offered. They are well able to excavate their own holes, so may not have been interested, reserving their efforts for breaking and entering to supplement the larder. Starlings habitually take over old woodpecker holes, most often after the constructors have finished with them. The two pairs in boxes in 1988 brought off only 8 chicks between them.

George Wood and Alex Coxhead have ringed a number of birds in Coed-y-Bedw during the 1980s and 1990s, using mist nets to catch adults and marking youngsters before they fledge, this leading to some interesting recaptures, giving information on movements.

A pied flycatcher caught in a mist net here on 7th June 1989 was found to have been ringed 45 miles (72 km) away, in Rifton Wood, Stoodleigh, Devon, just over 2 years earlier, on 31st May 1987. Another nestling from a brood of 8 ringed in Coed-y-Bedw the same day was recovered the following summer (19th May 1990) 34 miles (54 km) away at Nags Head, Parkend in Gloucestershire, where she had taken up residence as a breeding female.

She was not the only wanderer, another ringed in our reserve on 11th June 1992 turning up at Nottswood Hill, Longhope, Gloucestershire on 27th May 1993. This traffic works both ways, pied flycatcher number H 642123, ringed at Nagshead on 4th June 1992, being found breeding at Efail Isaf, just north of the Garth on 27th May 1993. More often birds return to their natal area after migrating away for the winter. Thus four ringed in Coed-y-Bedw on 6th and 7th June in 1989, were re-trapped there two years later, 2 on 25th May and 2 on 4th June in 1991.

A visit to Nagshead in May 1994 revealed the pied flycatcher habitat there to consist of much more mature woodland than Coed-y-Bedw, with mighty oaks planted at the time of Napoleon - for more oak warships when they matured in the year 2000, should we need them! These oaks were in prime condition, none having rotted to produce nest holes, so Nagshead birds, like ours, were dependent on the provision of nest boxes. The Nagshead ornithologists had found that in lean years, when caterpillars were in short supply, the pied flycatchers did better in the open, grazed woodlands more like Coed-y-Bedw. Where dense scrub grew, in the absence of sheep, this housed a big population of warblers and other caterpillar-feeders, so that they were in competition for the meagre resources.

Sheep are a useful management tool in many situations, but unexpected factors are involved once we start tampering. Woodland managers must decide between favouring these very special pied denizens more characteristic of Mid-Wales, or going for greater diversity of the more commonplace. When mankind accepted his 'dominion over other creatures' he took on great responsibilities.

A nuthatch ringed on 17th May 1991 turned up a few miles away at Treforest, Pontypridd on 27th November the same year, killed by a cat. The nuthatch ringed in the reserve on 17th May 1989 did better, and was found back on site on 12th May 1991. Nuthatches do not travel as far afield as many species, one ringed at Efail Isaf in 1991, turning up the following winter in Pontypridd, a few km away.

A great tit ringed on 12th May 1990 was brought in by a cat at Cefn Bychan, Pentyrch, only 2 km away just 6 weeks later - this a part of the quick turnover entailed in predator:prey relationships in the food chain - of which the domestic puss is lamentably part. Another great tit, ringed on 24th May 1990, had a better run for its money, being found dead on Garth Hill 3 years later, on 18th April, 1993.

A blue tit ringed in Coed-y-Bedw on 6th June 1981 was brought in by a cat at Rhiwbina, half way to Cardiff 5 months later. Another, ringed the same day at Taffs Well, turned up on Garth Hill more than 4 years later, on 23rd July 1993, freshly drowned in a pool. It is remarkable that such tiny vulnerable creatures manage to find a living and escape all the hazards for so long.

I am indebted to George Wood and Alex Coxhead for details of ringing recoveries.

4. Insects: the more obvious Species

Insects do not force themselves on the attentions as do screeching jays and scolding wrens, but can scarcely be overlooked when the woodland is in full flower in May. The massed garlic flowers prove an irresistable lure for seekers after nectar and pollen and for the robber flies and crab spiders that gain a living from the flower feeders.

The aromatic heads swarm with furry bees of various sorts, but these do not stick with one species, some having pollen baskets crammed with bright orange pollen being tempted onto the stands of bluebells, with their pale cream pollen. Both ground-cover plants supply a range of wasps and hover and drone flies which dress in similar black and yellow stripes to deceive enemies.

With these hovering hordes are orange-bodied and black-bodied sawflies whose green caterpillars feed on alder, sallow and birch, together with the alder wood wasp, whose females have a long ovipositor for inserting eggs deep into the orange alder timber.

Most of the common galls caused by Cynipid wasps on oak trees have been noticed in the reserve, along with a quite uncommon one, the pink wax gall or bud gall caused by *Trigonaspis megaptera* on tufts of epicormic shoots sprouting from oak boles.

Four of the 50 or so fly species identified here by the experts are gall midges, the galls more apparent than the perpetrators. Clouds of tiny owl midges or moth flies *(Psychoda)* swarm through spring and summer and 8 species of *Hilara* have been named. These are Empid flies, which catch other insects on the wing, the amorous male passing the female a food parcel wrapped in silk to keep her occupied while he does what is necessary to perennate his kind.

Down by the stream on sultry summer afternoons insects impinge more forcibly upon the senses. The Tabanids, known variously as clegs, stouts, horseflies and gad flies, are hard to ignore. When breasting the almost invisible clouds of midges on a muggy May day, it is small comfort to know that they are so gossamer-light that many fail to break through the elastic surface film on emerging from their aquatic pupae. These drown under the invisible barrier before doing any bodily harm, becoming food for pond skaters and trout instead of birds.

Glance among the fool's watercress in late May and you may see large craneflies laying their eggs in quiet pools. They do this dragonfly fashion, dipping the tail tip repeatedly beneath the surface. Smaller ones may be laying among the *Eurhynchium riparioides* moss of the stream or the *Hydrohypnum luridum* of the margins.

A real speciality by the water in early summer is the giant lacewing, *(Osmylus fulvicephalus)*, Britain's largest and a rare species, found also at Cwm Nofydd, east of the Taff. They are sluggish fliers, easily caught in cupped hands as they flap past and liable to settle on the person in lieu of a low branch. The patterned wings are longer than the body and span 5 cm (2 inches) when spread.

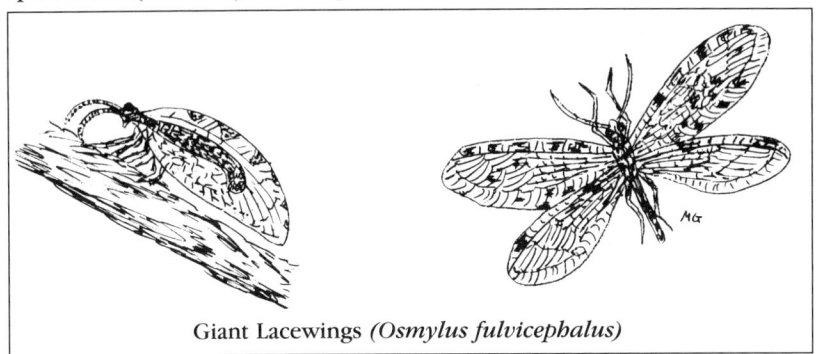

Giant Lacewings *(Osmylus fulvicephalus)*

Common green lacewings *(Chrysopa)* range more widely and have a longer season on the wing. Male scorpion flies *(Panorpis communis)* cock bulbous-tipped tails menacingly but harmlessly over their backs. Both sexes have long snouts and feed on carrion as larvae and adults.

The three familiar species of whites and speckled woods are the only really common butterlies, but orange-tips and brimstones appear in spring, along with the occasional comma or other Vanessid. Nineteen species have been recorded in the reserve, the most dashing the silver-washed fritillary flipping high among the branches. Clouded yellows turned up in the 'clouded yellow year' of 1983, wall butterflies sun themselves, appropriately, on the walls of the ruined house and graylings frequent the nearby tip.

Most interesting are the purple hairstreaks, which feed almost exclusively on oak, as their scientific name *(Quercusia quercus)* signifies, but have been found also on sweet chestnut and sallow. They are difficult to spot, as their whole life is spent in the treetops. The flattened brown caterpillars with zig zag patterning can sometimes be brushed from lower branches and adults occasionally get grounded and can be examined in the hand. A caterpillar collected on 5th June 1981 pupated 2 days later and emerged to display the most beautiful purple-blue iridescence in sunlight. A cryptic property of this elusive insect is that it appears black when the sun goes in, the colour being wholly refractive.

Visiting entomologists beat the branches to dislodge leaf-eaters and their predators into a white collecting tray held underneath. Wriggling across the white sheet will be caterpillars of Tortricid and Noctuid moths and numbers of loopers or Geometers, that emulate dead twigs when in the branches and include abundant species such as the mottled umber.

Winter moth caterpillars may evade capture by letting themselves down on silken threads and climbing back up when the danger is past.

Nights in the reserve in 1981 and 1985 with a moth trap enabled the wardens to knock up a list of 63 moths, the biggest and best the poplar hawk moth. Some, like the large and lesser yellow underwings, are more often encountered on the neighbouring fields, where the 'woolly bear' caterpillars of drinker and oak-eggar moths feed among the grass, but all were atracted to the light.

The oak hook-tip and scalloped hook-tip were more characteristic of the wood, their curve-ended wings as distinctive as the pink petal pattern of the peach blossom moth, whose caterpillars feed on bramble leaves. Three 'prominents' were lured to the trap: iron prominent, swallow prominent and coxcomb prominent, along with the related figure-of-eight and rare lobster moths, which last is named for the weird pose adopted by the larva when threatened. Not content with waving spidery legs at a potential predator and raising its swollen, lobster-like tail menacingly, this mainly beech-feeding caterpillar reinforces its defences with a punitive jet of formic acid.

Much the commonest group of moths is that with looper caterpillars and not the least of their attractions are the evocative names which early lepidopterists chose to give them. Some in the reserve are satin beauty, July high-flier, scalloped oak, feathered thorn, great oak beauty, small fan-footed wave and swallow tail. A few of the adult moths are visible by day, these mostly pale coloured ones like light emerald and large emerald and the yellow brimstone moths which rest blatantly on tree trunks. Almost fly-like in their delicacy are the clouds of longhorn and goldwing moths hovering around bushes with wings glittering when the sun is out.

5. Beetles, Bugs and Others

Best known of the beetles are the ladybirds. As voracious feeders on aphids , they are friend of farmer and gardener alike, but of little use as food for others, as their bright warning colours show. Seven-spot ladybirds are the most familiar, but there are 2-spot, 10-spot, 12-spot and 14-spot here, most occasionally exhibiting colour reversal with red spots on a black background instead of the usual black on red. The two-spot shows a whole range of different patterns and, confusingly, of number of spots - with sometimes as many as 14 black spots on a yellow background, this being Britain's most variable kind.

To confuse matters further, two similar beetles have been found in the reserve, the ladybird mimic *(Endomychus coccineus)*, boldly spotted with black on red but with longer, clubbed antennae, and the false ladybird *(Chilocorus renipustulatus)* with 2 red spots on black, but rounder than a 2-spot ladybird and with an all-black head.

Another, quite similar, with black spots on yellowish wing cases, is the four-spot carrion beetle *(Xylodrepa quadripunctata)*, which hunts the caterpillars of oak roller moths among the oak leaves.

The eyed longhorn *(Rhagium mordax)*, a yellow beetle with black eyespots hiding among fallen leaves, is longer of body and antennae and is a wood borer. Its larvae mine radiating galleries between the bark and the timber of fallen oak and beech, as do the notorious elm bark beetles, carriers of Dutch elm disease, on elms.

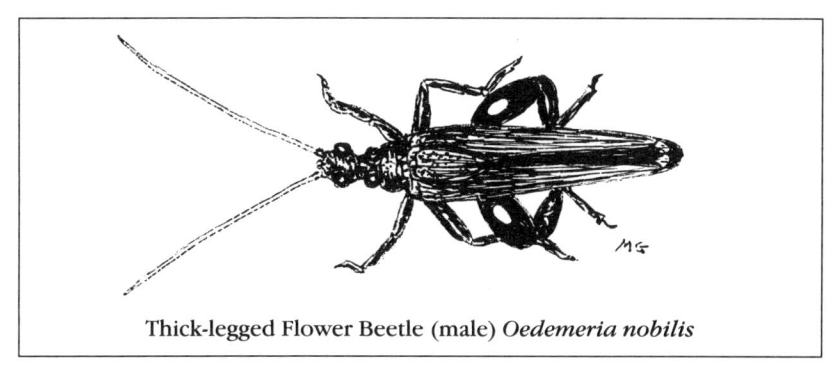

Thick-legged Flower Beetle (male) *Oedemeria nobilis*

The beetle most often encountered is probably the red-brown skipjack or click beetle *(Athous haemorrhoidalis)*, which skips around the bracken and turns somersaults when handled. More conspicuous, again in red and black, are the two cardinal beetles, *Pyrochroa coccinea* and *Pyrochroa serraticornis*. Equally colourful, but resembling mobile green peas, are the tortoise beetles *(Cassida rubiginosa)*, which frequent the anthill area of the old tip, favouring thistles. The wing cases and thorax give a smooth oval outline which hides the head and all but the tips of the legs like a tortoise carapace.

Carnivorous rove beetles *(Philonthus* or *Quedius)*, like small devil's coach horses, have the remarkable facility of folding the long wings away under the abbreviated wing cases when they alight, cocking the tail up to ease them in - as when squirting a jet of repellent fluid at a would-be predator. Another active taker of prey is the scuttling black ground beetle, *Nebria brevicollis*, which can be disturbed from under stones.

Mottled beetles sitting around on alder leaves tend to tuck the long snouts which distinguish them as weevils in under the thorax when at rest. Beech weevils *(Rhynchaenus fagi)* are smaller. Light green tree weevils *(Phillobius calcaratus)* cease to be light green as they grow, shedding the scintillating golden-green scales from the wing cases to become a dull brown. They are likely to be moving in tandem in early June, remaining attached when picked up.

Broadly flattened hawthorn shield bugs *(Acanthosoma haemorrhoidalis)* and parent bugs *(Elasmucha grisea)* have been recorded. The latter, which live on the birches, are among the few insects which afford their young parental care, overseeing both eggs and nymphs during the vulnerable life stages, although not saving all from the tits.

Most easily identified of the bugs is the red-spotted black froghopper *(Cercopsis vulnerata)*, which frequents the sallows in the valley bottom, vaunting its warning colours to ward off enemies. The related froghoppers *(Philaenus spumarius)* are the cuckoo-spit insects, whose nymphs hide in a frothy mass of bubbles. *Cercopsis*, sometimes called firebug, spends its nymphal stage underground, sometimes as much as a foot down.

Capsid or Mirid bugs come in many colours, green, yellow, brown or black, plain or speckled, large or small. Most suck plant sap but a few are carnivorous. *Psallus* species in Coed-y-Bedw confine their attentions to the oaks.

Other bugs which are exclusively sap suckers are the leaf hoppers, the subject of many years' study by Michael Claridge, whose intimate knowledge of the group gained here has taken him often to the Phillipines and other far flung sites to help solve problems related to the devastation of rice crops by leaf hoppers. He examined 7,399 specimens from Coed-y-Bedw, belonging to 36 different species. One of the rarest of these rejoices in the name of *Limnavuoriana sexmaculata*, enough to put most people off studying such a complex group.

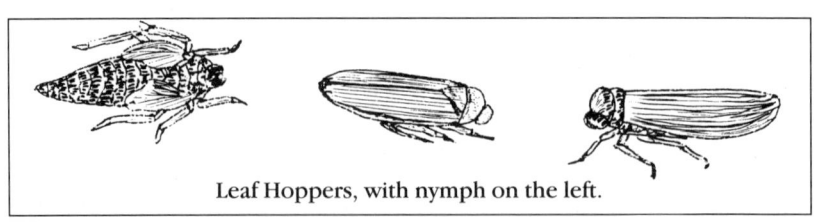

Leaf Hoppers, with nymph on the left.

They are certainly the province of the expert, their colour patterns very variable and, although most are host-specific, occurring on only one kind of tree, they cannot be identified by their host, as up to 20 species have been found on a single tree type in the reserve. Numbers are quite revealing:- 19 on alder, 16 on oak, 16 on sycamore, 14 on hazel, 13 on wych elm, 12 on birch, 12 on rowan, 8 on hawthorn, 7 on field maple and only 2 on ash. Needless to say, some proved to be new county records.

Their manifestation to the layman is in the whitening of the leaves from which they have sucked the green cell contents, leaving only the colourless cell walls. Like other insects, they need to shed their skins as they grow, and it is interesting to observe that they do not let go their hold even when this major process is taking place. Indeed, the sucking stylet, plugged firmly into the leaf tissue, is the only thing they have to pull against as they wriggle free, withdrawing the legs one by one to leave the empty husk balanced on its nose, still plugged into the food supply.

There are other, even more obscure, insect groups present, but one needs to be with someone like Claridge to have them pointed out. They include the spring-tails *(Collembolans)*, not all of which have a spring in the tail, also the book lice *(Psochoptera)*, which browse on algae, lichen, fungi and bacteria on tree trunks, be these dead or alive.

Cynthia Merrett, 'spider woman' at the National Museum of Wales, has found a species of spider in Coed-y-Bedw which is a second record for the triple county of Glamorgan. This is *Sabacon viscayanum* subspecies *ramblaianum*, found only before on Gower, but in several other sites since. Among the many spiders listed is one new to Glamorgan: *Robertus neglectus,* and there are velvet mites , *Eutrombidium*, making up for lack of size with their bright scarlet colour.

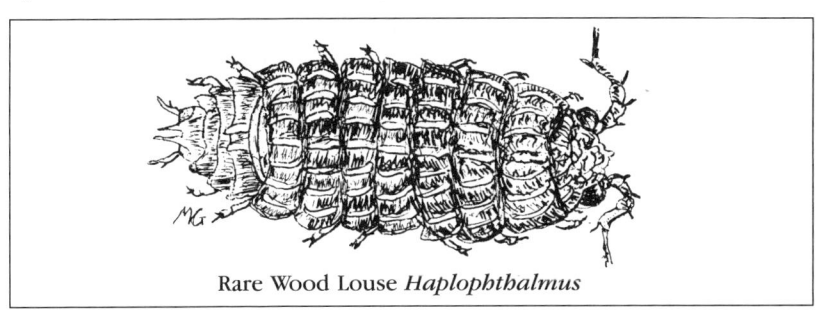

Rare Wood Louse *Haplophthalmus*

June Chatfield, the National Museum's 'Snail woman', has listed 47 different snails and slugs, which enjoy the moistness of the leaf litter, and has discovered a rare woodlouse, *Haplophthalmus menge*i, which is a second record for Wales. Commoner woodlice present are *Oniscus asellus, Philoscia muscorum* and *Trichoniscus pusillus.*

Helping them to recyle the plant debris are herbivorous millipedes, *Glomeris* and *Cylindroiulus*, which run the gauntlet of carnivorous centipedes, including *Lithobius*.

Chapter 4
THE UNDERGROUND WORLD OF THE LITTLE GARTH

Introductory

The Little Garth forms the western side of the Taff Gorge, where the Taff, first as a glacier and then as a river, lowered itself down through the most resistant of the ridges delimiting the south of the Coalfield. The rim of Coal Measure and Millstone Grit rocks to the north withstood the scouring by ice and water less well and eroded back to form the broad basin containing Taffs Well, with Gwaelod y Garth straggling up the slope to the west.

Both sides of the gorge have been quarried, so the land falls away almost vertically into the now wooded Ty Nant Quarry on the Garth side and to the A 470 roundabout under the wooded heights crowned by the thirteenth century Castell Coch, which was almost completely rebuilt in the nineteenth century. The conformation of the pristine gorge before the quarry men got busy with their pickaxes and dynamite must remain a mystery.

The Little Garth - or Garth Wood - rises to only 590 feet: the River Taff at its foot lies at 100 feet. As so often with Carboniferous Limestone, underground rivers have carved out natural caves. Because of its content of iron ore, the hill is now riddled with man-made caves, in the form of mine tunnels and shafts, also a mighty underground lake.

Its mineral wealth makes it the most commercially valuable part of the limestone ridge and, indeed, of a much wider area. The overall thickness of these South Wales beds decreases from Tenby in South Pembrokeshire, through Gower and Porthcawl to Cardiff and Gwent. Dolomitisation has occurred in the Cardiff area and the Dolomite beds are thickest at the Taff Gorge - 300 feet deep under Garth Wood and said to be "worth a fortune".

The Dolomite, which is rich in magnesium carbonate, goes west to Creigiau, where it disappears under glacial drift. This material also overlies the softer Old Red Sandstone to the south, which has worn down almost to the level of the coastal plain, so that the south-facing scarp of the Little Garth rises abruptly from the lower land of Morganstown and Radyr.

Man had moved in by Neolithic times and the first to exploit the minerals were men of the pre-Roman, Iron Age. (Some locals refer to the nineteenth century as another 'Iron Age'). Roman artefacts belonging to the first and third centuries AD have been found, the Romans particularly interested in the silver associated with the galena or lead ore accompanying the iron east of the Taff.

The oldest iron forge of which we have tangible evidence dates from 1620 and large scale iron works were functioning from the start of the nineteenth century until closure in 1884. Minerals won from the hill in modern times are Dolomite and poorer quality limestone. The old Barry Railway line passes under the Little Garth in a tunnel, to debouch onto the Taff Viaduct, built in 1898 and demolished in 1970.

Most of the land around the great scar of today's quarry is clothed in beech wood. Charcoal found on ancient hearths has shown that beech was present in the indigenous forest - in one of its most westerly sites as a native tree - and 34 hectares here have been designated as a Site of Special Scientific Interest on this account. Early records show only the sale of oak from the woodlands, so beech may have been favoured by the selective felling of others. The even-aged beech stand on the south face is the result of replanting.

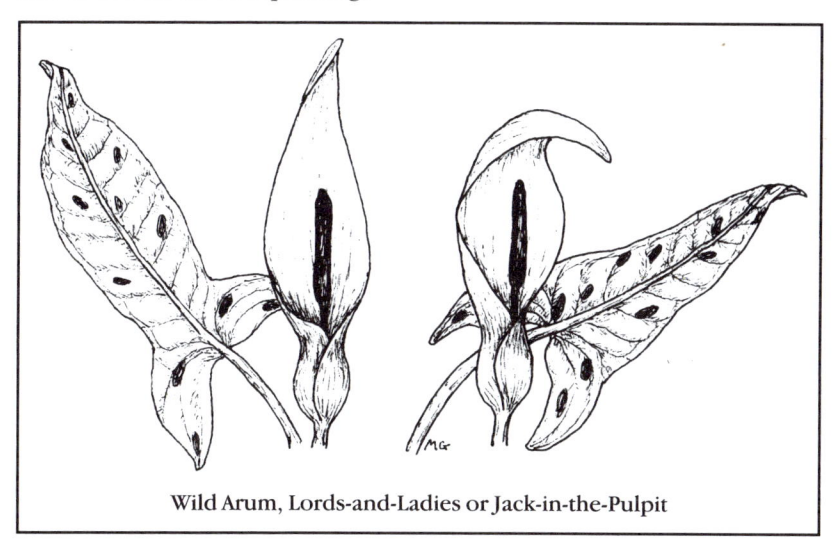

Wild Arum, Lords-and-Ladies or Jack-in-the-Pulpit

Ground flora is that of a classic beechwood and includes rarities such as yellow bird's nest and bird's nest orchid, which can tolerate the deep shade cast by beeches. Having no chlorophyll of their own, they are not dependent on sunlight.

Fauna is also interesting, this being probably the southern limit for nesting redstarts and pied flycatchers; birds which epitomise the oakwoods of Central Wales. Old and new quarry cliffs in the vicinity provide safe sites for peregrines, buzzards, kestrels and ravens, while ancient timber is vulnerable to the hammering of home-making woodpeckers. There is a rich invertebrate fauna, with snails and others needing generous amounts of lime particularly favoured.

1. Rock Formations and Cave Dwellers

Garth Hill is part of the uptilted rim of the basin cradling the Coalfield to the north, so the limestone beds dip predominantly in that direction: actually down to the NNW, at 40 degrees. All is not that simple, however, and travellers through the gorge on the A 470 can see one of a series of asymmetric folds on the roadside rock face.

A syncline (downfold) plunges at about 10 degrees to the NW and another plunging to the west can be seen on the face of the old Ty Nant Quarry which was dug into the riverward flank of the Garth. The disused railway tunnel through the south east of the hill passes directly under the trough of a syncline and geologists think the rocks were exposed to at least two phases of folding.

A major fault in the north of the current quarry (Walnut Tree Quarry) dipping to the east at about 80 degrees is infilled with silt and clay, while another small fault and thrust occur in the east.

Beds outcropping on the south scarp show the blocky cleavage of the main limestone. The softer Lower Limestone Shales (which have worn away east of Castell Coch to create the scenic valley of Cwm Nofydd, north of Rhiwbina) are covered over by glacial deposits and are invisible on the Garth side of the river.

The drift-covered Millstone Grit of Coed-y-Bedw to the north lies unconformably over the highest limestone beds, which are of shelly Seminula Oolite, only partly dolomitised. Oolite is so called because of the tiny egg shaped particles visible to the naked eye, and can be seen cropping out in the north of Garth Wood.

Limestones are often categorised by the fossils they contain, but dolomitisation destroys most of these during the recrystallisation process so this is not easy here, although some of the strata contain Crinoids (sea lilies) and Goniatites (coiled, snail-like creatures).

Angular unweathered fragments of fine grey Dolomite are embedded in other rock types in places to form a pseudo-breccia. Identified in the cementing matrix are white Dolomite, sparry Calcite, red Haematite and blue-grey argillaceous or clayey sediments. Semi-transparent white Calcite rocks scattered over the ground may have the pointed form of Dogstooth Spa, each crystal growing round a nucleus of red Haematite - which is ferric oxide, as in rusted iron.

Haematite is the best quality iron ore and the basis of iron mining. Aeons ago it seeped down more or less vertical joints from a previously overlying rock, now worn away, the mineral deposited as the drainage water oozed along the cracks.

Pieces of shiny metallic galena (lead sulphide or lead ore) can sometimes be found on the ground, although more often in the Draethen Woods to the east. This material and the heavy pink or white Barytes (barium sulphate) are thought to have seeped up the joints from a granite magma below.

Reddish Haematite gets hydrated to yellowish Limonite and this to ochreous material, from which yellow ochre used in the paint industry comes. Remains of this process can be seen at the lower end of the Heol Goch road along the northern flank of the hill.

Natural caves form in lines along the course of underground rivers and are produced as a result of solution of the limey rocks by pounding water. If tapped by a mining tunnel water could come gushing into the workings, but those exposed on the north west face of the modern quarry were less catastrophic.

Some of the Calcite (calcium carbonate) crystals lining the cave walls are as much as 8 inches (20 cm) across and are sometimes stained brown with a fine coating of iron. Large Dolomite crystals may be coated with snowy white carbonate: other crystals are of Quartz (silica dioxide). Layers of calcareous Flowstone are deposited by water seeping over rock faces.

Cavers enter the system on the south-east corner of the hill above the Ty Nant Inn, after a steep scramble to within 50 feet of the ridge top, 300 feet to the west of the Ty Nant Quarry. The main chamber is 100 yards long, 50 feet high and 20 feet wide at its widest, with smaller passages leading away.

Rock falls have filled the chamber with boulders and debris to a depth of 20 feet, making going difficult. M S Hussey, who excavated here in 1964-65 (Trans. Cardiff Nats. Vol. XCIII (1967)) thinks that at least some of the falls must have occurred during the period of human occupation.

Earlier finds, by T E Lewis of Morganstown in 1912 (unpublished), were deposited in the National Museum of Wales. They include sherds of Late Bronze Age, a knobbed pot, Romano-British sherds and metallic objects of Irish origin from the Dark Ages.

Two flint objects assigned to the Neolithic period have been associated with a human skeleton, found in a 20 feet deep crevice. John Ward, a former Keeper of Archeology at the National Museum, believed the cave to have been a Neolithic burial chamber.

Subsequent exploration by R E M Wheeler (also unpublished) revealed more coarse grey Romano-British pottery, hearth stones split by fire and charcoal fragments.

Both investigations found numerous bones of cattle, pigs and sheep and/or goats, charred by cooking fires or broken for their marrow. Cattle would have been reared on the fertile lowland of Morganstown just below, the pigs in the wood and the sheep on the hills. Weaving tools found suggest that wool as well as meat was utilised, while grinding stones indicate that these late Bronze Age inhabitants also grew corn.

The work conducted by Hussey in the 1960s involved the shifting of quantities of loose boulders and was blighted by several rock falls, burying hard-won terrain. Digging in at floor level of the first chamber was more fruitful, yielding bone tools and Bronze Age pottery. Further in, before excavations were abandoned on safety grounds, the cavers found more Roman and Romano-British pottery and traces of Dark Age and Medieval (12th century) occupation.

Bone tools unearthed include a weaving comb and needle and awl in near perfect condition, also some unworked flint slipped into a crevice and later sealed over by natural tufa - between the Stone Age and the Bronze Age. Later calcification was found above Bronze Age deposits, this natural cementing continuing into modern times wherever lime-bearing waters give up their carbon dioxide to the air and deposit their load of minerals.

There appears to have been a period of long abandonment, following which came Roman artefacts judged by C. Boon to be from the first and third centuries AD.

Metal objects from the Dark Ages were of both bronze and iron, some iron studs fixed to thin iron sheeting thought to be from the soles of heavy boots. Pots from this period were interpreted as imports from Gaulish or Frankish manufacturers, suggesting either foreign trade or immigration.

There was no prolonged residence in the cave after the Dark Ages, the Norman finds, including clay pipes, probably left by folk taking temporary refuge within. This would be the approximate time of construction of the eleventh century motte built on the still extant mound close to today's Garden Centre at Morganstown.

2. Cave Formations and Invertebrate Life

The LESSER GARTH CAVE is the best known of the systems penetrating Little Garth Hill and the only one to have yielded artefacts from early cave dwellers. It is thought to have originated as a resurgence, draining water from the heart of the hill away into the Taff Gorge, through an exit now partially blocked by boulders.

A length of 580 feet (180 m) has been explored, this no easy task, as the vertical range between the highest and lowest passages is 50 feet, the

21. Ramsons or Wild Garlic

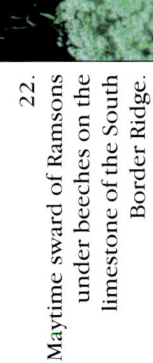

22. Maytime sward of Ramsons under beeches on the limestone of the South Border Ridge.

23. Sylvan path through the Little Garth beechwood

24. Wild Arum, Cuckoo Pint, Lords and Ladies, or Jack-in-the-Pulpit

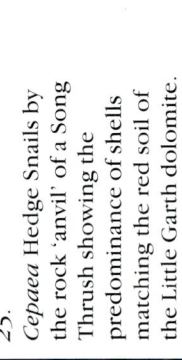

26. Red Cardinal Beetle

28. Greater Bee Fly

25. *Cepaea* Hedge Snails by the rock 'anvil' of a Song Thrush showing the predominance of shells matching the red soil of the Little Garth dolomite.

27. Green Tiger Beetle

Cave Cranefly, *Limonia nubeculosa*

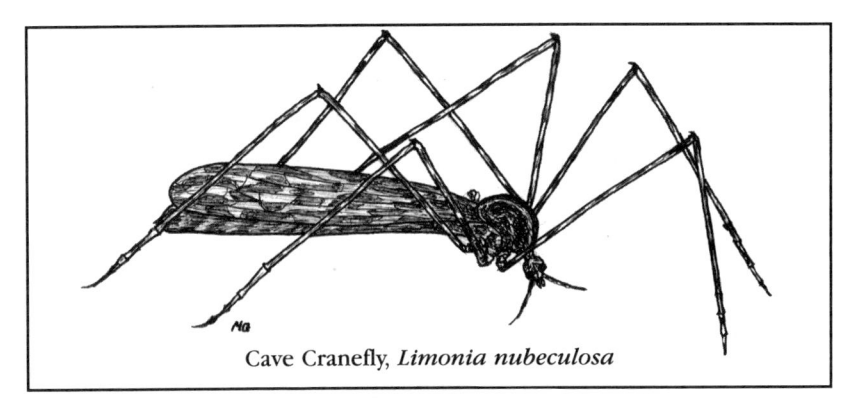

ascents and descents much repeated in the sussing out of a route through. Cavers require more agility, courage and determination than the average man, especially when breaking new ground - often quite literally. To be the first man in - ever - must quicken the pulse and the adrenalin flow.

As in the others, aeons of dripping water in the Lesser Garth Cave has fashioned some intriguing mineral formations. Tony Oldham, in "The Caves of the Southern Outcrop" (1985), refers to large amounts of flowstone and clusters of small fan-like curtains well in from the entrance; with a splendid stalactite pillar of over 20 feet near the start of an ox-bow, with more dripstone and several crystal pools.

The OGOF TYNANT FECHAN is the smallest cave system, at 75 feet long, and lies northward, towards the wooded hill summit. It is a 'crawling cave', with only one small chamber.

Further on again, near the top of the Heol Goch road to Pentyrch (B 4262) is OGOF CEFN BYCHAN. Entered from the base of a farm refuse tip, this is 100 feet long with two chambers, one 40 feet high, the other partially filled with mud.

OGOF GRISIAL, also 100 feet long, leads off the north side of Walnut Tree Quarry. It was exposed by blasting in 1981 and has since been destroyed by blasting. Exploration before its demise led to a 15 foot chamber showing fine examples of dog's tooth spar.

OGOF PEN-Y-GRAIG, 380 feet long, leads in from one of several holes in the wall of the old Ty Nant Quarry on the western flank of the Taff Gorge. It includes two large chambers and one smaller one. Passages are ornamented with long white straws, stalactites, columns, dripstones, white helictites and crystal pools. Straws, suspended from the roof, are hollow and parallel-sided, with water trickling down the centre instead of the outside, as with stalactites. Helictites are similarly small and slow-growing, but seem to defy the laws of gravity, twisting in odd directions for no apparent reason.

OGOF FFYNNON TAF in the south-east of the quarry and north-west of Lesser Garth Cave, was discovered by quarrymen in 1986 and is the longest according to present knowledge, at 613 feet with a vertical range of 30 feet.

As so often, a number of attempts were necessary to determine its full extent, apparent blockages being penetrated on subsequent visits by more serious digging, tighter squeezes and longer wriggles. This led eventually to Oliver's Secret Garden, where the explorers were rewarded with views of some splendid stalactites, these illustrated in John Adam's "Ogof Ffynnon Taf: New Finds under Quarrying Threat" in "Descent: The Cavers' Magazine" (1986). Formations in 358 feet (109 m) of canyons beyond these, were dominated by a bright orange pillar christened Surah's Column.

Skeletons of cats, ordinary domestic Moggies *(Felis domesticus)*, were found further on, through a larger chamber and more passages past the Toll Gate. Two were very old and one was cemented to the rock by natural calcification, the bones adding a extra quota of lime to the flowstone. The cavers entered from a breach exposed on the quarry face and it remains a mystery how and why the cats should have penetrated so far underground, to the same spot but at different times, when there is no evidence of prey.

Ogof Ffynon Taf is the only cave system in which signs of vertebrates have been found, although it would be surprising if small animals such as mice, birds and toads did not occasionally seek shelter in the others.

An eastern arm of the cave is referred to as the Bat Chamber, the name probably arising from the presence of lesser horseshoe bats, which are the most usual species found in caves and are easily distinguishable from greater horseshoe bats.

Quarrying has now destroyed the entrance to this fine cave system but a new way in has been found along a narrow tunnel from the Lesser Garth Cave. It is that one that is best known to zoologists.

In the absence of sunlight to sustain green vegetation, it contains a preponderance of animals over plants. The basis of the food chain is organic debris washed in from outside and boosted by microscopic fungi and bacteria which can live in darkness.

Observations on the invertebrate animals have been made by the late Jeff Jefferson of University College, Cardiff, Phil Chapman of the BBC Wildlife Unit, Bristol and Julian Carter of the National Museum, Cardiff.

The most exciting find was the rare white cave spider *(Porrhomma rosenhaueri)* made by Jefferson and Chapman in 1982. This was the second record for Britain, the first also made by Jefferson, at Ogof-y-Ci on the Nant Glais, a tributary of the Taf Fechan in the southern part of the Brecon Beacons National Park - in the same river system and the

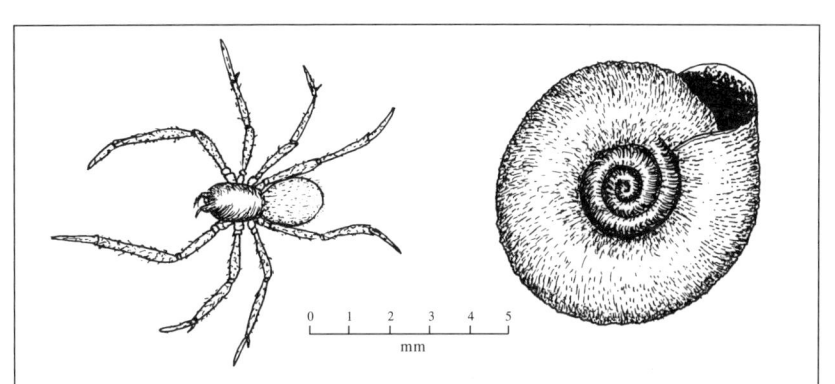

Rare white cave spider *Porrhomma rosenhaueri*. lacks eyes and pigment, and is recorded in only 2 caves in Britain - both in South Wales.

Rounded Snail *Discus rotundatus* sometimes found in caves.

same deposit of Carboniferus Limestone, but the sites are unconnected as the strata dip deeply into the bowels of the Earth below the South Wales Coalfield in between the South and North outcrops.

A few records have come from Ireland, otherwise it is a species of mainland Europe. There have been some half dozen sightings in the Lesser Garth Cave, of half a dozen together on one occasion. This is the only one of Britain's 590 or so species of spider that lives exclusively in the unlighted zones of caves.

Porrhomma belongs to the money spider group (*Linphiidae*) but differs in being eyeless and having almost no pigment. Two others of this group occur in caves, although not exclusively so, but these have some body colouring and rudimentary eyes. One of them, *Porrhomma convexum* lives alongside the white one at Ogof-y-Ci and turns up in Somerset, Derbyshire and Yorkshire caves. Within these it has a white abdomen and juveniles may be pure white, but specimens found in the open wear the more usual black and grey camouflage uniform of more everyday spiders.

With plenty of flies around, it is odd that the cave *Porrhomma* feeds almost exclusively on springtails. These are caught in a delicate sheet web. The builder hangs upside down below the web, responding to the vibration of an alighting springtail by jerking the victim off its feet and racing to the spot to deliver a lethal bite from below. Then the prey is dragged through the net and the nutritious contents sucked out (Chapman (1982) "Cave Life", Part 4.) The spread of their eight slender legs enables them to progress across the surface film of pool water.

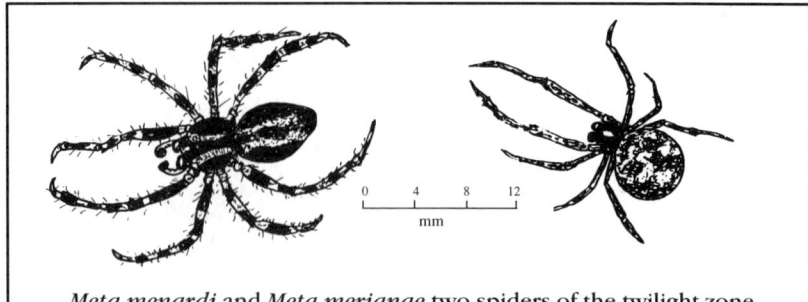

Meta menardi and *Meta merianae,* two spiders of the twilight zone within the cave entrance.

The other two spiders present are *Meta menardi* and *Meta merianae*, orb weavers of the family *Metidae* with an affinity for dark places, from damp cellars to disused rabbit burrows. Both are threshold species living inside and outside the cave, although individuals may spend their entire lives inside. They have lost neither colour nor eyes.

Meta menardi, which penetrates further into the dark zone than the other, comes in two shades of brown, with oval abdomen and spiky, stripy legs. *Meta merianae* is darker, with light patterning on the rounder abdomen. It is smaller, 6-9 mm as opposed to the other's 13 mm, the males of both smaller but much larger than *Porrhomma*, which is only 2.5 mm long, excluding appendages. Their webs are small, with few silk strands at the hub, and are fashioned to catch both flying and crawling prey.

Another threshold animal is the lens shaped rounded snail *(Discus rotundatus)*, which is commoner outside than in, seeking dark refuges under stones, rotting wood and leaf mould - a partial troglodyte, like the wren, which is named *Troglodytes troglodytes* for its propensity to creep into small dark holes.

Jefferson published his findings here in "The Limestone and Caves of Wales" (1989), Ed. T D Ford. His list embraces thirteen species, the three spiders, two moths, four flies, two Isopods (like woodlice) a beetle and the aforementioned snail.

Both the moths have a wing span of 1.5 inches or more. The more colourful, the orange herald moth *(Scoliopteryx libatrix)* is commonly found in the twilight zone of caves, mines, tunnels and other orifices, often with wings and torso glistening with drops of condensed moisture. The patterned coppery coloured wings are folded across its back when at rest, giving it a narrower outline than the spread wings merit.

The other moth is the tissue moth *(Triphosia dubitata)*, its mottled golden brown scales appearing a drabber grey in the subdued light.

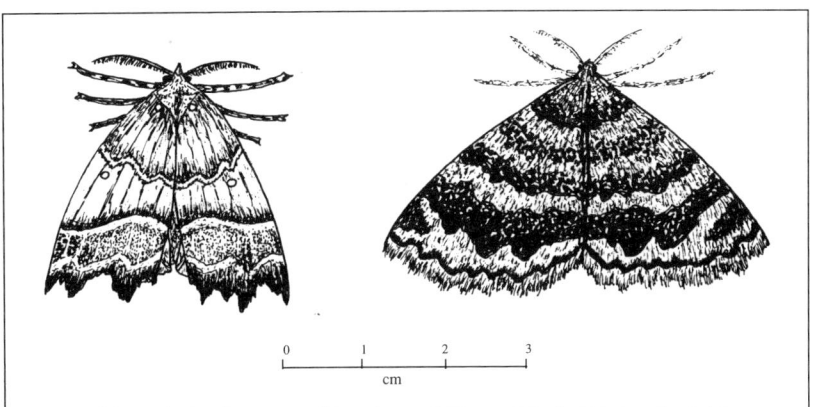

Herald Moth, Scoliopteryx libatrix *and Tissue Moth,* Triphosia dubitata, *spend most of their adult lives within the entrances of caves or mines.*

This rests with wings half spread, to give a triangular outline. In both species it is only the adults which come into the caves and then only into the entrances. Caterpillars of the herald moth feed outside on poplars and willows, those of the tissue moth on blackthorn and buckthorn.

Both types fly into caves or mines soon after emerging from the chrysalis, to settle or walls or roof. Heralds become very torpid, tissues less so. Jefferson suggests that for part of the time in this state of semi-hibernation there is a 'diapause' or period of suspended development in the ovaries, which is necessary before the female can emerge and lay eggs on the food plant.

No-one has come up with any reason as to why these should be the only two of over two thousand moths and butterflies in Britain to take to life in caves on a regular basis. (The 51 peacock and 32 small tortoiseshell butterflies counted aestivating (the summer equivalent of hibernating) in just one of the dark underground ammunition stores on Flatholm Island which they had invaded in the heatwave of 1983, were a one-off. They are the epitome of brilliant summer days, but the brilliance had got the better of them on this occasion, drying up the flower nectar, and they had resorted to the relative cool of emergency stations.)

Another summer visitor to caves, including the Lesser Garth, is the largest of the two-winged flies, *Limonia nubeculosa*, a cranefly with prettily mottled wings. Few craneflies feed when adult, so the absence of suitable food inside would cause them no inconvenience. (Jefferson (1982), "Cave Life," Part 5, "Life in the Twilight Zone."

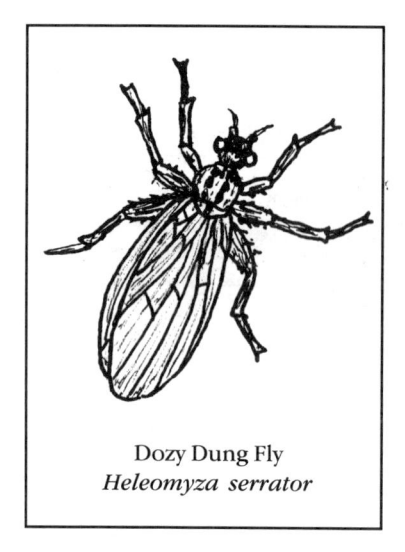

Dozy dung flies, Phil Chapman's name for *Heleomyza serrator*, occur in both threshold and dark zones and are present throughout the year. They resemble common house flies, but are leaner and brown, the product of larvae living outside on sheep dung. The 'dozy' applies to their astonish capacity for inertia. As Chapman rather picturesquely puts it (Chapman (1982) "Cave Life", part 4:

"They are not in caves just to hibernate. They never seem quite to cotton on to the coming of spring. Even in midsummer, there they sit, still patiently waiting for Godot, until some unsporting fungus sneaks up and eats them for lunch."

Dozy Dung Fly
Heleomyza serrator

At some stage, they rouse themselves from their lethargy just sufficiently to copulate with a nearby fly of the opposite sex and, later on, the female will have to muster the energy to move out and find a succulent dollop of dung in which to lay her eggs.

A lot fall prey to the fungus but nothing, apparently, eats them, in spite of the abundance of bodies of both the quick and the dead. Chapman suggests that larvae, after fattening on the sheeps' leftovers, might burrow into the soil to pupate and drop into crevices, from where the flies crawl into caves which may be too humid for their well being.

Squadrons of mosquitoes *(Culex pipiens)* (a species which rarely bites humans) settle at the cave entrance. In autumn mated females move inside for the winter, emerging in spring to sup the blood of a victim, usually a bird, and lay their eggs in pools and puddles outside. Only some behave thus, because there are three or four generations a year, so this diapause only occurs in every third or fourth life cycle. Nevertheless, it seems to be as necessary as the blood meal of the *Anopheles* mosquito that attacks humans if the reproductive vigour of the population is to be kept up.

The fourth type of fly under Garth Wood is the olive brown web-spinning fungus gnat *(Speleopta leucogaster)*. In this instance it is the larval feeding stage which dominates the scene. Long glistening white maggots spin tangled webs which usually become sprinkled with water droplets from the super saturated atmosphere. These are not so much webs to catch prey as a scaffolding to climb around on in pursuit of non-elusive food in the bacteria-rich sediment washed in by the drainage trickles from the world above. The species has not yet been found outside caves.

The gnats are reminiscent of that other, more famous member of the *Mycetophilidae* or fungus gnat group, *Arachnocampa luminosa*. These are the New Zealand glow worms, which festoon the roof and walls of the Waitomo Caves in the North Island, casting a mysterious glow over a fairytale world, to the delight of boatloads of tourists moving slowly across the waters below.

It is the silken webs which are bio-luminescent and these dangle into space to catch midges and other flying insects. The 'Arachno' part of the generic name refers to the spiderlike spinning of the threads, whose luciferin, basis of the glow, is a waste product of digestion, which produces light when acted on by an enzyme in the presence of oxygen.

The cave water louse *(Proasellus cavaticus)* turns up in caves as commonly as ordinary woodlice do in damp cupboards but, unlike those, is confined to this type of habitat. Members of our South Wales race reach to 8-9 mm as against only 4 mm in the Mendip race across the Bristol Channel. The isopods scuttle over the rocks on their ten short legs and another, *Androniscus dentiger*, has been recorded here by Jefferson.

Cave beetles are for the most part intruders from the outside - ground beetles, rove beetles or diving beetles. Only one has turned up in the Garth caves, this, *Choleva spadicea*, being a Coleopteron or ground beetle. Springtails are tiny, diverse and little known, so none have been named here.

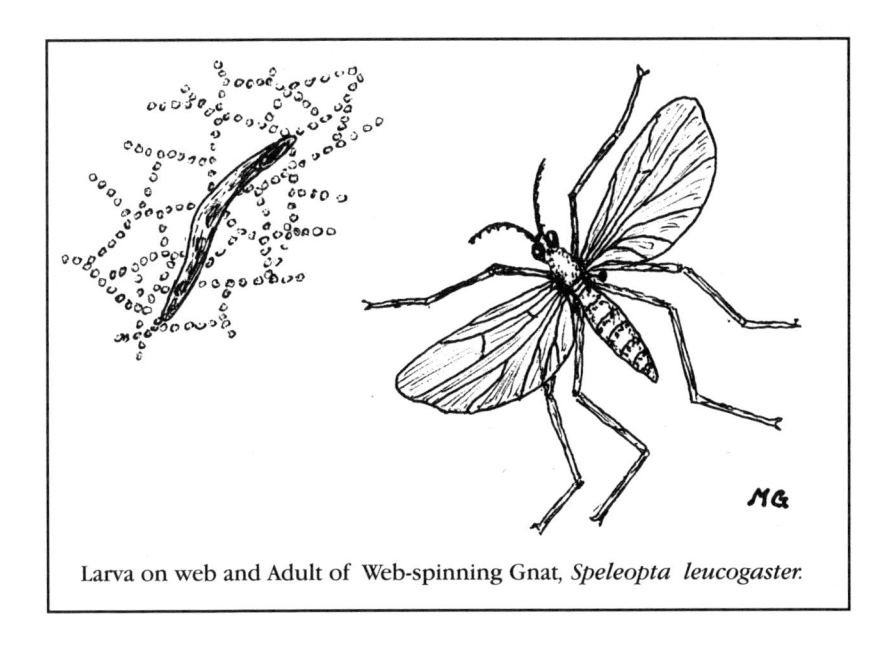

Larva on web and Adult of Web-spinning Gnat, *Speleopta leucogaster.*

3. Early Iron Mining

The body of iron ore cropping out on the Little Garth was of vital importance to the Iron Age community of 2,000 years ago. Concealed, as it must have been, by topsoil and leaf mould, it is interesting to speculate how they discovered it - given the sparseness of the population at the time.

Iron was also essential for the equipping of the Roman legions in the first to third centuries AD and the newcomers no doubt put the indigenous people to work winning the metals they prized, both here and at Machen and Draethen a mile or so to the east, where silver, lead and zinc were also there for the taking.

Ore bodies are not thought to have impinged on the caves where the early inhabitants lived and worked, but fragments of iron have been picked up in these. Evidence shows that a craftsman was working metals in the dry passage connecting the two main chambers of the natural cave system during the Dark Ages. He was melting down copper, bronze and gold as well as iron, in small hard pottery crucibles.

Hussey (1967) writes. "In this work we find the influence of Ireland, which suggests that the Taff Gorge was then a trading route into South Wales."

Haematite occurs in the belt of dolomite from Llantrisant to Machen, where almost half of the rock is haematite and up to 40% of the haematite is workable ore: a much richer source of iron than the rounded ironstone nodules found in local Coal Measure rocks.

The northern ironworks that grew up around Merthyr, Dowlais, Blaenavon and Ebbw Vale had only the poorer ironstone to draw on locally, the northern limestone outcrop not so richly endowed as the southern, and not dolomitised. Their ironstone formed 20% or less of the country rock and was of inferior quality. It was often in the form of nodules or bells which fell from the roofs of the coal mines, a hazard to those within (who were known as 'colliers', the term 'miner' refering only to the men of iron.)

Nodule mining showed small profit, entailing as it did the man-handling of quantities of waste, so the cheapest possible labour was employed, often in the form of women and children. Some use of this material has been made in the south, as at the Brass Vein Level by the River Taff below Gwaelod village, and iron pits were opened in the Coalfield rocks across the river at Graig-yr-allt.

Walkers in the woods on the Great Garth, north to Gedrys, can find exfoliating, rust-stained iron nodules among the woodland floor debris, their outer layers peeling away in a small version of onion scale weathering.

View to the North through the Taff Gorge, showing the river, road and rail routes, and the old viaduct spanning the Gorge with the Little Garth to the left.

Latterly the northern iron masters contracted out for better quality iron and ore was supplied to them from the Little Garth, first by canal and then by railway. It is on record that at one period most of the Garth ore went north with only about a quarter being smelted in the local Pentyrch forge. Later still the northern works transferred to Cardiff to utilise imported ore.

Little is known about the winning of iron, if any, between Roman and Elizabethan times, when charcoal was used for smelting and English iron workers from Sussex and Kent started moving to Wales as their local timber supplies diminished - the government keen on keeping a nucleus of oaks for the navy. ("Hearts of oak are our ships, hearts of oak are our men" are words frequently chanted about those rumbustious days in our childhood.")

Iron was mined at Mwyndy, Llantrisant, as early as 1539, with other enterprises starting up during the next few decades at Merthyr, Aberdare, Llanharry and Bridgend (E.L.Chappell, "Historic Melingriffith").

In 1565 Edmond Matthews of Castell-y-Mynach in Creigiau and Radyr, employed Henry Sydney and a German, John Bowde, to open up iron works on the Little Garth, which he owned. Guns were manufactured and, ten years later, in 1575, Matthew's enterprise was in trouble with the privy council for exporting ordnance in violation of a monopoly held by Ralph Hogge. Matthews leased the forge to another but the authorities caught up again in 1616 and subsequent petitions were turned down, the works being closed in 1625. Most of the early artefacts were of timber, even water conduits being of hollowed logs, sometimes halved lengthways, so tangible remains are few.

The mine pit was originally sunk on the top of the Little Garth, but eventually became too deep to work safely. The enterprise was re-opened in the eighteenth century by the Blakemore-Booker Company, which came to own coal mines, iron forges, rail tracks, the Melin Griffith Tinplate Works and much more. Furnaces were updated in 1740, when charcoal was still being used for smelting - one acre of forest supplying enough fuel to produce three tons of iron.

By 1815-1830, when new furnaces were built and renovations undertaken, coke was taking over from charcoal, although the two were used side by side for a while. Much of the coal feeding the steam boilers came from the Coed-y-Bedw Colliery closeby, which was producing coal from 1827 to 1913.

A tunnel was driven in from the north side of the hill to near the bottom of the mine pit, and more tunnels pushed westwards, eastwards and downwards to a depth of 400 feet or so.

The incentive for the mole-like tunelling, deeper and deeper into the bowells of the hill, was that the area of heamatite was greater at greater depths. Also the best haematite, containing 39.63% of iron occurred lower down. The deep workings extended at least 450 feet (140 m) to east and west of the addit, which was driven in about 1840.

Ore was worked by stoping, the miners working from a tunnel constructed alongside the ore vein. Although the haematite body is extensive, it is irregularly shaped, so all is not plain sailing, even without the faults and folds.

The dynamic owner of the Booker-Blakemore enterprise had died in 1858, passing the reins to his son, Thomas William Booker. Soon after this the method of processing steel was discovered and, in common with other iron masters, the new owner regarded the cost of conversion to this process to be prohibitive.

More than 50% of the firm's capital was tied up in the iron works, which became a liabilty, imported Spanish ore from Bilbao being of higher grade and more suitable for steel, which was, in turn, more suitable for tinning. From 1875 steel gradually ousted iron as the basic material for tin plate. Another setback this year was the gas explosion in with serious loss of life in Llan Mine (the site of today's Old Drift Garage), which Booker also owned.

Booker's sons carried on mining iron ore until 1884, around the time that the industry in the north of the Coalfield moved to the Dowlais Works and East Moors in Cardiff, to utilise the new imports.

Various solutions were tried at the Little Garth, but the works were eventually shut down by the end of the nineteenth century.

Such deep workings had become a source of wonder to the public before the final closure of the Booker:Blakemore empire in in 1884 and visits were organised for those wishing to learn more. One such is ably described by F.G.Evans (1872, Trans Cardiff Nats. Soc. Vol.III p. 42). He tells the story as follows:

"The mines amply repay the trouble of inspection. Visitors are conveyed through the tunnel in a covered carriage kept for the purpose and carry a lamp to enable them to examine the sides of the rock as they go. Having arrived at the end of it and become accustomed to the subdued light, they begin to perceive surrounding objects. Close by a powerful engine is in motion to pump up water and raise the minerals. Men and boys, horses and trams are seen flitting around and a hum of voices and the sound of hammers greet the ear. A car is in readiness to take them down the shaft to a depth of 170 feet. In the quick descent there is no time to observe much, but there may be noticed in passing a blacksmith's shop that looks as if it were suspended in mid air, where the tools of the workmen are sharpened. Below numerous lights are seen. These are the candles of the miners engaged in blasting the rock........."

He describes much more before finally emerging into the main outer pit *"which bears some resemblance to the crater of an extinct volcano. In frosty weather its walls are adorned with massive icicles."* (Like those of the exit from the A 470 road cutting under Castell Coch hill today.)

There has been talk of opening the mines once more for public viewing, entering through the northern side tunnel, but there will be no flickering candles nor hum of miners' voices now. An alternative exit would need to be constructed and other safety precautions taken and the project is likely to remain in the formulative stage as yet - perhaps until blasting in the modern quarry ceases.

In 1926 there was a partial revival when the West of England Ochre and Oxide Company operated at Little Garth, making paints from yellow ochre and red oxide. Material was stored on the side of the Pentyrch Road where the old bridge crossed onto the lower section of the modern Coed-y-Bedw Nature Reserve.

John Tyler worked here for 7 years until 1933, digging out ochreous material with shovel and bucket and pushing it in a wheelbarrow to the tram, which was manhandled out of the mine with no assisting power. Even at this late date the men worked below by the light of candles.

Ventilation underground was good, sometimes too good. Tyler reports that in cold winters there were icicles 60 feet long in Big Pit, so thick that he failed to circle them with his arms. Unlike coal mines, however, there is no methane emission, with its associated liklihood of explosions.

A new company started mining for ore in 1936, after the underground lakes had been pumped out, the necessary electricity produced by smelly diesel engines balanced on a raft. Many of the old miners' tools were exposed on the lake bed. The new venture failed, the mine was closed and the pits filled, with more spoil dumped in the lake, hiding their floors should the water ever be evacuated again.

4. The Iron Mines in Modern Times

Drainage is primarily by ground water systems and surplus water had to be pumped out when work was in progress. Vast depths have accumulated in the shafts since mining ceased in 1884.

Many of the underground water tables are 'perched', the water not continuous throughout. Some drains westward along the ridge to the vast underground reservoir which is tapped for modern use at Schwyll - the onamatopaeic name of the waterworks by the River Ewenny near Bridgend.

A modern show piece is the lake, 250 feet (76 metres) below the ground surface and 200 feet deep. It appears as several, because the cave roof dips in places to water level, and one part, where sunlight strikes the surface, is known as The Blue Waters.

Until the mid 1990s water was pumped up from the underground lakes to the quarry, which succeeded the mine, for the washing of aggregates, the water returned for the silt to settle out. Now the screening process after crushing has been improved so that the finer particles can be extracted and marketted separately without the need for washing. (There is no such handy source of Water in Tarmac's quarry at Creigiau, where aggregate washing was never practised.)

The present entrance to the mine is along a tunnel cut in the early 1840s to allow more or less horizontal access to the working level from the foot of the hill. It was built on a slight gradient, allowing surplus water to drain out of the interior, and is currently occupied by a shallow stream. During periods when the water emerges impregnated with lime there is some fascinating tufa deposition here.

Lime in its soluble form is calcium bicarbonate. On emerging into the daylight carbon dioxide is given off, leaving the insoluble calcium carbonate, which precipitates out as a chalky white crust on leaves, twigs and stones on the bed and margins of the stream. Limey rods are seen to have blades of grass through their centres, the nuclei of deposition - while calcified roots and branches, fruits and feathery tufts of moss adopt the fantastic shapes of rare porcelain.

At other periods, for no obvious reason, there is no tufa formation and crystal clear water runs over uncoated pebbles. My visits have been too infrequent for me to be able to relate these tufa-free periods to heavy rainfall, diluting the lime content or speeding up the flow so that there is no time for the solids to settle out.

I have seen no tufa recently, so perhaps the spasmodic extra concentrations of lime came when the quarry men returned water used for washing the finer particles from the crushed aggregate, this adding more free lime than that leaching into the flow from the tunnel walls.

At best the deposits were poorly cemented, the sometimes cream-coloured, papillose surface resembling the fur which accumulates inside kettles in hard water districts. Collections of petrified leaves and twigs tended to crumble eventually in storage. The petrifying process was swift enough for few of the previous autumn's leaves to remain uncoated by the following March.

The landmark for visiting this site was the roofed brick edifice to the left of the tunnel entrance known as "Smoky Joe's" from the graffiti over the entrance. It was used as sleeping quarters over the years by a series of squatters, but was demolished in the early 1990s. Originally it was the powder magazine, the nearby stables and workshops having been demolished long since.

Once upon a time this now secluded woodland glade was humming with activity, the tunnel being the main point of entry for mine equipment and exit for the products.

John Tyler, author of "Iron in the Soul", the story of the Little Garth Iron Mines, published in 1988, found the keystone of the arch leading into the passage. It was inscribed "1842". The completion of this new route meant that iron ore had no longer to be hauled to the tops of the shafts or the Big Pit and trundled back down on horse-drawn trams along the network of tramroads through the Garth wood and across the Pentyrch Road, from where it still had to go to the Taffside Pentyrch Iron Works (now the Heol Berry housing estate and green), along a track parallel to the Pentyrch Road and down a steep incline into the furnace yard.

Two of the four opencast pits on the top of the Garth can still be seen, with traces of old walls and the relics of the lifting gear. One is the main shaft, site of a historic photograph of Dr. Mungo.

This is an impressive hole in the ground, lined by tall beech trees, harts tongue ferns and other shade-tolerant plants. A smaller orifice leads away into the moist darkness at its base. An attempt to fill this in with quarry rubble, on safety grounds, was abandoned when the historic value of the site was pointed out, and a stout barbed wire fence was erected around the whole area, in lieu.

In the event of the mines being reopened to the public, this main shaft is envisaged as the alternative entrance. At present the land between it and the access road along which trucks thunder to and from the quarry is in a sorry state, as abandoned by a cement company formerly based here. There are plans to cover over the debris and landscape the area.

The main feature of the site to the late 1990s is a fabulous old beech tree perched on the brink, with a sizable portion split away and lying alongside. It is as large as they come and still thriving, but even such giants cannot live for ever.

The other existing orifice is the one directly above part of the underground lake which allows noontide sunshine down to illuminate the "Blue Waters". This is currently the main pumping site, with the pipe emerging by the old walls shoring up the gravelled vehicle track alongside. Fat 'penny bun' Boletus toadstools burst from the leaf mould under the bordering beeches here.

It is possible to clamber a little way down and members of the Fire Fighting Service carry out rescue practice on the ridge of land between the shaft and the modern quarry brink. This, too, has been wired off from the over adventurous public since vandals went down and stole a valuable length of cable which they could have hauled out only with difficulty.

Material accompanying the ore which came by the improved route to Smoky Joe's, was dumped on new sorting beds just below the tunnel. These rubble heaps are now moss-covered and colonised by vigorous wild arum instead of the more usual hart's-tongue ferns which often take over such sites. When sheep had regular access here in the 1970s, tree seedlings were nibbled off a few inches above ground and the plant cover remained low, featuring wood avens, wood sanicle and dog's mercury.

During World War II the tunnel itself and the shafts were used for storing high explosives and other nearby ruins are the remains of shelters built for the men who guarded these.

Explosives have moved on since the years of the black powder that was used prior to the advent of gelignite, stuffed into holes made by a two to three man team with sledge hammers.

Previous to that lime was used, presumably burned calcium oxide or quicklime, stuffed into holes strategically placed along the strata. When wetted and sealed this expanded as it changed to slaked lime (calcium hydroxide) splitting the rock apart. This was at a time when the miners went to work down ropes, hand over hand, and put bars in the wall to make primitive steps.

In the very early days it is likely that rocks were split by lighting a fire against a desirable face and then throwing water onto the heated cliff section.

By the late 1980s, Steetley, the company then working Walnut Tree

Quarry, had partially filled some of the old shafts with quarry waste, blocking access to the western lakes. Permission was being sought in the early 1990s to extend and deepen the quarry, endangering the entire iron working complex and threatening to destroy a heritage that Roger John (1990, "Community Link" July) describes as a fairy tale world with rainbows forming on drops of water as they fall from the chamber roofs: "The magic of the underground experience taking on a quality greater than reality."

The deep-set labyrinth is still extant in the late 1990s. Long may it remain so, as a monument to the intrepid men of our industrial past, who risked their lives daily on dangling ropes and crazy ladders - a source of wonderment in our present button-pushing feather-bedded age. Last century's workers, weary after a day's toil, would seek leisure time rest. Today's workers after a day bent over a desk top computer, are more likely to seek exercise!

The Welsh Mines Society maintains that these are the only large scale iron mine workings left in Wales and are of unusual importance in industrial heritage terms. An initiative was inaugurated to persude CADW and other organisations to ensure their protection, as a major education and tourist resource.

Assets to be exploited are the iron ore caverns and lakes, the natural cave system occupied in prehistoric times, the ancient beechwood and the surface evidence of centuries of industrial activity. With Castell Coch just across the gorge and the partially renovated Taffs Well Spa with its newly laid out gardens just upstream, the region could become one of Wales' main tourist attractions. What a pity the tall connecting railway viaduct was demolished in the 1970s! With the renovated Nant Garw Potteries and Museum a little further north, this might, indeed, have been a titillating enticement at "The Gateway to Wales" to lure travellers moving west from England along the M4 motorway.

Some fine calcite crystals on a chunk of dolomite found in Nant Llwydrew

Chapter 5

THE DAYLIGHT WORLD OF THE LITTLE GARTH

1. Modern Quarrying

The first quarry to nibble into the south-east corner of the Little Garth Hill was the Ty Nant Quarry, named after the Morganstown stream - as was the local public house. History does not record the site of the tree that gave its name to the modern Walnut Tree Quarry which has disembowelled the eastern end of the hill. There was also a Walnut Tree Inn near the railway station and a notice on the Taffs Well signal box: "Walnut Tree Junction", the name applying to the whole district.

Along the ridgetop, half way to Pentyrch, is the old Ton Mawr Quarry, no bigger than the Ty Nant, despite the name, these both mere fly bites in contrast to the spreading forty acres or so of Walnut Tree Quarry.

The Ty Nant Quarry ceased working long ago and has been taken over by naturally regenerated scrub woodland and rock plants. Walnut Tree Quarry has recently changed hands but continues to be worked on a massive scale, extracting stone for the metal industry and less valuable aggregates.

The Ton Mawr Quarry, unworked for many years, has recently been re-opened by the farmer owner, octogenarian T.S. (Sammy) Rees, under the management of staff made redundant by the larger quarry nearby. In late 1997 the workings were still quite shallow, at one level only, and the output modest. Planning permission allowed the enterprise to go down for 30 feet, but there was argument as to whether this was 30 feet from ground level or from the former quarry floor! If the quarry comes up for sale it is likely that the larger one alongside will buy and put it into abeyance until their own excavations curve round to engulf it and set things in motion again.

Early quarrymen on both the Garth and Castell Coch sides of the Taff River burrowed into the sides of the gorge, widening the gap that came to be the throughway for canal, feeder, railways and roads linking the coalfield with the coast.

Initially limestone was burned to quicklime and slaked for agricultural use. Although a seemingly extravagant use of dolomite, the high magnesium content proved an asset in preventing the sort of magnesium deficiency disease which killed my favourite cow, Duchess, during my farming days of long ago.

Remains of the line of kilns where the Ty Nant limestone was burned are still visible on the side of the road linking Morganstown with the Ynys roundabout and the road crossing of the Taff. The arched stone entrances face outwards towards the highway, getting progressively lower northwards, due probably to a change of gradient when the unsurfaced road was made up. In summer they are swallowed up by an exuberant annual growth of Himalayan balsam, emerging again in winter.

During the 1930s the quarry owners, Thomas Edward and sons of Taffs Well, produced limestone chippings for road stone and railway ballast. Stone from the quarry crossed the unmade road by a bridge to the old Pentyrch and Melingriffith Railway. This ran from the Rhyd-yr-Helig Mine north of Gedrys along the west bank of the river to the Pentyrch Ironworks, past the Ynys Ford (subsequently replaced by two bridges) to the Melin Griffith Tin Plate Works. Loads were taken aboard at the Pentyrch Sidings opposite the Ty Nant Inn, to link eventually with the Taff Vale Railway.

Already, before the 1920s, the potential of dolomite on the Little Garth had been realised by Captain Burns, a Cornish tin mining engineer, who mined in a small way for silver-lead ore on the other side of the gorge. He started working it, burning the rock in cupules discarded by the Ebbw Vale Steelworks.

There was a valuable market for dolomite to line the furnaces used in the Bessamer Process, where steel was made by blasting compressed air through molten iron to burn out the excess carbon and other impurities. A new furnace was built at viaduct level with a railway siding linking into the Barry Line.

Steetley Quarry Products took over in the mid 1940s and opened up the Walnut Tree Quarry in a big way until the merger with Redlands Aggregates P L C took place in 1992. Best quality rock was also used for fire-resistant bricks in the Sinter Process of steel making where the iron is welded to form a homogeneous mass by heating without melting. Most went to the Margam Steelworks in West Glamorgan.

On a quarry visit in 1971, geologists from the Nature Conservancy Council enthused about the quality of the dolomite - the best in Great Britain, some consisting of 43% magnesium carbonate and most of the rest calcium carbonate. East of the Taff Gorge the more valuable beds are contorted and faulted so the quarries on that side have more problems with working. Cefn Garw Quarry south of Castell Coch closed down, but aggregates were being hauled out from there again in the late 1990s.

Other South Wales deposits have too many impurities, such as silica, or too little magnesium, or the deposits are too small to merit extraction. The nearest significant deposit is in Derbyshire.

Poorer quality material from Walnut Tree is used for road stone, river revetments, land fill and limestone dust for concrete blocks or to mix with Liassic limestone products in coastal cement works. The price doubles for every twenty miles of transport, so this inferior stone is a viable proposition only for local use.

A corner of Walnut Tree Quarry in December 1984, with a view over the coastal plain.

Nothing is wasted. In 1997 even the screening southern bund of clayey earth was being dug up and sold to cover over a landfill site for rubbish, the bund to be rebuilt from other poor quality overburden as this became available.

The best metallurgical quality rock is found at the greater depths so inferior material has to be removed first, its sale making the concern economically viable. Unlike the mass of junk mail that keeps our postal system economically viable, it has a value in its own right, principally on account of its hardness. It is prized for the foundations of heavy buildings and major trunk roads needed to support the new trans-European juggernauts and for structural concrete generally. Lighter aggregates, as from coal waste, lack the high crushing strength and cannot be subsituted.

Other spin offs have been the Glamorgan Brick Company, a firm producing ready-mixed concrete and the supply of stone to Wimpeys for making asphalt used in the M4 motorway.

The proposal by Redlands in 1994 to produce asphalt on site was vigorously opposed by the local community, on the grounds of anticipated pollution by tarry deposits, dust and carcinogenic fumes containing polycyclic aromatic hydrocarbons, which quarry personnel maintained posed no threat. The matter has still to be determined at the time of writing, but no asphalt has been produced here up to the year 2000.

The local pressure groups had already fended off applications to extend the bounds of the quarry north into the S S S I (Site of Special Scientific Interest) in 1976 and again in 1988, this threatening to jeopardize the northern skyline of the hill as well as damaging the scientifically important beech wood.

The thorn in the flesh throughout has been the old outdated planning permission granted in 1947 and 1949, when post war needs were great and today's sensitivity to environmental concepts were still firmly in the future. Implemented as they stand, the quarry owners could remove the entire south and east flanks of the hill and with them the majesty of the Taff Gorge. Steetley had agreed not to jeopardise these faces, but rather to burrow downwards. So far, Redlands is keeping its options open!

Removal of the already narrow rim on these faces would expose half a hundred acres of land almost at river level and the gorge would be no more than a memory. When T C Cooke wrote his BSc Environmental Geology Thesis in 1977 (unpublished), the quarry occupied only 30 acres, working at 3 to 4 levels with 40 to 50 foot faces between each. At that time 70 workers and 100 hauliers were employed, removing a million tons of rock a year or 20,000 tons a week.

The enterprise is now much bigger, the various tiers and truck roads set out map-like as viewed from the broad track around the quarry rim, the precipice topped by a line of massive boulders. In the 1980s the stepped cliffs were being blasted and removed at 5 to 6 levels; by 1997 there were up to 8 levels in the main pit, plumbing greater depths. The proposed quarry extension in the 1980s and 90s was for 5 hectares.

The gently simmering controversy in the late 1990s involves the provision of a new access road to keep the heavy trucks off the hill leading up to Pentyrch - the traditional exit over the years. Those who live north of the hill favour the idea formulated in 1988 of a tunnel emerging into the old Ty Nant Quarry in the south, involving the least

Tufa deposited on bed of stream emerging from mine addit at Smokey Joe's.

visual impact and the felling of relatively few trees; all trucks to leave northwards and across the Taff onto the A 470 trunk road. Those who live south of the hill favour a new alternative of a much larger scar on the face of the gorge with a heavy duty road running down the face of the hill to the Ynys roundabout and Taff crossing direct.

This exit is deemed impractical, trucks coming out of the tunnel and down an impossibly steep gradient to debouch immediately onto the roundabout. The Ty Nant route wins but is unlikely to be in use before the turn of the century. Tree felling had commenced in February 1999

The healing of this scarred face of the hill when the burning and crushing plant were removed at the end of the 1980s, was undertaken by A D A S for the Ministry of Agriculture, but was a non-event. The slope was terraced and planted with beech saplings, but in the absence of topsoil or organic matter of any kind, these refused to grow. Even the grass and weeds between are threadbare and nothing big enough to be visible from below had grown through the 1990s, despite repeated efforts by experts to solve the problem.

This east face of the gorge is crossed by a culvert taking drainage waters from the floor of the working quarry. From the tall narrow ridge of land separating quarry and gorge, the walker looks down the 8 ranks of quarry cliffs to an almost flat floor where rain water collects in wet weather. This percolates gently to the south-east corner of the great amphitheatre, depositing silt as it goes.

A hole blasted in this corner leads the water through filter beds into the tunnel of the old Barry Railway line, along which it is piped to emerge where the railway formerly debouched onto the Taff-straddling viaduct south of the failed beech saplings. By the time the flow reaches the Taff, suspended solids are negligible, as checked by inspectors of the environmental arm of the Water Authority which succeeded the N.R.A. (National Rivers Authority).

Now, in the late 1990s, the railway tunnel is blocked both ends to exclude walkers, a necessary safety precaution as blasting gets ever closer. The quarry floor is becoming progressively lower, as the better quality rock is removed, this facilitating the exit of the future access route from this corner.

Twenty feet more and the working will be at the same level as the river, but with plenty of solid rock between according to the experts to prevent the Taff from seeping through and flooding the hole.

Quarry extensions and the landscaping of the surrounding land have been the subject of ongoing discussions for over 20 years now, with input from the various conservation bodies and Forestry Commission, but these matters are always well away in the future. (Admiring the map of the renovated Tarmac Quarry site with central lake at Creigiau Quarry open day in 1997, I learned that this was not to be for at least 30 years yet!)

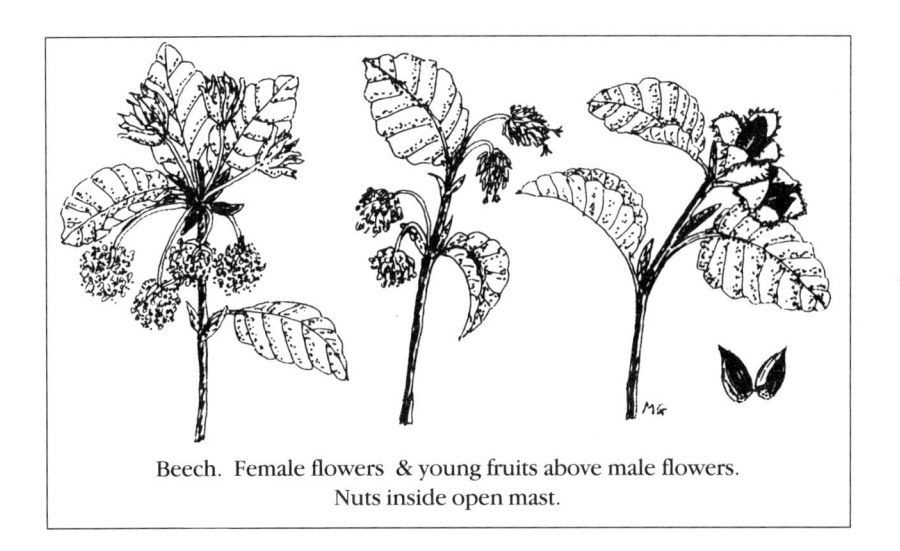

Beech. Female flowers & young fruits above male flowers.
Nuts inside open mast.

2. Nature Moves Back in to the Working Quarry

The old adage "Nature abhors a vacuum" applies in quarries as on other inert material where there are no contaminants sufficiently lethal to inhibit life. Certain plants are remarkably tolerant of the flying dust stirred up by the constant succession of laden trucks. Visibility is completely obscured as these leviathans trundle past, to have their undercarriages washed by rising water jets beyond the weighbridge.

Beech trees are noted for their efficient leaf mosaic - horizontally placed leaves on horizontally placed branches intercepting every ray of sunlight - and every fall of dust. The welcome rain sluicing the cloying accumulation from their shiny surfaces converts the ground to mud, so that boots rather than eyes and nostrils get clogged up. Photosynthesis must be curtailed in dry spells, but the beeches survive.

Incomers, their seed swirled around in the slipstream of the trucks, often have fluffy fruitlets, arrivals including hemp agrimony, ragwort, dandelion, thistles and willow herbs. Perhaps, like marine organisms awaiting the rhythm of the tides for their bursts of activity, they do most of their growing on sundays when the din and the dirt are stilled or when welcome showers arrive without obscuring too much of the sunlight.

Far and away the commonest shrub is *Buddleja*, the butterfly bush, and with it are the butterflies. These hasten through the dustiest parts but linger marginally to sip the honey-sweet nectar, body hairs protecting their respiratory spiracles and averting asphyxiation. Cottony, wind-blown sallow seeds settle and germinate in the early summer months. By late August there are veritable blizzards of the tiny two-winged seeds of birch, slipstream or no slipstream, and these, too, are quick off the mark to put down roots when they come to ground.

Spoil heaps and mounds of chippings welcome colonists, perforated St. John's wort being among the most colourful after the orbs of early coltsfoot have transformed to pendant balls of fluff. Spikes of rosebay reach upward in fiery splendour before shedding clouds of parachuted seeds onto the wind.

Newly crushed chippings are apricot coloured until the rust weathers out to give the blue-grey shade seen in weathered cliff falls on Glamorgan's yellower Liassic Limestone bastions. More earthy heaps show mini versions of classic capstone erosion after heavy rain, with angular pebbles balanced atop slender columns of soil which they have protected from being washed away with the rest.

A former garden near the quarry office was cleared to give more parking space, but peripheral plantings still struggle under the shroud of dust: peony, *Fuchsia*, *Mahonia*, Rose of Sharon and pampas.

Birds are more mobile than plants and may move in well ahead of them, even onto newly blasted cliff faces if cosy niches present themselves.

Jackdaws are commonest, substituting newly formed crevices for the chimney pots which they occupy throughout the Valleys. With the wily

Wild Solomon's Seal is conspicuous in the beechwood east of the Taff Gorge.

intelligence of all members of the crow family, they have learned about blasting. When the men who detonate the explosives retire to the rusty iron bunkers to set the bang in motion (observing it through pillar box slits) and the sirens sound their warning, the jackdaws leave their nest holes for the safety of the open air. As the dust settles they return to their chosen sites - or another if these are no more. Ravens often occupy cliffs in working quarries and there are ravens about, but they do not nest here.

The star turn in recent years has been a pair of peregrine falcons. They have chosen a more stable site on the north cliff, tucked back, as so often, in a vegetated niche a foot or so high, with another nearby as look out post for the partner off duty. Sometimes they are to be seen on the more verdant cliffs of the Ty Nant Quarry, bringing their prey in there to eat in peace during March and April of 1997, but there was no sign of nesting there.

Alternatively, these birds may have been the pair which had set up home in Cwm Lleyshon Quarry at Draethen, a few miles along the South Border Ridge to the east, but whose nest was dislodged by a storm in the early part of 1997, causing them to desert. Sometimes they were joined by another tiercel. Or perhaps they were youngsters, not yet ready to nest.

The backing cliff at Ty Nant is still fairly open, but every niche where the peregrines could get a suitable toe-hold is right for colonising shrubs to get a roothold, so they were possibly squeezed out. All our Glamorgan birds occupy vertical sites where they can swoop out unobstructed by plants.

While it is suspected that birds formerly nested in Ty Nant Quarry, they need a large hunting territory and there has never been more than one pair at a time on the Little Garth. No doubt they sometimes meet up with the Creigiau Quarry family over the heights of the Great Garth, but there is plenty of room up there for both.

Always they are noble and it is especially rewarding to be able to view them from above as they sail effortlessly out from their eyrie below the rim. Jeff Watkins, a Redlands Quarry employee, keeps an eye on them and tells how he watched the falcon kill the local kestrel. Like members of the crow family, they seem to enjoy mobbing the resident buzzards but take little notice of the jackdaws where, maybe they feel outnumbered. Or is it just a matter of taste? We ourselves enjoy the odd pigeon pie on occasion but would never consider eating a member of the crow family. (During my war-time farming days wood pigeons were a serious agricultural pest and we were often out with twelve bores or point two two rifles saving the crops and filling the pie dish.)

Wood pigeons usually manage to give the peregrines the slip by veering off into the cover of the beeches, where the dramatic hunting stoop of up to a hundred mph would come to grief in the tangle of branches. Racing and passenger pigeons tend to rely on their speed for escape, and remain in the open, where they are more likely to fall victim.

Ornithologist Richard Smith observed the falcon swoop out from her eyrie and grab a passing green woodpecker, but the nearby remains pointed to pigeon as the favoured prey.

Jeff Watkins has recently taken over Cwm Farm from his aging father. The land abuts onto the south of the Little Garth and Ty Nant and was encroached upon by the big new housing estate of Radyr Gardens in 1996. Like crofters and smallholders elsewhere, he has had to seek another source of income, leasing some of his land to neighbouring farmer, John Llewellyn and more, along with the stables, to local horse owners. So the industrial landscape gradually takes over from the rural one and matters are not going to improve now that the parish of Pentyrch has been sucked into the clutches of Cardiff City.

Peregrines have made a remarkable come-back from the brink of extinction on a national scale since the toxic chemicals formerly in common use on the land were banned and their prey is no longer full of poisons. No longer are the eggs soft-shelled and breeding inhibited, so there are youngsters looking for new sites to supplement the traditional ones on mountain and coastal crags.

In 1995 the Walnut Tree Quarry pair hatched three to four eggs but only one youngster, a male, left the nest. They had changed sites that year to a more open one alongside a broad ledge and not too difficult to get down to by a determined enough marauder, so they may have been interfered with.

In 1996 two young were brought off successfully, but there were none in 1997 and only the tiercel was seen mewing from his ledge and soaring forth on reconnaissance flights during the latter part of the summer. Perhaps he was the extra tiercel in the Ty Nant Quarry, and the other two his offspring of the previous year. Without ringing, these are things we shall never know. There was no breeding in 1998.

Local ornithologist, Cliff Woodhead, who keeps an eye on local bird specialities, thinks they may have been squeezed out of their chosen slot by a burgeoning Buddleja bush. Any hope of an offer from a quarryman to remove it was dashed when the imparting of the news produced a response of:

"Oh, so they've got a window box this year, have they?"

Maybe an R.S.P.B. peregrine ringer can be persuaded to abseil down the short distance from the top and remove the obstruction in time for the 1999 season. Man has formulated so many hazards to their past welfare, it is only meet and proper that he should make some small amends.

Cladonia chlorophaea and *Peltigera praetexta*
Two of the more spectacular lichens on mossy boulders. Ty Nant Quarry

3. Rehabilitation of the old Ty Nant Quarry

Directly above the Morganstown allotments behind the Ty Nant Inn is a good place to obtain an aerial view of fifty years of quarry reclamation by the wild. A short scramble up from the north-eastern allotment brings the viewer to the brink of a sheer drop, impressive in itself but only a fraction of the height of the towering dolomite face to the left. Like the better known McDonnell Ranges in Central Australia, this cliff catches the morning sunlight and reflects it back in an ever-changing kaleidoscope of reds - from magenta through crimson and burnt sienna to orange. White birch trunks stand in for those of the Australian ghost gums.

In autumn shimmering drifts of old man's beard claw their way up, but the main cliff is sprinkled only sparsely with Buddlejas and others able to force their roots into the cracks left by the blocky cleavage.

Beech and ash trees have survived the rigours of wind and soil drought on the summit, but are tight-leaved and stag-headed, creating a tattered skyline. The old quarry floor, invisible under its cover of trees, is still at an early successional phase, dominated by Buddleja, birch and sallows, these overtopped only intermittently by the ash, beech and sycamore which will take over eventually.

Obliquely across the valley is the matching face of the Taff Gorge, in shadow when the Garth is high lighted and a deep purple, but changing to apricot pink in the afternoon light. Castell Coch snuggles among beeches half way up to the right.

Standing here on a September day, I looked down on the rufous back of a hunting kestrel and the flashy white rumps of a pair of chasing jays. The throaty cronk of a raven drew my gaze to the black hunter, sailing out from the cliff and the plaintive wailing cries of birds closeby must have been those of young raptors.

A footpath leads east and north around the quarry edge behind the Ty Nant Inn, leap-frogging over close set hillocks and tip slides and through relict woodland of quite gnarled and ancient beeches. This follows above the riverside road, past a motley of ivy-grown ruins of brick and stone, to emerge onto the road just beyond the row of lime kilns. This exit was obscured in summer, like the kilns, by the sagging boughs of elm, guelder rose and dogwood drooped across the stand of Himalayan balsam, until the trees were felled early in 1999,and the exit blocked with fencing!

Sorties can be made through thickets of saplings and creepers and over old spoil heaps to level stretches of the old quarry floor. This marginal woodland is spread with a white sheet of ramsons or wild garlic flowers in April and May and has served as a reservoir of wild flowers which are spreading across the abandoned acres. The garlic understorey follows close behind the taller shade-givers, the size of the plants dwindling on the advancing front as seedlings germinate to form tiny new bulbs.

Viewed in sunshine, the jumble of big mossy boulders humping out of a counterpane of garlic and dogs mercury, seems to have been magicked from the industrial leftovers by a weaver of old time fairy tales. There are white bluebells as well as blue, abundant wild arum, occasional broad-leaved helleborine orchids, primroses and violets. A mesh of brier and bramble arches tentatively across moist patches carpeted with balsam seedlings.

Shrubby aliens jostling with the pioneering Buddlejas and birches are two going by the name of Japanese honeysuckle - *Lonicera nitida*, actually from China, and *Leycesteria formosa* from the Himalayas. Both tempt birds with edible berries and there is no shortage of takers to oblige by spreading the seeds around.

Tremiscus helvelloides Fungus

The central amphitheatre must have been a hard standing, as few herbs have managed to get a roothold in the carpet of moss and field daisies. This thin film is often waterlogged, suggesting solid rock below. Little mounds of tarmac and slabs of concrete surface among the remains of camp fires and cricket wickets. Lime loving flowers increase peripherally, pink centaury and knotted figwort merging into a fringe of perforated St. Johns wort, ploughmans spikenard and wild golden rod.

When the May sun shines these are alive with brimstone, peacock and small tortoiseshell butterflies, the second generations of these dancing creatures thriving on the purple tassels of Buddleja in late summer, when they are joined by a humming chorus of hover flies and bees.

A buzzard is likely to come mewing out of the quarry woodland and the inevitable flock of jackdaws can be more than forty strong. Chiff chaffs arrive quite early in April, followed by willow warblers and common garden birds find refuge in this seldom disturbed haven, which is so much more three dimensional than most. The towering cliff fends off the westerly gales and a degree of shelter from the easterlies is afforded by the formidable cliff just across the gorge.

Even by midsummer the sapling tree growth was insufficient to exclude all the dappled sunlight by the early 1990s, but the wetness still favoured the moss growth more characteristic of deep shade. Pencil thin ash saplings as much as 2 m high wore socks of moss creeping 20-30 cm up from the ground - like pin men in gum boots. So crowded were they where the winged seeds had spun to earth and germinated, that they remained as

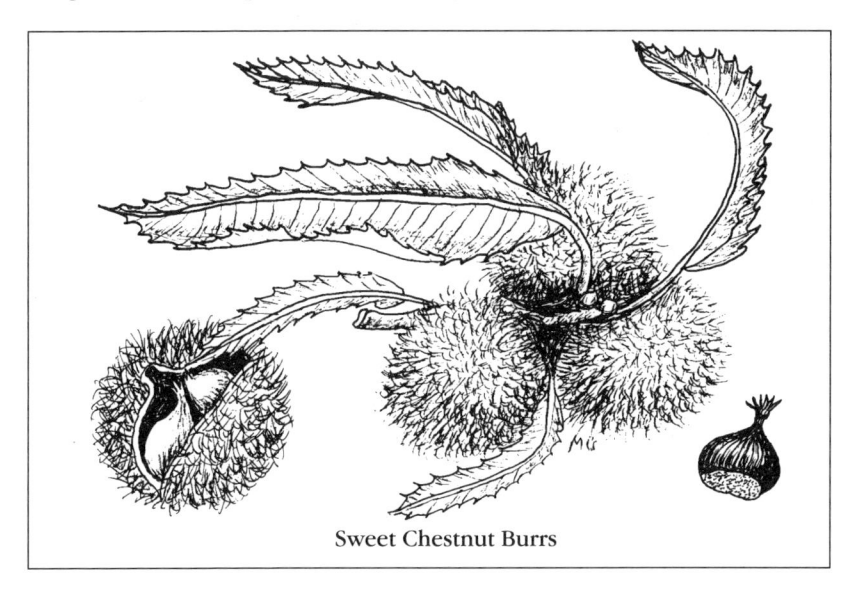

Sweet Chestnut Burrs

slender whips to 4 m and more, simulating a bamboo thicket. Wood sorrel is the usual coloniser of mossy tree bases, but here it was violets.

Thick moss carpets on tumbled boulders and sodden logs held sufficient moisture to encourage lichens of damp grassland. Slabs of dogs tooth lichen, *Peltigera praetexta* mingled with one of the cup lichens, *Cladophora chlorophaea*, which bears secondary brown-tipped branchlets around the rims of the hoary grey-green cups.

Fungi benefitted from the sogginess and an especially exciting find in August 1994 was the orange-red jelly fungus, *Tremiscus helvelloides*, the lobes folded one against the other and much fleshier than the common orange peel elf cup. This newcomer to Wales, first found in 1973, was always associated with industrial sites, mines, quarries and railway sleepers, until it spread into Llanwonno Forest along man-made tracks in the late 1980s. Usually on old or burned timbers, many of them imported from the Baltic, one of its strongholds, it was not infrequently turning up along the line of limestone quarries in the southern Brecon Beacons, but this was my first record in the south - again on the Carboniferous limestone.

More everyday fungi included creamy yellow *Panellus nidulans*, a rather sticky little 'oyster of the woods', emerging from a fallen beech, and brackets of *Stereum gausapatum* and thin, concentrically zoned *Polystictes versicolor*.

Some fungi were nibbled by mice or slugs, but the most evident food remains were those of grey squirrels. These favoured raised feeding sites, flat-topped boulders spread with a mossy tablecloth instead of the usual tree stumps. Remnants of the feasts in August consisted mainly of neatly split hazel nuts opened prematurely and with scraps of unripe flesh adhering to the still green shells. As I examined them more pieces of shell pattered down on me from a disturbed diner, chattering his annoyance from the tree above. He finally moved off to strip bark from green spindle twigs

My attention was diverted to a lone rabbit gnawing at the wood sedge growing among the small burrows of bank voles. A long drawn out battle was being waged between a wall brown butterfly and a wasp, the two floundering among the nutshells, taking turns on top. The butterfly finally flew up and away, apparently unhurt, to my surprise.

The main crop of nuts was left to ripen and overwinter, to feed a variety of creatures up to March the next year. Shells whose contents had been extracted through neatly nibbled holes had been tucked at the foot of boulders by bank voles or wood mice. Shattered shells beside guano splashes showed where birds had been taking their share.

The long displaced boulders used by the squirrels had weathered to a deep reddish purple. Smaller stones, recently split by heat around the camp fire embers, showed sparkles of orange haematite and yellower limonite.

Syrphid hover flies fed on the wing at most flowers but invariably settled on the teasel heads. Here were so many close-packed florets that it would have been a waste of energy to hover while sampling them all. Bumble bees favoured the flowers of self heal and wood sage. Insect life dwindled in the deeper shade, where ivy was taking over from the moss as principal ground cover, but a garlic glass snail (Oxychilus alliaris) among some harts tongue fern spread the garlic smell beyond the edges of the garlic patches.

In April incoming migrant birds mingle their songs with robin, blackbird and song thrush. Three churring mistle thrushes took avoiding action as the peregrine sped past but none took much notice of the more familiar outlines of buzzard and raven over the cliff. Corvids of one sort or another, probably magpies or jackdaws, had been scuffing up the moss in search of food items. Fruit eaters had paid in kind and a plethora of currant seedlings was springing up - the fruit probably filched from gardens.

Derelict sites such as the Ty Nant Quarry are ideal wildlife habitats, seldom visited by man, usually ungrazed and not bothered by modern farming practices. The scenario after the new ingress-exit road is made in the early 2000s is best left to the imagination. A larger repeat of the Ty Nant sequence in the Walnut Tree Quarry would not be for many years and is unlikely anyway unless the local authorities have evolved alternatives to landfill sites for domestic rubbish by then. People with waste to dispose of seem unable to resist holes in the ground. I was told when I visited Redlands Quarry in 1997 that the quarry company could get more income leasing the site for landfill, as it stood, than by quarrying it!

"Particularly if we accepted builders' rubble and put it through our crushers to sell back to them!"

I can never understand why garbage, if it has to be dumped, cannot be put on level land which, when covered over and planted, is little changed. In my book, scenery consists of ups and downs, leafy dells and bosky hollows. Fill in all the landscape features and the landscape becomes featureless - an East Anglian style prairie, devoid of character and prettiness. The 1990s natural rock garden of the Ty Nant Quarry speaks eloquently to this theme.

4. Plants of the Little Garth Beechwood

The dip slope on the north side of the Little Garth is almost as steep as the southern scarp face, because of wearing away of the soft Millstone Grit in the Coed-y-Bedw Valley alongside. The eastern face, cut through initially by the Taff, is steeper than either, but gradients level out in the west as the hill merges with the general east to west ridge flanking the Coalfield.

The fine beech hangers of the steeper slopes and the summit form the SSSI, so designated when this was found to be the most westerly native beechwood in the U K. Recently Professor Smith of the University of Wales Botany Department in Cardiff has been finding beech pollen in prehistoric peat deposits further west, indicating a withdrawal eastwards.

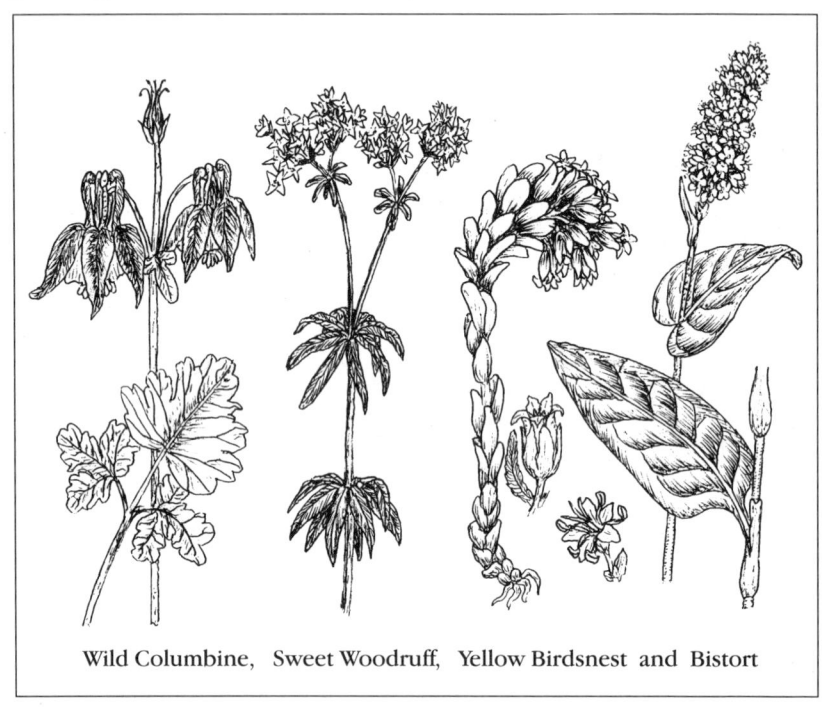

Wild Columbine, Sweet Woodruff, Yellow Birdsnest and Bistort

Although essentially a south-eastern species, like hornbeam and lime, beech grows quite well almost throughout Britain when planted, but the discovery of beech charcoal in an ancient hearth established it as a genuine native on the Little Garth. In view of the intensity of industrial activity here, both past and present, it is remarkable that any has survived. Ironically the largest trees and the densest stands are those currently under greatest threat, adjacent to the quarry.

Livestock are seldom present, but in any case, beech is more resistant to grazing than many. It is a little known fact that the famous Epping Forest beechwood was a limewood until commoners were allowed to graze their animals there, preventing regeneration of the lime. Nearer, in the other special South Wales beechwood at Clydach Gorge - currently threatened by projected widening of the Heads of the Valleys Road - lime trees survived the early coppicing regime but succumbed to later grazing.

The limestone substrate which favours beech becomes progressively covered with Boulder Clay towards Pentyrch in the west. Here tree species are more varied, including birch and sallow, which are precursors of beech, and weed trees like sycamore. By 1993 the first two had already reached 8-9 m high where the old Barry Railway line abuts onto the demolished Taff Viaduct.

Little Garth beeches show considerable genetic variation, making them too diverse for all to be good timber trees and marking them out as a self sown native stand. Trees planted for timber are selected for various growth characteristics and are often from German stock. A character of many here, and one not found in Chiltern beechwoods, is a buttressing of branch bases, many having a bulging protuberance on the underside at the point of emergence from the trunk. In addition to beech there are some fine straight-stemmed field maples, limes, wych elms, pedunculate oaks and sweet chestnuts, all self regenerating.

Following former marginal encroachment of agriculture, natural regeneration, augmented by planting in the South, has been remarkable. The western summit remains open, the fields unmown and ungrazed for long periods during the late 1990s, so that meadow grasses and herbs have been able to flower and set seed.

Formerly there were more. Entering the woodland from this side, one soon comes across overgrown, stone-faced banks topped by lines of trees, these the old field boundaries which kept marauding livestock from the coppiced wood. The leading edge of the advance illustrates the way in which woody plants appear on new ground. Beeches lag behind birch, ash and sallow, with their wind-distributed seeds, as do oaks - beechmast and acorns needing help from animals if they are to get far from the parent trees. Fortunately their saplings are able to grow in the shade of the others but the first comers, unless they have got away to a good start, cannot tolerate the deeper shade cast by the late comers.

Bracken grows ahead of the tree pioneers on open land opposite the farm buildings in a bend of the quarry road. Ash, its acutely angled branches spearing directly upwards, pushes easily through the ceiling of bracken fronds, but the spreading branches of beech saplings are likely to get trapped below during the growing season when the fern cover is reinforced by massed Himalayan balsam.

Relic earth and stone walls also bound the ancient 'main road' through the wood, now a hollow, stone-floored track, its surface as much as 2 m below the adjacent ground in places. The old hedge shrubs died out as the tree canopy closed overhead, pleached hedge trees pushing up to join the encroaching trees or becoming spindly, with no seedlings able to replace them. Subsequent erosion has exposed old beech roots which clasp the soil or neighbouring ash boles as flat, smooth-barked grey slabs, like those of tropical strangling figs.

Another legacy from the past is a pair of old charcoal burning platforms. These are discernible because of artificial levelling, as accumulating leaf mould usually masks all trace on the flat. Having identified the site, it is possible to find flakes of charcoal below the litter layer. Some charcoal burners carried their own soil from woodland to woodland, this sealing the smouldering heaps better than what they might be able to scratch up on site. Their residue, and the ash, gave a better soil texture, more conducive to plant growth and also to excavation by badgers and foxes. (When coal replaced wood as the industrial fuel this was converted to coke by burning in a restricted air supply on a similar principle to the burning of wood for charcoal.)

Cord wood to be ignited was likely to consist of branches 3-5 cm across, cut from coppiced stools on a rotational basis of 14 - 15 years - the wood divided into 14 - 15 plots to ensure continuity. Any species could be used but smaller wood, often hazel or willow, might be cut more frequently for hurdles, rick pegs or other farm uses. Some of the Little Garth beeches are multi-trunked as a result of coppicing although a single standard was usually left to grow on while the side shoots were lopped. Beeches do not take kindly to this treatment as they age because the bark thickens over the dormant buds which can no longer push through, as they can through thinner, younger bark. Some trees were left as standards or 'maiden trunks'. This type of woodland management died out with the appearance of fencing wire, polythene rick sheets and other modern artefacts.

Coppicing kept the above ground parts of trees eternally young, the basal stool too restricted and too actively alive to suffer much fungal damage. Often fungi pose more problem to the forester than to the forest, usually attacking only the dead heartwood while leaving the peripheral sapwood to grow on. Thus old hollow trees can bear a full complement of leaves with unobstructed upward passage of water and minerals and downward passage of manufactured carbohydrates.

Ganoderma applanatum can cause heart rot in old trees. Its sporing bodies are firm shelves or brackets more than a handspan across, each white top covered covered by a thick dusting of cinnamon coloured spores fallen from the brackets above and redder than the quarry dust.

This was one of no less than fifteen different kinds of fungi growing on a single beech discovered when walking directly up from the corner of Heol Beri Green in December 1984. Some, like candle snuff and dead men's fingers, were black, with the texture of charcoal. There were four species of jelly fungi, including witch's butter and little mauve branches of *Coryne sarcoides*, a few pustular ones, like coral spot and orange *Dacromyces deliquescens* and even jew's ear, which seldom grows on trees other than elder. Frilled orange slabs of *Phlebia radiata*, oyster of the woods and a variety of brackets completed a remarkable collection, many of them supplying food for the lesser animal life and a graphic illustration of the ongoing process of the recycling of assets.

These were in a part of the wood where two species of flowering plants join in the recycling process so whole-heartedly that they can skip photosynthesis altogether. These are the pinky-brown stands of bird's-nest orchids *(Neottia nidus-avis)* and the rarer yellow bird's-nest *(Monotropa hypopitys)*. Both are saprophytes, utilising nutrients from dead organic matter in the leaf litter. In place of normal roots they have a bird's nest like tangle of mycorhizal appendages holding the fungi which dissolve goodies from the soil and make them available to their plant partners, although gaining no photosynthesised carbohydrates in return, as do the mycorhizal partners of forest trees. Presumably a place to live is sufficient reward.

Other rather special plants here are broad-leaved helleborine orchids, the tall pink spikes of bistort or snake troot, wild columbine or granny's nightcap, tutsan, wood spurge, sweet woodruff and sweet violets along with the commoner kinds in the primrose season. Among more

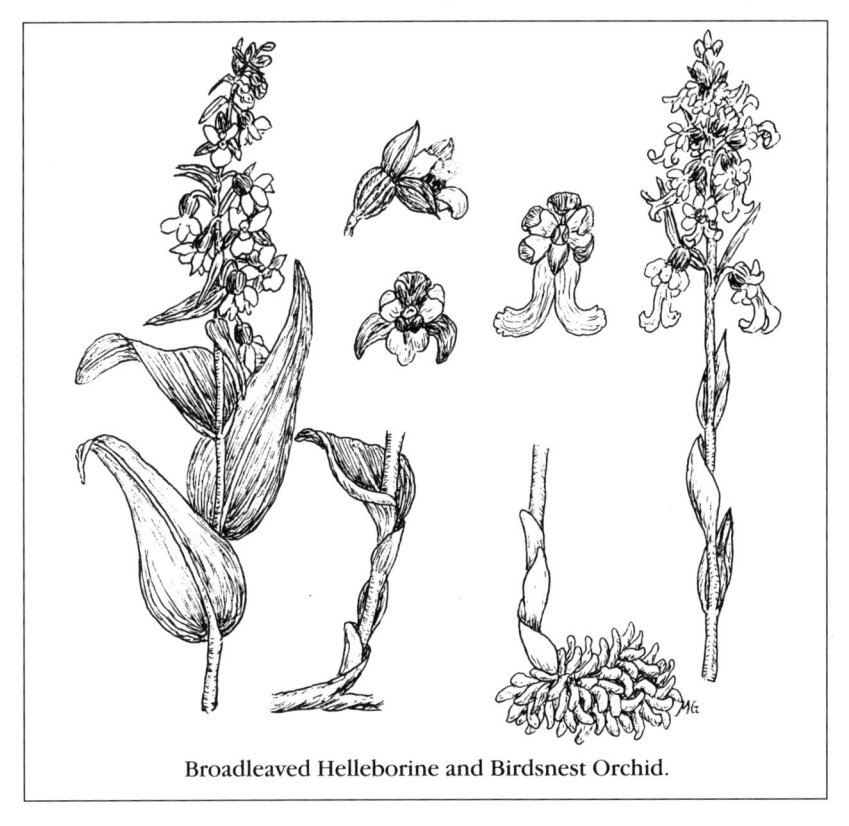

Broadleaved Helleborine and Birdsnest Orchid.

widespread species are bluebells, wood sorrel, red campion, pig nut, yellow archangel, bugle and marginal ploughmen's spikenard, calamint, cowslip, mullein, agrimony and the inevitable black bryony, wild clematis and honeysuckle. Wild solomon's seal is much rarer than on the eastern side of the Taff Gorge and Herb Paris has not been found.

Soil at the top of the slope tends to be dry and crumbly, the lime content flocculating the clay to create a habitat suitable for wood sanicle and wood speedwell. Nutrients and organic matter wash progressively downwards and the deeper soils of lower slopes favour ramsons and hart's tongue ferns, although these two clothe the entire eastern slope above the Ynys roundabout, which is awash with white garlic flowers in May and June.

The limey downwash is halted by the track up to the viaduct end opposite the Gwaelod-y-Garth turning and precipitates out on the vertical bank as rippled slabs of tufa decorated with mini stalactites. This coats unstable wet soil, so the whole lot sloughs away at intervals.

Fallen beech leaves are slow to decay and form an acid leaf litter when they do. Wood anemones are scattered throughout, on deep soil and shallow. Windflowers some call them, their scientific name from the same root as the anemometers with which we measure wind strength. Although characteristic of ancient woodland, anemones can be shaded out by dense growths, as of holly or yew. Seeds are sparsely produced and are said to remain viable for only ten years, so a programme of coppicing every decade gives them a boost, along with other woodland understorey flowers.

Most beat the shading factor by making the bulk of their growth in spring before the upper leaf canopy expands and when the soil under trees can be several degrees warmer than that in the open. The beechwood floor can seem very bare in summer when the leaves of lesser celandines, anemones, bluebells and ramsons have withered, leaving only a sprinkling of less showy flowers like enchanter's nightshade and wood avens.

5. Fauna of the Little Garth Beechwood

Walkers are fewer on the Little Garth than the Great, so wildlife suffers less disturbance. Badgers are present, sometimes crossing Heol Goch into the Coed-y-Bedw Reserve. This is not a busy road at night but there are still traffic casualties, as in May 1998.

Local foxes are regularly sought by the Garth Hunt, but the complex of mined and tunnelled hillsides which this ranges over are so full of hideouts that few are caught. The wily residents are more conversant with the wealth of bolt holes than is the baying pack, members of which can be encountered trotting disconsolately across Heol Beri Green when their fellows and the pink-coated huntsmen are making a decorative frieze on the summit of the Garth Mountain.

There are hunt days when no foxes are sighted - except by those not involved in the chase. Horses and riders enjoy their gallop, the hounds are exercised and the fox gains experience in giving them the slip, with everybody happy and no harm done.

Walking the woods in May 1990 I met up with a fox whose sheer bravado marked him out as a character. Broad browed and bushy tailed, he was melanistic, with much black on the shoulders, flanks and tail and no white tip to the brush. When I passed among the trees he lay low: when I emerged onto the quarry road, where humans belong, he trotted jauntily out behind me, crossed and followed just within the wood, with a great rustling of dry leaves under padded paws.

He made a brief investigation round the base of an old beech where I had photographed fungi and sniffed along the path I had walked three hours earlier. As aware of my past movements as of my very obvious present ones, he seemed quite unworried. I began to wonder if he shared a quarryman's ham sandwiches at lunchtime.

He gave the impression of being well able to elude the pack of motley rough coated hounds that surges along my lane on winter saturdays, but, sadly, he was no match for modern machines. Travelling the M4 a week later I saw the remains of a large melanistic fox on the hard shoulder just south of the wood. There was no mistaking the black hairs among the tawny red.

Dr. Holly of Merthyr Tydfil, who is conversant with the history of hunting, writes of melanistic foxes being introduced into Glamorgan from the continent around the 1920s by the Llewellyn Brothers, one of whom was associated with the Cwm Dare Hunt and the other with St. Fagans'. These were virile animals, expected to give the hunts a better run for their money than the indigenous ones. The fine physique and sharp wits of the individual who shadowed me had not saved him from the destructive march of civilisation.

1971 saw rabbit numbers beginning to recover after the Myxomatosis check, but there were noticeably more 'bush rabbits' then, sheltering above ground - the type that survived the contagious plague better than the more crowded burrow dwellers.

They tend to be 'woodland edge' species here and there is a big population some years in the partially cleared ground around the quarry brink. These animals are small and dusty, scooting across the barrens between sleeping quarters in hazel scrub and dining quarters on abandoned wasteland. Watching them, I have wondered how their incisors stand up to the red grit which coats everything edible. Perhaps the dust explains their marked preference for grasses, whose vertical leaves retain less of the fallout. Broad-leaved plants most likely to tempt them are birch seedlings.

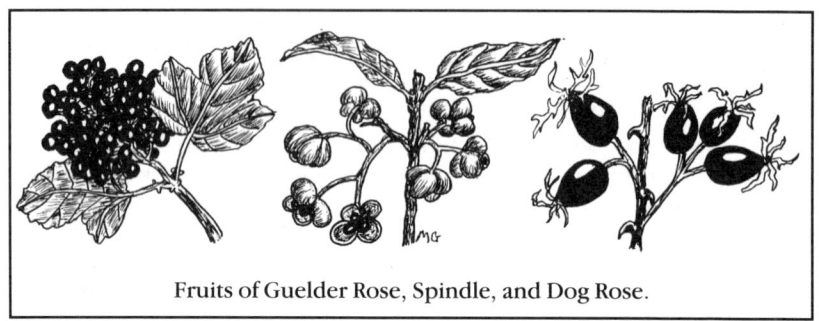

Fruits of Guelder Rose, Spindle, and Dog Rose.

Molehills are red and almost stoneless on the shallow soils, black where displaced leaf mould accumulates. Proceeding quietly, one occasionally sees a slight heaving and a brief glimpse of a twitching snout. Apical holes show where others have emerged during the hours of darkness, not too wisely if the nightly hooting of tawny owls means anything.

Mossy banks have a good peppering of small rodent burrows, with plenty of holed beech and hazel nuts and cherry stones among the leftovers of birds and squirrels.

Grey squirrels are never far to seek. 1984 was a mast year for oaks, with a glut of unusually large fruits. By 7th December fallen ones had started to germinate, their fleshy roots red or white, depending on light intensity, and reaching 5 cm or more although few had turned to penetrate the soil. Many were half eaten.

The banquet seemed too generous for squirrels, mice and jays alone and had attracted a big flock of wood pigeons. The platform nests which these build among the twigs are sometimes too flimsy to hold all the blatantly white eggs, whose shells may be found below.

Most common woodland birds are present as well as the less common wood warbler, redstart and pied flycatcher. Nuthatch, tree creeper, bullfinch and wren are commonplace. All six tit species are present, although marsh tits tend to outnumber willow tits, which turn up more frequently on the other side of the river according to local bird ringers, George Wood and Alex Coxhead.

Although feeding on the grassland outside, green woodpeckers nest in the ancient trees, some of which are fantastically contorted. Great spotted woodpeckers often use smaller timber. I have come across a five inch diameter birch trunk with so many nest holes excavated in it that it had broken through in two places - the top severed first.

Most characteristic butterflies are the shade-loving speckled woods, the spring broods marked with buttercup yellow, those emerging in high summer with primrose yellow. Clouded magpie moths commonly fly by day.

A walk in May, when the floral display is at its best, may reveal vestal cuckoo bees *(Psithyrus vestalis)*, dressed to resemble the buff-tailed bumble bees *(Bombus terrestris)* which they parasitise. The rightful bumble bee queen chosen to host the young generation is callously killed when she has produced enough workers to bring up the 'cuckoo's offspring in the luxury to which they are accustomed.

The more lively, clear-winged Bombus queens emerge from hibernation in March, when temperatures are still too low for most invertebrates. They zoom from flower to flower collecting pollen and nectar to fashion the 'marzipan balls' of bee bread with which they furnish their nests in mossy banks.

More sluggish, the darker winged cuckoo bees emerge at a more leisurely pace in May. Their flight is erratic as they seek among the sprouting vegetation for a bumble bee's nest in which to lay their eggs. The urgency of the fast flowing notes of the well known *"Flight of the Bumble Bee"* would be inappropriate if dedicated to the cuckoo bees.

At woodland edge and quarry brink in April and May the bee parasite is the greater bee fly *(Bombylus major)*, hovering motionless over the preferred blue flowers, mostly of ground ivy or forget-me-not, as it probes with the non-retractable proboscis for nectar. The plumply hairy black and yellow striped body looks more like that of the bees which nurtured it as a youngster than its relatives, the true two-winged flies - represented here most noticeably by gangling craneflies and biting clegs.

Easily recognised as they scuttle along the path ahead of the walker and take short, erratic flights, are the bright green, yellow speckled tiger beetles *(Cicindela campestris)*. The fast moving adults have only a few short weeks above ground after two boring years as a larva clamped to the wall of a vertical burrow waiting to grab a prey animal unlucky enough to walk across its entrance.

Outside the wood the sunshine which highlights the yellow of early colstfoot and broom and the later perforated St. Johns wort and ragwort, favours a variety of invertebrate life. Money spiders spin webs under earth banks, their resilient silken threads criss crossing in seeming disarray with no radial symmetry. These become covered with fine red dust from quarry blasting and soil collapse, but remain effective in trapping ants falling foul of the trip wires above. When prey arrives the spider comes racing out along the underside of the web, tummy up, to grab it.

Woodland rides are of apricot red rendzina soil littered with apricot red stones and apricot red fragments of snail shells, all apparently painted with the same ferruginous pigments. The shells are most apparent where the sun filters through the leaf canopy, to be reflected back from the shiny interiors. They occur in profusion along selected lengths of track falling within a song thrush's territory. Any rock fragment might serve as an anvil for a thrush to break open its snails, but these are commoner on the tracks, particularly the sloping ones which are washed free of soil and debris by becoming water courses in wet weather.

Shells are mostly of brown-lipped hedge snails *(Cepaea nemoralis)*. Developed to match their environment in an evolutionary bid to escape bird predation, they resemble few others in the county. Yellow and brown stripes are the commonest pattern elsewhere, yellow on sand dunes and pale pink among blue-grey lichens. These richly hued ones are quite special. I saw no plain yellow ones in the gloom of the beechwood and the few brown and yellow striped ones stood out like sore thumbs on the ruddy background.

Included in the remains were a few light brown, dimly striped shells of copse snails *(Arianta arbustorum)*, blending well where shaded by ivy and sanicle leaves, but not as totally invisible as the others, be these penny plain or humbug striped. I made an unscientific assessment of the leftovers at one anvil.

Copse snails comprised 8% of the sample. Of the hedge snails 48% were a light translucent red striped with brown, 43% were plain red and 9% were yellow with broad brown stripes. Of the half that were stripy red 75% bore narrow pale stripes and the others fewer darker stripes.

What had I shown? That the bulk of the snail population wore the most cryptic colours so that they would not be seen, or that the bulk of the snails actually taken wore the most cryptic colours which had failed to save them? Or that there were simply more reddish snails in the population as these had a higher chance of survival, and so were more freely available to become casualties? I should, of course, have gone again at dawn or dusk or in the rain and counted the number of snails on the hoof (or stomach) to compare the quick and the dead, but I haven't got around to it yet.

Half a dozen or so ungrazed meadows take over from the woodland where it merges into the ridge on the outskirts of Pentyrch, some of them abutting onto a row of sweet chestnut trees bordering the wood. They are well furnished with footpaths and stiles and crossed by an ancient tree-bordered track.

Of long standing, they are typified by yellow rattle, burnet saxifrage and spotted orchids. Legumes sustaining the common blue and small heath butterflies include birds-foot trefoil, yellow pea, tufted vetch and a variety of clovers. Composites favoured by the August hosts of meadow browns are knapweed, yarrow, cats ear and hawksbeard . Small coppers and whites divide their attention between cinquefoil, silverweed, buttercup and centaury. Other flowers are eyebright, self heal and various umbellifers.

The most interesting plant encountered here - in August 1997 - is a rare St. Johns wort, *Hypericum X desetangsii*, of which there are only scattered records through England, Wales and Southern Scotland. It is a hybrid between the common perforated St. Johns wort and the spotted *Hypericum maculatum*.

Hedgerow Honeysuckle

Chapter 6

CREIGIAU. DISUSED MINES AND RAILWAYS IN THE WEST

Introductory

Having looked at the core of our region in the Great and Little Garths, our survey now moves anti-clockwise round the west, south and east from the left-hand top corner of the map. The north-western boundary of the Caerphilly Mountain Project Area follows approximately along the 300 foot contour beyond the divided upland block. In the north-west it embraces the Tyn-y-Coed Woods, situated on Middle and Lower Coal Measures, and contiguous with the woodlands of Craig Gwilym to the north and Coed-y-Creigiau to the south.

These more northerly woods are traversed by part of the 21 mile long west to east 'Ridgeway Walk' from Coychurch Higher to Caerphilly Mountain, as this curves north between Rhiwsaison and the Garth Mountain. The scenic long-distance path was established by the Taff-Ely District Council in 1979 and follows the ranges bounding the south of the Coalfield, encompassing some fine views as it goes.

It passes east from open moorland on Mynydd-y-Gaer in the neighbouring district of Ogwr, to similar open moorland on Caerphilly Common in the Rhymney Valley District (Grid references SS 969 860 to ST 157 857). Where possible, it utilises upland parish tracks of great antiquity, old tramroads of the industrial era, narrow woodland trails and broader Forestry Commission rides over the hills, but it has to drop into a more urban environment to cross the Taff Valley.

Today all is pleasantly green and rural, following the grimy industrial past of these north-western woods, but the threat of change is not entirely lifted. While there is usable coal in the underlying rocks, there is always the chance that someone will want to dig it out. In the 1970s and 80s it was rumoured that Craig Gwilym was scheduled for opencast mining by the National Coal Board. There was great public concern, with the three councils, county, district and community, ranged shoulder to shoulder against the proposals, which proved in the event to be a false alarm. The N.C.B.'s consultation maps classed Craig Gwilym as "An area undergoing investigation: an established prospecting site not intended for working at the present."

Subsequent discussions in January 1983 confirmed that there were no current plans for any new working sites in Mid Glamorgan - which is scarcely surprising in view of the subsequent closure of all the deep mines because of loss of markets. The joint councils, nevertheless, made it clear that any subsequent proposals for open-casting at Craig Gwilym would be fought at every stage.

Thus have our aspirations changed from the less affluent days, when there were more green places not submerged under bricks and mortar and populations would happily sacrifice some of them to bring work and prosperity to their area. Perhaps it is not the aspirations which have changed but the people. Vast new housing estates at both Creigiau and Pentyrch have transformed these once isolated villages into dormitory suburbs for commuters to Cardiff and beyond. Commuting early in the 20th century was mainly by miners boarding the early train for the mines at Pontypridd when those on the Garth closed.

During the industrial era this western part of our region was well endowed with railways, all of which have exchanged their rolling stock for walkers and horse-riders, although a few stretches have become flooded, overgrown and impassable. The main passenger line and a busy mineral line ran parallel through or past Creigiau Station, diverging to north and south to connect with the network of railways serving this southern part of the Coalfield

The old station lies between the Creigiau Inn and the entrance to quarry and playing fields, the road to Pentyrch humping up over the two railway lines in quick succession. Our railway walks start here, from a village amenity area used for such social functions as the community firework display on Guy Fawkes night, when public-spirited villagers pay in advance for the merrymaking, trusting that the coins dropped into the collecting buckets will reimburse them.

1. From Mines to Mammals in the Tyn-y-Coed Woods

Tyn-y-Coed has emerged from its clanking industrial past to become a pleasant amenity area, furnished with carparks and picnic sites, wayfarer paths and nature trails. It is managed by the Forestry Commission, but is essentially of broad-leaved trees, oak, beech and sycamore, with only scattered plots of conifers, mostly western hemlocks, but including some cypresses and giant firs *(Abies grandis)*.

Today's verdure masks what was once a hive of industry between the crop workings of the Two-foot-nine coal seam and the Five-foot and Gelli-Deg (hard) seam with the Amman marine band running parallel from west to east. The geological survey map marks many disused bell pits, old coal levels and air shafts, and some of today's paths originated as mule tracks or tram roads. Yesterday's miners have been replaced by both wild and domesticated mammals.

The local badgers, which moved in when things quietened down, found easy digging in the piles of friable fly ash from the power stations, the contours of the heaps offering convenient slopes for burrowing into horizontally. By the 1980s the sett covered almost a quarter of an

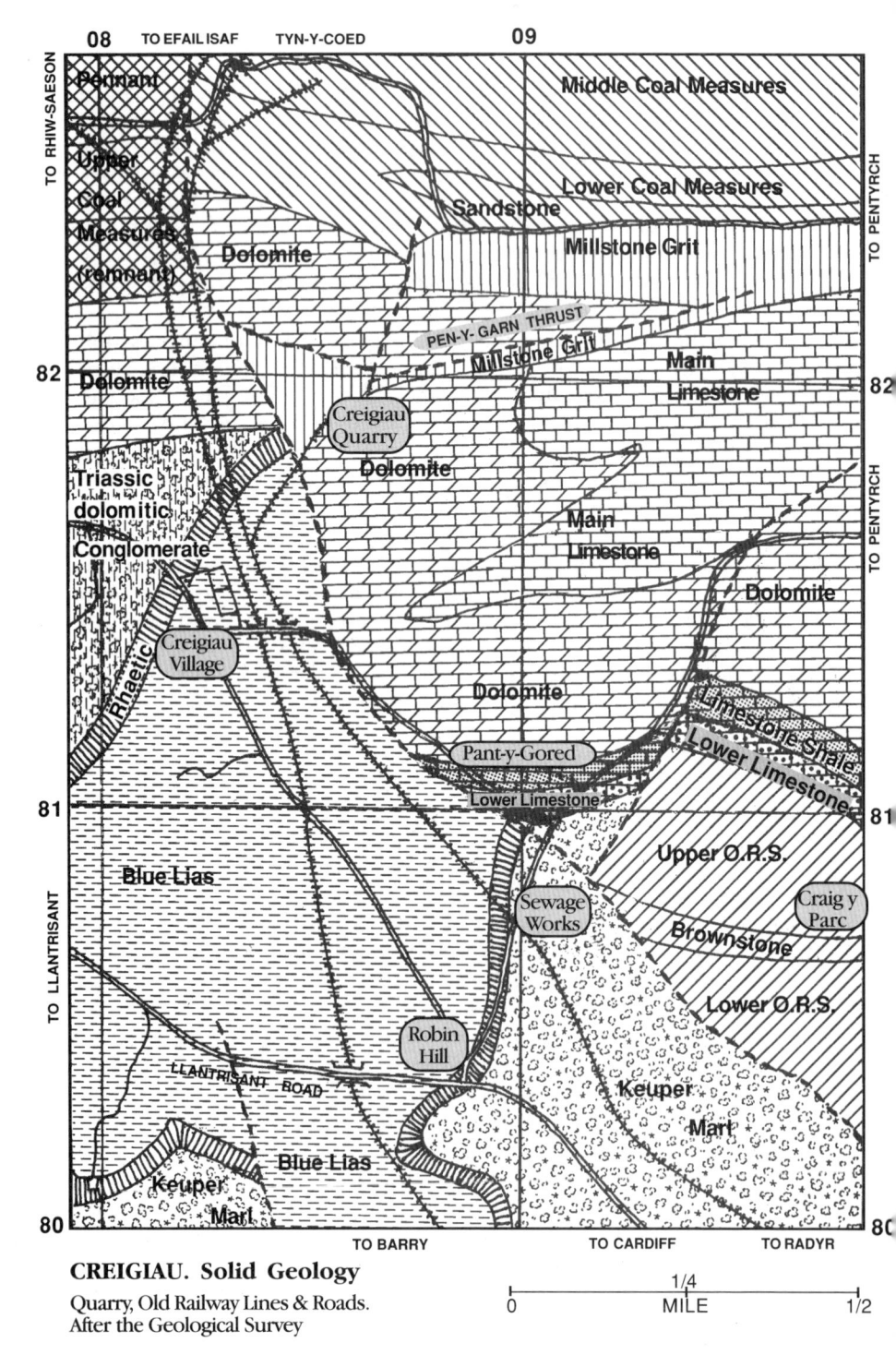

CREIGIAU. Solid Geology
Quarry, Old Railway Lines & Roads.
After the Geological Survey

KEY TO MAP

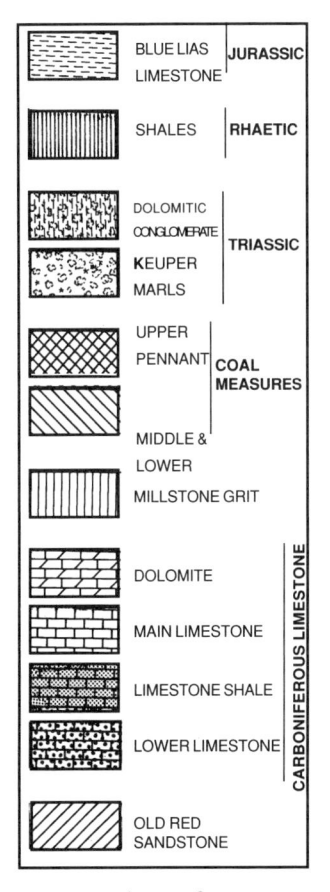

▭	BLUE LIAS LIMESTONE	JURASSIC
▨	SHALES	RHAETIC
▩	DOLOMITIC CONGLOMERATE	TRIASSIC
▨	KEUPER MARLS	
▩	UPPER PENNANT	COAL MEASURES
▨	MIDDLE & LOWER MILLSTONE GRIT	
▨	DOLOMITE	CARBONIFEROUS LIMESTONE
▨	MAIN LIMESTONE	
▨	LIMESTONE SHALE	
▨	LOWER LIMESTONE	
▨	OLD RED SANDSTONE	

acre and had not escaped the attentions of badger-digging vandals, who dug pits over a metre deep to capture the inmates for foul purposes of their own. Fortunately the wide ramification of tunnels offered sanctuary to most, and cubs were being produced through the nineties.

The population has been in residence for long enough to inaugurate the characteristic growth of elder bushes around the sett, these liberally ornamented with fleshy flanges of Jew's ear fungus. The woodland floor round about is pocked with latrine pits, where different badger food remains can be distinguished in the hygienically segregated droppings.

Soon after the making of the picnic sites, the canny mountain sheep started soliciting titbits from visitors, each generation of ewes passing the know-how on to their lambs. A less usual feature of autumn and winter in good mast years was the pasturage of free-range pigs in the woods, to hoover up the harvest of acorns and beech nuts.

This is a twentieth century re-enaction of the medieval practice of pannage. Having had some experience of piggy psychology during my farming years in the 1940s, I wondered what problems their rounding up might present when I first encountered them on 14th December 1984. None, it seemed. The herd leaders trotted up as soon as they spied my lone figure emerging from the undergrowth and wiped muddy (ringed) snouts companionably on my slacks. Evidently humans were an accepted part of their world, even while they enjoyed the privileges of medieval wild boars, and they would be happy to oblige when required.

William Linnard in "Welsh Woods and Forests", published by the National Museum of Wales in 1982, stresses the importance of pannage in the century from 1256 to 1356, when the fattening of swine on acorns, hazel nuts and beech mast was one of the most widespread sources of income from the forest. It was, however, an irregular one, entirely dependent on the occurrence of mast years. 1984 would yield high bounty, but in 1983 the cupboard had been bare.

In the more anglicised manors of South and East Wales, freemen would pay a fixed sum, say a penny per pig, and bondmen would be

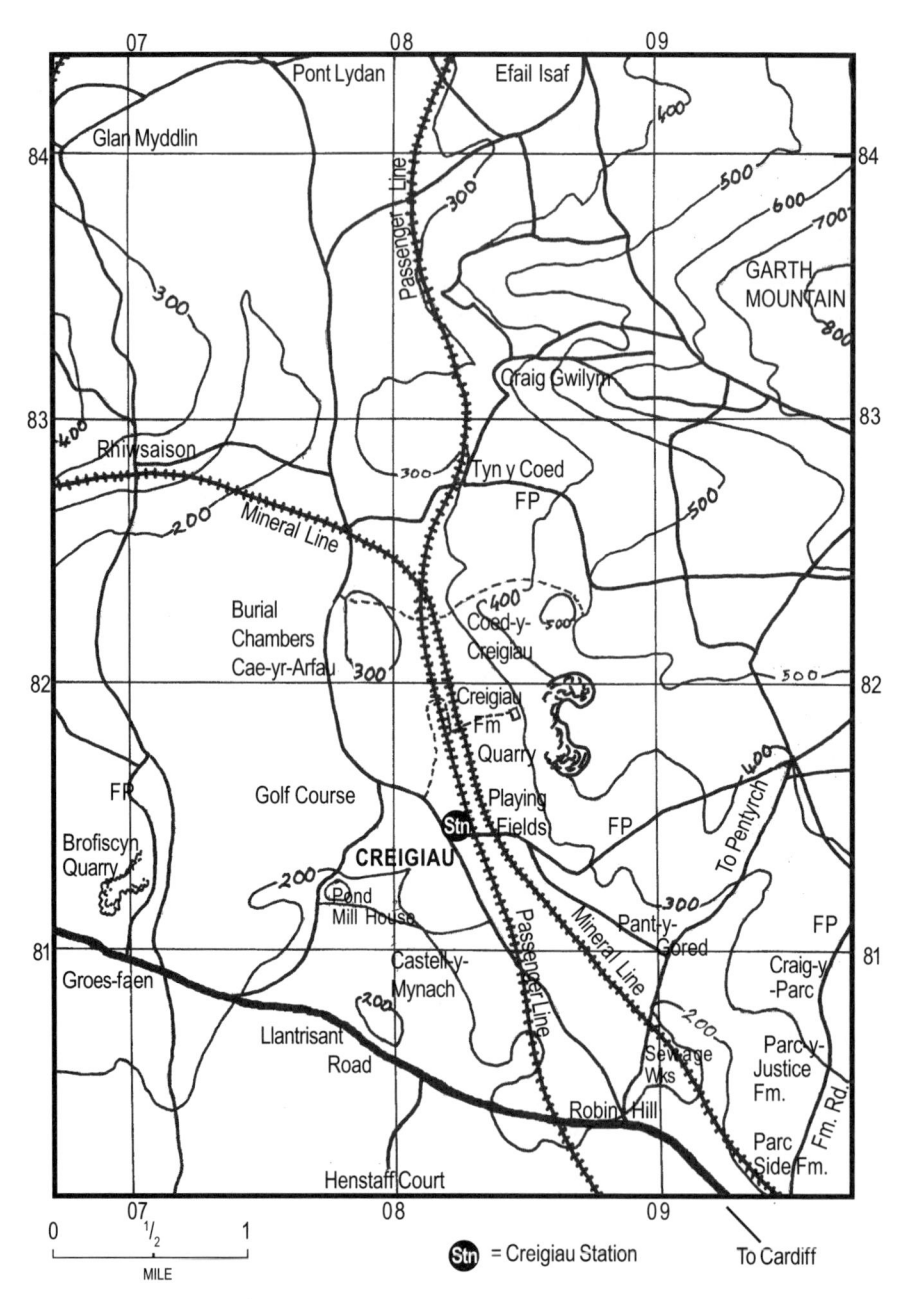

Creigiau Railway Lines, principal routes, and contour lines in feet.
The Western boundary of the Caerphilly Mountain Project Area follows the passenger railway line from the north to Creigiau Station and then the mineral railway line.

levied according to their head of stock. Pannage persisted in places until the present century, as at Allt-yr-Rhiw in the Ogwr Valley near Blackmill -one of the few woods still to have commoners' rights at the present time. The sharp hooves of the swine pressed many seeds into the soft soil out of harm's way, so that forest regeneration was helped rather than hindered. In 1997 free range pigs were quartering the hillsides and picnic site at Gethin Woods near Merthyr, but this was in June for the lush grazing, before the fall of tree mast.

Many may remember going out as children in World War II to gather acorns to supplement the rationed barley meal fed to pigs. Some, too, may remember the pigs gorging themselves on these unexpected and indigestible fruits of our national tree, and dying of colic. My veterinary friends tell me that this seldom happens when the animals are allowed to forage for themselves and take time about it, like the wild boars that grew up in the forest. A parallel may be drawn with the times when we make pigs of ourselves, stuffing down three times as much as we need, simply because it is put before us in a restaurant.

There is a full complement of bird life at Tyn-y-Coed, with a lot of jays helping the Large White pigs to collect up the acorns in mast years. Like squirrels, jays bury what they cannot eat straight away and, like squirrels, they fail to re-excavate all their caches, so they are effective agents in the spread of our native trees, achieving the otherwise puzzling transport of these large disseminules uphill.

Other noisy inhabitants are hammering woodpeckers and clapper-winged wood pigeons, which gather in winter flocks of fifty or so. More secretive ones are the solitary dunnocks and sociable goldcrests slipping unobtrusively through hazels draped with honeysuckle and clematis. Sunny woodland edges supply some good blackberrying in autumn and the spring can be bright with celandines and yellow archangel flowers.

2. Railway Routes and Creigiau Station

Railways were the lifeline of the busy Coalfield communities in the last century, linking them with the coastal lowlands for an input of farm produce and the coastal ports for the export of industrial products. To do this they had to break through the South Crop and the South Border Ridge. No less than five took a route through the Taff Gorge as the Glamorgan Canal had before them.

The uppermost railway on the eastern, Taffs Well, side was the Barry Line which tackled the gorge at a higher level - crossing well above the river on the Walnut Tree Viaduct, emerging from a cutting on the east and plunging into a tunnel on the west. The eastern leg of this route, with its expansive views, has been pressed into service for walkers and cyclists as the Taff Trail and the Three Castles Cycle Route embracing Cardiff Castle, Castell Coch and Caerphilly Castle.

Next down is the broad ballast track of the recently abandoned Rhymney Railway and below this the long-forgotten stretch of the Bute Railway between Nant Garw and Coryton. The still functional Taff Vale Line switches from side to side of the flood plain in keeping a straighter course than the meandering river, which it crosses above and below Gwaelod-y-Garth, a village which had its own mineral railway as well as a feeder canal west of the river.

No more ways through the ridge presented themselves to the railway builders until the land mass drops to around 200 feet in the Creigiau area. Two lines concern us here, the passenger line curving in from the east north of the Great Garth and the mineral line curving away to the east south of the Little Garth. These two stretches of track follow roughly below the 300 foot contour line marking the edge of the upland and were chosen as the western boundary of the Caerphilly Mountain Countryside Project area.

The lines lie just west of the Creigiau geological fault, which strikes across the land from the north to the south-east. This brings the newer Liassic and Triassic rocks of the Vale of Glamorgan north into Creigiau on the west side, resulting in greater geological diversity here than elsewhere in our area.

Creigiau Station lies on the younger Liassic limestone, the railway tracks passing off this to both north and south across a narrow belt of Rhaetic rocks to the red conglomerate or Keuper marl of the New Red Triassic sandstones. Northwards they move rapidly onto the older dolomitic limestone and so to Coalfield rocks, the regenerated vegetation along the way reflecting the increased acidity of the substrate, although modified on the track itself by the limestone ballast. Both lines miss the outcrop of Upper Old Red Sandstone to the south, these ancient Devonian rocks petering out east of the fault, where they form the steeply sloping Craig-y-Parc Woodland.

The passenger line through Creigiau was double-tracked, connecting industrial sites at Treforest in the north through Efail Isaf and continuing south through St. Brides-super-Ely and Drope to Barry. It went into a deep cutting at Tyn-y-Coed, where the 300 foot contour bulges west across its path from the Great Garth, and this cutting is permanently flooded now that it is no longer drained for the rolling stock. A pleasant, primrose-bordered section between Wenvoe and Cadoxton was appropriated in 1982-83 as the main Barry Docks Link Road to the M4 motorway via Culverhouse Cross, bringing yet more heavy freight from the railways to our overworked roads. Volunteers from the Glamorgan

Wildlife Trust rallied round to salvage some of the primroses and transfer them to safer sites.

North of Creigiau the single track mineral line branched west across Llantrisant Common and east to Brynteg and Tynant towards Pontypridd, the stem of the Y curving through Rhiwsaison to Creigiau and on south of Radyr to Fairwater, where it joined the main line west of the Taff to Cardiff.

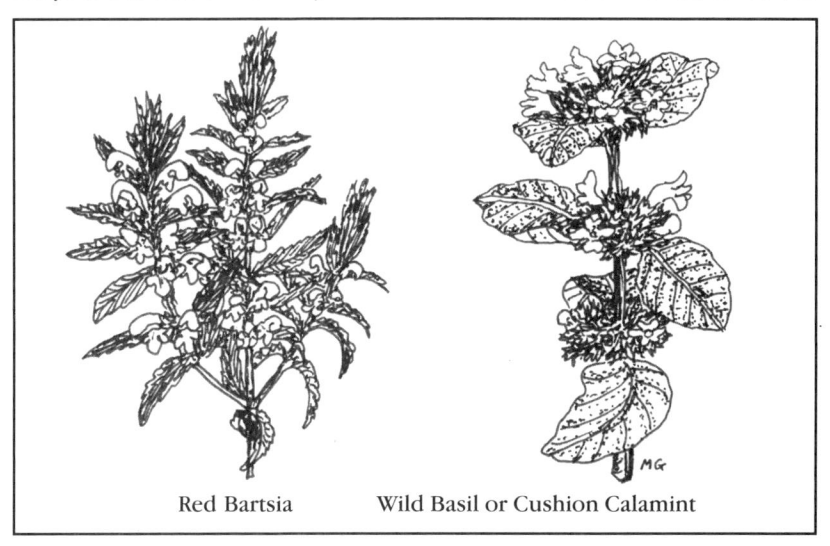

Red Bartsia   Wild Basil or Cushion Calamint

Two branch lines joined it from the east at Tyn-y-Coed, one from the crop workings of the Rhondda No. 2 coal seam and one from the South Cambria Colliery. Another further south connected with the Creigiau Quarry, this carrying one train a day north from the quarry during the first half of the 1970s, south in the morning empty and back north loaded at night. Originally the quarry products went south, avoiding reversal at the acute-angled junction of the lines.

Access to the extraordinarily long station platforms north of the Creigiau to Pentyrch road can be gained on the level at the south-west corner or by entry under the road bridge from the south - this last just passable with a bit of a scramble by 1999. Ornamental shrubs, clinging on in the face of competition from the wild, tell of the former station master's pride in his little kingdom. Laurestine bushes *(Viburnum tinus)* flower through the long winters, with little orange bells appearing on the Berberis in April and May. Rambler roses climb among English and Irish yews, sporting red blooms in June, and little green flowers appear on the Japanese spindles *(Euonymus japonicus)* in warm summers.

Because walkers use platforms rather than track here, native woodland has annexed this section of the track. By the 1980s the old iron way had disappeared under a tracery of silver and downy birches, grey and goat sallows, and the inevitable mauve-tasselled Buddlejas with their attendant bees and butteflies. Ash saplings were pushing through - precursors of the woodland-to-be if they were allowed to remain. Already their bark was nibbled by rabbits below and squirrels above.

A selection of herbs had moved in, the blue field scabious contrasting pleasantly with the yellow of meadow vetchling, wild parsnip and perforated St. John's Wort. An intruder here was the pearly everlasting *Anaphalis margaritacea*, whose woolly white shoots carpet woodlands in its native New England. It is thought to have been introduced into Britain in cemeteries, for the 'everlasting' quality of its papery white daisy flowers, but it has become a characteristic 'railway plant', bordering many lowland lines and some right into the Brecon Beacons.

The more heavily trodden surface of the platforms, an uncompromising plant habitat at best, was infiltrated by smaller creepers during the early decades of neglect. A soft felt of clovers, tares, bird's-foot trefoil, daisies, grass and moss advanced inexorably across the bald masonry, holding moisture, trapping seeds and making the way easier for those that came after. Among the less hardy which benefitted were hemp agrimony and hogweed.

A decade later, in the mid nineties, foot traffic had increased and the platforms were more open, the softer growths trodden out and hardy stonecrop creeping over bare stone faces. In May 1994 dogwood was bursting with flower buds along the platform edge and a path had been opened up through the 6 m high birch:sallow spinney between the platforms, probably by young athletes headed for the playing field beyond. Greater stitchwort, herb Robert and bush vetch bloomed among the Irish yews, while the little ashes of a decade earlier were now sturdy young trees with a crop of baby sycamores jostling for space in between. All the western platform but the marginal coping stones were overgrown with woody species by 1999

Part way along the platforms a track diverges eastwards, taking horse riders and mountain bikes through the belt of woodland to the mineral line as well as sportsmen to the grass pitches and tennis courts. It circumvents a giant black poplar, one of several, with heart-shaped leaves a soft bronze colour in May. A bifurcation about 2 m up gives the rugged, ivy-draped trunk a circumference of at least 8 m.

Beyond was the lime-green exuberance of beech and sycamore, in the resplendant aftermath of their dramatic bud-burst, which is so ecstatic compared with the tardier opening of oak and ash. Here was a relaxed landscape, working out its own destiny, claiming back land lost to the industrialists. It might be wasteland to would-be developers, but it was the elixir of life to the locals exercising themselves and their dogs in the May sunshine.

29. Rosebay Willow Herb and Hemp Agrimony.

PLANTS OF THE BEECHWOOD RIDES. AUGUST 1999

30. Greater Willow Herb or 'Codlins-and-Cream'

31. Creigiau Farm from quarry entrance. View to Caerau Hill, near Llantrisant.

32. Creeping St. John's Wort

33. Bistort

34. Creigiau Tennis Courts and Allotments on the newer, soft Lias Limestone beside Carboniferous limestone quarry.

3. Old Passenger Line to the North

The line that had served the people before is serving the people again, offering dry-shod passage in both directions from Creigiau Station. The mineral line, although lying only a few metres lower, has always been partially flooded but was almost wholly submerged after the wet winters of 1993-94 and 1998-99. It is still passable, but preferably with the aid of horse or bicycle.

In our anti-clockwise survey of the parish boundaries, it would be logical to start our railway walks at Tyn-y-Coed in the North. Practical considerations override logical ones , however, and we start, like the villagers of old, at Creigiau Station.

It is still posssible to join the line at Tyn-y-Coed where the road from Rhiwsaison crosses its deep cutting. In the past this involved a steep scramble down from the carpark. By 1994, when the gradient down had been eased by heavy use, the carpark has been closed, leaving room for only a few vehicles at the roadside. It is still capaciously multi-partite and open within but contains only one burnt-out car, the entrances firmly blocked by heaps of tarmac, rubble and tree branches to thwart the drug-takers and glue-sniffers. So much for those blackberrying sorties!

With the mineral line so close, it is convenient to make a circuit north from the station (Map reference ST 084 815) up one line and down the other - if the gumboots reach high enough. So many woodland paths link the two that the simple loop can be modified in various ways and dog-walkers are not confined to the proverbial dog's walk, following the same scent home.

In the 70s the railway ballast was sharply uncomfortable underfoot, but soil had filtered down among it in the 90s during the burial process which conserves our archeological remains and the going was easier. Foot traffic had kept the invasive vegetation at bay and natural gradients had been ironed out by the track-layers, as on canal towpaths by the 'navvies' - the original 'navigation men'.

Moving onto the first embanked section, a silvered woodland pool below to the west reflected two big multi-trunked trees in May 1994, a sycamore in full leaf and an ash with red and green shoots pushing unwillingly from black bud scales. Alongside was yet another new housing estate encroaching back into the wood. Where do all the people come from? Ingress paths from this accounted for some of the current usage and should justify the preservation of this ancient workaday route in its new amenity guise.

Tender leaves unfurling in spring are the basis of many food chains, providing a bonanza not only for the creatures which munch them, but for those which live inside, causing the anomalous growths known as galls.

Leaf rosettes terminating some of the goat sallow twigs in the station are called camellia galls and are caused by a midge, *Rhabdophaga rosaria*. Another midge, *Iteomyia capreae*, produces oval pouches between leaf veins of the same bushes, forming green humps above and red hollows below. Quite often the eggs are laid in parts of the plant already attacked by the bean-gall sawfly, *Pontania proxima*, so that one gall forms directly on the other. More familiar galls appear on the oaks: soft pink oak-apples, hard brown marble galls, succulent red currant galls and the short-stalked crimson discs of spangle galls on the leaves. All these we saw within the space of a few hundred yards on an early summer walk with entomologist Michael Claridge in 1985.

A shallow cutting through the Dolomite beyond revealed pale veins of calcite and barytes in the 70s, but these were hard to locate by the 90s, when increasing shade and heavy rain had encouraged the growth of moss and algae over the dark red rocks. Much was, and still is, ivy-draped. The little tufts of rusty-back fern, wall-rue and maidenhair spleenwort of the 60s were being overtopped by larger ferns - polypody, hart's-tongue and male fern - by the 70s and were more shrub-grown by the 80s, In the 90s the vegetation had gone full circle, with the larger plants shaded out by the thickening tree canopy and the tiny, undemanding ferns free to grow once more.

Out in the open pioneering wild strawberry runners were still looping their way across the ballast from the bordering ribwort and ox-eye daisies. Bumble bees were pollinating their flowers in May, preparing a luscious but tediously gathered harvest for July. By then the germander speedwell, brightest of the blue 'bird's-eyes', would be

Common Blue Butterfly on Bird's-foot Trefoil

backed by a lace-work of wild carrot and the pink and white of wild roses. Later the scarlet hips would shine against a backdrop of wine-red dogwood leaves and the fluff of old-man's beard, which pulls itself aloft by grasping at all and sundry with twisting leaf stalks.

The bordering woodland was disorderly and unmanaged, but triumphantly alive after decades of stress. In the limestone stretch field maples and sweet chestnuts appeared in the shrub layer and May-time carpets were of white ramsons or wild garlic. On the Coal Measures guelder rose was commoner and the ground carpets were of bluebells.

Both wood types were vibrant with bird song in spring, when incoming warblers added melodious notes to those of thrush, blackbird and robin and tits busied themselves with endless caterpillar hunts. The leaf canopy muffled outside sounds, but the distant notes of cuckoos filtered through and the raucous cries of jay and crow.

A pair of water-logged Coalfield pastures impinged towards the track from the west, the tussocky purple moor-grass and rushes speckled with the yellow of lesser spearwort and creeping buttercup and interrupted by clumps of gorse and bramble. The flickering wings of speckled wood butterflies and gyrating forms of green longhorn moths *(Adelia viridella)* of the deep shade gave way in the paddocks to the dancing forms of orange-tips and green-veined whites, frequenting especially the mauve flowers of lady's-smock or milkmaid. A herd of cattle came sploshing through: guernsey-coloured continental steers and black and white Friesian heifers, wearing football socks of pale mud pulled well above their hocks and only partially washed away as they waded through ponds surfaced with white-flowered mud crowfoot *(Ranunculus omiophyllus)*.

The bridge which took the passenger line over the mineral line disappeared long since, but it is worth commenting on the structure of the bridges still standing. The main masonry of all is dark red conglomerate from the Radyr Quarry near the shunting yards towards Cardiff. Pennant Sandstone forms the steps alongside the southernmost and the road wall, which is topped with coping stones of moulded black slag. The next to the north has the arch lined with four courses of glossily dark bricks and the parapet of concrete blocks set on bricks. The northernmost bridge features the Radyr conglomerate and slag coping stones but the Rhiwsaison road crosses in an iron trough, with panelled brick parapet on the south and breeze blocks on the north. Strangely, the southernmost bridge on the mineral line, which leads south past Radyr Quarry, is of sandstone from the North, with the road again in cast iron troughs.

Planks have been laid across the water where the two lines cross. A badly eroded path leads back to the higher level of the main track, but this, too, becomes submerged as it enters its cutting and is crossed with the help of stepping stones near a fine clump of cat's valerian, before the way climbs roadward through wood anemones, moschatel and dog's mercury.

Standing on the Rhiwsaison road bridge high above the cutting one looks down onto a broad waterway which is more canal than railway. It is clear now of the obstructing branches of the 60s and 70s but looks as though a rubber dinghy might not be out of place for the next stage. It was frozen solid, a veritable skating rink, in February 1983.

4. Old Mineral Line to the North

This line was less negotiable than usual after the wet winters of 1993-94, 1994-95 and 1998-99, but over the last three decades it has yielded some fascinating finds to well-shod parties of biology students. It crosses a watershed north of the junction with the quarry line, water flowing away in both directions along the marginal ditches or the track itself. Level stretches provide placid water where the walker sends water boatmen and water crickets billowing to safety on the bow waves from his boots, and sumps where silt is deposited over the firm standing, as where the two lines cross.

Below Creigiau Farm the walled drainage system is still functional, the bulk of the water being led off under both rail tracks through stone-arched culverts. The ensuing dry section is short, just as far as a second cross culvert, then one is splashing again between stands of shade horsetail, bittersweet and angelica, bordered by wild currant bushes.

A fascinating pioneering growth in the water is stonewort *(Chara vulgaris)*, a crusty green alga which romped through the limey stretch from the early days, taking up lime from the water and incorporating it in the branched axis and the whorls of lesser branches, to give a crisp mass which crunches underfoot like cornflakes.

In deep water in winter the fronds are green and grow to 24 inches long, preferring fast clear flows, but persisting among marsh horsetail in bright orange, iron-fouled seepages. In shallow water in summer, this unusually robust alga is greyer and adopts a very different form, with fronds only an inch or two high and closely packed to form a bristly mat. Its chief associate is a dark, curled liverwort *(Pellia endiviifolia)*, just breaking surface beneath slabby growths of another, *Conocephalum conicum*, with the golden saxifrage of the banks above.

Watercress can be gathered here, but beware the fool's watercress which grows among it. Here too are narrow-leaved water parsnip and blue-flowered brooklime, overtopped by yellow iris and meadowsweet.

A posssibly more fertile stretch alongside Creigiau Farm, with its springtime lambs and calves, can be wriggling with tadpoles in spring. Freshwater shrimps are everywhere, with water beetles and water boatmen. Where mud accumulates in sluggish sections caddis larvae build fragile tubes of silt grains and Chironomid midge larvae thrive, even where the surface is rainbow-hued with bog iron ore.

Caterpillars of July high-flier moths *(Hydriomena furcata)* feed on sallow leaves. These slaty-grey 'loopers' with pale transverse stripes form cocoons inside folded leaves which they sew together with silken threads. Tortricid moths, too, stitch up the sallow leaves for purposes of their own and Coleophora moths make themselves little caddis-like tubes from fragments of other sallow leaves. These protrude erect from the leaf surface, the little caterpillar standing on its head to munch the tissue below.

Alders, also, have their complement of insect life. Woolly aphids *(Eriosoma lanigerum)* hide under patches of white wax which they secrete on the leaf stalks and from the shelter of which they feed. Similar infestations on garden plants are referred to as 'American blight'. The principal users of the alder leaves here are mites, *Eriophyes laevis-inangulis,* makers of the upstanding red nail galls.

Spotted Flycatcher

Figwort weevils *(Cionis scrophularia* or *hortulans)*, both the slug-like larvae and the long-snouted adults, find a living on the water figwort. Warningly coloured red and black 'fire bugs' *(Cercopis vulnerata)* suck the watery fluids ascending the stems of various herbs. Most sap-suckers feed from the sugary fluids descending from the leaves, so these attractive little creatures have to work extra hard to absorb the necessary solids from this dilute solution.

Coltsfoot and barren strawberry can be flowering as early as January, followed by lady's smock, primroses, blue bugle and a few marsh orchids. Kidney vetch, creeping cinquefoil and mouse-ear hawkweed are at home on rocky limestone cliffs and do well on the few dry stretches of limestone ballast. Deeper soil behind supports red campion and Queen Anne's lace, followed by agrimony and melilot.

In 1994 it was still possible to leave the wood over a heap of tarmac to the lane leading to Creigiau Farm. Under the bridge a neat, horse-width track had been cut through the marsh vegetation, giving a hard if wet passage along the bridleway. The railway lines were still in use north of the quarry in 1973, long after the bridge at the line intersection had disappeared. In 1983 the rails were still there, but the quarry branch line was fenced off. By 1993 the rails had gone and most sleepers were thrown back onto the banks. The fence had also gone, but the line separating cow pasture ffrom playing field was a solid mass of brambles between overgrown hedges and quite impassable.

In February 1973 the brambles were neatly cut back by hand and the grass verges were used for hacking, gallopping and pony jumping. The quarry branch ended with two sidings headed into a cliff green with hart's tongue ferns, where the geological fault had brought the marly (unquarried) Millstone Grit up against the limestone.

Grass and elder twigs by the big hoppers where the crushed stone was loaded into the trucks, were grotesquely 'sculptured' with a thick coating of solidified limestone dust, simulating living fossils. Rain and dew had converted the clinging dust to cement, making individual grass blades 2 cm or more wide before the weight of stone caused breakage. Astonishingly the tissue was still green underneath when the crust was chipped off, suggesting a rapid build-up. Perhaps the unseasonal warmth helped, elevated coke-covered heaps of chippings alongside glowing like mounds of burning charcoal and bursting momentarily into flame in gusts of wind.

In 1983 it was easy enough to walk on south of the road bridge, although there was no access from the Station Cottages on that side of the road. By 1993 the path was still discernible in thick undergrowth beyond the bridge, but a machete would be needed to force a passage.

It is sad that these railways have fallen into disuse, when their role in reducing the pressure on the roads is so much more vital than in their heyday, particularly now that the Creigiau Quarry is working again after a period of quiescence. Nevertheless, it is good to see how rapidly Nature heals the scars. There is an inborn tenacity here, a persistence by renewal of that living thread of continuity that seems to survive the worst that we, the users and stewards, ·can throw at it.

5. Old Passenger Line to the South

Although lying just outside the boundary of the Caerphilly Mountain Countryside Project area, the redundant passenger railway line from Creigiau Station southwards continues to embrace the country park theme of rural amenity. It provides a well used walking trail for $1^1/_2$ miles, until brought to a halt by the embankment of the M4 motorway.

I had frequently walked it during the 1970s and 1980s, but the building of two vast new housing estates, around Castell-y-Mynach and north of Robin Hill, had fundamentally changed the once self-contained village. It was with some trepidation therefore, that I sought out this walk again on a sunny day in August 1993.

I need not have worried. It was there still, almost unchanged, thanks to the vigorous efforts of local country lovers and dog walkers. My 1993 plant list was little changed from those of 1973 and 1983. Shrubs had encroached further across the flowery 'wasteland' by the station houses, but there was still plenty of play space for individual and corporate functions such as the firework display.

The shaggy sward of cocksfoot and tall oat-grass was gilded with the yellow of wild parsnip, delivering up its nectar to greedily sipping bugs and beetles. Blatantly flowering ragwort supplied meadow brown butterflies with sweets and drifts of pink hemp agrimony would sustain the Vanessid butterflies far into the autumn. The soporific hum of bees rose from the red clover sward alongside the hard standing and hover flies in distinctive liveries of black and yellow stripes hung suspended over traceries of wild carrot, burnet saxifrage and upright hedge parsley flowers. Some of the high fliers were getting snapped up by hawking swallows.

Goat sallow and dogwood, draped with the first autumnal fluff of old man's beard, were advancing from the line of lofty ashes and sycamores hiding the houses to the west. The thistly paddock fronting the station houses to the east lay at first beyond a richly fruiting bramble thicket, then a dark woodland, penetrated by a network of little paths. In the secret interior of this youngsters could disport themselves as youngsters have through the ages, with triangular wooden platforms nailed firmly in the trees - well beyond the reach of earthbound adults - camp fire sites and improvised furniture in the clearings beneath.

When they left for other pursuits the wildlife took over. A vole had tunnelled under a discarded corrugated iron sheet, a jay screeched, a green woodpecker laughed and a moorhen honked from the sandy-floored stream snaking between modestly elevated banks at the old wood boundary - now crossed by spontaneously regenerated trees. Darker parts were floored by ivy, spiked with the strawey stalks of the springtime bluebell crop and softened by spreads of enchanter's nightshade and red campion. Woodland changed gradually through open spinney to attractive parkland, its grass as green as that of the fields beyond, where the mineral line diverged progressively further from the line that I had lately left.

Past woodland management had involved coppicing - of the plenteous field maple as well as the now stout-trunked hazel and lofty, gangling hawthorns. The month-long dry spell just past had resulted in films of downy white mildew on oak, maple and hogweed, while orange rust fungi had affected some of the sallow leaves. Dogwood in the shade was lax and green-twigged, simulating spindle: that in the open was bushier, red-stemmed and purple-leaved. A tiny reedbed bordered by hemlock water-dropwort occupied wet ground under alders, while creeping buttercups carpetted damp depressions among wispy briers and bur-fruited wood avens.

The underlying rock is Blue Lias throughout, supporting a wealth of limestone flowers which are usually forced to give way to agricultural monocultures, as the Lias yields fertile farmland. In the unkempt grass above the Creigiau road were the purple of two species of knapweed and two of vetch among broad stands of rosebay willow-herb.

The bridge taking the railway across the road had been dismantled since my early walks, the road straightened and widened and supplied with a central white line and a tarmac pavement. But the path continued, obliquely down the tall bank and up the other side by several tracks, some more scrambly than others, to join the little changed pathway along the embankment beyond. A kissing-gate was installed later.

Sometimes the way was open and flowery, with magnificent stands of large field scabious, agrimony and wild basil or cushion calamint. Blue butterflies sipped from the yellow pea flowers of meadow vetchling, bird's foot trefoil and black medick; meadow browns and hedge browns from perforated St. John's wort and fleabane. Farm vehicles used the first lap by Llwynioli and the short grass carpet here was sprinkled with mauve-flecked eyebright, red bartsia and yellow trefoil. Where the railway ballast showed through there were wild strawberries and herb Robert: where rabbits congregated the lawn-like turf which they kept mown was studded with dove's-foot cranesbill and field daisies.

A young rabbit sat erect on one such sward, not abroad in daylight because of an urgent need to feed, but just sunning himself, at one with his little world. A long ear twitched as a large white butterfly almost touched down on the handy perch, and there was a slight flinching as the chiff chaff which chased the butterfly zoomed uncomfortably close. He sat his ground, and I mine, until a pair of buzzards appeared overhead, riding an August thermal, and apparently unconcerned with prey, but posing enough of a threat to send the youngster bolting for cover. (Was this instinctive, or had he been well taught by the doe who mothered him?)

Sometimes the path narrowed to thread between tall shrubs sufficiently like woodland for the butterflies to change to speckled woods and green-veined whites. These sections were alive with song birds, come for the flies which converged on the shelter. I sat for a while with binoculars at the ready.

A family of greenish yellow willow warblers was busy among the sloe branches picking off invisible minuteae as they fattened up for their impending migration south. Another family came bustling through: long-tailed tits this time, constantly chattering and constantly on the move, as they would be long after the warblers had left for sunnier climes. Then came a blue tit and a song thrush.

Willow Warblers and Sloes

Soon to be leaving was the spotted flycatcher, whose favourite ash perch was out in the open, so that its fly-catching sorties were fully visible. Again there was no urgency about feeding in this prolific environment and the bird spent most of its time preening, stretching first one wing and then the other as it tweaked the feathers into place under armpits and on shoulders. A subdued tinkling drew my attention to a goldcrest behind a stand of flowering corn sow-thistle and a dunnock foraged at ground level, but proved no match for the spurting grasshoppers. Easier to catch were the frog-hoppers on willow herb and toadflax and the little flies congregated in the buttercup flowers. 'Noises off' came from bickering blackbirds, cawing crows and startled wood pigeons.

Thirty years earlier, when I had lived in Creigiau for six months, I had watched the nightly congregating of a huge flock of Corvids - crows, rooks and jackdaws - over these fields, as they gathered to roost in the wood beyond the railway line. They continued to do so for many years. Perhaps they still do.

To both sides of the Llantrisant Road bridge, with its high-fenced stock pen built conveniently beneath, the track is elevated on an embankment high above the neighbouring fields and pierced by a farm track at one point. The 'permanent way' may have been constructed with material from elsewhere, but the ballast was of limestone and the vegetation was essentially one of limey soils.

The tall banks were wooded and there were buddlejas alongside the path, one with white flowers instead of the usual mauve. Beyond was grassland, even the fields once devoted to maize for silage being under grass leys now, these newly mown. Two field ponds glinted from the pleasantly undulating, partially wooded land near Henstaff Court, their position tallying with two small limestone quarries marked on the geological survey map. A little flock of mallard rose from one, circled overhead and dropped down to a smaller pool near Pencoed Farm.

Young cattle, black, white and tan - Friesian, Charolais and Hereford - grazed placidly, attracting flies which attracted a twittering cloud of swallows. Gates splotched with blackberry-stained guano and pip-filled crop pellets allowed them briefly onto the track as the embankment lowered, the hoof marks suggesting that they usually just crossed, but they may have helped to keep the path open while glutting themselves with the lush white clover and vetches: a useful function, as the pressure of walkers tailed off with increasing distance from Creigiau.

There was a broadening of the hard standing at one point - old sidings perhaps, as there seemed no cause for a station. Colonisation of the ballast was at an earlier stage here, with a low sward of ox-eye daisy seedlings, ribwort plantain and mouse-ear hawkweed, grading back to rough hawkbit *(Leontodon hispidus)* and smooth hawk's-beard *(Crepis capillaris)*. Among the dark mosses were two interesting lichens, the tapered grey-green goblets of the slender pixie-cups lichen *Cladonia fimbriata* and crisped ginger-tipped fronds of one of the dog's-tooth lichens, *Peltigera rufescens*.

Some fine viewing points occur along the embanked section where bordering tree growth thins. To the north-west is the ancient hilltop town of Llantrisant, dominated by its church, to the north-east the pimpled tumuli atop the Great Garth. The beechwood of the Little Garth merges into the striped tree-planting pattern of Craig-y-Parc where the Old Red Sandstone dips out of sight, while the white bauble of the water tower stands poised above Fairwater to the south.

A few years later row upon row of broad-leaved trees had been planted in a series of plots alongside the railway line and Llantrisant

Road. Already there was a rash of new brick houses near the road crossing. Was this landscaping in readiness for more?

6. The Swallowing up of the Old Mineral Railway to the South

South of Creigiau Station the Caerphilly Project boundary follows the mineral line as this curves away to the south-east, through Capel Llanilterne, to Tyla Morris and alongside the M 4, separating Morganstown within from Radyr outside. The industrial track, now interrupted by the sewage works, continued east, turning south in Radyr to join the Taff Valley Line on the Cardiff side of the shunting yards.

It ran more or less parallel to the passenger line from Creigiau Station to just north of Robin Hill, where it left the Blue Lias to cross a narrow band of Rhaetic rocks. From here its easterly trend, like the fault, passed over the agriculturally amenable Keuper Marls, with the less tractable Devonian Old Red Sandstone rising north-east of the fault as the Craig-y-Parc hill.

South of Creigiau Quarry the line was closed to traffic around 1963 and it is worth placing on record the changes during the subsequent thirty years as this less-than-permanent-way has been reabsorbed into the landscape. Investigations were carried out in 1973 (4th February), 1983 (21st July) and 1993 (11th September).

"February fills dyke, either with the black or white". My 1973 exploration was too wintry and too wet to yield much in the way of animal activity, but it stressed the importance of the old drainage system as the ditches alongside fell into disrepair. Water seemed to be everywhere, some of the sources appearing on the Ordnance Survey map as 'rises' along the line of the fault, where new rocks abut onto old. Only one, just south of the quarry, is named, this being Ffynnon Dwym.

Raised only slightly above sodden woodland, the track was bordered in parts by narrow reedbeds, with the flopped remains of giant horsetail and hemlock water-dropwort. Flote grass lay suspended over massed water starwort in iris bordered pools to the west. Already sallows were closing in across the track and it was only just possible to force a passage by the old piggery. A broad swathe had been cut to allow cattle across to drink at the recently cleared, fast flowing stream.

The going was drier across the road by the new sewage plant north-east of Robin Hill. All the species of the passenger line were here in a sward of sterile brome, crested dogstail and yarrow, plus a few other lime-lovers like salad burnet among the wintry remains of red bartsia and fairy flax. Invading woody plants included downy birch, guelder-rose and a few little oaks.

Damper sections were lusher, with sedges and three kinds of rush, soft, hard and sharp-flowered. Shining leaves of lady's smock and brooklime gave promise of spring colour, while crackly haulms of greater willow herb indicated a glory passed. It would not be long before this became an alder-sallow spinney.

The next lap, between two breached stone bridges carrying muddy cart tracks, lay below Craig-y-Parc and was more substantially wooded. The unmetalled ways were no longer used, their gates overgrown with bramble and their central grass strips with hazel saplings, but fresh dung showed that ponies still used them, keeping the way sufficiently open for me to squeeze through the diminished growths of winter.

Primrose plants bordering the ballast were flourishing; those advancing across it into brighter light were more compact. Bluebell leaves remained marginal, insufficient soil having accumulated on the track to accommodate their bulbs. This was the domain of superficially creeping wild strawberry and ground ivy, with seedling violets and germander speedwell. Only the barren strawberry was flowering as yet. The brightest hue was from the scarlet elf cups *(Sarcoscypha (Peziza) coccinea)* on rotting sticks.

Emerging into the fertile market garden lands of Capel Llanilterne, the line became more deeply recessed and waterlogged to the point of supplying important wetland sites for wildlife. Soil from the red

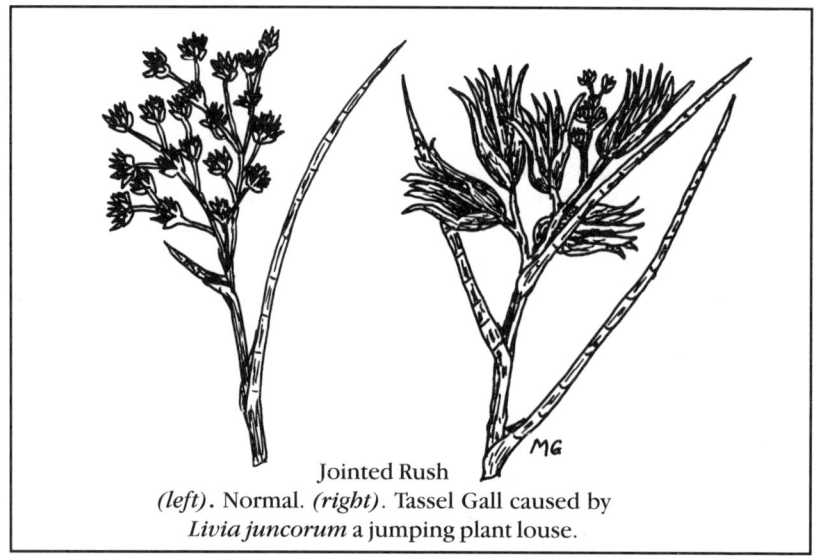

Jointed Rush
(left). Normal. *(right)*. Tassel Gall caused by
Livia juncorum a jumping plant louse.

Gerris Pond Skater

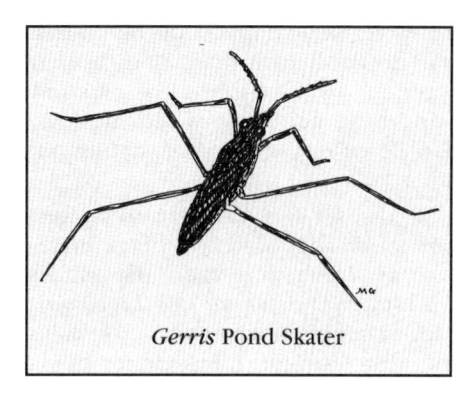

mudstone ploughlands had washed into the cutting to form poolside 'sandbanks' imprinted by the feet of moorhens. A farmer who had lost the hearts of many of his cabbages to wood pigeons and jays, had enhanced the watery theme by planting some weeping willows near his greenhouses.

Fertility filched from the brassicas and onions above benefitted the reedmace and angelica below, while lesser duckweed and a green algal scum utilised the surplus phosphates. Where not submerged, the layer of red soil over the crunchy chippings made the going easier and the cutting was more open towards the iron-sided bridge carrying the lane north past Parc Side Farm and Parc-y-Justice Farm to the path network of the Craig-y-Parc Wood.

By 1983 the stretch of line nearest the Creigiau Quarry road entrance had been swallowed up by head-high bracken, with emergent sallows and marginal oaks behind a wire mesh fence. Further on it was still open, leading first through wet, then dry woodland and on into open fields by the Pant-y-Gored road.

There was a nice example of fence line ecology here, the tall iris, angelica and alder of the one side chomped off short by grazing livestock on the other. Three streams converged on a marsh floored with flowering fool's watercress and narrow-leaved water parsnip, the water leaving in a single channel under banks ornamented with pink musk mallow among hart's-tonge ferns. A surprising component of the vegetation was the brookweed *(Samolus valerandi)*, which is more often found near the sea. Some of the bordering jointed rush had its flowers replaced by tassell galls, formed by the jumping plant louse or psyllid, *Livia juncorum*, while a few of the poplar leaves were affected by golden blotch disease, the outcome of infection by the fungus, *Ascomyces aureus*.

The richness of this wetland habitat, merely hinted at in February, was now very apparent. Water beetles scudded through crisp thickets of stonewort and *Gyrinus* whirligig beetles gyrated merrily around beside drifts of marsh bedstraw. With them on the elastic surface film were *Gerris* pond skaters, mostly juveniles.

I squatted to watch the numerous *Notonectid* back-swimmers, the water boatmen which live an upside down life in the pools. They hung quiescent for long spells, seemingly clinging to the surface film with the centrally attached legs, but had more likely popped up like beach balls, having to work harder to stay down than to float. They are air breathers and chose to do their preening on the surface, lying tummy side up, like sea otters, and stroking head and body with long legs. Every now and again one would dart down to the silty bed, letting out a stream of bubbles to lose buoyancy.

More dashing were the dragon and damsel flies. Largest and swiftest were the common hawkers *(Aeschna juncea)*, blue and black males with a yellow stripe on the black thorax. There were azure damselflies *(Coenagrion puella)* and common blues *(Enallagma cyathigerum)*, which are very hard to tell apart. Both have predominantly black females and predominantly blue males, the best distinguishing feature being the shape of the black mark on the male's second abdominal segment. They obligingly sat for sufficiently long on fleabane and water figwort for me to ascertain that both were present. A number were flying in tandem, the brighter male escorting his mate by the scruff of her neck to the sites he presumed most expedient for egg laying.

Blue-tailed damselflies *(Ischnura elegans)*, usually the commonest species, were rarer here, a few returning repeatedly to perch on square-stemmed St. John's wort - the marshland counterpart of the commoner 'perforated' sort. Eight large red damselflies *(Pyrrhosoma nymphula)* spent most of their time perched on lesser spearwort, unconcerned with mating. Males of the common darter *(Sympetrum striolatum)* were also red, but of heavier build, as befits a 'dragon'. These were more active, chivvying the buffish yellow females far across the paddocks, but seemingly failing to catch up with them, as I saw no signs of mating.

Many less striking creatures, from craneflies down, had newly emerged from the water: none of the biting kind. Muscid flies, *Mesembrina meridiana*, sipping nectar from angelica flowers, bore two yellow triangles on their wing bases and were less parallel sided than the common *Eristalis* drone flies, whose larvae are the well known rat-tailed maggots of pond beds. Their long breathing tube of three segments can be extended or retracted like a radio aerial to reach the surface and enable the animal to live in oxygen-deficient water. *Mesembrina* needed the combination of trees for sunning itself and animal dung for the laying of the single large ($4^1/_2$ mm long) egg.

Shiny seven-spot ladybirds were gorging themselves on aphids while *Opiliones* harvestmen and spiders occupied wet and dry habitats alike. *Crambus* grass moths crowded the upstanding marsh plants and the air was full of butterflies - meadow browns, wall browns and whites.

Footprints on the muddy shore told that water voles were about and it was a great thrill when a whiskery nose pushed out among the water mint and started nibbling some juicy leaves of flote grass. A decade

Water Vole

later a nation wide survey recorded these attractive animals - personified by 'Ratty' in "Wind in the Willows" - to have disappeared from 60% of their former known sites, due to loss of habitat or a build up of agricultural chemicals. Little enclaves like this, near the spontaneous emergence of springs and bordered by swamp woodland and old pasture rather than arable land, are likely to be their future stronghold.

The vole had gone by the time the grey squirrel came down to drink. This treetop denizen had been pottering on the opposite bank for some time, with no more than a cursory glance in my direction, before hopping down to slake his thirst. He leapt to my side of the stream, disappeared into a clump of nettles and emerged carrying a $2^1/_2$ inch diameter toadstool. Sitting back on his bushy tail, he held the rubbery prize in delicate forepaws, nibbling systematically around the rim and consuming most of the gills before his attention was deflected. He returned to the meal briefly, but seemed to find the stipe less palatable (as we do) and left it to continue pottering. Then a movement of mine startled a full grown rabbit, which scuttled past and sent him up the nearest tree, chattering angrily.

Before I left, this oasis in the drought stricken landscape had attracted a flock of ten linnets down to drink and several magpies, or the same magpie several times. Swallows, too, were dipping to drink in flight at the largest pool. Two manholes showed that the water was sufficiently permanent to be tapped for farm supplies - and more recently for the sewage processing plant.

Cattle sheltered under the stone and iron sided bridge across the road, where the churned mud was baked to the consistency of concrete. The hay racks and feed troughs beyond were in use, tiding the animals over the summer shortage of green herbage. Passage to the further moorhen pools was now barred by the securely fenced sewage plant cutting obliquely across, with piles of soil suggesting further construction.

In 1993 the farm gate across the track leading obliquely down from the west side of the road was tied only with orange binder twine, but led now into a very ordinary sloping grass field. Only the iron walled road bridge showed where the track had once been. Cattle had eaten away most of the trees above - to both sides of the bridge - and the bulk of the water had been diverted from the track and the deeply recessed alder spinney alongside to help service the sewage works.

Wetland species persisted opposite, comfrey and giant horsetail among them, but the second gate barred foot passage as well as vehicles. It was furnished with a notice. "Welsh Water. Eastern Sewage Department. Caring for the Environment". Another read "Danger. Deep water. Keep out.", the impregnable fencing making sure this instruction was obeyed. 'Caring for the environment' - yes, but at the expense of that vibrant community of a decade ago. So many new commuter houses - at both Creigiau and Pentyrch - must inevitably bring problems.

A recently opened garden centre of Creigiau Nurseries on the Llantrisant Road at Capel Llaniltene had been dumping garden rubbish in the cutting, posing a further blockage. East of here it was possible to look down from the next grey stone and iron plated bridge leading the old lane off the main road opposite the little grey church and view a completely open stretch of track far below. It was muddy to the point of waterlogging under ferny, nettly banks, but devoid of vegetation because of the shade of overarching trees.

Calendula marigolds and scorpion-grass forget-me-nots flowered along the edges of the iron trough above - bridge users warned by red and white notices signed by the British Railways Board that the laden weight of vehicles crossing should not exceed 24 tons. The old lane curved up past Parc Side Farm to join the concrete farm road to Parc-y-Justice and this the green lane to Craig-y-Parc. There were no market garden crops now, even the greenhouses and plant sheds were empty. Instead cattle and horses fattened on rich green clover fields.

Some of the locals regret that the railway line has been lost as a right of way. Perhaps one day it will be restored in the wake of the admirable 'Taff Trail' leading north from the Taff Gorge. There was talk in the nineties of re-opening it for rolling-stock from Creigiau Quarry, then of a new roundabout at the junction of rail, road and entrances to the quarry and playing field, but by the end of the decade nothing had happened except an enlargement of the earth-floored turning space.

36. Yellow Iris fruits flopped onto massed submerged Curled Canadian Pondweed

35. Yellow Iris flowers

CREIGIAU FROG POND

37. Five Moorhens and Greater Spearwort.

38. Saprophytic Bird's-nest Orchid

39. A splendid burl on a Creigiau elm. Sept. 1962 (valuable for veneers)

40. Broad Helleborine Orchid.

41. Old Ton Mawr quarry to the west of Walnut Tree quarry which can be seen on the skyline. 1988

Chapter 7

CREIGIAU FARMS, PONDS AND QUARRY

Introductory

Topography has an important bearing on life in the villages clustered around the Garth. At Creigiau we are down to the low elevation of Gwaelod-y-Garth, both villages having grown up between the 200 foot and 300 foot contours, whilst the intervening Pentyrch is between 500 and 600 feet. Creigiau lies on the windward side of the mountain, Gwaelod on the leeward, although more affected by chilly winds from the north-east. Needless to say, Pentyrch has a much harsher climate. It can be snowing and blowing up there when the other two thirds of the parish are relatively mild.

Contours were important to the early settlers, too, but for different reasons. It was pointed out in 1977 by Barry Davies of the Llantrisant and District Local History Society, that four of the most ancient settlements in Creigiau lie on the 275 foot contour line on the slopes of eminences. Inadequate implements and farming techniques limited Neolithic farming to light, freely draining soils, often on the tops of such rises, leaving the more sheltered but soggier lowlands to the woodland wildlife.

In the Neolithic period or New Stone Age of 4000 to 5000 years ago man was evolving from nomadic hunter to settled farmer. The lowland thickets of oak and ash would have catered for his hunting activities, the open tops for his farming. It is the other way round now, with working hours spent farming or labouring in the valleys and leisure hours rabbitting with gun and ferret on the heights, this applying throughout the Coalfield.

The most ancient building still standing, by several thousand years, if building it can be called, is the Cae-yr-arfau cromlech or burial chamber, which lies at 250 feet on the junction of limestone and Coalfield and is attributed to the New Stone Age. Limestone soils would be lighter, drier and more easily worked than coalfield ones, their occurrence here compensating for the lower altitude.

A preference for heights was also exhibited by the Bronze Age builders of the tumuli on the Great Garth and the Iron Age inhabitants of the promontary hill fort at Llwyn-da-ddu on the 400 foot eminence east of Craig-y-Parc.

We need to move on a few thousand years to the Middle Ages for our next surviving man-made artifacts. Barry Davies (1977) distinguishes five types of buildings erected in the fifteenth and sixteenth centuries, which saw the beginning of substantially durable stone dwellings for the peasants as well as the gentry, who had enjoyed them for some centuries.

Gentry houses surviving in Creigiau from that period are Castell-y-Mynach and Pantygored. Lesser structures of three units are exemplified by the "King's Head" Inn at Pentyrch, formerly Cae Colman. Smaller again were two unit structures, as seen in the Cae-yr-arfau farmhouse between ancient cromlech and modern golf course, this enlarged to three units in the eighteenth century. The eighteen foot square measurement commonly seen was probably determined by the size of the durmast oaks available for roof-trees.

Smaller again were single unit stone houses, the few which survive having no land attached, although originally crofters' cottages. Ty Bach, at Pantygored, is an example. Finally there were the one-room bwthyns, with cupboard bed in the rear wall. Twynygeirion Isaf on the Mountain Road is one now restored to residential use after a long spell as store and office for the Castell-y-Mynach Estate.

Moving to the recent past, we come to the time when the long-standing parish council, the oldest form of local government in Europe, became officially redundant with the Local Government Act of 1972, which decreed that it henceforth be designated Community Council to suit the now more secular world.

The Pentyrch Parish Council had a life of 80 years, the first meeting - five hours long and attended by 108 parishioners out of a population of only a few hundred - being held on December 4th 1894, in the Pentyrch School Room. This celebrated the villagers' emergence from control by vestry and vicar to government 'by the people for the people'. The last meeting, at the Gwaelod Village Hall, was on March 18th 1972. members soon adjourning to the "Kings Arms", to mourn or celebrate, as they felt inclined.

This chapter looks at the greener aspects of modern Creigiau, old and new ponds, overgrown allotments and neatly kept playing field and the major quarrying enterprise, recently re-started.

1. Cae-yr-arfau, Cromlech, Farm and Pond

There are several different spellings in use for this site, just north of the entrance to the Golf Course on the Creigiau-Rhiwsaison Road, and different origins of the name, such as "Place of battle, slaughter or arms" or "Field of the course", for chariot-racing or relating to herds and flocks rather than battles. I use the spelling on modern Ordnance Survey maps.

Only the east and west supportive slabs and the capstone of the cromlech remain in place today, with another stone on the floor. The north side, towards the old bridleway to the farm, was excavated in 1875, but the southern part of the mound of soil which covered it has

Neolithic or New Stone-Age Cromlech at Cae-yr-arfau, Creigiau

only recently been removed. A farm wall was built through it, incorporating the capstone, this formerly separating the field to the south from the track, but now running through the attractive garden of the big new house built on the old farm site by 1985.

Over the years the chamber, built for the ceremonial receipt of the dead, has been employed for the more mundane storage of coal, the slabs kept white-washed during this spell of utilitarian use. When I first visited, in August 1971, it was partially smothered in a summery exuberance of dogwood, bramble and hogweed.

The fifteenth century farmhouse stood proud, but much the worse for wear, with belts of white stonecrop flowering generously along the gutters. Elder saplings, metre-high brassicas, ivy, nettles and cocksfoot found roothold on the crumbling roof slates and wildlife, including nesting pied wagtails, had taken up residence in the walls.

A small pond in a mini-quarry behind the ruins was choked with nettles, ash, rubble and three old cars. It had been used as a dump and yielded an interesting series of old bottles and other artifacts when the Cosslett family, the new owners, cleared it during the early eighties and

Cae-yr-arfau Farmhouse - now demolished

131

transformed it into an interesting garden feature, with a stone seat placed against the low cliff in an embayment of lawn. They failed to save the farmhouse and barns for restoration, the foundations being unsound, and built a large brick dwelling with indoor swimming pool in its place.

The old bridleway had been moved north towards the horse paddock and stables and widened as the entrance drive, whilst the cromlech was incorporated in a little garden alongside. Two kinds of ivy climbed the marginal slabs, with herb Robert and ivy-leaved toadflax where the capstone slid into the fabric of the restored wall behind. In May 1994 green alkanet, with brilliant blue flowers, passed into budding bistort or snake-root and these into garden flowers - *Epimedium* and *Primula* - beside the narrow stone path.

The entrance drive and straight alignment of hedges east of the road lie along the boundary between limestone and coalfield soils. Garden and golf course are largely on the freely-draining limestone. The horse paddock on coalfield soils to the north was decidedly soggy and yellow with the flowers of marsh-loving creeping buttercup after the wet winter of 1993-94. At its foot was a fine pond, fed by the Nant Cessair stream, which shares its name with the Caesar's Arms Public House just beyond.

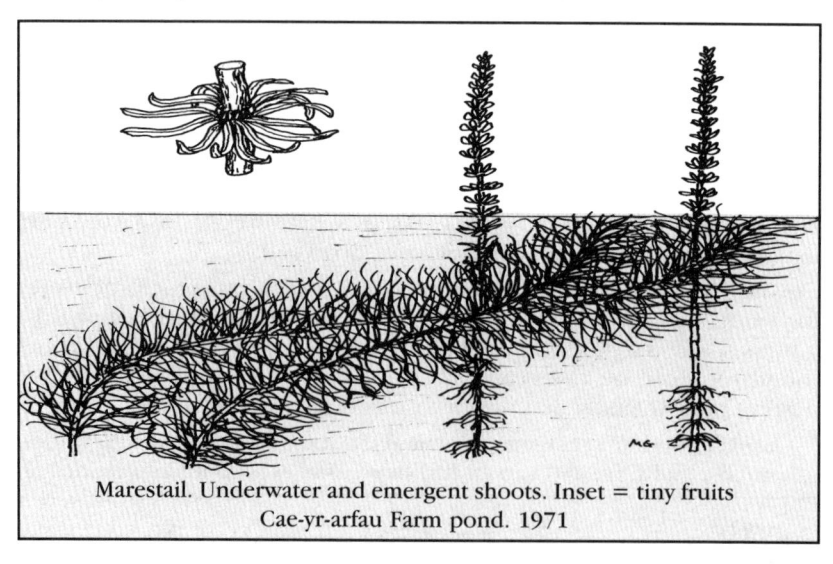

Marestail. Underwater and emergent shoots. Inset = tiny fruits
Cae-yr-arfau Farm pond. 1971

On my initial survey of this pond in 1971 I had been delighted to find a fine stand of mare's-tail *(Hippuris vulgaris)*. This is a rare species, a flowering plant that is often confused with the completely different horsetails *(Equisetum)*, which are fern-allies, a tail-over from the Coal Measure forests, bearing spores in cones instead of flowers and fruits.

The pond was kept open for cattle to drink and the mare's-tail occupied the centre, away from trampling hooves. Underwater parts, tassel-like and flowing gently with water movements, left no doubt as to why the name had arisen, but the shoots protruding above the surface were more like stiff bottle brushes, the whorled leaves shorter and holding tiny flowers and fruits in their axils.

Branched bur-reed was common, with water mint, water pepper and club-rush *(Eleocharis palustris)* almost equally so. Not often encountered, but both present here, were the two kinds of bur-marigold, the tripartite and the nodding. Others were various willow-herbs, persicarias and rushes, meadow-sweet and water forget-me-not. Almost wholly submerged were water starwort and marsh bedstraw, with the inevitable 'carrots', hemlock water-dropwort and fool's watercress marginal. The only species tolerating the edges of the lanes opened up by drinking cattle were brooklime and the little green toad-rush. Betony provided a touch of colour where the alders opened out.

When I sought out the site 23 years later it had improved immeasurably. Not only had it survived, but it had been dredged out and was four or five times the size, a good hundred yards long and up to nine feet deep in the centre, although not clay-lined, so liable to dry out partially in summer. The Nant Cessair ran in from the roadside through a smaller pond, which acted as a silt trap. then to the large one through a conical arch of decorative stone slabs.

An island crowned by an alder tree at the opposite end had been the further bank of the old farm pond. In its new private garden setting it was connected to the shore by a wooden footbridge with a hop vine encroaching onto a balustrade made from the two halves of an iron wheel from the winding gear of the Pentwys Colliery near Pontypridd. The twin wheel had gone to the Big Pit Mining Museum in the Gwent Valleys at Blaen Avon.

I saw neither marestail nor bur-marigold, but water plants had advanced rapidly since it was a silty sump with banks of bare soil (as seen in a series of photographs tracing its construction.) The floating leaves of broad pondweed *(Potamogeton natans)* were scattered over the surface, all others seen being marginal. These included reedmace or cat-tail and branched bur-reed, with a few others such as gipsywort, silverweed and figwort, including the uncommon yellow-flowered form, and many others of the original pond which had survived the bulldozers.

My visit was three months earlier than in 1971 and the kingcups, milkmaids and yellow iris were still flowering, augmented by garden plants, including some colourful azaleas, well clear of the limestone. A fringe of young alders less than a metre high would have to be checked if these and the grey sallows were not to hide the pond from view.

While I listed the flora a grey squirrel came gambolling out onto the fountain opposite. These are a menace in the garden and the soft fruit cage has had to be netted against them. A tail-bobbing pied wagtail watched for flies from a perch on the gunwhale of the moored boat. The three decoy pochard had attracted three mallard, a drake and two ducks, the one family of ducklings having dwindled from six to three. The nesting box erected for ducks had been taken over by moorhens, which reared three broods in it in 1993. Herons are frequent visitors and kingfishers have been seen.

I was shown a photograph of a grass snake swimming through the silty water when the pond was new. Apparently this ancient though restructured venue is teeming with amorous frogs at spawning time, these hopping, unobstructed, though rather exposed, across the lawns and invading the forecourt. Toads and newts also avail themselves of the stretched facilities and dragonflies emerge in season. My brief visit yielded few more invertebrates than a cluster of great pond snails, but most water insects have a flying phase and there would be no problems of colonisation. Fish, including brook trout, have been brought in by the inlet stream.

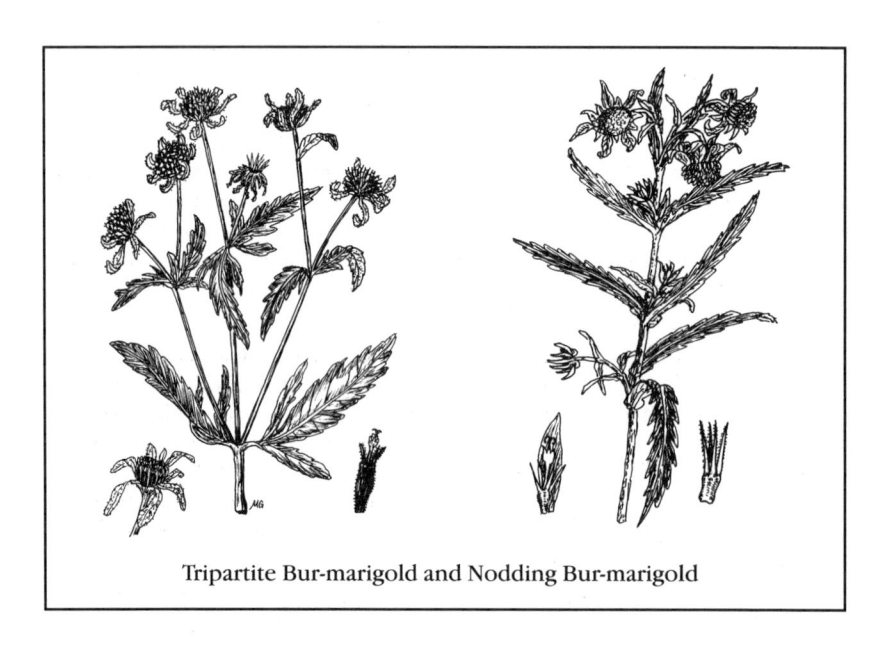

Tripartite Bur-marigold and Nodding Bur-marigold

2. Castell-y-Mynach Frog Pond

Cae-yr-Arfau and Cefngwarwig, a little to the east by the old railway line, were typical sixteenth century farms of 30-50 acres, but both were amalgamated into the Castell-y-Mynach Estates in the eighteenth century. Cae-yr-arfau, being nearer the road, was kept as the farmhouse and the other relegated to cottage status. It was at this time that Cae-yr-arfau was enlarged, the addition of the atypical rounded chimney thought to be a possible spin-off from the recently acquired techniques for building industrial stacks.

The Castell-y-Mynach family had become united by marriage with that of Pantygored, the other large estate, towards the end of the sixteenth century. Their rambling, whitewashed farmhouse still stands, imposing in its solidity. The roof of one wing sags slightly with the weight of the years and its mellowed stone tiles, the other has been spruced up with new grey slates.

Castell-y-Mynach Farmhouse

The stone barns have been tastefully restored as superior dwellings and a meeting hall, one having to be dismantled to ground level in the doing. Home paddocks and further fields were swallowed up in the early 1980s by a rash of new houses and this once dominating landmark is now hard to locate in the maze of residential roads leading nowhere. A fragment of unkempt green remained - hopefully destined for landscaping rather than yet more development. But no! By 1999 houses covered the whole, bar one last plot hard against the old garden wall, this already cleared for more foundations. It seems that nothing is sacred.

With the coming of so many new residents on the Castell-y-Mynach estate and the growing realisation of the value of wetlands for wildlife, amenity and education, a new pond was constructed. It lies against the northern link to Creigiau from the Cardiff:Llantrisant Road, at the end of Ffordd Dinefwr, which winds through the complexity of residential cul-de-sacs jig-sawed across the former farmland.

Although in the line of run-off of the Cae-yr-arfau stream and fifty feet lower, it is in a different catchment. The Nant Cessair swings away west from Cae-yr-arfau to fill the big Mwyndy or Maindy Pond on the Llantrisant Road between the two Miskin turnings, before joining the Afon Clun to add its quota to the Ely.

The new amenity pond is fed by Nant Coslech, which flows from the quarry, past Creigiau Farm and under the two railway lines, to tumble down through the woods below the church hall and post office, augmented by another spring marked by three manholes beside the garage. Water is led off above a little weir along a short leat to what soon became known to village children as 'The Frog Pond', and then back through a subsidiary woodland pool. From here it is culverted under the road, past a wet woodland inhabited (in 1994) by grey squirrels and pied flycatchers, then back again to the east side, past the old Mill House and on south as part of the Ely catchment.

In February dawns and dusks the pond can be heaving with randy frogs, exploiting the still water where their spawn will not get washed away. They achieve a skilful disappearing trick as the sun comes up, but leave parts of the pool brimming with spawn. The Community Council has taken the site over from Ideal Homes and installed seats for Mums to enjoy a respite while their offspring indulge in spells of pond-dipping.

Great Pond Snails in Creigiau Pond

When visiting in August 1993, I was intrigued to observe that a page from an exercise book floating on the smaller woodland pool had been taken over by no less than fifteen great pond snails *(Lymnaea stagnalis)*. Although true water snails, these have lungs and are air breathers, so have to pop up to the surface at intervals to obtain the necessary oxygen. They were using the paper as they might have used a water-lily leaf, but were quite ridiculously conspicuous, their normally camouflaged shells standing out like sore thumbs.

Fortunately the white 'plate' on which the meal was laid so temptingly, would not support the weight of the local song thrush, which had to view it from a distance, like an urchin peering through a cakeshop window. Two snails had failed to make it to the raft and were crawling upside down along the surface film, buoyed up by a bubble of air, or so it seemed. When a bubble was expelled by one, it sank immediately out of sight. These big southerly snails need abundant lime to build their shells and can only live in hard water such as this.

The current flowed briskly through this second pool, around alder trunks whose swollen bases were enmeshed in vagrant aerial roots, also seeking atmospheric oxygen, mangrove-fashion. Their shade excluded most aquatic plants, but the main pond was so overgrown at that time that it resembled a lush sward, necessitating a notice: "Danger, Deep Water".

Much of the plant mass was very edible-looking watercress. Lesser water-parsnip crowded the southern edge, with some yellow iris and woody nightshade. A rampant growth of golden-plumed sweet reed-grass *(Glyceria maxima)* with variegated white-striped foliage had taken over the roadward side. The streaky leaves resembled those of 'gardeners' garters', which sometimes takes off in gardens, but that is the variegated form of reed canary-grass *(Phalaris arundinacea)*, which has mauve or white flower heads. There was flowering fleabane and water mint and a fine spike of greater spearwort, an overblown buttercup which is rare in the wild and was probably planted here.

Clearance was carried out by the Caerphilly Mountain Countryside Service in the winter of 1993-94, the clods removed evidently dumped on the other side of Ffordd Dinefwr, as a fine display of water plants flowered there in 1994 at a higher level than the wild garlic, wood anemone and sanicle of the tall wooded bank where the Nant Coslech looped back to this side of the mainer road.

Fish disturbed during clearing operations included trout fry, three-spined sticklebacks, eels and a well-fed goldfish. Young men in their mid twenties reported catching bullheads in the feeder stream when they were boys, but have not seen these for years. Another task tackled by the workers at this time was the repair of the bridleway leading

Broad-leaved Pondweed in late July.
(Top) The upper 20cm of a metre-long stem growing in deep water and supporting the young stages of China Mark moths.
(Bottom) The land form on an almost dry pond bed.

upstream between garden fences. Plans for autumn 1994 included tree planting and the installation of a wooden platform to facilitate pond-dipping.

The cleared pond held no underwater vegetation by midsummer the next year. Only in the fast-flowing outlet stream were there sunken rafts of pea-green water starwort under banks of greater willow-herb and hemlock water-dropwort, with splaying stems of giant horsetail. Fewer marginal species remained, but these would advance all too rapidly.

We are on a geological boundary here, where Lias rocks change through Rhaetic to Trias, and some of the new houses in the lower south-west were built on a marsh, entailing much pile-driving and the laying of concrete rafts during their construction.

Castell y Mynach Farmhouse
(l) North & West faces (front), and (r)South & East faces (rear)

3. The Playing Field Complex

Aspect as well as waterlogging is important. Just a mile away at Crofta, on the lane to Miskin Manor (now a hotel and country club), vines are currently grown. They occupy a south-facing slope with thick hedges and shelter belts of tall trees protecting them from chilling winds. There is another vineyard at Llanerch, these 1990s enterprises a revival after a long gap since vines were grown at Castell Coch and Sully in the eighteenth and nineteenth centuries.

More everyday crops were formerly hand-tilled on allotments in the village heart, between the stretch of Nant Coslech following Woodland Crescent and the Creigiau Inn. This plot is now wooded and flanked by a children's playground, with new allotments being worked since 1980 alongside the old rail branch to Creigiau Quarry, to the delight of the local rabbits. Next to the neatly aligned vegetables there are tennis courts and another children's play area, and so to the impeccably mown playing field.

In early February 1984 most of the pitches were submerged under a reflective flood, with water gushing in from the quarry hill above and out onto the mineral railway below, but mostly it is in a fit state to support the vigorous play for which it was intended.

Little is allowed to flower on the grass sward. When Vickie Williams of Tyn-y-Waun, Mountain Road, found over a hundred bee orchids in a corner of the Pentyrch Playing Field in 1981, regular mowing was deferred until July, to allow for a fine display of flowers to delight non players strolling the boundaries. Exactly a hundred different wild flowers were listed in the field during April of that year, including unusual ones, like goldilocks and crosswort along the hedge and heartsease and field madder by the clubhouse.

There are no bee orchids on the Creigiau playing field, but it is a rewarding experience to walk around the periphery observing the wealth of blooms and their attendant insects. A beating of the bounds at the end of July in 1985 resulted in the knocking up of a flower list scoring not far short of the Pentyrch century. The day was overcast, but there were meadow brown butterflies everywhere, sipping the sweets of meadow flowers whose farmland counterparts have succumbed to the intensive methods practised on agricultural land. Families of tits swung through the bordering trees and six lugubrious carrion crows probed the turf for leather-jackets.

The roadward margin was a hedgerow community with hazel nuts and ripening haws attracting squirrels and blackbirds. The lacy hogweed flowers were a delicate shade of pink, an irresistable lure for the red and black soldier beetles, which seem to spend the whole summer in copulating pairs. Yellow spires of agrimony rose among purple knapweed and the heady perfume of meadowsweet lay heavy on the humid air - a focus for gossamer-light clouds of hover flies.

A riot of rosebay willow-herb romped through the pink-flowered brambles where I turned the corner by the old mineral railway. Tall hemp agrimony was crowned with more pink among angelica and greater willow-herb, whilst lesser stitchwort swarmed up the wire fence, sprinkling it with tiny white stars. In the unmown corner under the big oaks, silky-headed tufted hair-grass overtopped the wood soft-grass while tufted vetch and yellow pea straggled over the bushes, all enmeshed in the bristly clutches of cleavers. Capsid bugs fed on the thistle tops and small copper butterflies on tormentil flowers. The bordering stream was brimfull with summer rains, the spillover nurturing marsh woundwort.

Displaced soil by the tennis courts exhibited an early successional phase, with more flowers and less grass. Yellows predominated, with silverweed and creeping cinquefoil, perforated St. John's wort and cat's-ear. Purples, pinks and whites were provided by self heal, centaury and yarrow, pushing up where coltsfoot had flowered in March. Grasshoppers and froghoppers spurted all ways and gatekeeper butterflies sipped from bird's-foot trefoil.

The hedge separating the tennis courts from the quarry branch line represented woodland edge, with dogwood and field maple among the hazel. Black bryony and hedge bindweed surged over them all from a ground layer of hemp-nettle, hedge woundwort, campion and upright hedge parsley.

Rough grassland by the allotments afforded yet another habitat - and was no place for hay fever sufferers, with the feathery topped bents and fescues all presenting pollen simultaneously. Ox-eye daisies had been largely replaced by ragwort, with its almost inevitable tiger-striped cinnabar moth caterpillars. Both large and small skipper butterflies were busy pollinating the thistle flowers, ensuring a good supply of seed for goldfinches and siskins in winter. Large whites probably had more of an eye (or nose) for the brassica crops over the hedge, but the painted ladies had more catholic tastes.

The brackeny slope leading up to the quarry is a relict woodland site, with burdock, bittersweet, ground-ivy and speedwells beyond a fringe of salad burnet. Spoil tips beyond were a riot of purple buddleja and pearly everlasting at this season, with glorious splashes of pink musk mallow among calamint and eyebright. Grayling butterflies sat around among the last of the wild strawberry crop waiting for the sun to break through. Bees and drone-flies patrolled the nectar-bearing herbs, sun or no sun, with buzzard and kestrel providing a sky patrol above.

It is not necessary to chase around after an elusive ball to enjoy what the Creigiau playing field has to offer. Visits in spring, summer and autumn could bring the plant list to well over a hundred, so long as over-zealous groundsmen forebear the use of herbicides. Even in winter it can be fun identifying animal tracks in the snow and searching out their meal leftovers - nibbled nutshells, torn rose-hips or owl crop pellets.

4. Creigiau Quarry: History and Working

The Creigiau geological fault runs across the western entrance to the quarry and is followed by the entry route from the bend in Station Road. Softer Liassic limestone towards Creigiau village has been eroded down over the years to form the allotments and playing field and the level grazing land of Creigiau Farm. The harder Carboniferous limestone has withstood the ravages of time and rises abruptly towards Pentyrch, with the quarry biting into its western face.

The wooded hill which is being disembowelled is Coed-y-Creigiau in the north and Craig Ffynnon-dwym in the south, with the spring surfacing near the bend in the road. Northwards the quarry workings abut onto Millstone Grit, so all extensions must be to the south or east, or directly downwards, where a considerable reserve of suitable rock remains to depths of up to a hundred feet below the present floor.

The quarry was opened in the 1870s in the ownership of the Welsh Brick, Slate and Lime Company, to provide stone for the building of Cardiff Docks. When Guest-Keen moved its steelworks from Dowlais at the head of the Taff Valley to East Moors at its mouth, it earmarked the main output of limestone and magnesian dolomite for its blast furnaces and bought the quarrying enterprise outright. Two trains a day ran to East Moors in the Cardiff Docks area, carrying 5,000 tons of rock a week.

For a period dolomite went by road to the Margam Works of the Steel Company of Wales, but this function was soon taken over by Steetley, which was quarrying similar material from the Little Garth. East Moors took the whole output at that time, so when these works were closed the quarry went into decline and was itself closed in December 1977 by the British Steel Corporation, which held the lease from the Wingfield Estates until the year 2017.

Immediately prior to this the corporation had been considering investing a million pounds in new plant at the quarry, to supply their Margam Steel Mills, but when the market for steel declined, due to world over-production, this scheme was abandoned and the lease offered to other operators. The 'carrot' was eight million tonnes of proven reserves of dolomite suitable for the steel industry and with planning permission to remove it, but there were no takers.

Creigiau N. Railway bridge. May '94

By 1983 vegetation growth on the cliffs and crags of the irregular rock faces had transformed the site into an extended rock garden, full of flowers, birds and insects and a veritable treasure trove for naturalists.

That was when the Taff-Ely Borough Council threatened to take over the whole complex as a rubbish dump, and the Creigiau and Pentyrch Conservation Society rose in opposition.

When an interested quarry operator made tentative moves to re-open the quarry, the council mooted putting a compulsory purchase order on it, to keep their options open for dumping. In the event, however, no such horrific plan was implemented and the site passed to Tarmac Roadstone Ltd., which held the multi-million pound contract at the docks - bringing the history of disposal of the quarry products full circle to its beginning if stone is used in the Cardiff Bay Development Scheme. This was in mid 1983, when the reserves at Cefn Garw Quarry below Castell Coch were almost exhausted and closure imminent.

By 1993 the refuse disposal problem had been re-located to the smaller quarry at Tyn-y-coed near the Caesar's Arms, where a sophisticated "Refuse Transfer Station" for household waste was proposed. The quarry was owned by the Cossletts of Cae-yr-arfau, who extracted small quantities of stone from it for current building projects, but let the bluebell-covered slopes and nesting buzzards relatively undisturbed. The refuse station would involve new vehicle access from the Llantwit Fardre Road, portacabins and latrines for the staff, a steel building for bulk refuse containers and an open area for the recycling plant. It all proved more 'Council pie-in-the-sky', foundering principally on the difficulty of access from the narrow lanes. With luck, the bluebells and buzzards may carry on as before.

Extraction by Tarmac at Creigiau Quarry was delayed until 1987, when a small operation to remove 100,000 tonnes in 20 weeks was inaugurated. This material was blasted from an existing face, crushed, screened and stockpiled, with the use of mobile plant. In 1987 and 88 some 25 loaded lorries left the quarry every week day, reaching the Cardiff Road via Robin Hill, to avoid passing through the village centre.

In 1992 Tarmac requested permission to re-open the old mineral railway line as a haul road, to relieve pressure on this Pantygored-Robin Hill route. The Community Council was all in favour, subject to compliance with conditions such as the provision of a footbridge across to the playing field, the strengthening of culverts and provision of a suitable tree-screen where this did not already exist.

Discussions continued into 1994, when a new roundabout at the bend in Station Road was proposed as the point of access, to avoid re-opening the old quarry branch line and the stretch alongside Creigiau Station. It seemed that only the houses on the Pantygored Road were to benefit. At the time of writing, this scheme, too, seems to be foundering. How much more sensible if the railway had never been abandoned and the stone could go all the way by rail!

In September 1991 Tarmac held an 'open day', when interested villagers were able to view the development plans and be taken on a conducted tour. *"We have nothing to hide!"*. Eddy Bailey, geologist and conservationist who escorted one of the parties, reckoned that there was enough marketable stone here to last more than his lifetime, only 25 years of which had passed to date. He claimed to have been instrumental in saving a high spoil bank near the offices which was "lovely with self-sown flowers and shrubs in spring.", while the supervisor, who came of farming stock, had saved others and a skyline spinney, by diverting quarry roads and dumping to avoid the best stands of trees.

Tarmac had inherited a cluster of separate 'holes' or quarry bays, some dark red with contained iron, others grey. These comprised the main charm of the complex of leafy cliffs that so many of us had enjoyed rambling around in the late 70s and early 80s. Future working would inevitably destroy the magic by removing the ridges between, but would not be straightforward. At least three faults pass through the area, disrupting the beds, which lie at different angles and embrace a number of useless clay 'gulls'.

Creigiau rock is no longer used in steel-making. Most of the product now is for roadstone or river revetments, so the chemical composition of the rock is less vital than formerly. Large lumps are used for gabions, which are rocks confined in wire 'baskets' to stabilise road banks and river bends. A range of smaller sizes is produced by the excruciatingly noisy crushers, right down to the dust, which is mixed with shingle-sized 'gravel' for the cement works, to supplement the Liassic limestone dust which is the main ingredient of local concrete.

Hammers in the giant crushers have to be renewed every three weeks, at a cost of £6,000 a time. We were taken through the various phases of work carried out by the nine employees, from the initial measurement of surface irregularities with lasers to the blasting from the cliff brink and scooping up at their base.

Rue-leaved Saxifrage

Spring Whitlow Grass

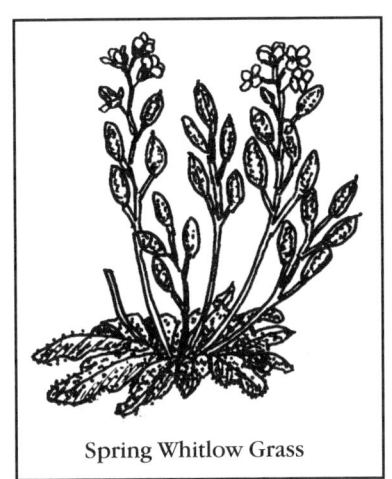

The current building recession had curtailed sales and there were stock piles everywhere, with pioneering plants pushing up irrepressible green shoots. One of the more mature heaps had been taken over by pearly everlasting, another had yielded a diligent picker several pounds of wild strawberries during the past summer.

Two public footpaths have had to be diverted.(The Ramblers have employed a man to walk some 200 miles of local paths to seek out closures or unacceptable deflections). Several pleasant walks remain around the back of the quarry and it is still possible to explore within, after reporting at the office and picking up a 'hard hat', preferably on a sunday when maintenance work is the main activity.

Nobody knows what the future will be, but at least the ultimate indignity of burial of those imposing cliffs under a mountain of trash has been averted. Tentative colonistion of open limestone faces by plants, as of mobile sand dunes, is infinitely more colourful and exciting biologically than the overall coverage of grass or trees in mature or 'restored' communities. It repeats the original colonisation of our ice-scraped landscape when the glaciers finally withdrew 10-12,000 years ago. While life remains it will move in - if we let it - whether on cliff or spoil heap, pool or rock slab.

5. Creigiau Quarry, A Decade of Reprieve

When quarry working lapsed in 1977 after a century of rock-shattering activity, the return of the vegetation was immediate and unstoppable. Phalanxes of creeping stems advanced on a broad front and longer hops were achieved by wind-borne and bird-borne seeds.

Some plants were there already, co-habiting stoically with the roaring machines. These had found man-made niches away from the competition that they are usually faced with in choking rye-grass swards and more generously lighted than on the unoccupied ground in the shade of oak or beech.

Raven, crow and fox had got acclimatised to the racket and learned to ignore it, hunting over piles of rubble where more timorous creatures - mice, voles and rabbits - crept out to forage under cover of darkness when the noise was stilled. Then, for ten years, Mother Nature had her way, unchallenged, and she is hanging grimly on since blasting recommenced in 1987. Even the mightiest machine is no match in the long term for her tenacity.

During the lull fluffy seeds of pussy willows and winged ones of downy birch wafted up abandoned cliffs and put down roots. Ants collecting tasty titbits from the Buddleja spikes dropped some on the way home and started new colonies to delight the nectar-seekers of subsequent years. Thistle down, 'blown' dandelion clocks and silky drifts of rosebay and other willow-herb seeds sailed to inaccessible crevices and spread nets of green to catch the falling disseminules of others.

Limestone dust settled out among the shoots, neutralising humic acids seeping from the dead remains and making everything right for the micro-organisms and tiny soil animals that sustain ground beetles and other carnivores. The ground beetles helped to sustain the jackdaws and little owls, shrews and hedgehogs, and these attracted feral or fireside cats, prowling in pursuit of food or fun.

'New' habitats have been in short supply since the final withdrawal of the ice and the course of early colonisation on sites scraped bare by bulldozers re-enacts that on ice-scraped faces. Nowadays there are more potential colonists waiting in the wings, ready to exploit the new opportunities, so the saga is more varied and interesting. Many, quite unable to carve themselves out a niche in established communities, can find a brief living here, until the more aggressive oust them once more.

On 5th February 1984 some fine clumps of primroses were flowering on a south face west of the main workings. Wild arum leaves were unfurling among the hart's-tongue ferns of the spoil tips, with hairy bitter-cress and barren strawberry flowers on otherwise sterile gravels. Old robin's pincushion galls on wild roses had been ripped open by predators, as had the hips themselves, their cheesy flesh spurned by finches interested only in the seeds within.

The ravens which habitually nest on the cliffs were rolling and cavorting in courtship flight against the steely February sky and thirty noisy jackdaws came rollicking out from a sheltered face. Two buzzards soared untrammelled in the north wind above the eastern cliffs. They came to ground during a sharp midday shower, but were sailing again over the woods when the sun broke through in the afternoon.

A kestrel hung, watchful, its hawk eyes probing the furthest embayment of the old workings. His sort were not the only mouse-eaters: the ground was lightly strewn with fox scats, impregnated with wisps of fur. A jay screeched, a magpie cackled and wood pigeons indulged in their monotonous "You two fools, you two".

An unbelievably tiny wren with an unbelievably loud voice trilled and chattered to any who would listen - and one could scarcely not. A robin delivered its always welcome winter song and a blackbird shrieked alarm at the close approach of a carrion crow. I enjoyed the unusual sight of five bullfinches together, handsome birds with rosy breasts and white rumps. Usually these move in pairs, both summer and winter, unlike the tits, which travelled through in chattering flocks.

A grey wagtail foraged ankle-deep in water spilling fast and shallow over rock slabs, as busily as if it was on river shingle. There seemed to be water everywhere, static puddles, moving sheets and well-defined streams, some disappearing into culverts, some bursting irrepressibly through the cracked rock from underground springs. Pied wagtails were also finding something worthwhile, presumably washed in from elsewhere, as the streams were too ephemeral to have life of their own.

By May 1986 the Carboniferous faces were as floriferous as any in the Derbyshire Peak District. Ploughman's spikenard, common mallow and perforated St. John's wort sprouted from vertical and horizontal surfaces alike. Lowlier were the gently perfumed banks of sweet woodruff and more blatantly aromatic wild garlic and Jack-by-the-hedge. Primrose and cowslip grew side by side, giving opportunity for hybrid false oxlips, more beautiful than either. On cliffs offering minimal roothold, tiny rue-leaved saxifrage pushed up among spring whitlow-grass, but the human eye, like the foraging insects' was drawn to the yellow mats of bird's-foot trefoil and creeping cinquefoil.

Nesting was in full swing by now, the ecstatic bursts from the resident wrens only part of the spring chorus from warbler, thrush and finch. The reverberating call of green woodpeckers echoed between the cliffs and a sparrow hawk dropped, arrow-like, onto a chaffinch, but missed.

Bristol Fach - now demolished.

By late July the wild golden rod and paler wood sage were romping over the spoil tips, hiding the tail end of the strawberry crop. Cushion calamint bore mauve heads almost as big as those of the wild marjoram alongside and nodding thistles bent elegant inflorescences over beds of knapweed and pearly everlasting. Grayling butterflies divided their attention between hop trefoil, eyebright and centaury, while large skippers and slow-flying bumble bees were drawn to the scented spreads of wild thyme.

These assets have withdrawn only marginally in the face of current quarry working. When the rock reserves are finally exhausted, or economics decree, they will move back to recreate the colossal, three-dimensional rock garden which graced that decade of neglect - unless our successors choose otherwise. The potential for a flower-decked "Pocket Park", picnic site and play area out of the wind will be obvious, and, hopefully, grasped.

The riotous colours and sun-kissed dust inside the quarry savours of a Mediterranean landscape. On a hot day it is almost a relief to retire from the shimmering heat reflecting from the cliffs to the cool shade of the surrounding beechwoods. Once the fine spread of bluebells has faded here, there is little intrusion into the sombre green light filtering through the efficient leaf mosaic.

A fine place to stroll is Craig Ffynnon Dwym south of the quarry, approached up the track where the entrances to playing field and quarry debouch from the public road. This was destined in the 1930s to be a motor road from Creigiau to the Pentyrch School. Its construction was inaugurated by Lt. Col. Wingfield, the land owner, to give employment to men thrown out of work at the quarry during the depression, when the steel industry which took most of the product went into abeyance. There was already a footpath here, leading uphill from Perrott's market garden, but a lot of rock had to be shifted to make the gradient suitable for vehicles, and who better to do it than quarry men?. After a year, with the job half done, the men returned to work at the quarry, and the route relapsed to bridleway status.

It leads through trees and over fields to Bristol Fach (Brysta Fach), a low thatched cottage demolished in the 1980s. The name arose because it was the storehouse for leather brought across the Channel from Bristol for distribution to local cobblers and saddlers.

Deviation from the path can be made through more interesting terrain around the back of the quarry - whose cliffs were firmly fenced off by the British Steel Corporation when they owned it. The no-man's-land of the clifftops, spared the depredations of livestock, holds a wealth of surprises for the curious, and those with time to stand and stare.

Chapter 8

THE SOUTHERN SLOPES

Introductory

The "three saucers" concept of rock strata comprising the South Wales Coalfield - from the Brecon Beacons to the Coastal Plain - is not so sharply defined in our region as it is at the eastern end of Cardiff's green backdrop of hills. For an initial explanation of the lie of the land, geology students are taken to that end of the Caerphilly Mountain Project area, where the three ridges - of Coalflied rim, Carboniferous limestone and Devonian old red sandstone - are clearly delineated, with steep-sided valleys between.

The uptilted South Crop of the Coalfield there is manifested as Rudry Common, its grass and bracken-clad moorland falling away south, past the coal miners' line of old bell pits, to the Millstone Grit valley and rising again to the Caerphilly-Draethen Road. From here the land climbs, green and cultivated, to the high wooded ridge of limestone, with its frosting of old man's-beard in winter, before dropping precipitously to the softer, eroded limestone shales.

Contours close together again on the climb up the dip slope of the old red sandstone ridge to Craig Llanishen, whose scarp face falls abruptly to the coastal plain. By the time the group has walked up and over all three from the Caerphilly Basin across Rudry Common to the Ty Mawr Inn in the south, there is no doubt in anyone's mind about the separate entity of the rims of the three geological saucers - and the ensuing beers will have been well earned.

Things are not so neatly explainable west of the Taff Gorge, but the pattern is still there. The Coed-y-Bedw valley nature reserve lies between the two northerly ridges, but the old red sandstone is manifested as two separate eminences. In the west is the 450 foot high wooded hill of Craig-y-Parc, rising only 100 feet above the valley separating it from Pentyrch to the north, but 250 feet above the Llantrisant Road to the south.

The second knoll is occupied by the Iron Age hill fort of Llwynda-ddu. This lies at 400 feet, but the land falls only to around 360 feet in the north, before rising again to 573 feet on the hill west of the Little Garth. Southwards the Llwynda-ddu mound drops sharply to 200 feet at Tyla Morris, from where the descent across the coastal plain is more gradual.

Both hills are composed of the hard conglomeritic layer which caps the upper old red sandstone. The softer rocks eroded away to the north are the narrow belts of lower limestone and limestone shale bordering the harder dolomite of the Carboniferous series. Those worn down to the south are the brownstones and lower marls of the Devonian series, which were subsequently partly covered by glacial drift.

Looking down on Pentyrch village from the west end of the Great Garth

The valley separating Craig-y-Parc from Creigiau and followed by the Robin Hill Road to Pentyrch is home to an interesting old quarry near Pantygored Farm. This cuts into thickly bedded crinoidal limestone and contains an old lime kiln. Crinoids are fossil sea-lilies (animals, not plants) and tell of the rock's beginnings under the waters of a coral sea some 300 million years ago - conjuring up visions of Australia's Great Barrier Reef for the more imaginative.

1. Craig-y-Parc Woods

The Craig-y-Parc Woods roll smoothly upwards to their 450 feet like an upturned basin when viewed from the south, their weather-resistant conglomerate the same rock that crops out as the 'capstone' on the summit of the Brecon Beacons north of the Coalfield.

Cutting across the lower south-western slope is the Creigiau Fault, bringing these harder red rocks up against the softer red mudstones of the Triassic Keuper marls, a wedge of which is interposed between the hill and the Pantygored quarry. The fault continues parallel to the old mineral railway line and the Llantrisant Road, leaving older rocks against the southern skirts of the wooded hill. Closest to the rising ground are the sandy brownstones and to their south are the softer red marls, both belonging to the Lower Old Red Sandstone series. The farmland between the wood and the road is bisected by the fault, with Parc-y-Justice Farm on the Old Red rocks to the north and Parc Side Farm on the New Red, Triassic, ones to the south.

Until the early 1990s the hill woodland was in the hands of the Forestry Commission, but only the lower southern border was extensively planted with conifers. The vertical striping arising from the planting pattern of broad-leaved trees is apparent from the road below at bud burst in spring and leaf fall in autumn, but is masked by the overall green of summer and in the leafless phase of winter. The area was one of many sold off by the Commission during the 1980s and 90s, the new owner taking over in 1993. Most is too steep to be used for purposes other than forestry and he hopes to upgrade the wood by removing diseased trees and planting new ones as necessary.

Craig-y-Parc is well endowed with public footpaths and a convenient circuit can be made from the western road junction near the 15th century Pantygored farmhouse on the Pentyrch-Creigiau road. This follows the southern flank, to turn north on the lane near Tynewydd and back west past the Craig-y-Parc School for spastics and so down the northern and western slopes.

This path-cum-bridleway leaves unobtrusively at a finger post between the new British Telecom Building and the Sewage Works (map reference ST 090 808), threading at first through the rumbustious growth of a derelict water meadow. To the left is a sea of bracken, alleviated by hemp nettle, perforated St. John's wort, upstanding hogweed and scrambling yellow pea. To the right is a veritable riot of tall marsh plants which defies penetration by man or horse when at its summertime height. Green spears of sedge and iris punctuate thickets of meadowsweet and greater willow-herb, while comfrey and large field cranesbill give seasonal colour. Butterflies and other insects abound in summer, but, by the end of winter, it is a stark wasteland of withered and collapsed stems.

When I came this way on a brilliant September morning in 1993, I was plunged suddenly into gloom on reaching the wood. It was bordered by the fast flowing brook which is stepped down across the garden of Rhuddin above and services the sewage treatment plant below - with the help of another from the alder carr across the road. A new wooden footbridge surfaced with non-slip wire mesh took me across: riders use the gravelly ford alongside.

From here on, whatever the weather, gumboots are a must, but the path is well used and walkers create their own detours where riders have made the main passage untenable. A lesser path to the left follows directly uphill: I took the more level one straight ahead.

To my left sunlight filtered through the lacy canopy of a lively green ashwood: to my right was the blank emptiness of an almost mature stand of conifers, where the ground supported no green leaf and no animal stirred. The only relief was where a few failed trees had been replaced by sycamore and fugitive sunbeams penetrated to hazel bushes and splaying fronds of broad buckler and male fern. A little pile of leftovers showed where a grey squirrel had been feasting on the nuts.

The sky was a brilliant rain-washed strip of blue, highlighting yesterday's raindrops, which scintillated on whiffling strands of spider silk strung across the path. It was saturday, but no riders had yet passed this way. An orb spinner sat among sparkling dewdrops on her gossamer 'cartwheel', and should soon be rewarded for her labours, as the air was full of dancing mayflies, glinting gold in the light rays with long tails adangle. More spiders let themselves down on silken threads. In spring such absailers are likely to be caterpillars - the mainstay of tits and warblers - but those which had escaped the birds had metamorphosed into moths long since, the tree leaves only tender enough to support them when young.

My feet fell soft on the carpet of leaves alongside the sloshy bridleway and the day was young, the song birds still in good voice, although it was not the singing season. There were many liquid notes among the squeaks and scuffles, interrupted by the clamour of carrion crows. A dark shape materialised from a dark corner as a buzzard weaved a dexterous path through the boughs into the open, where thermals should be building up to carry it aloft.

As I ascended, the conifers gave way to an even-aged stand of sycamores with red campion and orange sulphur tuft toadstools punctuating the green of violet and wood sorrel. Blinding shafts of light penetrated the beeches ahead and I found myself looking across the greenest of green clover fields. Two horses came bursting from a group of eight, with much whickering, and gallopped headlong to the shade of another beech, imbued with the rejuvenating aura of the sunshine after rain and the sheer exuberance of being alive.

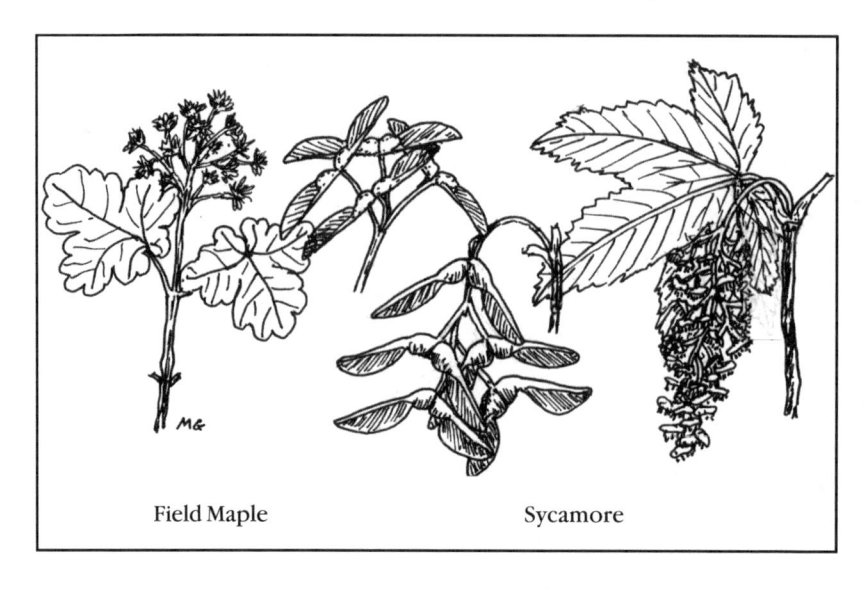

Field Maple   Sycamore

Hornbeam, in March, May, and August.

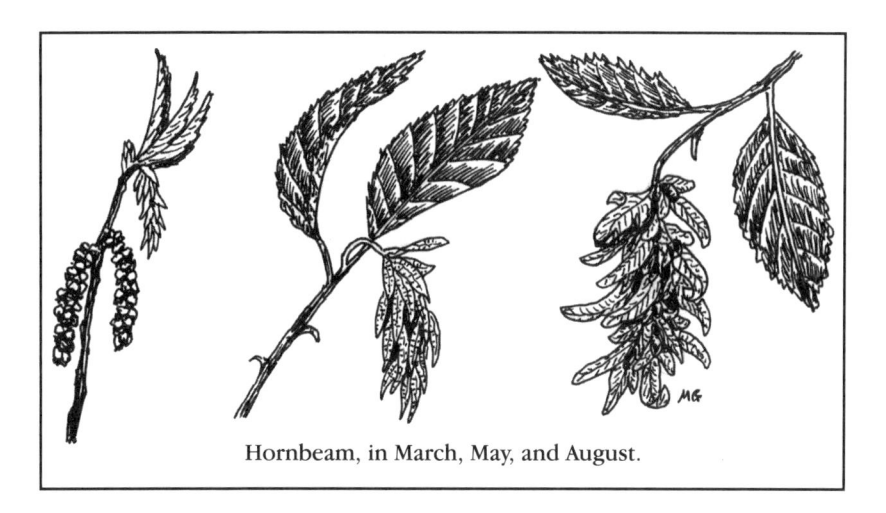

I watched them through the gnarled branches of an ancient lime tree, its mighty trunk lopped in the past, half way between coppicing and pollarding height, but this was long ago, the regrowths now almost trunks in their own right. One, practically severed from its hold, had fallen into the wood but still bore leafy twigs. Limes are difficult to kill once their tenacious roots gain a hold, although regenerating poorly from seed in our less than warm climate. Lopping ensures that their above-ground parts are always young and the roots continue to supply them with water and minerals long after the old trunk has hollowed with age.

Young lime leaves are irresistable to aphids, which siphon up more sap than they can comfortably hold in order to get sufficient protein from the sugary fluid - which oozes from their backsides to drip on all and sundry. But the honeydew phase was over, the leaves sprinkled only with the empty white exo-skeletons of the departed, possibly sucked dry themselves by the ladybirds that help to keep them in check.

The land fell away to the south, rising again in a spacious view. Drifts of foxgloves were a reminder that these soils of both the old and new red rocks were more acid than the adjacent Carboniferous ones. Freed from the choking conifers alongside, the wood burgeoned with holly, hazel and hawthorn below oak, ash and beech, with greater stitchwort, wood avens and herb Robert at their feet.

The path narrowed between encroaching brambles, then debouched through a little gate into a rough paddock where a green lane led down between high hedges to the old stone buildings and new polythene greenhouse of Parc-y-Justice Farm and on to the Llantrisant Road. A castellated stone wall draped with fruiting Clematis and

Cotoneaster reared from the upper corner of the paddock. This shored up a corner of the lawns of the fine terraced Craig-y-Parc gardens, with their walkways, staircases and balustrades of natural stone.

The splendid old gabled house was built by Tom Evans, a coal mine owner known as Tommy Glo Bach (Tommy small coal), who imported the stone from Somerset, transporting it by horse and cart from Cardiff Docks. The premises passed to the National Coal Board for office accommodation before being converted to the School for Spastics and other disadvantaged youngsters.

The walk can be shortened here by heading up under the oaks of the woodland edge and through a gap between the yew hedge of the garden and a wooded ridge. Only the inner faces of these fine yew hedges are trimmed. Here, alongside rolling sheep pasture, branches splay out at head height bearing a prolific crop of waxy pink fruits - providing shelter for the sheep but keeping the foliage out of their reach. This route emerges at the school carpark where the road makes a right angle bend.

The longer loop east leads along the foot of the paddock, with its meadow buttercup, knapweed, burnet saxifrage and ribwort. Meadow brown and common blue butterflies can be put up from the tangled grass on days too dull for them to fly spontaneously. Again one walks beneath overarching boughs of a lop-sided hedge - of sycamore and hazel this time - grown up after repeated ancient pleaching and cropped back by stock on the further side. The arched boughs simulate woodland sufficiently for the germander speedwell of the open to change to wood speedwell in its shade.

A dilapidated stile leads into a grazed sward of similar composition but with, the Yorkshire fog, cocksfoot and bent grasses grazed short; then up under ancient oaks to another giving acess to the lane. The steps down are prone to disappear under nettles by autumn, but the yellow arrow plaque nailed to the post marks this as one of the "Pentyrch Circular Walks".

The citizens of greater Pentyrch 'parish', and, indeed, Cardiff as a whole, are immeasurably blessed by the wealth of rural walkways at their disposal - so numerous that none gets overworked. The local Community Council had a blitz on footpaths during the 1980s, getting the waymarking renewed and producing an updated map of the astonishing number of ancient rights of way which are available for individuals and the corporate walks advertised in the local quarterly journal "Community Link". Many of these were led by the late David Jenkins, who busied himself in between by opening ways that become overgrown and repairing collapsed stiles and gates.

Turn left at the stile towards Pentyrch and left again at the corner of the lane where two more routes offer themselves: right to the old hill fort and straight on towards the Garth. The left option brings the walker back to Craig-y-Parc. The cherry laurel hedge by the corner house gives way to hazel on the right and a phenomenal holly hedge rises 15-20 feet alongside the undulating sheep field to the south. This lane takes only single line traffic, so the banks have to be trimmed back, but dog's mercury and wild strawberry thrive in spring and by September the right hand side is beautified by wild marjoram and field scabious under shorn dogwood, these lime-lovers reflecting the influence of the bordering limestone shales on that side.

Straight on past the entrance to the school, the walker is lured through the broad gate to the left rather than the lesser trail to the right, but this is a circular path used by the school and leading back into the gardens. A Forestry Commission notice points out that the track had been surfaced for the use of wheelchairs (it was being re-surfaced by a team of pupils and helpers when I passed in September) and was not to be churned up by horses's hooves.

Some fine beech, ash and sycamore trees persist here in a matrix of even-aged saplings, a few of them fallen, with new trunks rising in sequence along the old. The track debouches onto a levelled barbecue site, like an old charcoal burner's platform, surmounted by rain shelter, picnic table and circle of benches round the fireplace, with the woodland falling steeply away on three sides. The thicket below as the path curves back east along the southern flank of the hill can be alive with birds: flocks of tits and finches, tinkling goldcrests, cooing pigeons, scolding blackbirds and the music of robin and song thrush. The narrower, more northerly path wends its way down along the junction of conglomerate hill and limestone shale paddocks, and so back to the starting point near Pantygored.

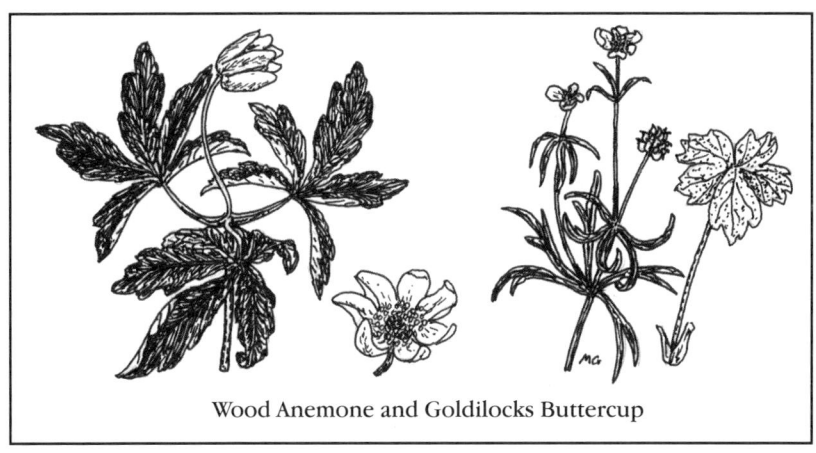

Wood Anemone and Goldilocks Buttercup

2. Old Pack Horse Road and the Llwynda-ddu Iron Age Fort

A few days later, on an equally blissful September morning, I extended this walk eastwards to the next road and beyond, around the tump marked as "camp" on the map and crowned by the Llwynda-ddu Iron Age Promontary Fort.

I followed a short length of made-up lane from the bend in the lane north of Tyla Morris, where I had previously turned back west to Craig-y-Parc (Map Ref. ST 100 808). Beyond a lone house this dropped steeply from 425 feet to 210 feet into the valley of the Nant Gwladys. The stream bounds exuberantly south beneath the alders of Coed-y-Wern to skirt the west side of the Prince of Wales Hospital at Rhyd Laver on its way to St. Brides-super-Ely to join the River Ely at St. George.

It was soon apparent that this was an ancient route, its origins briefly masked by the road makers above. Cart width and stony floored, it had become deeply recessed into the woodland by centuries of use, the banks heightening as I descended until I could no longer see over the top.

The only folk met throughout the morning were two local ladies on horseback, who informed me that this was part of the old pack horse road from Radyr via the iron age fort, across hill and dale to Llantrisant. I was further along then, near the old camp, and the information came in response to my comment on the antiquity of the hedges and query as to whether this was an old parish road. But that section was very different - sunlit and flowery - this part was gloomy to the point of eeriness, the earth banks faced with liverworts and topped with ivy and ferns. The former pleached hedges had relapsed into lines of kinky-based ashes and sycamores, suitable terrain for hobgoblins, any lesser components long since the victims of shading.

The track functioned as a shallow watercourse for a tributary of Nant Gwladys, but the stones had been scoured free of silt, so no mud wallowing was necessary. Most of the mini boulders were granular and purple-red - the flaggy sandstones of the Upper Old Red Sandstone Series - some were speckled with glistening white inclusions of quartz - the quartz conglomerates of the 'capstone' - a few were perforated with elliptical holes where limey inclusions had dissolved away - the honeycomb sandstones as seen north of the coalfield where the Heads of the Valleys Road crosses the Taff Fechan Gorge.

They made for rough walking and I was not surprised to find a cast horse shoe. Were the pack mules shod, I wondered. Probably they were, as even the geese were 'shod' with a simple mixture of tar and sand when being driven to market. Few passed this way now, to judge by the excited curiosity of the fat steers in a paddock falling steeply to more woodland in the north. Theirs was the only grass, the rest was wooded.

A broken terra cotta pipe suggested a former culverting of the Gwladys brook under the track, but the crossing had reverted to a stony ford, bordered by golden saxifrage and draped with woody nightshade berries. This was an alder wood, with ash and hazel and a little dog's mercury among hart's tongue and other ferns. The mule track ascending eastward from the stream functioned as another tributary.

At a T junction I turned right, to emerge at an overgrown "Footpath" sign in the slaughtered margin of the wood by the Pentyrch to Rhyd Laver Road. Felled trees had been replaced by elder and other shrubs and the whole had taken on the look of a tropical jungle, except that the enveloping tangle of lianas here was massed with the white trumpets of greater bindweed instead of the blue ones of morning glory.

I have explored this valley woodland in April, when its waterlogged floor is bright with the pink flower balls of marsh valerian, which gets overtaken by the meadowsweet, angelica and hemlock water dropwort of summer. There were celandines and wood anemones then, with budding bluebells and early purple orchids. A pony paddock had been carved out and there were other disturbances, but the loss of tree cover had not yet affected the flowers. Woodland species persisting included vetches, speedwells, primroses and yellow archangel among the bird-sown currant bushes in the roadward edge. Alongside my downward route there had been little apart from arum and three-nerved sandwort, but passerines sang from shady and sunny parts alike.

The next section of the pack horse trail leads to Lwynda-ddu House and is metalled, the banks as tall as before but the hedges kept in trim. They are mainly of hazel and field maple but are topped here and there by tall oak, beech or ash. Holly, elder, field rose and bramble were laden with fruit, but the black bryony berries outshone them all and there were still clusters of flowers on the honeysuckle.

Despite the narrowness of the lane, which necessitated a shaving of the banks, I counted 31 flower species on them, plus 3 ferns and various grasses. It was 22nd September, but there were still blooms on the buttercups, bush vetch, wild strawberry, wood avens, red campion, herb Robert, enchanter's nightshade, broad-leaved willow-herb, rosebay, foxglove, hemp nettle and nipplewort, while the slender St. John's wort was in excellent form. The lady on the horse said "You should see it in spring". I could imagine it, when the greater stichwort, hedge garlic, sweet violet, yellow pimpernel, yellow archangel, wood sorrel, butterbur and many more were in flower.

The lane climbed to the Llwynda-ddu knoll at over 400 feet on the Upper Old Red Sandstone, where a field gate gave access to the slightly hollowed paddock surrounded by a low grassy rampart, with broom bushes scattered among the yellow flowers of cat's ear along its western flank. The old fort entrance is thought to have been on this side, between two of the big oaks spaced along the ridge, although the deep ditch and outer bank is better marked at the other end. Llwynaddu means the Black Grove and the site is thought to have been used by the Romans as a 'marching camp' for their legions pressing west.

It occupies a commanding position, well chosen by the ancient defenders, who would have had unobstructed views west to the Craig-y-Parc Woodland, north to the upstanding dolomite ridge and east to where the land falls away to the Taff Valley. The Ely Valley and the coastal plain are spread beyond the brownstone slope to the south. The only occupants of the hill fort at present were two horses, their feet disturbing the summer's crop of grasshoppers, craneflies and spiders. A relic of the past was a small round-ended trough hollowed from a single block of sandstone under the tattered hawthorns of the eastern ditch.

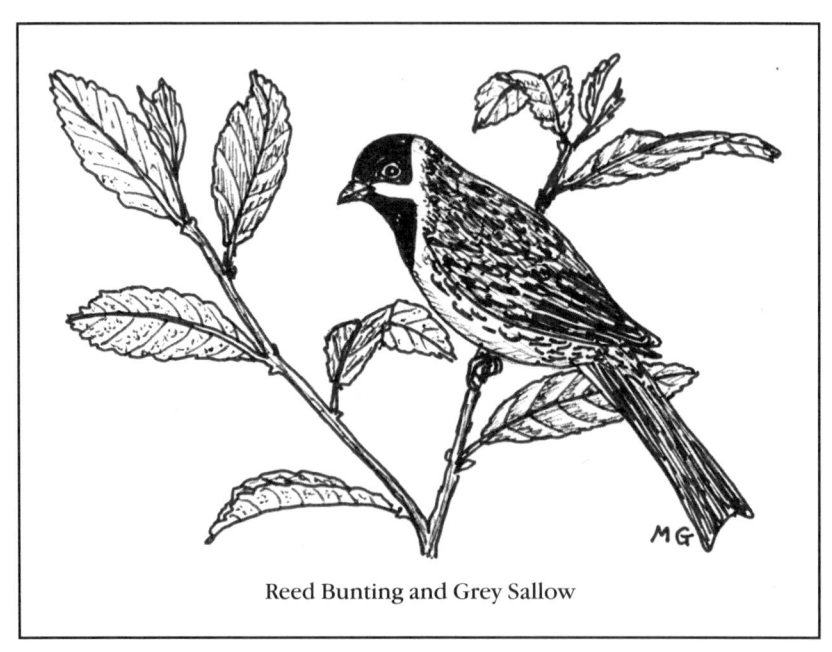

Reed Bunting and Grey Sallow

The public right of way goes slightly beyond to a cross roads, where two left turns bring the walker down across the fields by a few battered stiles to the Pant-y-caerau Garden Centre, which is on the bordering limestone of the Carboniferous ridge.

A little way up the Pentyrch Road from the garden centre is the Cwm-y-Fuwch Quarry, cut into Dolomite with barytes veins, its entrance shrouded in undergrowth. Behind the pink-flowered Himalayan balsam and white-fruited snowberry would-be investigators are greeted with a notice on a rusting iron shed: "Dangerous Quarry. No right of entry". Nature has taken over and few road users can know of its existence.

Back a few steps from here, a gate by Llys-y-Coed House leads west onto a broad grassed track fenced off from the horse paddock along the foot of the wooded limestone scarp. This crosses the tumbling waters of Nant Gwladys, which make a delightful feature in the garden alongside. Three modern manholes on the path are evidence of the utilisation of underground water at the junction of two rock layers. There is good blackberrying to be had along the first stretch and good bird watching along the whole.

The sun was hot and I was clad for autumn. Past the first hedge gap, I moved into the edge of the ashwood, discarded a layer and lay down to enjoy the tail end of summer. A late warbler was fidgetting among the maple twigs just above: a jay was feeding on one hawthorn and a robin singing from another. A gentle tapping impinged on the silences between the snatches of song - a delicate tapping in search of bark beetles rather than a rapid communicative drumming. The greater spotted woodpecker revealed itself later in a looping line of black, white and crimson.

A wood pigeon indulged in a spell of springtime cooing, chaffinches chinked and tits cheeped. Some carrion crows sailed out to harry the two buzzards that were minding their own business against the brilliant rain-washed blue over the valley, but failed to flurry them. A noisy flock of house martins went twittering across and the call of a yaffle came echoing eerily over the hills as I drowsed off. When I roused a squirrel was busy with a hazel nut closeby, having accepted my recumbent form as part of the landscape. He scuttled up a beech as I stirred to trek over the sheep paddock, climb a ricketty gate and run the gauntlet of a large mob of fat but placid beef cattle, back to the footpath sign at my starting point.

160

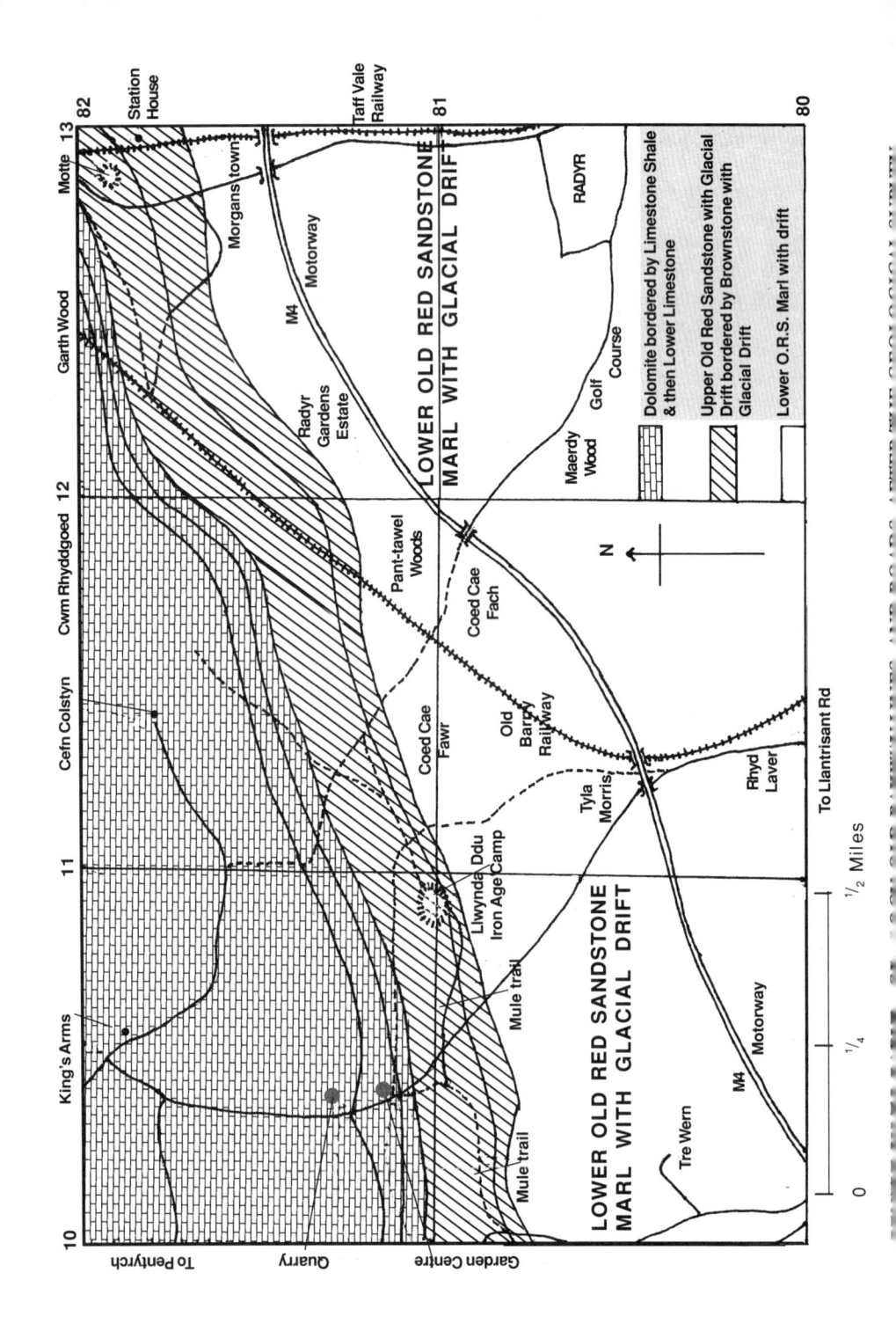

3. Coed-Cae and Pant-tawel Woods

The Llwynda-ddu loop can comfortably be added to the Craig-y-Parc walk and can be extended eastwards from the hill fort to the woodland complex of Coed Cae and Pant-tawel. For those who like to take life more easily or linger to observe the emergence of secretive wildlife, the Pant-tawel stretch can be approached across the M4 footbridge near the Radyr Golf Course (Map reference ST 113 812), or along the old Barry Railway line from the Ty Nant Inn at Morganstown.

The woods lie above Lower Old Red Sandstone Rocks, but these are covered by mounds of glacial drift, with the old Barry Line cutting through their centre. They were brought to public notice in 1976 when the M4 was being built and Wimpeys were seeking planning permission to dump subsoil from the motorway in them.

Local residents valued their high amenity value and local natural history expertise was marshalled to assess their biological potential. The evidence proved sufficient for permission to be witheld and, hopefully, the woods are now protected in perpetuity, although they have changed hands and been threatened with building development, Tree Preservation Orders have lapsed and been renewed and the C E G B has felled a swathe of timber to accommodate an electricity power line. Always this nibbling away of prime sites has to be watched. An important loss in the 1980s was the public walkway along the section of railway line from Rhyd Laver. Pant-tawel translates as *'The quiet hollow'*, but that was before someone thought up the motorway!

In her assessment of the flora, the late Dr. Mollie Percival (botanist at Cardiff University who had the rough shooting rights and visited regularly over fourteen years) classified the site as *"A Western Atlantic type woodland with holly and ivy and a good shrub layer of hazel, elder, spindle and honeysuckle."*

Red squirrels had lived there up to 1950 and there was an isolated sighting in 1976. Mammals currently present include fox, stoat and weasel, and there are green and greater spotted woodpeckers, woodcock and pheasant. The damp hollows provided important refuges for grass snakes and amphibians and the rare great crested newt as well as frogs and toads. She commented on the rich fungus flora, listing 31 of the larger species in her report.

Of special interest are the bird's nest fungus *(Cyathus striatus)*, two fairy clubs *(Clavaria (Clavulina) cristata* and *C. cinerea)*, stinkhorn *(Phallus impudicus)*, scarlet fly agaric and death cap *(Amanita muscaria* and *A. phalloides)*, the big edible parasol *(Lepiota (Macrolepiota) procera)* and brackets such as the dryad's saddle *(Polyporus squamosus)* and oyster of the woods *(Pleurotus ostreatus)*. Wood anemones, which

161

Shaggy Inkcap or Lawyer's Wig fungus *Coprinus comatus*

form the principle spring cover on the woodland floor, may be affected by the anemone smut fungus *(Urocystis anemones)*, whose spores burst from the leaves as black pustules. Roy Perry of the National Museum of Wales has identified others, as well as lichens and mosses.

Dr. June Chatfield, also of the National Museum, investigated the snail populations and came up with a list of 19 species, many of these from the dank sides of the old railway cutting - which might have been the first to be lost if dumping had gone ahead. Snails and slugs are not everybody's favourite creatures, but can be indicators of dampness, acidity and other features of the habitat.

Some will rasp away at the shells of their fellows when lime is in short supply, even to the extent of killing them, and some of the shells of the rounded snail *(Discus rotundatus)* were found to have been treated in this cavalier fashion by their contemporaries. The hollowed glass snail *(Zonitoides excavatus)*, which is similar, but lacks the ribs on the shell, is indicative of the acidity of the boulder clay and/or leaf litter covering what is a predominantly limey stretch of country.

The point snail *(Acicula (Acme) fusca)* is of particular interest in being one of only two operculate or lidded land snails in Britain. The other is the better known land winkle or apple snail *(Pomatias elegans)*, so common on the limestone of the Glamorgan Heritage Coast. The point snail is, veritably, "a winkle come ashore", living only in very wet sites among shaded moss and rotting leaves.

Oniscus asellus and *Trichoniscus pusillus* are two species of woodlice which enjoy the acid dampness, along with craneflies *(Tipula paludosa)*. The large black, garden and hedgehog slugs *(Arion ater, A. hortensis and A. intermedius)* are here. Drier parts favour harvestmen and spiders, green-gold weevils and ground beetles.

Spring is the best time to visit the Coed Cae Fawr Wood to the north- west of the old railway line, when the pools are aglow with kingcups and golden saxifrage and the banks with bluebells and anemones. There are three kinds of violets here, the common heath dog-violet, the early wood violet and the sweet violet, which last can be pink as well as the usual white or rich purple. Moschatel, woodland loosestrife and pignut follow, with an abundance of marsh plants where some of the western poplars have fallen and lifted their roots to leave little pools. Three species occurring here at 300 feet above sea level instead of the more usual 700 feet are petty whin, ivy-leaved bellflower and meadow plume thistle, bringing the May flower list up to 86.

Coed-Cae Fawr, also known as the Tyla Morris Woods, can be approached by heading east along the old pack-horse road from Llwynda-ddu hill fort. Within the wood this path is joined by another ancient track leading north-west by the southern end of Craig Hir Wood (the wood of the long cliff) and across fields to emerge at Greenhurst by the King's Arms Public House in Pentyrch. A little beyond the track junction an iron farm gate takes the public right-of-way onto the rolling grassland of Cefn Colstyn Farm, past two ponds and on to the Little Garth Woodland - the walk described in our next section.

The united paths lead south-east, sunk deep beneath the general level by centuries of wear and muddy as a result, but walkers have worn a higher, drier track alongside. While the woodland floor is most colourful in spring, the opposing hedgerow attains its full potential in autumn, when the maple leaves change through the yellow adopted by the hazel's to a peachy red: when the hollies are loaded with festive berries and the blackthorns and whitethorns with the subtler shades of sloes and haws. Trails of black bryony berries loop across hip-bearing briers and the silvery sheen of old man's beard lightens dark corners.

A narrow paddock with some splendid oaks lined up along its centre intrudes into the wood just before the broadening of the path to 7 m where it crosses the old railway line to become Pant-tawel Lane. The railway cutting is so deep and so filled with trees that its bottom is invisible from the stone-capped brick parapets of the bridge, which, like modern bridges taking tiny lanes across motorways, seems a mightier construction than circumstances required. From here on the lane is surfaced to serve the white Pant-tawel Cottages, with their clustered parked pleasure boats, and to take motorised trailers across the motorway to Morganstown.

The accompanying map shows Coed-Cae Fach Woods and Pant-tawel Woods lying between the cuttings of the old railway and the new motorway, with Coed-cae Fawr towards the northern ridge in the west.

Coed Cae Fach lacks the sheets of celandines, anemones and bluebells so well seen in Pant-tawel and the best kingcup pools were fenced off in 1976 on land earmarked for the motorway and new houses to the south. The boulder clay mitigates against lime-lovers and the ramsons or wild garlic and bistort or snakeroot of the northern hedges are replaced by more acid-tolerant lousewort and foxglove. (Bistort flowers, under the name of Easter ledges, are used to make Easter puddings in Cumbria and the Yorkshire Dales). The 96 different flowers listed here in May include bugle, sanicle, marsh valerian, devil's bit scabious and yellow iris. Guelder rose is common and fallen timber is characterised by charcoal textured pustules of the fungus, *Hypoxylon fragiforme*.

Pant-tawel Wood proper is more diverse, the drier, beech-dominated part qualifying as a bluebell wood. It is undulating, the beech of the knolls passing through mixed oak, ash and sycamore to birch, alder and sallow in hollows, which again hold impressive stands of marsh valerian.

Enter the wood by the path leading north-east alongside but high above the motorway. This provides a visual feast of colour in the fall, but an abomination of unrelenting noise rising from traffic which, mercifully, is invisible through the screening poplars. Telegraph wires overhead ensure that this bit will remain open to the sun, allowing the tawny bracken of autumn to rise 2-3 metres above the path and a riot of shrubs and semi-shrubs to border the woodland, with its berry-bearing hollies reaching unplunderable heights and ensuring winter sustenance for birds.

Slip through a large gap in the fence where the wood begins to narrow, ignoring the public path leading on across the fields, and circle back towards the railway. This path leads into a great amphitheatre of magnificent beeches, some with two or three short massive trunks, others real timbermen's trees, with tall boles rising straight and true before any major branching occurs. After the spring flush of flowers the ground is largely bare, carpeted with the copper coinage of bronzed leaves. This could be Burnham Beeches, despite being so near the recognised western extremity of beech as a native tree in Britain.

An old field boundary bisects the beechwood, this part mossy bank and part tumbledown wall, with smaller trees to the east, on land probably released more recently from grazing. Crossing this, the path descends into the now less deep railway cutting and can be followed all the way to the Ty Nant Inn at Morganstown. Broom bushes flower alongside in spring, western gorse in autumn and, since the 1940s, the almost inevitable Buddleja in summer.

This is a haunt of sparrow hawks and there are plenty of passerines to sustain them. Summer sees missel thrushes as well as the smaller snail-bashing song thrushes, marsh tits as well as the common garden species. Haw hedges and undulating grassland attract fieldfares and redwings in winter and I have watched a field vole trotting bodly over the snow here in broad daylight in search of fresh greenery or succulent roots.

In December and January flocks of goldfinches and greenfinches busy themselves on the seed heads of thistle and burdock. The more secretive bullfinches of the hedgerows concentrate on the dried out blackberry pips. House sparrows around Cwm farm prefer mugwort and can be watched rolling each tiny seed around in the beak as much as 4 times to de-husk it, before swallowing the kernel and shaking their heads to get rid of the chaff. It seems a lot of work for small reward. Wood pigeons are flocking at this time, magpies are everywhere and pheasants can be flushed from the long grass.

Foxes by an old pleached hedgerow tree.

4. Permanent and Seasonal Pools

Both the old Barry Railway and the new M4 Motorway sweep northeast from their intersection with the road crossing between Tyla Morris and Rhyd Laver. The railway heads for the line of hills, disappearing into a tunnel, to emerge high above the Taff Gorge, which it crossed on the Walnut Tree Viaduct, now demolished.

The motorway stays south of the ridge, intially in a cutting and then on an embankment, as it descends more gradually than the surrounding countryside to cross the River Taff at a less spectacular height, but still above the valley roads. Between the old and new routes is undulating pastureland, the bedrock lost under hummocky glacial drift, particularly in the west. The mounds are terminal moraines, dumped by the moving ice of the valley glacier as it finally melted on its passage south to the sea.

We have lost the rim of the outermost rock saucer here, the more resistant layers of the Old red sandstone being moulded onto the flank of the dolomite hill of the Little Garth, and extending south beyond the railway in their more easterly section. The brownstones and marls merge imperceptably into the coastal plain.

Their covering of boulder clay follows the gentle undulations and is sufficiently impermeable to hold water in its hollows, some from surface run-off and some from underground aquifers, where water bubbles out at the junction of two rock types. Some of the resulting ponds are permanent and tree-bordered, others are ephemeral 'winterbournes', appearing seasonally to swallow up hedges and fences and then disappear, like the turloughs of the Irish limestones.

The drier, western part of this farmland is classified as Grade 3, the more waterlogged section alongside the old Barry line as Grade 4. (Grade 1 is the most agriculturally productive, grade 5 the poorest.)

A line of springs emerges along the junction of limestone and sandstone, similar to other spring lines east of the Taff. Those at Cwm Nofydd, between Rhiwbina Hill and the Wenallt, succour areas of wet fen, draining off into streams. The Morganstown ponds here have no outlet streams and the soil is insufficiently peaty and alkaline to form fens, so water builds up in winter to spill over as topography dictates.

When water level in the lowest and largest of the seasonal ponds rises above hedge height, as in 1982, the spillage cascades across the derelict railway to supply a linear pond below, while two other substantial bodies of water sit in hollows of the land rising to the brink of the M 4 cutting beyond.

Ponds which remain, year-round, are bordered by trees and used by livestock for drinking. Water pepper, silverweed and flote grass choke the shallow end of one but, as the banks heighten the water deepens, supporting greater water-plantain, water starwort and lesser duckweed. Voles tunnel between the roots of bordering hazels and wrens forage at the base of a venerable pedunculate oak. Hawthorn and holly berries supplement those in the hedges for resident and wintering thrushes. The soft silts, where leeches lie in wait for water snails, are imprinted by the feet of heron, duck and moorhen. This is one of two permanent ponds south of Pentyrch where mallard and teal fly in at dusk to feed and can be flushed by late walkers.

The other lies closeby to the west, over a stile near a small gate, and is bigger, less tree-shaded and so better vegetated. There are big oaks both ends and some sallows in the north, with good access for stock. Moorhens breed here, and possibly mallard, as these ducks are often flushed in pairs. A fine show of trifid bur-marigold occurred in late summer in 1993, when there were broad patches of fool's watercress and brooklime and a western ridge of mint with a little gipsywort, starwort and duckweed.

The path curves south-west from here, through a gate by a water trough where the level is controlled by a ballcock, and on past a long-abandoned disc harrow to an old well, covered now by concrete. Hard by is a ground level concrete drinking trough and the urgent sound of fast flowing underground water issues through the cracks. Sited in a depression, but not at the lowest point, this area is covered with stones, from the size of footballs to huge slabs of quartz conglomerate, probably moved back from cultivations and serving to fill a former quagmire.

Another three ponds to the east are seasonal, devoid of trees and much more visible from above. I watched children sliding on thick ice on these in the hard weather of February 1986 and saw only the tips of metre-high fence posts protruding above water during the wet spell of December 1982. At that time three further hollows up the hill towards Pentyrch retained a day-long lining of snow, when the white blanket had melted from the rest - suggesting the chill imparted by a water-logged soil.

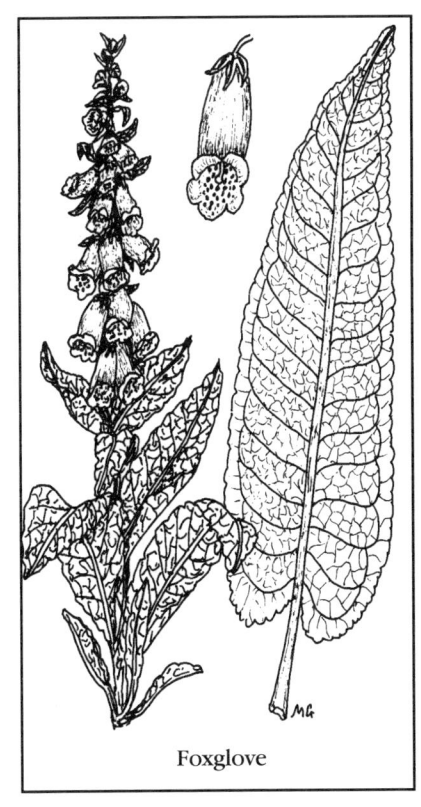

A decade later, judiciously placed drainage channels had helped some of the excess water into the linear pond along the embanked side of the old Barry Railway. This empties into a large woodland pool where moorhens nest when water persists into the summer, deferring its annual dwindling to a leafy quagmire scattered with fine bur-reed and angelica plants.

Just beyond is Cwm Ffynnonau Farm at Morganstown, the farm name translating appropriately as *'The valley of the springs'*, but usually shortened to Cwm Farm. Water leaves by the vigorous stream flowing past the Ty Nant Inn and followed by an often muddy track lined with elm, holly and hazel. In recent decades these have been joined by the dreaded Japanese knotweed, whose hollow stems the local boys soon learned to fashion into pea shooters when it started on its all-conquering invasion. Where

Foxglove

the stream leaves the pond it is crossed by the broad, walled farm track which was formerly bridged by the Barry line, but now climbs a ramp to join it.

The railside wetland is where children go for frogs, toads and newts, but a series of small woodland-edge pools towards Pant-tawel also harbours amphibians. During May, when marsh violets, lady's smock and wood sorrel are in flower, large and small tadpoles from different broods cluster rounds islets of splay-based alders, the trees formerly known as clog-wood because of their suitability for making the everyday country clogs - precursors of the gumboot. By September these have metamorphosed into adults and gone into hiding, while the only flowers are those of lesser spearwort, wavy bittercress and woody nightshade.

Although the seasonal ponds had not filled by September 1993, much of the rushy grassland between railway and woodland was ankle-deep in water, with rainbow-hued bog iron ore on tiny puddles occupying hoof prints. The wiry patches of hard rush had been left alone by the livestock, but soft rush, the less common of the two here, had been chomped off half way up. Both rose from a thick moss layer and sheltered hairy willow-herb and toad rush. Thirty years before the eastern end of this field had been covered by an 'alluvial fan' of gravel washed down from the quarry above, but these scars have healed.

Field fungi enjoy moisture but not water-logging and do better on the higher slopes. They are typified by wax-caps, the various *Hygrophorus* species, and more fragile frilled domes of poisonous *Panaeolus semiovatus*. I have found robust puffballs *(Lycoperdon caelatum)* ten centimetres across in December. Although exposed to weeks of rain, snow and frost and overlain with sodden oak leaves, they could still emit clouds of bone-dry, cocoa-coloured spores when tapped.

5. Loop Walk South of Garth Wood

The boundary separating Mid Glamorgan and South Glamorgan Counties between 1974 and 1996 extended well north to the east of the Taff, leaving the Cefn Garw and Blaengwynlais Quarries with the coastal plain, but dipped south in our area, so that most of the Little Garth (Walnut Tree) Quarry was in Mid Glamorgan. A pleasant two mile stroll from the Taff Valley through the calcareous beechwood of the Little Garth's lower northern slope was entirely in South Glamorgan except where it deviates north along the western slope to Ton Mawr Quarry and back into wetter, more acid birchwood with foxgloves. The homeward route, south and east, is in the parish of Morganstown, by pond and pasture and along the old Barry Railway line until this disappears into its tunnel below the outward route.

A convenient starting point is the Ty Nant Inn opposite Pugh's Garden Centre at Morganstown, with ample parking space and ample liquid refreshment on return. A knobbly path leads up to the wood between the Ty Nant Inn carparks and the allotments. Our route goes left from here but there are two possible detours.

Straight on up, almost to the summit, brings one to the entrance of the famous Garth Cave. A shorter ascent to the right emerges on the low south brink of the old Ty Nant Quarry, with the purple dolomite cliff towering majestically to the west and sheltering a young woodland of Buddleja, birch, ash and sycamore. Opposite, across the river, is the ruddy gleam of more naked dolomite, crowned by the fairy-tale castle form of Castell Coch. One cannot but wonder how much narrower and more impressive the Taff Gorge must have been before its walls were quarried back on both sides, making room for yet more commuter routes to follow the toll road, canal, works feeder and railways of the early days.

This little path leads on, over the humps and hollows of inumerable overgrown mossy spoil tips; a sequestered enclave of flowers, birds and butterflies. As beautiful as all old quarries are when left to themselves instead of being choked with our unwanted trash, this site is worthy of exploration in its own right.

Back westward, it is apparent that some of the beeches are very old survivors of past industrial upheavals, their smooth grey bark almost obscuring paired initials (carved by young lovers?) at the end of the last century. Bracket fungi on decaying stumps tell of some which have succumbed to the ravages of time.

Trees beyond are more slender; an even-aged stand originating in 1919 and replacing those taken for use in the first world war, when these slopes were almost clear-felled. A dilapidated notice at the start of the main trail warns that blasting may occur at any time between 8 am and 5 pm and advises caution when the sirens are sounding. No products of blasting have spilled down here, however, for many decades. Only at the far end of the wood are there the big mossy boulders of spills long past and loose chippings of more recent ones.

The beechwood is atypical in having a two tier canopy and healthy understorey. An almost leafless palisade of straight grey trunks separates the sunlit leaf canopy high above from the laxer canopy of younger beeches with hazel and field rose below. A low sward of beech seedlings forms a continuous carpet alongside the path, overtopped here and there by dogwood, false brome grass or wood sedge. Just uphill is a taller thicket of beech saplings approaching 2 m high.

Obviously there is a lot of surplus beechmast here some years, not adequately dealt with by squirrels, mice or tits, although there are plenty of these about. This might provide another opportunity for pannage - if a pig-keeper was willing to risk his animals straying into the quarry, to their own detriment, or the allotments to that of his neighbours' crops. None of the older beeches look set to fall for many years and, if one did, its close-set contemporaries would soon expand to fill the gap, so these young hopefuls are doomed to choke each other to extinction. Their mission is to add humus to the limey soils, the orange mounds thrown up by moles seeming singularly lacking in organic matter at present.

A few paths diverge uphill, one to a little quarry face where stone had probably been taken for building long before the steel industry disembowelled the hill behind. Others led into the thistly paddock

View east towards Castell Coch from Cwm Farm, Morganstown.

below. The main path passes over the old Barry Railway near its tunnel entrance, on a sturdy brick and concrete bridge scarcely wide enough to take a cart, whose wheel tracks were being usurped by hart's-tongue fern and seedling trees.

The next section is deeply recessed and can be muddied by tractor wheels and horses' hooves, with water ponded back behind the ridge used by foot traffic. Then it ascends past a breeze block generator house supplying high voltage electricitiy by underground cables to the rusty corrugated iron stone crusher above. Beeches give way to sweet chestnuts, long-needled pines and a few birches at the disturbed wood corner where paths diverge.

The right hand option terminates in heaps of chippings by the current workings, the left hand one, which I was eventualky to follow, leads down to Pant-tawel, but the one straight ahead is well worth exploring. The stile leads into an idyllic run-down paddock crammed with flowers, even so late into autumn as on my visit. A haze of white fairy flax replaced the more substantial blooms of eyebright: there was purple self-heal, red clover, pink centaury and yellow agrimony, with autumnal hawkweed in a matrix of fine grasses and bracken surging in on all sides.

Two paths lead north to Ton Mawr but are little used and difficult to follow beyond the first few hedge gaps. I returned to take the one across the deeply incised wooded valley of Cwmrhyddgoed, which demarcates the south-western flank of the Little Garth, descending from the 590 feet lost summit to 350 feet. A curved line of hazels surviving from an ancient hedge have been engulfed by woodland. Ducking under their arching boughs I threaded between cankered, coppiced ashes. The ash:birchwood beyond dropped steeply into what appeared to be a dry valley, although formed by water originally - in periglacial times, probably, before melting of the permafrost allowed the stream underground.

Forty long-tailed tits came loping into the birch above my head - a cloud of irrepressible sprites, from which emanated chirrupping trills and sibilant cheeps, their rounded forms smacking of the perennially 'baby bird'. Chaffinches spinked, a nuthatch whistled and the call of a green woodpecker came ricocheting through trees holding the inevitable chattering magpies and shrieking jays. A buzzard had sailed from the woodland edge as I entered and this spent the next hour circling over Radyr village, but I saw nothing of the resident peregrines.

I tried several paths, probably negotiable in winter but firmly blocked by bracken and bramble at this season, and finally returned to the cross roads at the corner of Garth Wood proper, taking the right hand fork of the left hand option, to descend between the wood extension and a belt of scrub. Mole hills were more organic here, linnets looped overhead, while speckled woods and the last of the hedge browns cavorted in the sun.

Sustained by juicy blackberries, I headed down between a flowering thicket of western gorse - the species of more acid soils - and the blue heads of devil's-bit scabious, which is less demanding of lime than are its close relatives. I had passed from limestone to the acid drift overlying the sandstone, with middle-of-the-road plants like knapweed, bird's-foot trefoil, yellow pea and eyebright predominating.

This land belongs to John Llewellyn of Cefn Colstyn Farm on the ridge to the north, the fine old seventeenth century long-house having recently changed hands. The wood to the west is Graig Hir, the wood

Western Gorse branches freely,
when not constantly nibbled by sheep

of the long cliff, but the land below is open and grazed. The path is not always easy to find, but passes close to one of the permanent ponds, with stiles and gates leading to the Coed Cae Woods, where one can circle back to the old Barry Railway for a more level return.

The track is mostly very wet, drying out as it approaches the more porous limestone to re-enter Garth Wood, and the western part can be a sheet of ice in winter. I sat awhile on a rusting disc harrow - abandoned from a former farming era - admiring the carpet of cinquefoil and mouse-ear hawkweed as I 'picked-my-own' from the surrounding brambles. Rosebay and wild carrot clothed the bank below, with the last few ox-eyed daisies and tufted vetch heads. Common blue butterflies, commas and large whites had replaced the speckled woods and hedge browns of the woodland edge and I spotted the odd small tortoiseshell.

Turning away from the track to Cwm Ffynnonau Farm, I followed the now less obvious railway line between increasing harbingers of the limestone such as dogwood and clematis, and ducked through a long tunnel of buddleja to pass under the bridge that I had crossed earlier. A few score yards along the rock cutting and I was passing under the ivy-draped arch leading into the spacious, double-tracked rail tunnel.

This was built in 1898 to take coal from the Rumney Valley to Barry Docks, and was closed in the late 1960s. The walls are stone-clad for the first few feet, then of natural rock, into which alcoves had been cut and arched with brick to provide sanctuary for a couple of men from the roaring passage of trains, the evenly curved roof continuing as far as light permitted me to see. Locals habitually walked through the tunnel when the trains were running and it was still possible to do so with the help of a good flash lamp, although part of the track forms something of a drainage sump. It emerges into a cutting at the end of the Taff viaduct which took the line across the Gorge for about 70 years until demolished in 1970.

No vegetation grew within, the scum of yellowish green algae on the rock soon changing to less light-demanding blue-greens and then fading out, while no plant-based soil had accumulated over the ballast. A little path connected with the outward route where fluttering bats and carolling song thrushes overlapped in the autumnal dusk.

During the early 1990s the eastern end of the railway tunnel towards the Taff Gorge was blocked by tall, impregnable iron doors, possibly to protect warehouse storage space within.

A year or so later a big new road, furnished with traffic lights, kerbs and tarmacadam pavements was driven through the valley south of the Little Garth. It started along the former stony track to Cwm Farm near the Ty Nant Inn, veering away from the old Barry railway line up the southern slope towards the M4 cutting. This was the access to the new estate of Radyr Gardens on higher ground to the west - red and yellow houses in a flambuoyantly laid out campus, and the likely precursor of more to the south - the unwanted developments bitterly fought by the inhabitants of Morganstown and Radyr, but in vain.

This area had been part of Cardiff for some years before 1997, when the three villages to the north - Creigiau, Pentyrch and Gwaelod - were sucked inside the city boundaries. Residents are hoping and praying that the rash of building is not the beginning of the end of the valued green belt that formerly kept the urban impact at bay.

Houses were still going up in Radyr Gardens throughout 1998, the twisting complex of roads giving each a different view - a fine panorama of still largely wooded hills, from Castell Coch frowning down on Tongwynlais, past the Wenallt radio mast and across the coastal plain to the ragged skyline of Redland's Walnut Tree Quarry in the Garth Woods.

The estate occupies the drier part of the drift-covered platform slung between Garth Hill and the Morganstown lowland, the westernmost houses separated from the cutting of the M4 by no more than the bush-lined footpath leading along the brink of the cutting to the little bridge from Pantawel Woods. Ground at the ends of the cul-de-sacs was scheduled to be landscaped into recreational areas with re-surfaced paths. Residual clumps of bushes hosted long-tailed tits, wrens and greenfinches even as building proceeded: an eminently desirable place to live but at the expense of more of the community's precious buffer zone.

The walk followed in this section had not been encroached upon, the developemnt lying south of the old Barry line. A new path and stile leads up to it from the estate road - which has been built across the middle of the pond where the track to Cwm Farm led up to the old railway. Two culverts take water under the road, from the watercress bed with hemlock water-dropwort above to that with bur-reed below.

Summer flowers on the newly raised embankment - foxgloves and wild garlic, white campion and hedge woundwort - illustrate the mix of imported soils, acid and alkaline, arable and woodland. Conspicuous in June among the yellow trefoils of the railway track, above sheets of flowering moon daisies, are the delicate cups of two-flowered cranesbill, an uncommon species.

Ruins of Ysgubor Fawr on morainic mounds south of the Little Garth

Chapter Nine

GWAELOD-Y-GARTH
ON THE WESTERN FLANK OF THE TAFF VALLEY

Introductory

Nestling in the lee of the Garth Mountain, Gwaelod-y-Garth enjoys a milder climate than the rest of the parish. Pentyrch and Creigiau are not only exposed to the prevailing westerlies but Pentyrch, at around 400 feet (122 m), is twice as high as Gwaelod's centre, at pub and post office cum shop.

Rain may be falling on unfrozen ground in Gwaleod while Pentyrch's frost-bound soil is becoming carpeted with snow. Topography and aspect are of vital importance in determining microclimates. No wonder the weather men cannot get it right for us all.

Gwaelod is divided between the rocky slopes moulded by the glaciers of past millennia and the alluvial infill of the plain below. Living within it, as I have done for the best part of four decades, its physical characters are difficult to assess: one cannot see the wood for the trees. It is necessary to be on the other side of the River Taff, with the gaze tilted upwards, to appreciate how its buildings cling to the mountainside.

The name implies that it lies at the foot of the Garth, but the elderly who toil up the Zig Zag path from the Pont Sion Phillips footbridge to 'Main Road' after visits to Taffs Well for doctor, dentist, chemist or public transport to Cardiff, dispute this. The hub of the village is well above that. The "South Wales Echo" of 1st February 1974 carried an article to this effect under the title: "Suffering: the Folk who live on the Hill". The opening paragraph by Alun Rees reads:

"Perched above the Taff Gorge, Gwaelod-y-Garth has a population of more than 500 and a large percentage of the villagers are getting on in years. But a trip to town has taken on the proportions and rigours of a route march - plus a few terrors."

Alun Phillips, aged 77, who had frequent need to visit Cardiff, spoke for many when he said: *"It's absolute murder for me walking back from Taffs Well up that path and it's worse for my wife."*

Approaching the footbridge along the path from the Taffs Well Inn and Junior School, it is very apparent how far the houses of Gwaelod struggle up the steep eastern side of the Garth Mountain - even now, when so many of the more elevated dwellings, the miners' cottages, have fallen into ruin.

The bulk of the houses along 'Main Road', including the pub and the shop, are lost to view among the trees. Below them are more trees, larger ones, clinging tenaciously to the precipitous slope delimiting

175

the Taff flood plain and merging upstream into the easier gradients of Garth Olwg, built to replace the miners' obsolete cottages on the Garth.

Downstream it grades into the Heol Beri and new estates of River Glade and South Glade. A few buildings are scattered above the notorious hairpin bend on the Mountain Road under the craggiest, though not the highest, part of the Garth.

From the Taffs Well side of the footbridge it is easy to spot the northward dip of the rock strata on the mountain top, the smooth green ridges aligned in sequence, like the defences of an Iron Age fort and matching their fault-displaced counterparts of Graig-yr-Allt on the eastern side of the valley.

When asked by the headmaster of Gwaelod Infants and Junior School for 150 words on the physical geography of the village for the children to translate into Welsh and put on their computers, I was sorely taxed to so condense the vagaries of the terrain and found myself resorting to a diagram.

The flanks of the Taff Valley, cut by ice and water over aeons of time, are set much wider than the river itself, which meanders from side to side of the great rift which it has carved through the Border Ridges.

In the heart of the village, where walkers tackle the Zig Zag, the Taff is on our side of the valley, cutting into the base of the mountain and leaving the broadened expanse of the flood plain to the larger settlement of Taffs Well on the other side.

Downstream, the often turbid flow loops away eastwards, making way for the old iron furnaces and brick works, now Heol Beri. After passing the Ynys roundabout under the garlic-scented heights of the Little Garth and negotiating the Taff Gorge, the river turns transversely away across the valley between Ynys House and Pugh's Garden Centre north of the Morganstown motte and back to hug the base of the scarp under the elevated settlement of Radyr perched on the brink above.

There is just room for the main valley railway line to follow along the foot of the cliff, where salmon filter through the new fish pass by Radyr Weir and black-headed gulls drift to the edge of the fall, picking titbits from the water surface, to repeatedly fly back and repeat the operation. Radyr Station is handily adjacent to the footbridge leading across to the Forest Farm Country park and Glamorgan Canal Nature Reserve, but the next road bridge is a long way down, at Llandaff North.

Upstream from Gwaelod is another big eastward loop of the river - from Gedrys and Maesbach on the west side to Nant Garw, with its famous porcelain kilns, now a museum, on the east. This leaves ample room on our western side for the fertile acres of Ynys Gau Farm and the marginal slopes of Garth Olwg.

Thus Upper Gwaelod lies on the ancient Coalfield rocks, some of

42. View from Pentyrch (top of Heol Goch) to the Garth Mountain (left) and Graig-yr-Allt. May 1969

43. View north from Garth summit. Efail Isaf (left), Church Village (right). August 1999

44. 45. 46. 47. Four of the ponds on the undulating glacial drift between the Little Garth and Morganstown. December 1982 Tree-bordered ones are permanent, the others drain away in summer. Note the drowned fence and hedge.

which are buried under glacial till, and Lower Gwaelod on the new river gravels with their topping of alluvial silt. 'Main Road' runs roughly along the divide between the two, as it climbs from near river level in the south to the 200 foot contour line through the heart of the village.

The accompanying map, emphasising this 200 ft and the 125 ft contours, gives an approximation of today's relationship of the River Taff to its flood plain, although the marginal rising ground obviously does not follow these contour levels exactly.

North from the village centre, the lane that 'Main Road' has become follows the contour, turning under the railway to meet the river where this converges once again on the western cliff at Gedrys and following it to the road bridge at Upper Boat. The river flats along this stretch are across the water and occupied by the Treforest Trading Estate.

Our winding lane was the main Cardiff to Merthyr road before the larger one was built through Taffs Well, that now superceded by the A 470 trunk road along the foot of the hills behind.

While the steep wooded cliff scaled by the Zig Zag path from the footbridge divides Lower Gwaelod into two separate entities, Upper Gwaelod is continuous, embracing the lower slopes of the Great Garth and the Little Garth and dipping into the valley between them at the hamlet of Georgetown.

Strictly Ynys Gau Farm lies in the parish of Llantwit Fardre but, tucked below the main village street as it is, it must be regarded to all intents and purposes as an integral part of Gwaelod y Garth, with Llantwit half a day's march away.

The aberrant boundary follows the wiggly hedge line of Salem Field below Salem Chapel in Village Main Street - a field that was smaller before the removal of sundry other hedges. It was said to have been established in the thirteenth century. Which came first, I wonder, the hedge or the political boundary - which does not feature on the tithe map of 20th August 1839?

1. The River Flats Downstream

The road into Gwaelod-y-Garth from the south runs along the top of the Radyr scarp, dropping almost to river level before crossing the Ty Nant tributary from Cwm Farm at the Ty Nant Inn. This stream has been diverted south, to burble along two sides of Pugh's Garden Centre, past the rugby field and some hay meadows and then under the motorway, to enter the Taff before this converges on the Radyr cliff.

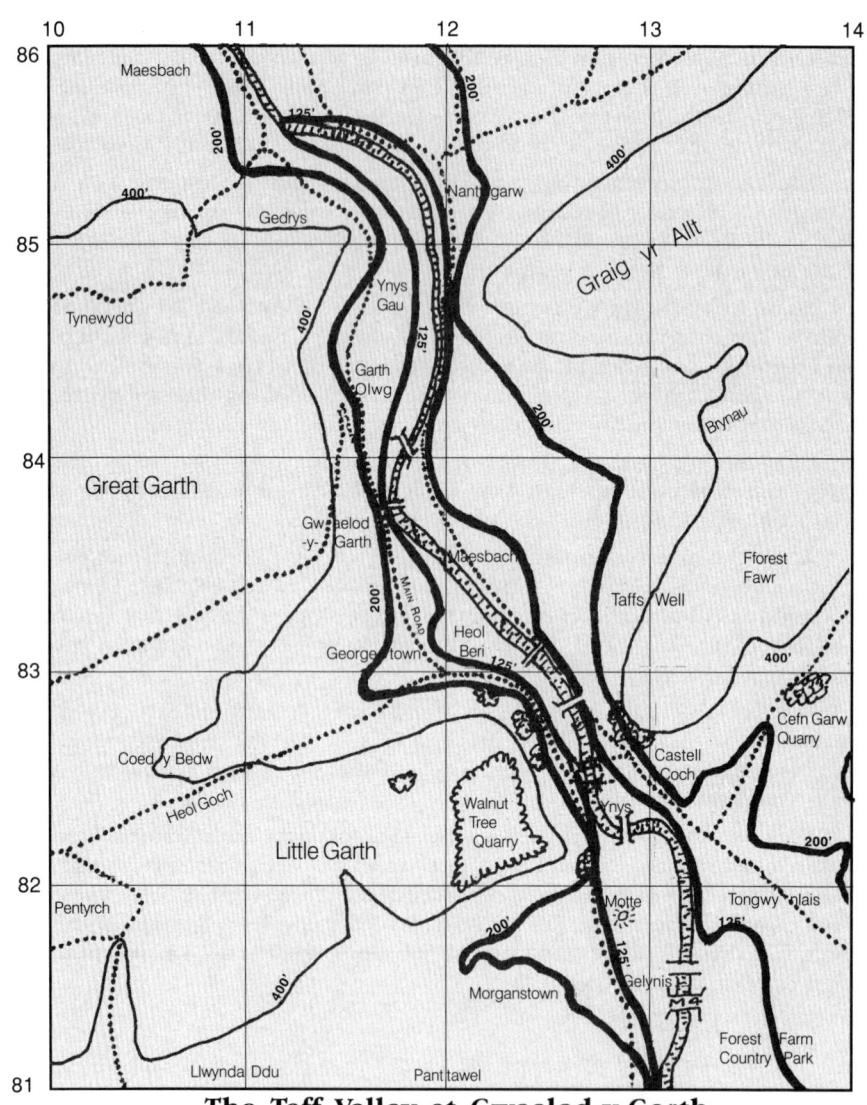

The Taff Valley at Gwaelod-y-Garth
(emphasising contours to show extent of Flood plain from Maesbach to Morganstown)

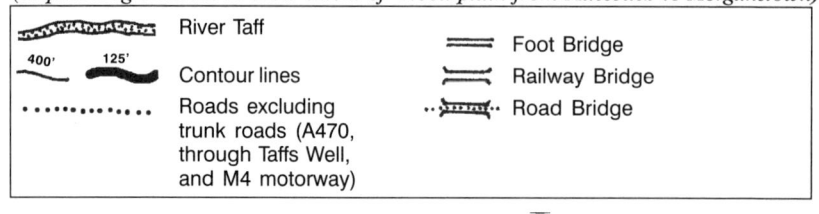

〰️	River Taff	═══	Foot Bridge
400' 125'	Contour lines	⇌	Railway Bridge
··········	Roads excluding trunk roads (A470, through Taffs Well, and M4 motorway)	··▭··	Road Bridge

178

It may have been used to power the corn mill near its mouth, where three tracks from the wooded scarp converged, but the mill pond and leat were destroyed when the railway was built. The mill was in ruins by the turn of the century and the cowman's cottage was later pulled down as being unsafe. A little way above was a water spout where the draft horses drank.

The stream is wooded throughout, flowing briskly over a clean bed and nurturing yellow irises and hemlock water-dropwort, with fine stands of giant horsetail and a few true reeds and guelder rose bushes on the calcareous clays alongside.

The hayfields upstream of the M4 crossing are bright with perforated St. Johns wort, knapweed and yarrow when late hay cuts are taken. They are bisected by a track from the Morganstown layby to the Gelynis Fruit Farm, whose 48 acres were split assunder by the intrusion of the embanked motorway in the 1970s.

Small in size and conveniently near retail outlets, Gelynis was traditionally run on market garden lines. Early on there were glasshouses with flowers, tomatoes and cucumbers, then lofty polythene tunnels with chrysanthemums. Old daffodil and tulip bulbs were set out in the orchard and along the adjacent bank of the Taff.

In the mid 1990s after a period of neglect it was planted with soft fruits, sweet corn, salad crops and vegetables and from 1997 the public has come to 'pick-their-own' strawberries, raspberries and beans. A plot alongside now bears upstanding vines. The stately stone barns, where barn owls and swallows nested in the hay lofts and house sparrows under the eaves, have been renovated. The whole site glows with hanging baskets, flower containers and strategically placed clusters of bedding plants, with red currants spilling over the garden wall near the site of the old toilet.

The ancient river sediments nourish good crops, as well as a prolific weed growth from the interim years of fallow, so seed eaters are catered for as well as the blackbirds, thrushes and grey squirrels which take their toll of the soft fruits. A mighty sweet chestnut tree, laden with burs in 1998 and 1999, stands in the riverward corner of the old orchard and is claimed to be as old as the house,- making it a veteran of 430 years.

Honey bees commute from hives in the garden to pollinate the flowers, massing to sip water from standing puddles when the weather dries out in summer. Their foraging season is prolonged by the proximity of the late-flowering riverside balsam.

Gelynis Farmhouse, with its impregnably massive walls and pleasant mullioned windows, is a Grade II Listed Building. It is old enough to have a legend of a ghostly blood stain, derived from a woman killed by Loyalist troops during the Civil War.

Part of the North face of Gelynis Farmhouse - August 1999

The old stone faced well in the forecourt descends to 26 feet (8 m), bringing it below the level of the nearby Taff, but with the slight current of an underground stream drifting through. The iron hand pump on its top is half hidden now by variegated periwinkle and dwarf conifers. A fox has been seen helping itself to the wild strawberries pushing out from cracks in the surrounding paving. Tested by health inspectors, the water was found to be of better quality than the mains supply and has been used to supplement this - for house and greenhouses - until quite recently.

The land was bought in 1570 by Hugh Lambert, an iron master from Tonbridge in Kent - from one Ton to another! He came here at the invitation of Sir Henry Sydney of Sussex, to work the Pentyrch Iron Mine and Forge. He, it was, who built Gelynis Farmhouse, which is approached from the Tongwynlais side of the Taff across the Iron Bridge.

This is now a footbridge, carrying a broad iron pipe taking water from the hilltop reservoirs above Tongwynlais, down under the river bank and through an inspection chamber to the bridge and so on to Barry.

In the mid 1990s the pipe ruptured between Mill Lane and Ivy House Farm, a parked vehicle subsiding into the washout to remain suspended. Repairs included the shoring up of the adjacent river bank, washed out by the spillage.

Prior to its use as a water conduit, Iron Bridge carried the Pentyrch to Forest Halt Light Railway line, which took coal from the riverside mines down the west bank from Rhyd-yr-Helig north of Gedrys through

Gwaelod and iron from Gwaelod's riverside forge to the Tin Plate Works at Melingriffith.

The existing structure was made well above the level of possible spates to replace an earlier Iron Bridge built in 1815. That was the year of the Battle of Waterloo and the bridge was named the Waterloo Bridge. It was destroyed in the phenomenal August flood of 1877.

The old grass-grown railway line bears off obliquely north-west, past Gelynis farmyard towards the Ty Nant Inn, as a hedged, grass-grown track, to meet the Taff Vale Railway at the Pentyrch sidings. The Old Station House, where some of the former freight was transferred to the main Taff Vale line for transport to Cardiff or Merthyr, is still inhabited. Vehicle access to it ceases on the wrong side of the railway line, the last lap across the track being achieved on foot.

The only road for vehicles to the Gelynis Farmhouse is from Morganstown, also across this main line, with its ten minute service of double-coached 'sprinter trains' slotted between the freight trains, thundering past to serve the new industry in the Valleys. These add their disruptive cacaphony to the constant rumble of motorway traffic, the more staccato notes as that pounds across the river bridge and the wind-induced hum and rattle of the bird scaring wires along the top of the raspberry rows.

The father of Mr. Bale, the current octogenarian occupant of the house, started farming the land here in 1906. His son tells how the forecourt was ripped up to bury the water pipe along the north side of the house, well ahead of the disruption of the motorway across the south. The railway runs a small field's width away to the west and, in July 1999, a new main sewer was installed across the bed of the Taff to a raised manhole at the junction with the fine red brick conduit some 4-5 feet diameter, built in Victorian times on the west bank north of the Iron Bridge.

Despite all this and the constant din, the visual prospect still pleases, with deciduous woodland rising beyond the intrusions to either side and a good view past Castell Coch through the gorge.

In recent years the Caerphilly Mountain Project Area has been extended south of the M4 on the west side of the Taff, right down to St. Fagans, but the boundary dips back behind Radyr, so the western Taff flood plain is excluded. So also is the Forest Farm Country Park on the other side of the river and the Long Wood of the scarp beyond. That area includes the Glamorgan Canal Nature Reserve but large chunks are currently being filched from within as a trading estate, extending from Amersham International to British Telecom and other large structures!

Upstream from Gelynis Farm and the rugby field is the Morganstown relic marked on maps variously as 'Castle Mound', 'Tumulus' and 'Motte'. Pugh's Garden Centre lies to the north of this eleventh century

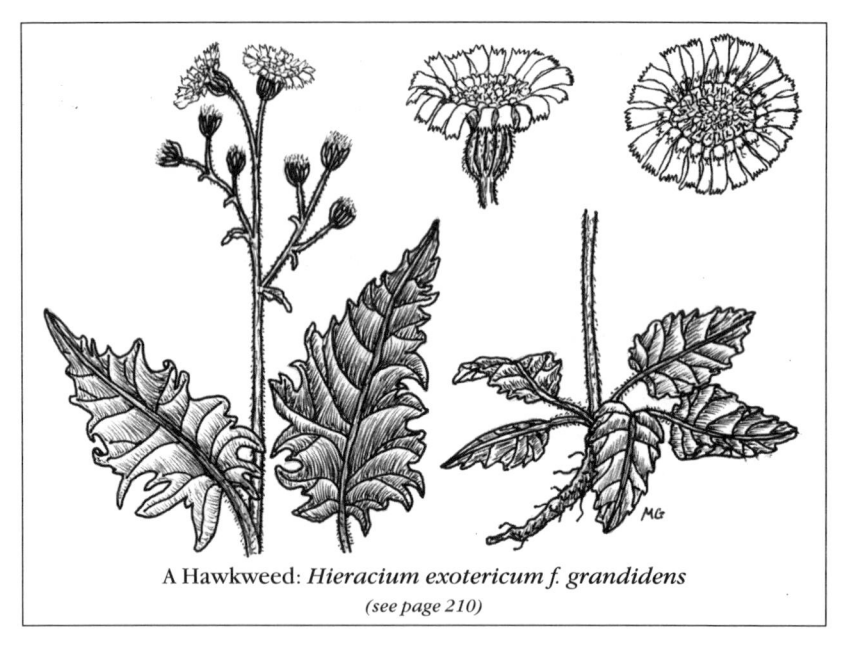

A Hawkweed: *Hieracium exotericum f. grandidens*
(see page 210)

feature and the old Station House to the east. Tradition has it that the motte was used by Parliamentarians to bombard Royalist troops occupying Castell Coch during Oliver Cromwell's war.

In the 1960s and 1970s the tree covered motte was visible from afar. During the 1980s it became hidden by alders and sallows and in 1988 downy birch and purging buckthorn were planted alongside to augment the cover. By the early 1990s brambles and nettles had formed an impenetrable barrier, but by high summer in 1998 several narrow paths had been pushed through, allowing access.

Within the outer defences most understorey plants are excluded by the heavy shade of the magnificent old beeches and sycamores rooted on top. The summit is carpeted with ivy and moss with a scattering of bluebells and primroses in spring.

The 120 ft (37 m) diameter motte is 18 ft (5.5 m) high, the scramble up its steep earth side eased by a few outstanding tree roots. Rhododendrons on the periphery now restrict the view and Castell Coch is no longer visible through the former tree gap.

In the 1960s and 1970s a marsh featuring yellow iris, angelica, marsh bedstraw, marsh ragwort and fleabane separated the motte from the playing field. Mints here were of particular interest. There was some exceptionally vigorous water mint *(Mentha aquatica)* and two of its hybrids. Peppermint *(Mentha X piperata)*, the cross with spiked mint, and verticillate mint

(*Mentha X verticillata*), the cross with corn mint. Flower heads of both the soft and hard rushes carried the tubular paper cases of little Coleophora rush moths and there were plenty of other invertebrates.

It is tempting to think that this is part of the old moat of the motte and bailey, but it is more likely to be a relic of the whole as it once was. By 1935 hundreds of tons of colliery waste had been manhandled onto the site by the men and boys of Gwaelod and the field ceased to be referred to as 'The Ynys' and was officially opened as 'The Cricket Pitch'. Now used for soccer and rugger in season, this has been a much used village asset.

When visited in the rainy July following the 1998 June floods, there was no standing water here, although everything was dripping with rain and swallows were swooping past at knee height over the short turf as they hunted low-flying insects, pushed down by the moisture-laden atmosphere. Where the mint and other water plants had bloomed there was now a tangle of meadowsweet and hemlock water dropwort, grading into the Ty Nant wetland at the foot of the western scarp.

There are no plans to open up this attractive piece of history for public viewing at present. Only those in the know can locate and climb the fort, that must once have been defended by a wooden palisade, and contemplate how the resident eleventh century Normans regarded the spectacular Taff Gorge hard by, before quarrying on both sides broadened it out. Is it a flight of the imagination to think that they might have been afeared to pass through it into the realms of the 'Valley Welsh', with such ample cover for snipers on either side?

Sadly the land between the garden centre and Ynys Bridge was destined for development. Already, by 1998 the Cardiff Aquatic Centre with the its tanks holding a fascinating range of freshwater fish and sea creatures was up and running, and beyond the high hedge of the yard to its north was a levelled expanse of man-made infill composed of river rounded pebbles. Closely aligned with the planned new exit from the Walnut Tree Quarry opposite stood a tall bill board advertising "*Ty Nant Court. New offices within a pleasant parkland environment*".

Pleasant it was still in July 1998, if the odd piles of bric-a-brac could be ignored. The drier part behind the tall roadside hedge was colourful with Buddleja, weld, ragwort, self heal, centaury and cinquefoil among coltsfoot leaves, spent spikes of great mullein and ephemeral scarlet pimpernels. Marginal to the inevitable perforated kind was a stand of the smaller elegant St. Johns wort.

Most of the rest was occupied by bushy, man-high alder saplings, some so closely juxtaposed as to be impenetrable. There were spreading puddles nourishing some of the plants brought with the river pebbles purple loosestrife, water figwort and various willow herbs.

Old Station House, Pentyrch, where the Pentyrch line joined the main Taff Vale railway under the old Ty Nant quarry.

This bulldozed platform occupies most of the natural river terrace between the Ty Nant Quarry across the road and the current level of the Taff flood plain, which lies some 15 ft (4-5 m) below its steep wooded edge. The 'parkland to be' commands good views of the surrounding beech hangers and one of the elevated covered reservoirs above the Tongwynlais houses. By February 1999, heavy machinary had moved in and the aspiring alder wood was no more.

It was possible before building commenced to slip through brambles, nettles and a wire fence in the south-east corner of the made land onto the Taff Vale Railway, 150 m or so north of Old Station House. Walking beside the line back to the Taff bridge, which is wide enough for four rail tracks although carrying only two, one looks down on the still extant exit of the old feeder that served the Pentyrch Forge and Tin Plate Works. This channel was formerly known as Forge Dyke or, by some of us later, as the Gwaelod Canal. Surprisingly, it is as open as it ever was, 8 - 15 ft (3-4 m) wide, its margins only lightly overarched by Japanese knotweed. It runs below the edge of a river terrace boosted by made land along the back of the new building plot, and slightly below the level of the Taff, in thick woodland. The river has dropped to meet it at the point of convergence on the upstream side of the railway bridge.

Easier access during the 1970s had revealed the extent of the river revetments employed to keep the two channels apart. This long tongue of land had become more thickly vegetated than I remembered it from 25 years before, the stone blocks hidden by a skirt of reed canary grass, water dropwort, 'Japweed' and alder. Swollen by the 1998 summer rains, the river was bounding past at speed, creating a cauldron of white water over the buffer of stones, but some swirled back into the silted backwater at the canal mouth.

A sketch map in John Tyler's "Iron in the Soul" (1988) shows the feeder entering the Taff downstream of the railway bridge in the early part of the nineteenth century, suggesting that the narrow intervening barrier might have been worn back since then. Its present entry above the railway bridge is close to a sharp bend in the river, where the full force of the current pounds this west bank, leaving a spreading pebble shoal on the inside curve opposite. Grey wagtails potter on this beach, bullfinches and the odd woodpecker cross the river while chiff chaffs and other summer migrants move in during spring, the adjoining western slopes being thickly wooded, the eastern bank a thicket of Japanese knotweed that got flattened by the 1998 spates.

A little below the railway bridge the Taff curves back south again, just as sharply, under the frowning walls of Castell Coch on the eastern side of the gorge. The kink in its course provided a convenient place for the shortest posssible crossing of the north to south railway, transversely rather than obliquely.

The ballast on the railway bridge was being colonised by Buddleja and the expected tree seedlings, along with bramble, Clematis, herb Robert, cleavers and the like, but, interestingly, also a special railway plant. This was the small toadflax *(Chaenorhinum minus)* which is rare and local and usually found only on railway tracks in Southern England.

The old canal, under its canopy of alder, elm and sycamore, was wide and open for its entire visible length, three quarters of a century after its useful life, having been periodically dug out, most recently to accommodate the 1998-99 floods, which gushed in from the river through two breaches in the barrier. Few water plants grow anyway in the deep shade of the trees, the standing water as dank and empty as any woodland pool.

All that is visible during low water is an elongated walled earth-floored gully within the wood, containing no water. Although quite close to the road, the Pentyrch light railway crossed to its roadward side at Ynys Bridge but was so close that it must have been destroyed when the road was widened. The concrete and brick abutments of the bridge which took rocks from the quarry over the road to the railway can still be seen among a tangle of branches at the foot of the Little Garth.

Mr. Bale of Gelynis remembers the railway crossing of the feeder as being on stout planks laid across the top of boulders between which the water swirled, the canal no longer navigable when he was engaged

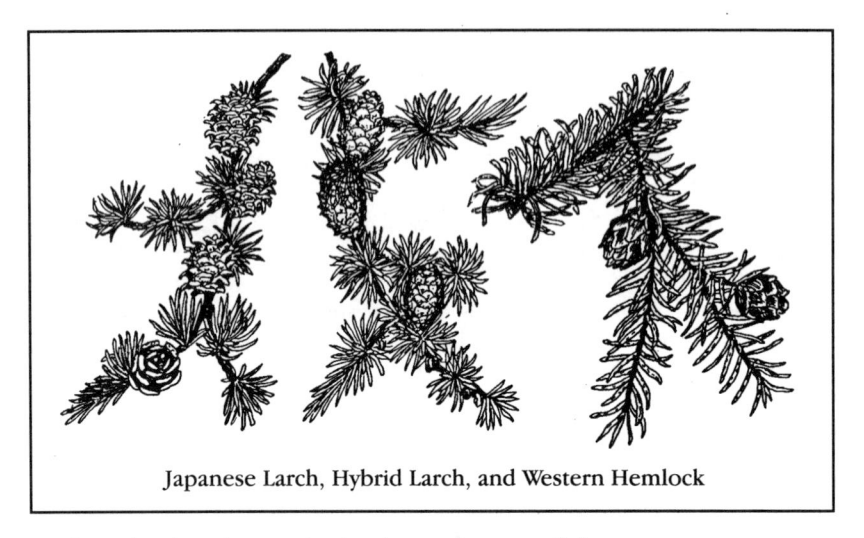

Japanese Larch, Hybrid Larch, and Western Hemlock

in those boyhood pursuits in the early part of the century.

It had not always been so. Following the period when pack horses took the Pentyrch iron south to the Melin Griffith tin works, tub boats were used. These passed along the Forge Dyke to enter the River Taff near where the Lower Portobello Weir was reputed to have been. No trace remains of this weir now. If present, it must have been above the dyke exit and the T V R bridge over the river in the gorge. The truncated canal barges or tub boats followed the river to Radyr Weir, which was built in 1774-75 to divert water into the Melin Griffith feeder, and followed on down the feeder to discharge their loads at the tin plate works.

Use of the tub boats was discontinued in 1815, when traffic was transferred to the Pentyrch light railway. This followed down the west bank to cut obliquely over the fields to Gelynys where the Taff veered away eastwards, crossed it by the Iron Bridge and proceeded down the east bank.

There were no wooden sleepers, the L shaped iron rails being bolted to a series of flat stones, each with a central hole penetrating six inches. Five inch oak plugs acted as rawplugs for the iron spikes holding the rails. The blocks were firmly rammed in place with gravel and small stones, the draft horses plodding along the middle of the track. Traffic was not all downstream, the Melin Griffith works sending tin plate back up across the Iron Bridge for transfer to the main T V R line at Pentyrch sidings.

In 1871 two saddle tank locomotives took over from the horses until the line closed in 1957. During the summer of 1998 industrial archeologists excavated a section of the old track and reassembled it by the riverside path near Radyr Weir.

When boats plied on this stretch of the river the walled channel leading from the southern side of the upper part of the Melin Griffith feeder curved back riverwards through what some believe to have been a lock or locks, the upper end of which has for long been marked by two badly rusted iron girders atop a stone wall.

A curved stone arch under which water from here re-entered the river a short distance below Radyr weir has always been visible, although most of the archway was filled with river-borne silt, its summit only about a metre above water level when the river was in spate. The intervening stretch was buried under the mounded floor of the riverside beech spinney until Cardiff Council personnel got digging in the summer of 1998.

They unearthed the curved tops of similar stone arches - one close below the girder-topped masonry at the start of what was either a lock system or a spillway for excess water from the feeder, and another about half way to its junction with the river. Was it roofed all the way when in use, as a spacious culvert, or did the lower arch mark the entry of an open channel to a tunnel under the Pentrych Railway to the river? Any boats taking this route could carry on down river to the deep section above Llandaff Weir, which is now the territory of the University and Llandaff Rowing Clubs.

During the January floods of 1999 most of the beech spinney occupying the suspected lock area behind the Radyr salmon trap was flooded. A channel had been opened up to allow the water to run off into the pit exposing the halfway arch. The torrent entering here gushed out into the Taff under the lowest of the arches, proving there to be an open passage between the two, under what is now the broad riverside path.

Upstream from here the new office blocks at Ynys Bridge have obliterated this section of both the Gwaelod Canal and the Pentyrch light railway. After its long run from the Upper Portobello Weir near the Zig Zag, the feeder had passed under the old Ynys Road by a fine arched stone bridge and on through what later became the alder wood occupying the river terrace. The alders were felled in the 1980s to make way for pony jumps, then, in 1988, the bulldozers moved in, destroying the bridge and bringing the modern office blocks, carparks and a short length of riverside road into being.

Between the cessation of early iron working and the mid twentieth century activities of coal washeries up-river, gudgeon, roach and eels are reported to have found a good living in the Gwaelod Canal, but the entire section through the old works above Ynys was filled in long ago.

The 1970s saw the building of a second road bridge over the Taff at Ynys, connecting the new A 470 roundabout under Castell Coch with a smaller one under Little Garth. Ynys House, huddled among protective

Excavating a new sewer on the west bank of the Taff at Gelynis. August 1999

tall trees, became hedged about by light industry at the blocked end of the old road, which formerly spanned feeder, railway, river, Taff Vale Railway and Glamorgan Canal on a close set series of five bridges.

Between river and T V R in the old days coopers made and mended wooden beer barrels and milled mortar for local building projects and the site is still in industrial use. Modern workshops beyond, packed back against the lofty concrete wall of the A 470 trunk road in the cul de sac at the end, were cut off early in 1998 when the railway bridge was being repaired, the staff unable to find another way in to work.

Both the new roundabouts are bright with ox-eye or moon daisies in early summer, but we had to fight the council roadmen (through official channels) to prevent these being mown down in their prime. There were other beauties on the Garth side then: the frothy pink flower heads of crown vetch *(Coronilla varia)* and sturdier ones of soapwort, but these were 'managed' to extinction.

Happily, a couple of decades later, the local authorities have shed their 'tidy parks' mentality for a greater tolerance of 'things natural' and road verges are beginning to bloom again.

The best example hereabouts is the huge Coryton Roundabout at junction 32 on the motorway, where this crosses the Cardiff to Merthyr A 470. Judicious planting of trees and shrubs on the fields which it encompassed at its inception in the 1970s has left many acres of meadowland, which are a riot of colour in season.

June 1998 and 1999 produced a wealth of common spotted orchids, many with inflorescences a full handspan long and one with a double spire in the upper half like a flower-decked tuning fork. A scattering of plants in the north-eastern section bore dark purple leaves and crimson flowers, and earlier this year there were many crosses with early marsh orchids in the western section, these showing hybrid vigour. Deep magenta pyramidal orchids had opened by the end of the month, these with fine cylindrical pointy-tipped flower spikes instead of the more meagre pyramids of poorer habitats. A few path-side bee orchids and twayblades remained from earlier successional phases.

Centaury and musk mallow added washes of pale pink, with a range of shades in the marginal tangles of broad everlasting pea, red clover and Buddleja. Yellow birds-foot trefoil provided a partial ground cover, augmented by meadow vetchling, creeping cinquefoil and silverweed, and pierced by turrets of agrimony and puffing seed heads of goatsbeard. Later came knapweed, fleabane, willow herbs and hemp agrimony.

Crimson robin's pincushions or rose bedeguars, caused by the Cynipid wasp, *Diplolepis rosae*, decorate the wild roses and bumper fruit crops ripen on dogwood and wayfaring tree. All these, along with springtime celandines, and colt'sfoot and the inevitable moon daisies, are becoming an increasing reality on road verges, in what was getting perilously near an almost flowerless landscape. With them come the butterflies, small coppers, small heaths, large skippers, meadow browns and common blues, with the spiky black caterpillars of Vannesids feasting on the nettles. Burnet moths and *Agelana labrinthica* funnel-building spiders are common.

Buzzard and kestrel hang overhead on the look out for small mammals and other birds use the cover, seemingly oblivious of the roar of traffic from the major road complex encroaching on the site - which is accessible by footways above and underpasses below. This is out of our area, across the river, but it is good to know it is there: a seed bank for future colonisation as habitats become available.

2. The Greening of the Old Iron Works

The ground on the narrow section of flood plain within the gorge is marked 'The Island' on the 1841 tithe map, but Ynys translates as water meadow as well as island. This former marshy land came to be islanded between the river and the Glamorgan Canal, which was

Short-tailed Field Voles

constructed across the base of the river loop under Castell Coch in 1794. (Back round the corner of the hill on the south facing slope under the castle was Lord Bute's nineteenth century vineyard, now a nine hole golf course.)

The presumed, although unverified, location of the sixteenth and seventeenth century Tongwynlais Iron Forge on the steep east bank of the Taff where the river turns south, suggests that the more spacious flats on our side might have been too waterlogged or subject to inundation: or was it merely to facilitate use of ore from the Castell Coch side?

Records show that Hugh Lambert, an iron founder, leased property in 1560 that later deeds identified as Old Furnace Farm and Ivy House. Phillip Riden (1992: *"Early Ironworks in the Lower Taff Valley"* Morganwg. Jour. Glam. Hist. Soc.) states it to be almost certain that the furnaces on the Tongwynlais - Whitchurch boundary were the works used by Sir Henry Sidney during the 1560s to produce iron for steel making. He took over an already existing forge in 1564. Tongwynlais must have been among the earliest blast furnaces in South Wales, if not the first. It was referred to as 'The Old Furnace' in the eighteenth century, when the Pentyrch one was in full spate.

In 1625 Thomas Hackett is documented as having a furnace driven by a water wheel at Tongwynlais, probably working iron taken from the dolomitised rocks of the Castell Coch ridge just behind, where the old iron extraction pits can still be seen.

The Reverend Lee Brown, in his *"Ffynnon Taf"* (1983), suggests that Ynys House was probably the farmhouse of the Old Furnace Farm, whose fields lay alongside the river, both upstream and down of Ynys. As a 'man of iron', it is probable that Lambert smelted the local iron before Hackett took over in 1625.

Work apparently ceased at the furnace in 1680. when its last lessee, George Hart, a merchant from Bristol, moved away to Caerphilly. In 1706 the enterprise was said to be in ruins. Nothing remains of the mighty water wheel that powered this mill until 320 years ago and knowledge of its site has been lost in the mists of time.

It is tempting to think that the stone housing in which it was located might be the two close set walls at right angles to the river bank in the garden of Ivy Dene House, the old lock keeper's cottage tucked in behind Ivy House Farm on the river bank. (Map Ref. ST 131 828). However, the nonogenarian now residing at Ivy Farm claims this to be an old outlet for canal water.

Even nonogenarians cannot remember back 300 years. Riden cites an account book of the 1790s referring to "Furnace Farm near Ivy House in the vicinity of which, according to local tradition, a furnace anciently existed." Most writings refer to it as being on the boundary between Tongwynlais and Whitchurch - the boundary marked by the Nant y Fforest Stream, previously known as the Gwynlais Brook. This stream currently exits to the River Taff through that very 8 metre deep walled gut.

The channel carried no water in July 1998, but a veritable torrent was gushing through after the October rains of that year, when sandbags had been placed alongside the brook higher up to curtail the flood gushing out onto Mill Road. Such spates would explain the cleanly scoured nature of the confining walls of this last lap to the river. The canal passing close behind was fed by this stream, which still supplies the main flow for the Glamorgan Canal Nature Reserve to the south. It is culverted under the village.

Ivy Dene and Ivy House are situated at the end of Market Street, the continuation of the appropriately named Mill Street - which leads from the hub of Tongwynlais Village up the hill past the entrance to Castell Coch on the beech-clad flanks of Fforest Fawr. There was a grist mill half way up the hill, powered presumably by the Nant y Fforest, and this is more likely to have given rise to the name of Mill Road than a possible iron mill at its riverward end.

The 6 inch to the mile geology map marks a 'mill' directly between Ynys House and 'Forge Hill' on the lower slope of the Castell Coch hill immediately above to the east (Map ref ST 129 825). If the name 'Forge Hill' related to the Pentyrch Forge, why was it not on the Pentyrch side of the river? This square of the Geological Survey Map was compiled from surveys dated 1873-78. Could that shed light on the lost iron mill site, although a little north of the parish boundary? The geologists do not mark the two nearby grist mills.

The second grist mill in Tongwynlais, on whose water wheel octogenarian Bale remembers clambering around with his school friends in pre-war days, is further south, nearer the Old Red Barn (now demolished) by the canal. The wheel was undershot, the driving water,

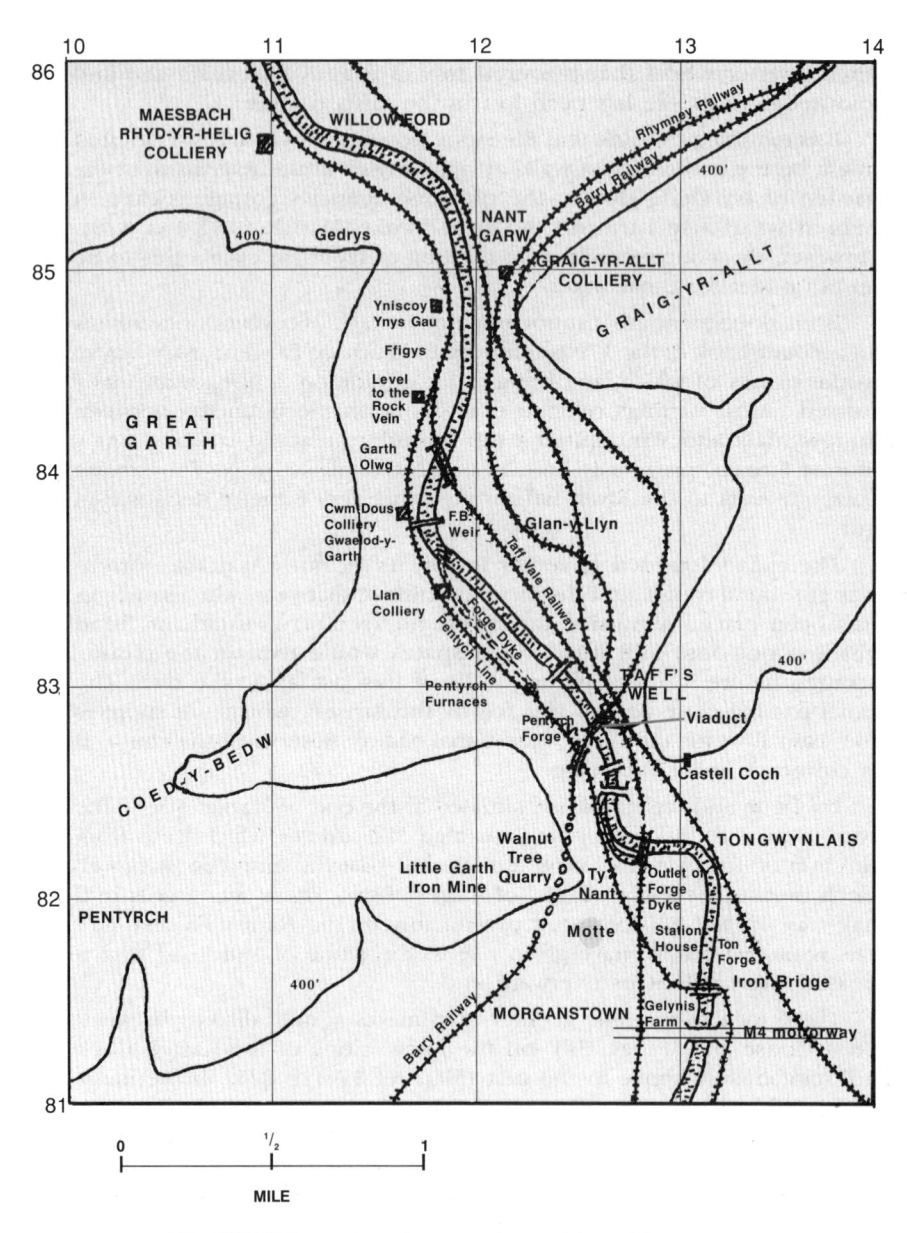

**OLD MINES AND RAILWAYS IN THE TAFF VALLEY
GWAELOD-Y-GARTH**

48. Gelynis Barn and old Ty Nant Quarry on Little Garth. August 1999

49. Gelynis Barn and working Walnut Tree Quarry on Little Garth. August 1999

50. Taffs Well Viaduct in the 1960s from Castell Coch. Walnut Tree quarry plant on Little Garth to the left, Great Garth right.

51. Iron Bridge and Castell Coch from the M4 motorway bridge over the Taff. January 1985

which he recalls as coming from the Glamorgan Canal close alongside, striking its underside to set it in motion.

Upstream, beyond the Taff Gorge, was the larger riverside foundry and forge in Gwaelod village. The clangerous racket of that old time industry must have been even more intrusive than today's roar of trucks and trains.

The blast furnace existed in 1565, possibly starting a few years later than the one across the Taff, and using ore from the Little Garth. Work was stopped by the government in 1602 because the guns being cast there for Denmark were finding their way into enemy hands in Spain. The Sierra Leone fracasse in 1998 was not the first occasion on which the authorities were worried about British made armaments getting into the wrong hands. Pentyrch furnace continued working, under different management and with various political hicoughs until final closure in 1616.

There is no record of activity here for the next 123 years, but the works were re-opened about 1740 and continued for nigh on 200 years, so the wild life has been well schooled to endure the noise. First came the furnaces, then the forge and, by 1891, the rolling mills.

Although situated firmly in Gwaelod-y-Garth, this hub of industry was known as the Pentyrch Works. The Nant Llwydrew from the Coed y Bedw Nature Reserve drove the furnace and the forge was at first powered by the tail race from here. Later, about 1790, the Forge Dyke was led off the Taff near the Zig Zag to power both an enlarged forge and the rolling mills.

The name of Portobello for the weir which ponded back the water for the dyke was derived from that of the Portobello Public House in Taffs Well, named (or renamed) in or soon after 1739 - the year when Admiral Vernon captured Portobello in the West Indies.

The reservoir on this power supply system, the Forge Dyke, is said to have been on the site of the present riverside football field. After powering the works the water was released through a series of arches, the last of which was the one taking it under the Ynys Road. Why did it enter the Taff so far downstream from there, I wonder? In view of the great length of masonry put in place to keep the two apart there must have been some good reason. Flood water pouring from the river into the dyke from two breaches in the 1998-99 spates suggests that this was the nearest place where levels were adequate to keep the Taff from flooding back in.

The Cwm Llwydrew Stream, which rotated two drum type water wheels at the blast furnace, emptied directly into the river - as it still does - now through a broad concrete pipe installed when the new houses were built in the 1980s. The reservoir or reservoirs where this water was held to maintain sufficient head was on the site of Heol Beri Green.

Derek Thomas of Heol y Nant has distinguished the lines of old embankments, suggesting that the water may have been ponded back in three basins. A big pond is shown on the site of today's green on the tithe map of 1839. The whole area became marshy before the ultimate infilling with industrial waste. Works downstream from here were replaced by the derelict car yard, which did nothing to enhance the scenery on the approach to the vilage during the 1960s and 70s.

The iron works, famous for its military ordnance, first functioned from around 1565 to 1620, the second from the 1840s to 1879 , after a peak production of 6,977 tons in 1846. Traces remained until 1930, when the Pentyrch Steel and Tin Plate Company moved in for a short while, only to fail in 1931 and sell out to the Melin Griffith Company, which never worked it.

Spoil heaps and derelict buildings persisted and the old engine shed against the road, with its arched ironwork superstructure, survived into modern times as part of the old car yard, but was finally pulled down. The tall ventilation stack, adorned by the symbolic eagle with sparkling beer bottle eyes, dominates the old photographs of the site and was blown up long before, but within living memory of a few to whom I have spoken.

This part of the ironworks was replaced by the Heol Beri Council Estate. The brickworks lay to the immediate northwest of Heol Beri Green and were independent of the iron works, using waste fireclay from Llan Mine until clay pits were opened in Maes-y-Gwyn Field across the road. Excavation of the clay shales here left cliff, humps and hollows overlooked by Maes-y-Gwyn House.

Scrape away the covering carpet of beech leaves and leaf mould and there is sticky clay still, some yellow, some grey, both as glutinous as the puddle clay used to waterproof the canal bed. Burrowing rodents work their way in beside tree roots for ease of digging. A load of curved bricks from the works chimney went to harp maker and museum craftsman, John Thomas, for the building of Pear Tree Cottage and his workshop in the village centre, before he moved away to Pembrokeshire in the 1970s.

Similar clay shales to those of the brick works were brought to the surface when ventilation shafts were being dug to serve the coal levels penetrating the Garth. The Ballards and the Phillips families living on the Mountain Road have both had to wrestle with this material in their gardens, which contain the upper ends of shafts, bricked for 3 m or more down. The late Mr. and Mrs. Ballard, keen gardeners at "The Nook", told how they laboriously added peat and sand over 15 years before they had their sticky clay 'tamed'. The shafts had been closed, but are said to have been reopened as air raid shelters during the war, then re-sealed.

Methane seepage from the mines into Garth houses, particularly bad in 1959, has been referred to earlier - this largely the result of the walling up of the mine entrances along the riverside. Gas built up, particularly in the Cwm Dous Mine tunnels, and seeped upwards through the soil, dissipating into the air, but becoming more concentrated if trapped in a confined space. Mrs. Hunt of the old shop at the bottom of Mountain Road, was fortunate in that her methane leak emerged in the family grate. She lighted a fire there and it kept on burning for three weeks with no refuelling: veritably the widow's cruse of oil. Replacement of brick walls by open metal gratings was done to let the gas out but has not, so far as I know, let roosting bats in, as in many other mines.

Enormous quantities of slag from the smelting process were dumped between the Taff and the Portobello feeder - as the Upper and Lower Oriel Tips. It took eight years, from 1892 to the turn of the century, to clear this, by pick and shovel and wheel barrows to railway wagons, to boost the foundations of the Cardiff, Penarth and Barry Docks and Barry Railway track.

In the 1960s our village octogenarian miner, Willie Charles Thomas, recalled with glee his rides on the engine engaged in this task. He remembered the railway viaduct from the Little Garth to Fforest Fawr being built across the works in 1898, when he was twelve. Its useful life was shorter than his own, just three quarters of a century before it was demolished in 1969-70. It was constructed for the railway carrying coal from the Monmouthshire Valleys to Barry Docks. Dismantling involved all but one pier on the east bank, left to commemorate Queen Elizabeth's silver jubilee. The operation culminated in the excitement of the removal of part of the track by helicopter, to save what lay below.

The footings of the Upper Oriel slag tip were for many years the location of the Swiss Holdings Piggery. Grassed rubble occupied the levelled zone between pigsties and river, this settled enough by the late 1960s to support semi-parasites such as yellow rattle and red bartsia.

Land fell away sharply behind the Heol Beri garages for about 20 ft (6m) into a wet hollow with willows leading on to the riverside field. Both were likely to go under water when the Taff was in spate and several attempts were made to bolster up the revetments with rubble and boulders to prevent this.

As part of the "Taff Valley Project" in the early 1970s, the Glamorgan County Council designated the zone as a potential recreation area, but these plans came to nought. Bulldozers moved in between the Heol

Beri Estate and the Thermocouple factory to the south, felling birch scrub with sycamore standards. Ground exposed near the road was dark with slag from former workings, that towards the Taff was the pale grey of power station fly ash, which had been used as a foundation material for the estate.

The Mid Glamorgan County Council, which replaced the other in 1974, took over part of the old car yard as a stock yard for sand and road chippings. Then came the Post Office security and bulk delivery services, Short Bros. Heavy Plant and the various others that now constitute yet another of the Trading Estates springing up through the Valleys.

Wasteland plants appearing in the 1960s and 70s on old works clinker heaps and the cinder track of the old Pentyrch Railway between the river and Heol Beri, included some that are more typical of limey sand dunes.

Grey Squirrel on a reconstruction of the old Pentyrch Light Railway track.

Upstanding from softly whiskery pink carpets of hare's-foot trefoil and mouse-ear hawkweed were the blue spikes of viper's bugloss and yellow ones of evening primrose, with extra prickly burnet roses. The old wooden railway sleepers are still visible athwart the path at the end of the 1990s, but the build up of humus has caused the sand plants to dwindle through intermediates such as yellow and mauve toadflaxes to more characteristic riverside herbs.

The pig farm site and adjacent flat land was owned by the Taff Ely Borough Council, which approved the building of 109 houses here on 19th December, 1984. A further build up of level became imperative and a layer of red topsoil was spread over the infill. The River Glade Estate had been built on this by 1988.

The disruption created by the bulldozers caused the female mallard nesting in the Coed-y-Bedw Nature Reserve to lose her way when she tried to bring her brood of ducklings to the river. The little ones were rounded up and brought to Doug Castell, who keeps ducks and other small livestock on the field above the new estate. Together he and Alan Lock, then warden of the reserve, got them down to the river. The mother duck was flying around in consternation throughout, but lost no time in gathering her bobbing charges and shepherding them to where others lounged on protruding rocks and half submerged boughs. Doug's comment: *"Ten to eleven ducklings. Why so many when mine only produce two or three?"* The hazards of the wild are such, especially since the arrival of feral mink, that the wildling would probably be lucky to finish up with two or three.

The builders left a riverside walkway for public use outside the high garden fences of the houses nearest the Taff. Tree planting was undertaken to stress the 'glade' connotation. South Glade Estate was a subsequent spillover towards the main road.

Northwards from here the land rises fairly gently from river to road where the contour lines dip westwards into Georgetown and Coed y Bedw along the Nant Llwydrew. The old dwellings and pony paddock at the bottom of School Lane remain much as before. The broad riverside walk occupies the levelled strip of land formerly followed by the Forge Dyke and the Pentyrch Railway, well above river level. Upstream the hillside closes in towards the Taff, leaving room for little else.

Iron Bridge, where the old Pentyrch line crossed the Taff south of the Gorge

3. Woodland swallows the Riverside Drift Mines

The Old Drift Garage occupies the wooded hollow below the village school where the river terrace begins to narrow northwards. The 'Old Drift' is the lofty bricked entrance to the tunnel penetrating the bank carrying the road as it rises towards the village.

Llan Mine here was a steep inclined drift arched with brick throughout. It is said to go 700 yards from the riverside gravels into the Lower Coal Measures under the Garth Mountain, tapping the Hard Brass Vein, the Fork Vein and the Wing Vein, so called because it kept 'disappearing'.

Three hundred men and boys were employed here, two thirds of them underground, working with naked lights. The 1875 methane gas explosion was in Brass Vein. The figures quoted vary, but it is likely to have killed twelve and injured five, some of these dying later from their injuries. The catastrophe was only three years after the mine's inception, in 1872. The explosion was thought to have been caused by a miner piercing the barrier between the current working and an earlier one alongside, where the concentration of gas had been allowed to build up - and ignited on contact with the lamps.

My 1970 notes record chunks of limestone from the firing kilns used for extracting the iron brought out from Brass Vein with the coal. The intense heat had produced bubbles and contortions and a splitting into layers a centimetre or so thick, probably following the original lines of bedding. These were colonised by a dozen or so plant species, including small bird-sown shrubs - elderberry, gooseberry, holly and hawthorn - and have long since been swallowed up by the woodland flora.

The surroundings, too, have moved on to mature woodland. There are some incredibly old birches here, with burls on their trunks and the twiggy excrescences of witch's brooms on their branches. Boles are so darkly furrowed that the typical white bark is confined to the upper parts and the trunks are huge, one dividing at the base.

These would have been the pioneer trees. Many have fallen and are so rotted that the burrowing beetles, millipedes and snails have abandoned them as having nothing left to offer. The fallen timber remains, drained of nutrients, the inert residue meat only for the ravages of fungi and bacteria which will recycle them on the woodland treadmill.

Oaks, ashes and sycamores have overtaken them now and there are some quite magnificent beech trees, with gnarled roots spreading across the eroding slopes. When these eventually fall a lot of the precariously perched soil will go with them. In some years the leaves of a few show little hairy growths which are caused by the gall midge, *Hartigiola annulipes*. Three mighty beeches by the Drift were felled in 1999.

Sheep do not venture here and regenerating tree seedlings include all these but no birch in the heavy shade. Holly, hazel and dogwood are pushing through, but only ferns really flourish in the low light and high humidity lower down - male fern, lady fern and broad buckler. Harts tongue ferns sprout from the greening walls shoring up the bank behind the old railway line. One true-breeding clump produced forked fronds over many years, another started to do so in 1997.

The two slabby liverworts, *Conocephalum conicum* and *Pellia epiphylla*, line sundry water trickles while conspicuous among the mosses are *Atrichum undulatum, Mnium hornum* and species of *Fissidens*. In better lighted parts the seasonal sequence of ground flora is from starry carpets of lesser celandine or more muted dog's mercury, through bluebells with yellow archangel to enchanter's nightshade with wood avens and herb Robert.

The riverside railway served other mines to the north. Closest is the Cwm Dous Mine, opened in 1847, just upstream of the Zig Zag path to Pont Sion Phillips footbridge and closed around 1913.

Beyond this again is the Rock Vein Mine at Ffygis opened in 1873. The date on the Salem Chapel just above - a private residence since 1978 - is 1871, so spiritual needs were given priority over more down to earth ones.

Lesser Spearwort and Creeping Buttercup

The stream from the big Water Board tanks up the mountain gushes down just north of the Zig Zag and another one empties from the gated entrance of Cwm Dous Mine. Marginal grasses stiffen with icicles during cold spells but the wet area explodes into a delight of golden saxifrage flowers in early spring, these a more acid greeny-yellow than the celandines hard by.

A subsidence higher up the slope may actually be into another level pushed in very close. This has been fenced about with wire netting to deter the venturesome, but is full of water and uninviting. In summer the pool can be dark with a scum of algae and flies mature from underwater larvae to cavort over the surface in a zizzing cloud.

Other springs seep from aquifers in the layered sandstone of the wooded cliff to join the pathside waterway which is furnished with stepping stones as necessary. Deeper parts of the converging waters are green with water starwort, fool's watercress and hemlock water dropwort, with the gentian-blue flowers of brooklime opening in midsummer. Marginal to these are milkmaid or lady's smock, lesser spearwort and forget-me-not.

The stone footings clustered about the Cwm Dous Mine are those of the old stables, dwelling and garden walls, which were abandoned in the 1920s when activity shifted to other levels.

The Ynys Gau Railway Bridge at low water, looking upstream, early 1970s before the alder fringe grew along the west bank.

Where the river bank swings away from the railway track that follows the foot of the cliff the way became overgrown and impassable in the 1970s. A branch path leads obliquely upwards to climb steep steps and emerge on the village street opposite the shop, but this, too, became impassable at the top in 1998. It is cleared periodically.

The only option then was to take the path to the high river bank and follow its undulations upstream and down to river level. A sizable tributary comes in at the junction of the woodland with the paddock accommodated by the divergence of river and cliff. The crossing into the field became progressively muddier and more difficult over the last three decades, so a diversion now leads to a drier crossing on the river-worn rocks at the stream's mouth.

Following outside the paddock fence under newly sprung alders and over a narrower stream, the broad concrete footings of the Taff Vale Railway bridge lead the walker underneath to follow the river all the way to Upper Boat opposite the Treforest Trading Estate.

This railway bridge and the one opposite Ty Nant Quarry where the Forge Dyke empties, were necessary because the Blakemore-Booker concern owning the Pentyrch Forge would not allow the line - which served rival concerns - to cross its land. With their consent the railway might have remained west of the river throughout this stretch, although it could have been a tight squeeze to fit it in through the central section. Quantities of coal waste had to be dumped to make a terrace wide enough to accommodate the feeder and the Pentyrch railway line.

When water level is high it is not possible to go under the bridge - nor practical to go over the line. Staying on the Gwaelod side of the railway there are two options allowing the walker to join up with the public footpath from Gwaelod Main Road to the old Rock Vein Mine at Ffygis.

One is along the base of the steep wood in the gully formerly occupied by the mine railway and now, in part, by a linear woodland pool. The other is on the broad track leading alongside the railway to the old mine buildings beyond the protruding shoulder of hill. This track is crossed for a considerable distance by deep mud-filled corrugations engendered by the passage of the Ynys Gau dairy herd over the years. The cows step from one gully to the next, muddying their udders in the process: walkers do their best to stay on the greasy ridges, muddying as little as possible.

The path to the mine from the Ffynon Ffygis end of the village is well sign-posted at the entrance stile but gets lost in the confusion of tracks around the overgrown mine footings. Formerly it crossed the railway line to join the long distance riverside path, but this was discontinued on safety grounds when the frequent service of fast 'sprinter trains' was inaugurated. Subsequent bramble growth now thwarts the most determined. Strangers go over the newly renovated stile, map in hand, to emerge later looking puzzled - an unusual experience in this Pentyrch Community, which prides itself on the upkeep of all footpaths. In the meantime there is good blackberrying to be had for those prepared to linger.

From the stately pines by the lane at the entrance to Ynys-Gau the Daren-ddu geological fault crosses the farm obliquely SSE to the Rock Vein Mine buildings, displacing the Rhondda No. 1 and Rhondda No. 2 coal seams a little further south on the west side, as does the main Tonglynlais fault followed by the river from below the village post office down to Whitchurch.

The mine tapped into the Rhondda No. 2 coal seam but, according to Willie Charles Thomas, headed towards a coal deposit separated

201

from the main vein by the faulting. After a while it failed, was re-opened and failed again: a white elephant, yielding little coal.

The subsidence along this shaft, through the Ffynon Ffygis Cottages and Owl's Valley (Cwm Dyllaen) around 1920 has been referred to in chapter 1. Cracks appearing in the Garth Olwg houses as a result of subsidence were more recent, during the 1960s, and thought to have been triggered by blasting in the new Nant Garw Mine, which crossed obliquely beneath Rock Vein some 500 m lower down.

Jack and Clive Francis, who have farmed the Ynys-Gau land over the years, tell of the missing cow that subsided with the shaft and had to be dug out, startled, no doubt, but none the worse. It was missing for some time, although only just below field level, out of sight in a vertical-sided hole.

"She went round and round trying to find a way out. We dug a slope on one side and she scrambled out on her own."

The rupture torn through the field over the shallow tunnel extended for almost 400 m, posing the question as to why the mine had not been opened 400 m further back. It seems the mine company owned only the entrance and had to pay the land owner higher dues for an open gully than a covered way to get the coal to the railway.

The collapse was fenced off and topped up with rounded river pebbles to prevent more accidents. The bare soil exposed in 1970 became

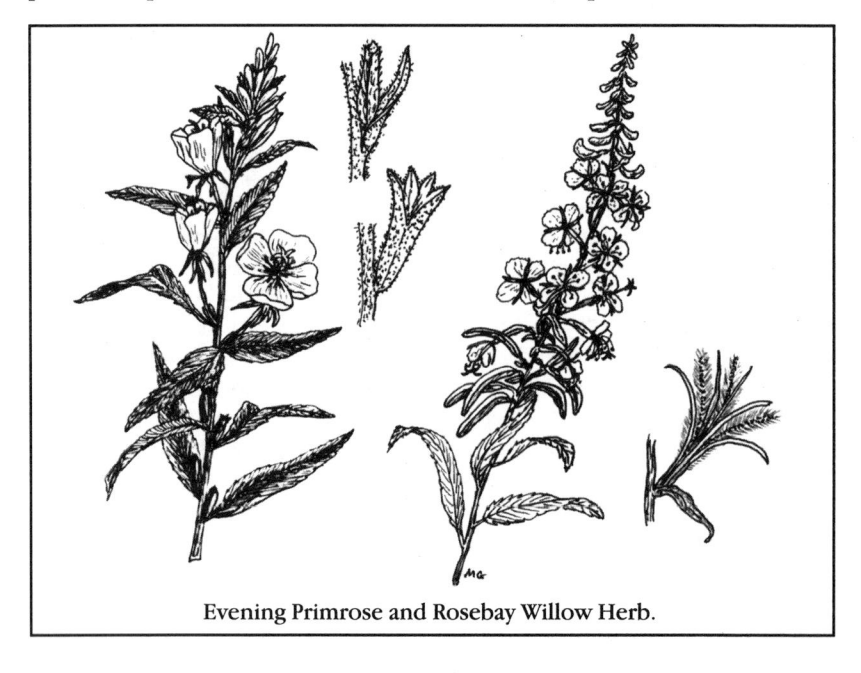

Evening Primrose and Rosebay Willow Herb.

colonised by foxglove and rosebay willow herb. It is now bush-grown.

The shallow tunnel was bricked for a fair distance in, but the roof had bellied with the overlying weight and Clive admits to never venturing very far in as a boy. The date 1873 is inscribed on the brick arch at the entrance, which was furnished with a grating to keep out other young adventurers, but they had levered this away by 1971 to get in. By 1974 it had been replaced by a wall.

Villagers had gathered watercress in the stream for as long as they could remember - until the 1960s, when the water disappeared - some said into the Nant Garw Mine, from where it had to be pumped out. The floor is now dry apart from the occasional plop of water from the roof.

A geological boring made into the garden of Ffygis House above the village street revealed 12 - 13 m of boulder clay overlying a further 12 - 13 m of bedrock above the mine.

After closure, faulting and collapse was not confined to this side of the river, the Taff bank having given way below the Swan Inn on the Taffs Well side. The wall built to repair the damage cracked and there were major dredging and walling activities going on during 1970 and 1971.

Enough coal was got out of the Ffygis mine before formal closure for significant slag heaps to accumulate. These are steep-sided and acid, supporting ling, sheep's fescue and mat grass under the broom bushes and birch trees of the developing woodland that was eventually to engulf the heath plants.

Dairy cows do not venture here but make their corrugated ways in the hollows between. Sheep, however, came to nibble the heather and wavy hair grass in the early 1970s. The lambs wore the khaki-buff 'collars' of the Welsh Mountain breed, which balks at little when there are edible morsels to be gleaned.

Boulders, rounded by ice or water, litter the ground outside, not far above river level, but well back from its present course a field's width away along the railway line.

A dump of white clay was brought for making a bridge to trundle waste material from the mine to the tip. The clay is impermeable, holding up rain water, but the cattle relish the marsh plants which it supports, particularly the flote grass, which they find vastly superior to the bristly tufted hair grass of the woodland floor. There were sidings here, and a railway junction, so the coal went away by rail on the Pentyrch line for local use in the forges downstream, or on the Taff Vale line to Cardiff or Barry for export. Remains of the nearby signal box are still to be seen beyond the bramble banks. After closure the stream from the mine flowed along the old Pentyrch track before entering the Taff.

4. Power Station Fly Ash on Ynys Gau Farm

Ynys Gau Farm occupies the entire western flood plain below the road from the riverside paddock downstream of the main line railway bridge right up to Willowford, beyond Gedrys. Above the road a sloping field cut from the wooded skirts of the Garth Mountain produces luxurious crops of hay.

The land is worked by Clive Francis, following in the steps of his father Jack. It is run as a dairy farm at the Gwaelod end until 1998, with beef production at the other and the occasional green fodder crop when remedial ploughing is necessary.

They have had to deal with a mixed legacy of soil types, some indigenous, some brought by the Taff Glacier, some by the river in post glacial times and some by man in modern times. All need different management.

Alongside the stepped pattern of alluvial flats flanked by higher river terraces are rounded mounds - eskers or drumlins, the moraines dumped in this section of the valley as the glacier slowed its grinding passage south and melted away, stranding the load of debris it had scraped from the hills to the north. When snow lies village children bring their toboggans to these smooth humps, to enjoy a mini-repeat of the Ice Age of 12-10,000 years ago which fashioned the slopes down which they hurtle.

Higher land intrudes onto the plain where the farm stands - as it did in the Ice Age - but it is loftier now than then because the ancient ridge of rock served to stay the passage of the moving force and caused the terminal moraine of earth and stones to be abandoned on top as the ice thawed and trickled away.

This barrier ponded back a lake three and a half miles long on the upstream side at Treforest, the waters escaping eventually through a gap in the ridge into what is thought to have been a smaller late glacial lake at Taffs Well.

A boring made at White Hawthorns by Professor Anderson of the University Geology Department in Cardiff, cut through 75 feet (24 m) of clayey silt from the old lake bed, covered by a thin, later deposited, layer of alluvial sand and gravel. These rested on bedrock at 53 feet (17 m) above present ordnance datum level thinned to north and south.

A boring just downstream showed rock at 95 OD - 42 feet higher - and another at Taffs Well went down 80 feet without reaching bedrock at all. Silty soil occupied this profile from 29 to 67 feet and is believed to be more lake bed sediment, with the old river basin shallowing again at the gorge. Obviously this ancient valley was more spectacular than the partially infilled one that we see today.

The natural infills that Clive Francis has to farm include sticky Boulder Clay brought by the moving ice, friable Glacial Gravels left behind as moraines or drumlins (the tobogganing sites) and fine silty river alluvium, but not the lake bed deposits as these are covered over. He has also two man-made soils on his land, the slag from the Ffygis coal mine and imported burned coal ash from the Central Electricity Generating Board's power stations.

The glutinous clay, ground to powder by the moving ice, but still containing pebbles, pounded and rounded in their passage down valley, puddles into a sticky morass under the hooves of his cattle and cannot be used in wet winters. The gravels of the mounds and ridges left behind when the meltwaters finally made off through the gorge are different. When he ploughs these to rejuvenate his 'permanent' grass leys, the four inch deep furrow changes abruptly from stony loam to heavy clay at their margins.

Between river and railway, where it is usually too wet to plough, the alluvial soil is black and fertile, growing good grass but holding up pools where the cattle drink and produce more quagmires.

Even into the 1990s the farm needed no mains water system, the livestock adequately supplied by clear running streams from the Garth and the field ponds held up on the lower land. The pond on the upper river terrace near the farm buildings gets very muddy and there were plans in 1992 to fence a bit off with a concrete standing for the cattle to drink, but this had to wait for a year when it was dry enough to get the heavy digging machine onto the land. In the meantime a ditch was dug by hand to drain away the excess.

Some of the more interesting water plants here are submerged red-tinged water purslane, emergent greater water plantain, angelica and tripartite bur marigold. One of the narrow riverside fields tapers back into a spontaneous alder wood.

The water supply for the house and farmyard is a well just above the bridge taking the farm track over the adjacent railway, this bearing a warning notice in the early nineties admonishing farm vehicles not to exceed a load of 3 tons.

This water is pure and never dries up, although getting uncomfortably low in drought years. The farmer had to pay £47 in the early 1990s - *"And £97 for a girl to look at the cowsheds"* to have water quality and hygeine checked as he was selling milk.

The well is spring fed from an aquifer and is culverted to the farm. It is a lesser version of the one which supplied the entire village until recent years, via the big iron Water Board tanks below the Mountain

Road. The frog ponds on the fields to the south are not spring fed. Like the lower mires, they are repositories of surface run-off, held up by the clayey substrate in this case and merging with the high water table on the lower land. The glacial gravels of the drumlins are the best drained of the natural soils, but Ynys Gau has a fifth type.

This is pulverised fuel ash (PFA) or fly ash from power stations, referred to as duff by the farmers. Jack Francis applied for this in 1958, to fill an unproductive hollow containing a pond, a marsh and an old walled garden by the entrance gate. Initially two and a half acres were involved, six lorries working five days a week for more than a year to fill the hollow to a maximum depth of twelve feet - much more having blown away across fields and gardens in the laying.

This was early days for crop production on duff and an article in the "Farmers' Weekly" of 14th March 1969 reports how local scorn was heaped on the project. *"That stuff is only fit for burying cats!"* quoth one agricultural advisor, but he was proved very wrong. In 1964 Jack Francis took 300 fifty six pound bales of hay from the two and a half acres and described it as the most productive field on the farm, while his son in the nineties takes two crops of hay or silage a year and uses the field for rotational grazing in between, speaking very highly of it.

Once fertilisers were applied and the grass cover established, it stopped blowing, packed firm after rain and held the moisture well. Milk was tested for taint for ten years, but no taint was found. There was a slight hicough when the turf yellowed from a severe infestation of chafer grub.

"I knew I shouldn't plough the duff" said the farmer "but I gave it two good harrowings, put seed on top, rolled it in and everything was fine."

The new sward turned out well and has maintained quality over the years but two snags arise from the loose texture. Cattle tend to pull grass out by the roots and burrowing animals find it an ideal digging site. This does not, however, detract from the value of the plot, which is the most productive in summer and the greenest in winter, as well as producing good 'early bite' in spring. Best of all, it doesn't poach: the dairy cows can be turned out there on winter days and fed in the field, without getting gummed up in mud or damaging the sward.

This saves the chore of carting their dung out from the barn, as farmyard manure is vital to add body to the powdery mass. The organic matter breaks down very quickly and what the moles throw up in their hills looks like unadulterated ash, despite the many applications of dung and general purpose fertilisers (nitrates, potash and phosphates) which have passed through it to the grass.

Moles only move in if there are earthworms to eat. The author's late cousin, Eric Gillham of the C E G B in the Midlands, who monitored

Moles in Clover

fly ash infills through Southern Britain, tells us that the fly ash on the old greyhound stadium just across the Taff has the distinction of being the first ash site in the country to support earthworms, so these and the Ynys Gau worms have a place in the literature, alongside those of Charles Darwin.

The floodlighted dog stadium, where bets were won and lost, occupied the former site of a big old colliery reservoir so water relations were good for binding the fine particles together and keeping the accumulating organic debris sufficiently moist to be useful to worms.

A stabilising layer of stony clay soil was spread over the ash there, which had been down about twelve years on 6th March 1974 when Roy Perry of the National Museum and the author were able to list fifty nine higher plant species and fourteen moss species on it. The list lengthened as the season advanced. There were a few marsh plants, such as fool's watercress but no acid lovers, the sheep's sorrel so characteristic of coal slag tips being replaced throughout by common sorrel.

The community off the actual race track was tussocky grass with European gorse and broom. Some had been burned, the flames exposing a labyrinth of short-tailed field vole tunnels among the shoot bases, these plant eaters finding the terrain as satisfactory as did the moles. The stadium has gone now, replaced by yet more houses!

No soil cover was applied on the Ynys Gau ash but rabbits, too, found this an excellent medium in which to set up home. Stabilised by creeping clovers and long-rooted dandelions, it compacts beyond the point of caving into the burrows or asphyxiating the inmates. Worms bring moles and blackbirds: rabbits bring foxes and buzzards, while the odd stoat and weasel are seen about. The varied soils, the steep wooded sides of the river terraces, ponds with frogs, riversides with herons, barns with swallows and kestrels and much more are part of the rich wildlife of Ynys Gau.

The duff field is kept as permanent grassland, like the riverine flats, the one too loose to plough, the other too soggy. More freely draining glacial soils are under long term grass leys, ploughed up only to rejuvenate them when the creeping buttercup, sorrel and thistles begin to take over. Perennial ryegrass with red and white clovers predominate on the cow pastures, with more of the taller cocksfoot and Timothy grass producing the fine hay crops from above the lane.

The southern paddocks, handier to the milking byres, are used by the dairy friesians, nurse cows since the late 1990s, the northern ones, best reached across the muddied farm bridge over the railway, hold the charolets and limousins for beef.

When the leys are ploughed a one year fodder crop may intervene. In 1985 the tobogganing field was planted to kale, which took badly on the lower slopes towards the mine, where there was a lot of sheep's sorrel and big patches of peppermint.

Millions of tons of pulverised fuel ash are produced annually by coal-burning power stations. Much is sold as building material, land

Rabbits, Dandelion, and Ribwort.

infill for new developments and reclaiming marshes and sea flats, but research was under way in the 1960s and 70s to explore its use on agricultural land.

Coming from the burning of fine coal dust, the duff consists of the burned clay and shales left after combustion of the organic fraction. Boron is made more soluble by burning, to the point of toxicity, but lagooning removes a lot of the soluble material and makes it more suitable for crops.

It is usually too alkaline for conifer growth, but field crops can be more tolerant, clovers, particularly wild white, and grasses, particularly perennial rye, especially so. As these are the mainstay of permanent pastures and leys, the problems are minimised. Farmers like those at Ynys Gau who were in at the beginning, maintain that it can't be faulted.

The beet and cabbage families, which thrive on alkaline seaside soils, do well on it. Sugar beet, fodder beet and mangolds, can actually benefit from the extra boron in moderation, but rye is the only tolerant cereal. After a few years of weathering, carrots, parsnips, celery, radishes and onions can be grown, but the usual macro-nutrients are in short supply, with nitrogen deficiency a particular problem. Clovers help by fixing atmospheric nitrogen, but more phosphates and potash must be added to maintain the necessary balance.

After a period of time the ash can be used for cereals or trees, with goat sallow the most amenable of the woody plants. The essential thing is to get the initial grass ley established as soon as possible, to prevent blowing.

Plant incomers to the Ynys Gau duff fields were as well satisfied as the worms, moles and rabbits. Buttercups, daisies and broad-leaved dock were well established by May 1992, when the sward was silvered by a continuous counterpane of puffing dandelion clocks. Dandelion leaves, which we sometimes add to our salads, ribwort plantain and some of the other new arrivals, detracted not at all from the value of the pasture. The experimental herb strips at the Aberystwyth Grassland Research Station have indicated the value of this sort of variety in the diet of farm livestock.

The rash of dandelions may have been spawned along the roadside - as the product of over close cutting through the 1960s and 70s. The council workers' mower blades were set far too low in those days, before the voices of the conservationists were heeded. Everything was shaved off at ground level, sometimes a little below it, leaving unsightly scars and destroying all but those plants with a below-ground energy store, principally the long fleshy taproots of dandelions and the basal stem tubers of the onion couch or tall oat grass.

For many years these two held sway on the lane verges, but the tide has turned at last. Driving north from the village in spring is now a real pleasure. Lesser celandines, wood anemones and cuckoo pints, all with root tubers of their own but less robust than the other two, have returned, along with lady's smock, Jack-by-the-hedge and many more.

Rather special is an unusual species of hawkweed, a metre tall and with unevenly dissected leaves (see p 182). This is very glandular in its upper parts and has been identified at the National Museum of Wales as *Hieracium exotericum f. grandidens (see p.182)*. Others in the 1990s are dogs mercury, germander speedwell, yellow pimpernel, yellow archangel, bugle, pignut, cow parsley, ramsons, bluebells and wood mellick.

Even discounting the wild rose, bramble and honeysuckle, seven woody species make up the hedges beside the Ynys Gau entrance lane. These are field maple, hazel, hawthorn, blackthorn, holly, elder and oak. Foxgloves join the greater stitchwort and herb Robert in the hedge bottoms and black bryony dangles its scarlet berries over the tops.

5. North to Gedrys Wood and Rhyd-yr-Helig Colliery at Maesbach

From the sharp hairpin bend on the Mountain Road above the Gwaelod-y-Garth Inn, a path sets off across the crowded contours of Craig-y-Lan, with deciduous woodland above and coniferous plantation below (this felled in 1997). It divides by a sentinel beech, the lower route dividing again with the two upper forks leading to Lan Farm.

The Lan Farm buildings are set a little back from a craggy pennant rock face supporting some statuesque beeches - the start of the rough terrain beloved by badgers. Open land stretches from the farm to the Garth summit, providing grazing for mountain sheep and the riding ponies that have been based at Lan over the years.

Northwards the ground falls steeply to a kink in the River Taff, which turns south at Nant Garw, this slope occupied by Gedrys Wood, with its old quarries and abandoned mine shafts, spilling down from Gedrys Farm above.

Gedrys is a broad-leaved woodland, left intact when the adjacent conifers were planted around 1962, and it shows signs of ancient coppicing, with some of the larger trees multi-trunked. It ascends from 150 feet to 500 feet, quite precipitously in parts.

The lane access to Lan Farm on the level ground above crosses a delightful mountain stream, spawned in the rushy tree-strewn pastures of the northern Garth. It pursues a tinkling passage through an open-floored, stock-dominated durmast oakwood, the banks golden with celandines at the back end of winter.

This is the Gedrys Stream, which runs parallel to the Ton Teg Lane in its lower part and joins the Taff at Willowford. In the doing it has to cross the lane from Gwaelod, which winds sinuously down under the dense tree canopy, to dive under the Taff Valley Railway at the bend in the river. When the stream is in spate the little bridge is taxed beyond capacity and several truckloads of pebbles can get strewn across the highway, barring traffic. In August 1985 the road itself was washed away below the crossing.

Although bounded by lanes on three sides and a broken fence on the other and with a few footpaths, Gedrys Wood is little disturbed and has been studied over the years by parties of ecology students from the Pontypridd Polytechnic (now the University of Glamorgan). Most seems to be little troubled by farm livestock except at the summit where the Lan Farm ponies nibble at the alders, stimulating the sprouting of bunches of epicormic shoots. This area is swampy and the alders are elevated on spreading mangrove-like bases. Water flushing down onto the track formed a thick sheet of ice at the end of February 1986, which was said to be the coldest February for forty years, with even the wintergreen bramble leaves wilted.

There is a good mixture of woody species, with oak, beech, birch, rowan, holly and alder buckthorn. Ferns and mosses are characteristic, including soft shield fern and hard fern and the Sphagnum moss which denotes acidity. Shade horsetail thrives, the lateral whorls of branches branched again, bringing it more into line with the scarcer wood horsetail than the more familiar field horsetail - a pernicious garden weed.

An average bluebell wood, with violets and wood sorrel in spring, less common valerian and broad-leaved helleborine orchids appear later in the summer. A garden ragwort *(Senecio fuchsii)* is naturalised.

On that frigid February visit we flushed two pairs of wintering woodcock from the leaf litter. A flock of redwings was moving through and one of the resident buzzards was mewing overhead, having given up waiting for a thermal. Blackbirds rummaged among the crisped leaves for fugitive grubs, all cocks, as is usual in winter, but each about his own private search, with no attempt at flocking. Fox tracks led under bushes and grey squirrels had been ring-barking some sycamores.

There was no snow cover to protect the plants, just hard black frost, the air too parched for dew to crystallise out as rime or hoar frost. Ice had congealed over some stretches of the stream, although most flowed too fast to freeze. Impressive icicles bordered the little falls and ice-cased sticks protruded at odd angles, like glass wands.

Timber was cut at the top early in 1989 and dragged out, leaving the ground badly churned up. Big trees, saved by orange paint marks, were left standing. By January 1990 massed foxglove rosettes were appearing, promising a bumper crop of flowers for 1991.

One of the woodland paths leads into the conifer plantation, which extended south along the mountainside to Gwaelod village before felling. It is traversed by a broad forestry road crossing the North Sea gas main on an iron bridge supported by wire netting cages of boulders. The steep banks are heathery and an apiarist kept his beehives on the trackside for many years before moving them to more flowery wasteland between road and river. Interesting flowers with the heathers are New Zealand willow herb and slender St. Johns Wort.

The lower southern part of this plantation, mostly western hemlocks, was harvested in the mid 1990s and the foxgloves came again on the clear-felled slopes behind the Ffygis end of the village. Rosebay willow herb, the other incomer after felling, remained sparse. Leggy birches were left standing but all others were taken - sitka spruce, douglas fir, noble fir, lodgepole pine, lawsons cypress and European and Japanese larch.

John Zehetmayr of the Forestry Commission pointed out that this mixture of species marks the woodland out as having been planted before the early 1960s. Policy since has been for monocultures of the most suitable species, in this case western hemlock and Japanese or hybrid larch.

Maesbach Farm on the slopes above Willowford, like Ynys Gau, Lan and Gedrys Farms, lies in the parish of Llantwit Fardre. Below the farmhouse is the Rhyd-yr-Helig Colliery, the best preserved of all the old mines, and several other smaller shafts.

Whilst student parties from Pontypridd concentrated on Gedrys, those from Cardiff - geologists and industrial archeologists as well as ecologists - were drawn to Rhyd-yr-Helig, a few hundred yards further up-river.

Rhyd means ford and the miners from the colliery crossed the Taff at Willowford immediately below, on the strip of land between railway and river. A ferry boat took them across when the water was too deep to ford. The building here is now a dwelling house, but was formerly an inn.

Rhyd-yr-Helig was a deep mine, unlike the drift mines described further south, but small pits were being worked here too from the beginning of the industrial revolution, as there is coal to be found at various levels.

The drift mines under Gwaelod village burrowed into the lowest coal seams, nearest to the underlying Millstone Grit. At Maesbach we are over a mile from there and the seams which crop out on the surface at Gwaelod are a long way underground as the strata dip into the Coalfield Basin. The deep mine at Rhyd-yr-Helig tapped into higher seams, the bigger, more modern Nant Garw mine (now closed, like the rest) was working the lower seams from the other side of the river.

Rhyd-yr-Helig coal went out by rail, the Glamorgan Canal which served the earlier mines being on the other side of the Taff. Nevertheless, it was one of the first pits to be opened in the Rhondda section of the Coalfield, though possibly not until about 1840. Closure was in 1876, leaving a generous accumulation of slag, from which the farmer is said to have made a mint of money, selling it for the foundations of the Lanwern Steelworks in Gwent.

Ivy Rinderspacher, who lived in the renovated cottage at the junction of the Gwaelod and Tonteg lanes where access was gained, said the commotion was horrendous.

"A constant stream of heavy lorries, day and night, as it was a rush job, with not a few collisions."

In the 1970s red (burnt) and black (unburnt) slag were still recognisable, but the mounded tip site was pleasantly vegetated with a young birchwood, the trees likely to be about ten years old and with other species infiltrating. At that time the old renovated stables were used for growing mushrooms. They are still boarded up and padlocked, but not abandoned. A fine growth of Russian vine *(Polygonum balschuanicum)* has engulfed the roadward end of the building.

Exposures of pennant sandstone around the mine show strata at unexpected angles, due to faulting with a westerly downthrow. Faults run approximately north to south, the biggest, the Darren-ddu fault,

The Old Engine House at Rhyd-yr-Helig Colliery, Maesbach, South Face 1984 (inset, enlarged) End of range of century-old Coke Ovens. 1972

followed by the valley. The river crosses over this on the Gedrys bend. Another runs along the hill just above the mine and the bigger Maesmawr fault passes very close to the Maesbach Farmhous higher up again.

The Llantwit number 1 coal seam crops out near the farm at the base of a thick sandstone bed and coal has been extracted from a few addits below to the east. The Rhyd-yr-Helig shafts passed through three named coal seams (Llantwit 1, 2 and 3) and four smaller veins. Two shafts are shown on the 1876 abandonment plan.

Despite possibly no more than 36 years of working, the waste heaps covered a huge area and there were a lot of buildings, many of their footings still recognisable in the early 1970s, when spontaneously regenerated woodland extended all the way to the road junction.

Most imposing was the stone engine house with arched entrances facing two ways from the elevated boiler flue and winding gear opposite the entrance by the central landing platform. Trees were establishing on top and roots of elms were plastered against the walls, nibbled and deformed. One specimen sporting three trunks had a churring mistle thrush nesting in a high crotch.

Old ivy stems had become calcified and cemented to the stones and lobed tufa dribbles were building up, as lime-saturated water dripped from the mortar. This wall was one of the pair encompassing the winding gear, each surmounted by an engine. The cable on the drum drew loaded trucks up from the now flooded mine and let them slowly on down the incline to the railway.

A series of domed coke ovens, their entrances facing downhill, were built of pennant rock and lined with double ranks of purplish sintered bricks covered with clinkery accretions. Soil and burned slag lay over the ovens, leaving open flues 30 cm square and similar sized channels running between them at ground level. Fern sporelings, mosses and liverworts, particularly Lunularia cruciata, were established inside, but no higher plants.

One of the buildings east of the track received a fast flowing stream which disappeared underground. A tree branch poked into the soft silt of the floor released a series of bubbles, the same happening in a small dammed reservoir above the engine house. This now held only just over a metre of water, due to silting, and fed two divergent streams. Floating duckweed and fool's water-cress occupied part while sinuous tracks of aquatic invertebrates wound across the mud between.

It became a ritual on party visits to the site to set fire to the pools - or rather the methane or marsh gas which they released when stirred. The bubbles were ignited by burning paper held on a forked branch. The bluish flame conjured up visions of moorland will o' the wisps in those unsophisticated times. Now it reminds us of the modern use of

The west corner of the Engine House at Rhyd-yr-Helig, showing the hidden arch. 1998

the methane emanating from the Cardiff rubbish tip at Lamby Way to generate electricity!

Another pastime here was water divining with a pair of metal rods held horizontally. It worked for nearly everyone, so much waters was held in the pennant sandstone aquifers. The slower the swing of the rods, the deeper underground was the water. We were told that the depth of each find was equivalent to the distance walked from the beginning of the swing to the coming together of the notches 10 cm from the ends.

Water bubbled from the ground at unexpected places after rain. Engineers regard these rocks as 'abominably wet' and refer to discontinuities where adjacent strata have been forced apart by water which is liable to emerge under pressure. Formerly it was even wetter, much of today's water draining into disused mines.

Across the valley, where the A 470 trunk road was being constructed, engineers were dealing with the water problem and the danger of slumping by constructing a horizontal series of zig zag ditches, leading the water to cross channels for culverting under the road and into the Taff. A drilling rig was boring into the hillside, tapping the water above the road on 29th January, 1972.

Current bedding in the Pennant rocks, showing as overlapping series of narrow beds, pointed to water movements in the sand from which the rocks were formed in Carboniferous times.

The entire site had been wooded for long enough in the 1970s for rotting timber to provide a good living for fungi. Brightest on drab winter days were the scarlet elf cups Wormwood and Mugwort on half buried sticks in the keyhole shaped entrance of the drainage sump, with attractive coral spot fungus on sticks leaning against the mine shaft buildings.

Wormwood and Mugwort

Pear-shaped puffballs *(Lycoperdon pyriforme)* sprouted from old timbers among the ruins and orange mushrooms pushed through the grass. Crustose species clinging to trees were mauve *Peniophora* on living hazel and white *Stereum rugosum* on fallen branches. Brackets included *Stereum hirsutum*, *Polystictus versicolor* and the familiar razor strop on birches.

There were always plenty of woodland birds about, including tree creepers, nuthatches, bullfinches and jays in winter, with the looping flight of greater spotted woodpeckers commuting over the ruins between stands of birches. In spring wood pigeons built their platform nests and the expectant chatter of young blue and great tits emanated from holes in the masonry. A blackbird built its nest in the rectangular drainage sump where water was pumped out of the mine, to be channelled down the wooded bank to rail and river level. Migrant warblers moved in to join the resident blackcap.

Passerine crop pellets of special interest occurred among the more usual March ones of large ivy pips. Stuffed full of the double-winged samaras of birch catkins, apparently undamaged in the drying black sludge, they were 2.5 to 4 cm long and rather less than 1 cm wide, the average size for thrush or blackbird pellets. Tits, goldcrests and siskins eat birch seeds, but these seemed to have been imbibed 'on the side' by a larger bird seeking more succulent morsels to have been cast out as waste.

The fox earths appeared empty in January 1972 but the characteristic foxy smell was overpoweringly strong again by March. These animals are regarded as vermin and are periodically shot by local farmers. Bank voles were spotted in the dead of winter entering the rubble heaps piled against the ruins, and there was a lively population of short-tailed field voles.

One of these, on 16th March 1972, was scooting along under a loose meshwork of dead sticks, which cracked underfoot. There was a veritable labyrinth of superficial tunnels here, covered by sufficient debris, even in winter, to be entirely above ground - like those exposed by the flopped remains of wilted grass when long-lying snow melts.

Lodged across as a protective ceiling was a weft of dead nettle stems.

On the runs themselves golden saxifrage sprouts were budding among the young nettle shoots of the ensuing summer. Later the whole would be lost under a 2m high stand of stinging nettles, with bramble arching in from beyond.

The kestrel overhead at the time seemed to be wishing us away so that it could profit from the bare season. Tawny owls which hooted here at dusk might prove more of a danger to the nocturnal wood mice which burrowed around the tree boles, leaving little heaps of discarded nut shells on their doorsteps.

Squirrel dreys occurred, and their split hazel nuts, while new mole hills had been thrown up in the dark organic soil among the ruins. Rabbits were on the increase in the early seventies, with plenty of feeding scratches here, but most of the warrens were in the woodland.

On that visit of 16th March 1972 we counted nine brimstone butterflies, all males, three peacocks and a small tortoiseshell. This was the second day of spring, after a spell of bitter winds and driving snow. The lacewings, winter moths and gnats, which had been about most of the winter, were joined by glossy green flies, brown weevils, chewing pollen from the bursting sallow buds and spiders supplying unwilling provender for the diligently seeking wrens.

In those days of nearly thirty years ago and a hundred years after the mine closed, Rhyd-yr-helig must have been one of the best examples of the takeover of industrial ruins by the plant and animal kingdoms. Sadly, the little community was to be cut short in its prime, in the name of more efficient agriculture. Were the neat grass fields that came to replace the felled and ploughed-up woodland in place when the miners moved in in 1840 - or was there woodland here then?

By January 1984 all trees but a few around the sorely depleted mine buildings had been removed. A vacant expanse of rough ploughland reached from the road gate to the four square engine house, with the severed butts and upended roots of trees and shrubs poking grotesquely into the wintry air. The old tree-bordered mine road along its levelled terrace was now a muddy farm track leading past the colliery to a sea of slush barring passage to the birch spinney beyond.

At the time of writing, in the autumn of 1998, the open slope is under permanent grassland, the ryegrass-clover mix pock-marked with dark green circles around old animal droppings. Rubble had been heaped to hide the western arch of the engine house and the trees on top recently felled, the timber piled against the flanks of the encompassing hollow. Some had been sawn into lengths to fill a breach in the summit, with young sycamores pushing through. The secondary or tertiary spinney atop the walls was now a scrubby sward of tufted hair-grass with hop trefoil, field speedwell, nettles, wall lettuce and other composites.

Traces of the calcified tree and ivy roots remained on the west and north walls, where only one stripling ivy plant survived among sparse maidenhair spleenwort, fern sporelings and a little *Lunularia* liverwort. All woody growth apart from a well-shaped alder and a beech tree had been cleared from the surrounding banks.

The main stream, newly guided straight across the slope in 1984, was used for watering livestock in the field above. Waylaid in a covered tank, it was piped to a trough consisting of an old bath above, the overflow near the top spilling the crystal clear excess back into the stream.

The old holly bushes alongside had been hedged by grazing stock into a dense wall of foliage, as evenly as by an accomplished topiarist. Even now, so late in the year, the new pale leaves expanding among the prickly ones were tender and soft, a pleasant hors d'oeuvre for a hungry horse.

Most of the pools had been drained, but there was standing water where butterflies, bees, wasps and craneflies came to drink, among water pepper and creeping buttercup. Persicaria with greatly swollen nodes grew in the lower stream where it tumbled over the still wooded bank to railway level. Here the meadow brown butterflies gave way to speckled woods, the carrion crows and chaffinches to a pair of wood warblers and wrens.

Beyond the now less muddy field corridor strewn with unripe but squirrel-mauled hazel nuts, the former birch spinney had been felled and left. The mounded, bronze-tinged plants dominating the whole area, apart from the furthest grassy corner where the horses congregated, proved to be water pepper, its sap too peppery to tempt the animals down the slope. This is an unusual dominant, suggesting a wetter soil than that existing after that rainy summer. With it on the broken, unploughable banks of the former woodland were foxgloves and common persicaria or redshanks.

Back in the mine field tree-lined hollows of old stream beds persisted and the hedges contained some magnificently contorted trees, beech, sycamore and alder, a fantastic legacy from former pleaching. These monuments of past husbandry, the uneven contours which no plough could touch and the sunlit, rolling grassland was exceedingly pleasant, and no doubt more profitable than the woodland of the interim period, although so much poorer in wildlife.

Outside the gate and stile a garden had been made opposite the cottages in the edge of the wild wood. Fuchsias, Hebes, Tree Mallows, Globe Thistles and some fig trees grew among Himalayan Balsam, while Montbretia, Herb Robert and Forget-me-not contributed to the ground cover.

Tongwynlais Village drowses beneath Castell Coch. View north through the Gorge. February 1972.

Chapter 10

THE RIVER TAFF

Introductory

Seldom in historic times has rainfall been less predictable than in the 1990s, when the media have bombarded us with announcements of *"the driest February or wettest July since records began"*. Topography still, however, exerts a vital influence. From a fluctuating average of 40 inches (just over a metre) a year in Cardiff at the river mouth, the figure more than doubles (to around 90 inches (2.3 m)) at 1,200 feet, where the Rhondda's contribution to the overall flow of the Taff gathers - even more in the loftier spawning grounds of the Taf Fawr and Taf Fechan in the Brecon Beacons National Park.

Peat bogs on the high tops absorb some of the water like a sponge. releasing it in a steady seepage to the upper tributaries, but much pours unhindered from rocky or eroded mountainsides. The pace of the river slackens only intermittently until it reaches the coastal plain, after breasting the gap between the Little Garth and Castell Coch. Low-lying fields like those at Ynys Gau are conveniently sited to receive any overspill and prevent the sort of flood damage to built-up areas that has occurred so often in the narrower valleys of the Rhondda.

The Taff catchment on the eastern end of the Coalfield plateau is higher than that for the rivers of West Glamorgan, so the mountains fall more steeply to the rivers and the rivers more steeply to the sea.

Coalfield shales of the West have yielded more readily to erosion than have the uncompromising Pennant Grits of the East, so rivers like the Neath have cut a wider, deeper channel after their descent down the steps created by alternating bands of hard and soft rocks in the "waterfall country" of the Brecon Beacons. For much of its length the River Neath meanders through marshy flatlands with a maturity scarcely achieved by the turbulent Taff until it reaches the cathedral city of Llandaff.

Although imposingly broad in these lower reaches, the Taff is largely un-navigable. It has too many minor rapids and is often too shallow because of the quick run-off, as it falls the 3,000 feet (over 900 m) from the Beacons to the sea in a distance of about 30 miles - gradients that make the river prone to sometimes catastrophic spates.

The hilltop drovers' roads were adequate for pre-industrial revolution purposes, but better transport was needed for the eighteenth century. With the principal iron industry and some of the earliest coal mines situated at the edge of the Beacons, around Merthyr, Dowlais and Hirwaun, the river valley provided the obvious through way to outlets on the coast.

Canals and light railways were built along the smooth, though sometimes soggy, valley floor, these followed by major railways and roads. In places the various highways converge closely against the river and we have already noted the crowding of the 5 bridges where the Ynys road crosses from west to east in the Taff Gorge below Gwaelod-y-Garth.

The first turnpike road down the valley from Merthyr to Cardiff was completed in 1771, utilising in part an already extant turnpike road from Cardiff to Caerphilly via Nant Garw. A passenger coach service was launched and, by 1840, mail coaches were running regularly. Users of the turnpike roads grudged paying the tolls, however, as shown by the 1843 Rebecca Riots.

1790 saw the start of the Glamorgan Canal, which was opened to industrial and general merchandise 4 years later, and the section of the Taff Vale Railway from Cardiff to Pontypridd was completed in 1840. The journey for loaded freight trains was downhill, the uphill return being largely with 'empties', so light engines could be used.

Then came wider roads through the valley towns, followed by the A 470 trunk road by-passing them. Our section through Taffs Well was completed during the early years of the 1970s, much of it along the course of the old canal, which had been laboriously levelled by the navvies (navigators) of almost two centuries before.

Last of the Pentych Ironworks. The old engine-shed in 1971, with the quarried face under Castell Coch across the river.

1. Physical Features of the River: Ferries, Fords and the Taffs Well Spa

The ancient pre-glacial river channel etched into the underlying rock is some 20 - 35 feet (6 - 10 m) below today's river level. Subsequent southward movement of ice and water brought sediments to the valley floor from the scarified country of the North.

With a later lowering of sea level, the modern Taff, born of the meltwaters, was rejuvenated and cut down through the riverine and glacial deposits, leaving steep scarp faces in the drifted material to either side.

When the sea rose again, to a height slightly greater than that at present, river flow was slowed and some of the load was dropped to partially fill this secondary valley. The Taff now had time to dawdle on its way to the sea and it meandered inconsequentially from side to side of the old rift.

When the force of the current was directed onto the outer curves of bends, the unstable banks were cut back. The loops encroached gradually seawards, wearing away the spurs of land between and the scarp faces that we see to day at Gwaelod and Radyr were left parallel to the overall line of flow.

In adjusting to another slight lowering of sea level, the Taff cut down into these river gravels to leave low river terraces along the foot of the scarps. Some have disappeared, but terraces survive in our area. Their steep riverward faces are usually wooded, with grassland above and below.

Bedrock surfaces in parts of the main channel, as around Quakers Yard and at Pontypridd just upstream of the Treforest Trading Estate, and downstream at Llandaff weir below Radyr. The ridge of rock surfacing at Ynys Gau and its role in capturing glacial debris has been discussed in Chapter 9.

Potholes have been created at Pontypridd where stones swirl around in hollows with a pestle and mortar action, as in higher limestone regions nearer the headwaters. On the slope above in 1970 and 1971 bulldozers excavating for the A 470 trunk road were unearthing beautifully rounded boulders up to half a metre long and half as broad, worn to impeccable smoothness as they were rolled around by ice or water over aeons of time. During the preceding century these had been hidden under rows of terraced houses, now demolished in the name of progress. Motorists had ample time to study them while waiting in traffic blocks at the Glyntaff Bridge.

The ancient lakes at Treforest and Taffs Well referred to in the last chapter were dammed back originally by ridges of bedrock. The Taff exploited the major north to south fault to wear its way through the South Border Ridge of limestone and dolomite at the Taff Gorge. The cutting alongside for the A 470 exposed a wrinkle fold showing the geological succession from the Old Red Sandstone through the overlying basal limestone shales. This clear sequence merited designation as a geological S S S I (Site of special scientific interest) which geologists come a long way to see. The tawny red dolomite just to the north has for long been a favourite with climbers.

Old Red Sandstone forms the wooded ridge above the 1990s houses and the Friendly Inn at Tongwynlais - and has yielded a rare plant fossil. Most of the village at its western foot is on the same fluvio-glacial deposit as the steep scarp of the Long Wood in the Glamorgan Canal Nature Reserve.

Mighty though the Taff is, water engineers have pitted their strength against the flow to change its course in Cardiff. In 1848, when Isambard Kingdom Brunel constructed the main London to West Wales Railway and station at Cardiff, his navvies moved a stretch of the river to combat the all too frequent flooding. The old river course came to be occupied by Westgate Street, with the Cardiff Arms Park Rugby Ground on the dried out land between the two channels.

More recently, further downstream, above the Clarence Bridge, a major loop has been by-passed, leaving an island where the lesser black-backed gulls nested among weedy ground flora through the 1960s and 70s until urbanisation caught up with them and they moved to the rooftops.

Aerial views of the flood plain between Castell Coch and Iron Bridge reveal the sweeping curve of an old ox-bow lake, now a damp hollow alongside a straight stretch of river. Had man intervened here, I wonder, blocking the upper end of the lost meander, or had the river in spate found its own short cut through a more direct flood channel?

To the end of the seventeenth century there were no road bridges across the Taff between Pontypridd and Llandaff. The first seems to have been built around 1815, with a sturdier one by Bole Farm in 1877. The footbridge to the Taffs Well (or Walnut Tree) Station was constructed in 1907, the first Ynys (or Walnut Tree) Road bridge between 1926 and 1930, these two replacing the previous ferry.

The early name of Taffs Well was Rhyd-y-bythel or Rhyd-boithan, rhyd being a ford. Other fords were Rhyd-Radyr, Rhyd-Fforest, Rhyd-yr-Ynys or Cil-ynys, Rhyd-Tywood, Rhyd-yr-bothos, Rhyd-yr-helig and Rhyd-y-felin, the last name still in use without the hyphens.

Edgar Chapell, in his "Historic Melin Griffith" (1940), records that pack mules conveyed their loads from the iron ore mines above Castell Coch to the Pentyrch Works by fording the Taff just above the Ynys Bridge. Those animals must have been very sure-footed, although the river was shallower then, with much of its water diverted into Forge Dyke. There were blocky stepping stones to help the humans across.

New and old Ynys bridges.
View from the crushing plant on the Little Garth, March 1971.
Note the anticlynal wrinkle fold beyond Ynys House.

Most fords were furnished with ferry boats for when the water was too high to wade - a chilly business, anyway, in winter, before the invention of gumboots! Even the ferries, which were hand-propelled, were unable to function when the current was running strongly. How those ferrymen would have enjoyed a modern inflatable propelled by an outboard motor!. Now that these are available, we have other means of crossing.

The highest ferry service functioning in historic times was at the appropriately named Upper Boat, with its black and white timbered inn alongside the incompatibly utilitarian D I Y emporium. Upstream from here crossings were by stepping stones or fords.

There was another ferry on the deep water ponded back by the Upper Portobello Weir. Although several rowing boats were moored on the Gwaelod side in the years before the first world war, the ferry boat proper was kept on the Glan-y-llyn or Taffs Well side. (Does this 'llyn' refer to the ancient lake, or just a broad stretch of river?) Gwaelod folk had to whistle for it. The fare was one penny, for the boat to be hauled across along a rope attached to opposing banks.

A fatal accident occurred in 1915 (or 1920 according to another authority) when it capsized at high water and was washed over the weir, together with the lock keeper's daughter, who had come to collect her groceries. The boat, still containing the shopping, finished up closeby, but she tried to swim for it. Her body, identified by her wedding ring,

ROAD WORKS IN THE TAFF GORGE. 1971

52. The new Ynys Bridge under the Little Garth quarry. February

53. The new roundabout and A470 under Castell Coch. November

54. View south through the Taff Gorge over Taffs Well, from Graig-yr-Allt. February 1971

55. View south through the Taff gorge over Heol Beri and the pig farm, October 1971 before the building of the River Glade and South Glade houses.

was washed up weeks later on the coast of Somerset. A few years afterwards the ferry was replaced by the Pont Sion Phillips footbridge a little downstream.

The Upper Portobello Weir is shown on the tithe map surveyed in August 1839 and the 1873 map revised in 1898. It was longer than the width of the river as it crossed obliquely, like the present Llandaff Weir. Water was channelled into the downstream corner on the west bank to be led off into the Pentyrch Forge dyke. When the sluices were open to direct extra power to the works, it made fording down river easier.

Nevertheless, by deflecting the main stream across to the east bank, the non-aligned weir caused recession there and a widening of the river channel. The Taffs Well springs, which had formerly surfaced in the middle of Cae Ffynnon, the Well Field, came to be sited dangerously close to the eroding river bank as a result. The Rev. Lee Brown (1983, "Ffynnon Taff") gives an account of the spa through the ages.

When G.W.Manby visited in 1802, he found several powerful springs rising from the bottom of the well at a depth of 3 feet (1 m), while a column of clear water forced its way up like a mini geyser at intervals of 3 - 5 minutes. Gas was forced out under pressure in a stream of bubbles. (G.W.Manby (1802) "An Historic and Picturesque Guide through the Counties of Monmouth, Glamorgan and Brecknock").

One later investigator thought this gas to be mainly nitrogen; another reported that it burst into flame if a light was applied - suggesting methane, as in the Rhyd-yr-Helig mine pools.

After the building of the weir, the springs were inevitably inundated by river water during spates. As much as 4 feet depth of river gravel might be washed in, but the force of the springs was able to clear this. Nicholson, in "The Cambrian Travellers' Guide" of 1840, states the well to be "Now in the middle of the river", with people wading out to reach it except when the water was low in summer.

Only one of the several springs was enclosed in 1861 - in sheets of iron, allowing three people at most to bathe simultaneously. By 1865 benches were provided. In 1891 Mr. Morgan, the owner, rebuilt in stone, to enclose all the springs, and opened the well in August to accommodate ten bathers at a time. The sex of the current occupants was advertised by the garment draped outside - trousers or petticoat.

The waters were used for bathing rather than drinking, being warmer than the Taff: 65 - 68 degrees Fahrenheit according to different authorities. This was just comfortable, although cooler than the Roman Baths at Bath, and produces a fine head of steam when the air is frosty. An alternative name was Ffynnon Dywm, the Tepid Well. Its chief although by no means infallible use was for the alleviation of rheumatism.

J.W. Thomas. who visited 75 years after Manby, was the first to analyse the waters (J.W.Thomas (1877) (Trans. Cardiff Naturalists' Society, IX).

He found them to be impregnated with iron (chalybeate) with a little lime and magnesia, non-smelly and staining the wall with rusty iron oxide. His records are of a resurgence from the Coalfield rocks below of 800 gallons an hour, from a depth which he estimated as 1,300 feet or nearly a quarter of a mile: hence the slight warming.

After a period of disuse during the first world war, the well was reopened and reroofed. Enthusiastic use was resumed, but dwindled, due to a lack of faith in its healing properties or a greater reliance on modern medicine.

Repairs to the river bank set the well building firmly on the eastern shore and a swimming pool was built by unemployed miners during the 1926 recession . Pupils from Radyr School and elsewhere were brought here for swimming lessons before the second world war. The project was a little too ambitious in that there was insufficient head of water to keep so large a volume continuously replenished. Also the river still took its toll. The final knell - of contamination and structural damage - was sounded by a spate in 1960.

Plants took over, germinating between the tiles and looping in from the margins. Buddleja, balsam, evening primrose and soapwort loomed large among the invaders, attracting hosts of butterflies, but, inevitably, the notorious Japanese knotweed took over eventually. The swimming pool was filled in, leaving only the downstream wall as a reminder of its existence.

By this time the river bank had been considerably heightened and strengthened to protect the Taffs Well houses from flooding. This process coincided with the removal of the weir in 1970 and release of the polluted, impounded water from behind it. The Water Board's J C Bs were driven back and forth across the stony river bed for many months that summer, pushing the river gravels to more appropriate positions to accommodate the flow.

During the seventies a path along the east bank had taken walkers directly to the well from the Pont Sion Phillips footbridge, past a gas storage tank, now replaced by buildings and kennels. This route was fenced off by high wire netting along the bank top in the mid eighties and access to the well barred. No longer was it possible to stand inside, where steps led down for about six feet into the yellow-green water from either end of the 'forecourt', to give it too grandiose a name. The outside of the building was an eyesore of defaced brick and concrete.

During the 1975 and 1976 droughts the water supply had remained constant, enabling the groundsman to beat the hose pipe ban and water the exceptionally fine turf of the bowling green, its mineral content having no ill effects. In 1985 he and local enthusiasts cleared the well to a depth of 13 - 14 feet (4 - 5 m), allowed it to refill and swam in it. Renovation of the spa was part of the much vaunted "Taff Valley Project", but was never implemented.

There was spasmodic lobbying of the Taff Ely Borough Council by locals to reinstate "Britain's smallest and cheapest Spa", but to date the building is sealed, awaiting the necessary finance. The rusty outflow of the 1970s and 80s under a concrete sill is now piped through the embankment into the Taff. Although the water is ponded back during spates, river water cannot enter by this route.

The building was embellished in the mid eighties, the new concrete roof ornamented with a turreted rim and a stepped top added to the adjoining part of the swimming pool wall. The two windows were bricked up and a metal door put in place. This was dented by bullets. The replacement wooden one had a panel ripped out to make it possible to see inside. An asset was the new ornamental garden made where the pool had been: an amenity, albeit a rather fossilised one, falling far short of its potential.

A carpark was made and the garden extended upstream to join it, with a picnic site beyond a padlocked gate leading behind the houses to the north. By 1998 the outside of the well house had been embellished with a facing of rocks, which continued down the diminished swimming pool wall, whose slabbed top gave convenient access to the flat roof where children played and stepped through green netting alongside onto the high flood defence and so down to the riverside path on the further side. Iron grids protected a new stout wooden door and the windows were now open to viewers through frameworks of glass fragments adhering in ornamental confusion to stout polythene.

The information plaque had been stolen from its stone cairn but the garden, with its paths of curved brickwork, was well tended. It consisted of a shrubbery of dwarf conifers, variegated and grey-leaved shrubs rather than a flower garden. Walking there on a damp September evening after rain, I was not surprised. The place was crawling with slugs, monsters up to 12 cm long, like those of my own garden across the river through that exceptionally wet summer of 1998. Most were garden slugs *(Arion hortensis)*, brown with an orange rim round the sole, others were black *Arion ater.* Scores were surging out over the sweet mown grass of the lawns from the river embankment to the south and almost as many from the ornamental shrubberies, their chomping, so disastrous to the flower gardener, helping the man with the mower.

Principal shrubs were *Cotoneaster, Hebe, Senecio greyii, Euonymus, Spiraea,* red-leaved *Berberis* and variegated laurel. Outside the well house were *Gunnera, Astilbe,* rock-rose and pampas, while genuine tropical castor oil plants *(Ricinus communis)* flowered and fruited alongside the bowling green, where there was less slug cover and some attractive bedding plants.

On the 1750 map today's Taffs Well Inn was named the Rose and Crown Ale House. This was not because the well was unknown then, because the building doubled up as the farmhouse of the small Ty Ffynnon Taf Farm, its home paddocks now accommodating the park, the junior school and a few houses.

During the 1970s and 80s the inn sign was of a man emerging from the well and another outside - lest the reason for the village name change from 'ford' to 'well' be forgotten. During the 1990s, however, this connection was lost. The new inn sign above the words "Ffynnon Taf" is of a Welsh lady in red flannel petticoats and high hat, against a background of river and mountain!

The spring bubbles inexorably on. There could be a reinstatement of the spa yet.

Construction of the covered reservoir above Tongwynlais, looking north through the Taff Gorge, February 1972.

2. Flash Floods on the River Taff

While the river may roar down with frightening velocity, there are times when it is so placid that a film of ice can form along its margins, this extending from the bank like a counter-balanced sheet of glass as the water flows away from beneath it. Sometimes several ice shelves will form overnight when a flood is subsiding. In recent years, even before El Nino took charge, floods have been more frequent than freezes.

"The greatest flood in living memory" mentioned by John Tyler (1988) in *"Iron in the Soul"*, as experienced by his grandfather, was on August 28th 1877. Sheep, pigs, cattle and horses were swept to their death and cornfields ruined. This was the spate that swept away the original Iron Bridge at Tongwynlais and made the Llandaff Bridge and turnpike road impassable. The L shaped row of iron workers' cottages and the mission hall on the low ground occupied by today's rugby field were flooded up to bedroom level, on this and a number of other occasions. With the Taff on one side and Forge Dyke on the other, they were particularly vulnerable and were demolished in the 1940s.

No year passes without some flooding, but certain spates remain memorable for their display of power. 1961, 1975, 1976, 1979, 1990 and 1992 stand out among those witnessed by the author. Alan Lock has photographs of the river roaring past Ynys Bridge at road level. 1975 and 1976 are best remembered for their long summer droughts, but the drastic water shortages came to an abrupt end with the September deluges.

My most spectacular flood viewing was at Blackweir on the Pontcanna Fields below Llandaff. Water poured over the weir in a shining arc, to swoosh up again in a smooth-backed wave to an equivalent height, the foaming crest tumbling forwards to sweep across the willow-clad island below.

Gwyn Davies, a former pollutions officer with the Welsh Water Board, recollects a spate hurtling through the river bridge at the top of the Treforest Trading Estate. A flotilla of big empty oil drums bobbing down on the flood were forced under the surface by the bridge and exploded on the downstream side - flying for 10 - 20 feet (3 - 6 m) into the air on release, like giant tiddliwinks.

According to national TV news, 27th December 1979 saw the worst flooding in South Wales for twenty years. E E C money was sought and the government offered local authorities finance to help clear the mess - if they could raise a matching sum. A hundred families received help from the Lord Mayor's Fund.

In Merthyr Tydfil two ladies were drowned and many more were cut off. In the Rhondda several hundred people were evacuated and housed in village halls. Sewage pipes overflowed and contamination of the mains water supply necessitated deliveries of drinking water by lorry. Trehafod and other main streets were under 5 feet of water, heavily impregnated with coal dust.

The Ynys Gau paddocks emulated the pre-glacial lake and the Heol Beri Pig Farm, now River Glade, was flooded out. In Llandaff North the road-river bridge was weakened and rendered unsafe. For two years single line traffic was controlled by traffic lights until the new oblique bridge was built just downstream.

Cloying black silt was stranded up to a metre deep over the riverside fields - just like the life-giving Nile floods we were taught about in our schooldays. Debris was strained from the water to this height by the wire netting round the Haley Park tennis courts at Llandaff North. Massed polythene, branches and other debris were caught up in riverside trees to a height of 5 m.

Some of Llandaff, along with Cathedral Road and other parts of Cardiff, were under water. Canton was hard hit, as was the Sophia Gardens Sports Centre. During the first few days of January, 1980, refuse men were collecting lino, carpets and furniture covered in black ooze, from outside the stately houses of Cathedral Road.

Supplying and controlling the quantity and quality of the mains water that we all demand is no mean task. In the early 1980s the principal effort was put into heightening the banks of the Taff and its chief tributaries, but no amount of work on the main channel could control the unruly tributaries which came bounding down the mountain sides to augment the flow.

From 7th to 9th February culverts were collapsing all over the Eastern Valleys, with TV spectaculars showing waterfalls running in at the backs of terraced houses built athwart the slope and out at the fronts. Water surged under the Ynys bridge within a few centimetres of the tops of the arches. Mountain Ash on the Cynon tributary of the Taff was cut off on 7th February for the second time in close succession, but the rush was spent in a couple of days.

Then came the spectre of water shortage, with the Water Board's efforts directed towards the location and repair of leaks in the main arteries. Major new sewage treatment works have been springing up around the county, along with the upgrading of the leaky sewage pipes that follow the river valleys too closely - an unadorned addition along stretches of the two Rhondda Rivers and others. The one mitigating fact is, that when these are overloaded with land drainage as well as domestic and industrial effluents, both dilution and speed of run-off are at maximum.

The phenomenally wet summer of 1998 alleviated the prospect of long term water shortage, but it was a sad day that year when the big black storage tanks on the side of the Great Garth above Gwaelod were ripped out, as obsolete. The indefatigable crystal flow had kept the village supplied with 24 hour a day tap water during the 1975 and 1976 droughts when others had their mains supply cut through part of each day. Now all that sweet water is running to waste, straight down the mountain into the Taff, to be lost in the salty Severn Estuary. And there was plenty of it.

Hemlock Water Dropwort washed out of the ground by the flooded Taff, December 1992

Rain continued right through November and the 1998 floods of the last week of October were once again deemed the worst for twenty years. Red alert warnings were out for all the South Wales rivers and lives were lost, one of a man who had gone to rescue his livestock and was swept away himself. At peak there was again neglibible leeway under the old Ynys Bridge and the field below the village centre was partly submerged.

13.5 inches or 329 mm of rain fell in the Rhondda in five days and householders in Aberfan on the middle Taff spent six nights in emergency accommodation. This latter disaster was caused by the rising of the Taff itself, not the tributaries that had triggered the destruction of the school in the disastrous tip slide of a couple of decades before.

1992 was as good an example as any of the unpredictability of the water supply. During the phenomenally dry April, May and June our rivers were low, but not actually drying out as many were in South-east England. In the late summer the soil became saturated and unable to deal with the 3 inches of rain that fell in 24 hours on 30th November from a slow-moving frontal system.

The Severn Tunnel was flooded, cutting Wales off from London by rail, with some of the 'sprinter lines' closed, roads under water and embankments collapsing. Flood alerts were issued for 28 rivers in Wales, these often too late to act as an early warning system for evacuation.

"The rivers just rise too fast!"

It was small comfort to receive the official bulletin reporting that, after four dry winters, the water had not penetrated far enough to replenish the underground aquifers and that most of the last three month's rain had been lost to surface run-off. Only then, in November and December, was the life-giving fluid reaching down to the sources of the springs and wells. I set out to explore up river and down, as far as the flooded roads allowed, and produced a report for the Cardiff Naturalists' News Letter which is repeated here almost verbatim.

THE TAFF FLOODS, NOVEMBER _ DECEMBER 1992

This was by no means the first time that the Taff had risen in majesty. We who live in the Valleys had seen it all before - as recently as two years back - but it is always impressive.

From an unruffled flow idling over glacier-smoothed pebbles, the river had become puffed up with importance and was showing its teeth. All through 30th November, 1992, it mounted steadily up the masonry pillars of the Taffs Well railway bridge, licking hungrily round waterside alders and forcing its coffee coloured armoury into the dolomite revetements below.

An uprooted tree was trundled down to be steered through an arch, caught in a counter current, entangled and dislodged, to speed on among the motley of polythene containers and empty drums. Marginal bushes upstream became islanded as water spread inexorably over the turf behind.

"Eleven feet above normal" quoth the media. There was a slight drop the next day but, by 2nd December, after 4 more inches of rain in 21 hours, the lost height had been regained, along with more, bringing it to 14 feet above par. Official records quoted 10 inches of rain in 3 days! No tree would have made it through the diminished bridge arches now.

It came as no surprise to hear the official announcement: *"The drought is over."* Only 5 months before there had been grave concern of water shortage. All through April, May and June I had been carrying cans of water to save my garden seedlings. In July the rains came - and the slugs - neither letting up for very long between then and Christmas.

Early showers slid off the bone dry surface, unable to penetrate. Gradually water percolated the crust: now the ground was saturated and it was sliding off again. It was grievous to see so much of the very stuff of life racing unused to the sea.

The ill fated first floors in Pontypridd's Sion Street and Taff Street went under, as always in floods, while William Edward's elegant curvaceous bridge alongside held firm - as it had since the first few abortive attempts to persuade it to stand up in 1756 - when it was claimed as the greatest single arch bridge in the world.

The curve of the Cynon, where road and river were re-routed during the removal of the burning tip at Cefn Pennar in 1988-89 overflowed, as the secretary of the Glamorgan Wildlife Trust had warned the planners that it would at the time. Inevitably the Mountain Ash Comprehensive School was closed, yet again, until the floods abated.

The Rhondda Rivers do not come from the rain sodden Beacons, but from the top of the Coalfield, in the 90 inch plus rainfall belt, but their tributaries fall a long way in a short distance. The worst manifestation was the land slip at Blaen Llechau above Ferndale, where mud and slurry let itself in at the back doors and out at the front, after breaking through the intervening walls. There were more landslips at Tylorstown on Rondda Fach and Pont y Gwaith on the Taff, while twenty homes in Pentre and Porth were reported to be in trouble.

In the bleak mid-winter of 2nd December I followed the foot of the Gwaelod y Garth scarp upstream to where it curved back to make way for a field where the land at the cliff base is under water for much of the winter anyway - a perfect spawning ground for frogs. Now water was surging in under the railway bridge, covering the rest except for a brief central hump, where a great gathering of gulls was busy gorging on worms and grubs flooded from their burrows.

A heron stood in a quiet backwater, driven from its mainstream fishing grounds and hoping that some of the fish might be swimming overland - Amazon Forest style. Water battling to get out where the wooded cliff bulged riverwards, was thwarted by the back-up from the Taff, engendering a circular dance of flotsam behind the bordering brambles.

When water level had dropped 12 feet down the bridge stanchions by 5th December, I splashed into the field to view the aftermath. It showed a text book example of the relationship of weight of particle carried to speed of water flow. Scores of featherweight polythene containers were stranded on the hump where the gulls had celebrated others misfortune. Dark silt lay on the slope immediately below and heavier light brown sand had drifted through the bramble fringe behind the riverside alders. The slope down the now hidden revetments to the river was covered with water-rounded pebbles caught up among the alder bases. There was no size sorting here: velocity had not diminished until the water spilled over the top.

Some of the molehills had been flattened; a few of the older ones resembled bristly white hedgehogs, the diminished mounds beset with the white shoots of creeping buttercup which hadn't quite made it to the light before the soil was swept away. Others were lightly frozen, crunching underfoot, but there were a few fresh ones along the higher riverward margin, proving that not all the moles had drowned in their burrows. A dark shadow slipped out alongside the stream - a mink was about its business, tracking down the less alert!

In mid afternoon on the 2nd I moved on to Radyr Station. The road dipping under the railway was under several feet of water, so I climbed the stairway to cross the tracks, encountering the massed commuters emptied from two sprinter trains making for the relief buses. No trains were proceeding further up valley. After breasting the human tide. I found no way off the further platform, the steps leading down into water, although the river footbridge beyond was high and dry.

The riverside path opposite was discernible by a double row of trees as the river watered the once thirsty allotments behind. From Radyr Comprehensive School at the top of the scarp almost the whole valley seemed to be flooded, with water lapping against the railway shunting yards. Radyr Court Road went under, and almost did so again in January, but now sports a new stone revetment and lawns replacing riverside scrub.

Approached from the Llandaff North side, the scene was as impressive as it was from above. Tangled marsh vegetation and grazed fields had gone under, the 10 feet tall thicket of Japanese knotweed just broke surface, while waterside saplings jigged back and forth as though in a high gale. Not all managed to hold on. A big log careered past at around 30 m.p.h.

A mallard caught off guard went ricocheting away across the maelstrom to scuttle ashore in disorder. The turbulence was too great for gulls and the cormorants had deserted their customary stance on the high tension wires by the old Tin Plate Works. As I photographed the ancient Melingriffith pump - or the quarter fraction of the mighty water wheel that remained above water - I spotted a whole flotilla of ducks which had found haven on the quieter water of the now united feeder channels.

A pied wagtail was scavenging along the driftline before turning in for the night and a blackbird uttered distracted staccato calls at imagined spectres in the gloom. Darkness overtook me as I scrambled along the grassy side of the inner river defences under the new houses. The outer defences had been topped south of the canal and 50 yards of the newly created riverside path was awash.

It was 10.30 pm when I drove back from Cardiff. The clouds had passed and an opalescent half moon hung in a starlit sky. (Like that during the total eclipse of the full moon a week later). A tawny owl called loud and clear from below the Gwaelod-y-Garth Inn, to be answered by another.

It was the start of the finish. Snow was forecast on land above 200 m and I woke next morning expecting a white blanket on the hills. Instead I found a white blanket in the valley, the pallid sun glinting off the top of a thick, cotton wool mist which obscured Taffs Well and extended a third of the way up Graig-yr-Allt Mountain. I left before it dispersed, but the next day it lingered until after ten.

Water level was down 6 feet by 3rd December. The rise and fall of our flash flood rivers can be as spectacular as the rise and fall of the Bristol Channel tides, second largest in the world. I hoped that those planners who wish to mar the admirable new development around Cardiff Bay by building the ill conceived and totally irrelevant Taff Barrage, were watching the forces at work and wondering how their proposed sluices would cope!

My explorations on the 3rd started at Tongwynlais. The Ironbridge tramway crossing stood firm and the path leading upstream from the first kissing gate had re-emerged, coated with a substantial layer of river-borne sand. This was yellow, rippled like a sea beach and with only the briefest wavy lines of drifted coal dust. It was imprinted with the pad marks of a large dog and a pair of hob-nailed boots that had got there before me.

A new load of shredded polythene had been sifted out by waterside bushes - a bizarre flowering of tattered, almost indestructible garbage that would mar the riverside for months to come. Japanese knotweed lay prostrated, headed downstream: many of the canes severed and voyaged on to pile in drifts 10 feet high below Radyr Weir, where empty drums bobbed interminably at the foot of the fall, trapped in an endless treadmill. Two big logs, patterned with the black mosaic of bootlace fungus, had escaped onto the path.

A mallard drake, flushed from cover, was carried out to midstream, to go hurtling down at an exhilarating pace, and chaffinches searched for water-borne seeds among the eroded entrances of water vole holes. All was bathed in sunshine, but not for long. Dark clouds hung heavy over the valley upstream and a lethal looking mass of purple-black was heading in from the west. I raced to shelter under the motorway bridge. Two dog owners raced in from the other direction and we reminisced on past floods as the ensuing deluge poured off the concrete to either side. The place we occupied had been under water yesterday.

They spoke of damage to the path further down, the lifting of the sealed surface, exposure of hard core, gouging of holes and drifting of sand and silt. If so much could be stranded here, how much more could pile up behind that monstrous mythical barrage - and who would clear it?

Pathside grass lay flat, neatly combed towards the sea, and an anaemic meshwork of underground ivy stems had been stripped of their soil cover. Hemlock water-dropwort plants had been ripped up and spewed out at the top of the weir, revealing their poisonous root tubers, which had acted as floats. Marginal tree roots looped out into empty air where soil had been scoured from behind.

Mike Wiley, warden of Forest Farm Nature Reserve, had come to close the sluice into the Melingriffith feeder the previous day, only to find the river flowing over the path and cascading down into the channel. The northern arm, under a fine show of polypody fern, sparkling with raindrops in the returned sunshine, had received a lot of the path surface, bringing it above current water level. More had drifted into the entrance of the ancient lock system, which was drier than I remembered it, while the stream carved itself a narrow channel against the opposite bank. A couple of magpies were searching the deposits for newly arrived goodies, while a carrion crow tucked into a substantial meal further along.

But it is an ill wind! The black-headed gulls were having a whale of a time. There must have been a hundred of them, spaced out across the river above Radyr Weir. They are often there, paddling upstream to waylay edible titbits floating down. Today none were pitting their puny strength against the smoothly rolling current: they were here for the ride. They floated sideways, turning downstream just 6 feet from the brink of the fall to take off, as into the wind, turn back and alight about 200 yards higher up for another free ride. There was no feeding: any debris was travelling at their own speed.

It was different with the cormorant, a young one, pale of throat and breast, which paddled vigorously in among the upstream gulls, overtaking them with ease. It took to the air with much splashing and flapping, well above the awesome brink. I wondered if it could fish in these conditions. At home in muddy estuaries, the turbidity would not have incommoded it, but the current strength might.

As I retraced my steps to Iron Bridge, a kingfisher shot past, a blue flash, brief but unmistakable. No doubt its nest hole had been inundated, but this was not the nesting season: it could find another refuge. A few pink flowers of herb Robert and red campion peeped from the banks and cow parsnip spread reassuring rose-tinted umbels in defiance of the oncoming winter.

Nature can cope with natural disasters. It is man's inadequate walls which suffer; those across the flood a deal more than those alongside. Maybe we shall be spared that barrage yet!

3. Water Quality, Fisheries and other River Life

Floods are not the only disasters that our lively river comes up with: droughts can be almost equally devastating, although less precipitate. At the height of industrial activity leats took water away to power machinary, leaving shallows and shingle banks. Nowadays the reservoirs on the mountain headwaters, constructed to sustain the growing population that is growing still, abstract quantities of water that do not re-enter lower down as the leat water did.

On 19th August 1976, the second of the two best remembered drought summers, the "South Wales Echo" featured the headline:
RIVER DRIES: EELS DIE IN THOUSANDS.

The lower Taff had ceased to flow and the stretch below Blackweir consisted of a necklace of pools and puddles on a denuded, boulder strewn bed. Below the 4 m high dam at Blackweir, which marks the limit of tidal infiltration, was a mass of writhing bodies, seething over each other and getting nowhere. These were adult eels, which the newspaper reporter described as being "on their annual migration upstream, meeting their first minor obstacle" in the form of the dry wall ahead. He had, of course, got his eels in a worse twist than they had achieved for themselves.

These fish were on their once-in-a-lifetime journey downstream, heading off to the South-west Atlantic to spawn, after several years of fattening up in the Taff. The upstream migration is undertaken by the tiny elvers or glass eels, which reach the Severn Estuary in March, tens of millions making their way up the rivers in April and May.

There is a thriving elver fishery in the estuary in early spring: 100 tons were taken in 1975 when water levels were still high enough for the little creatures to make their way inland. Another fishery in August and September exploits the adult eels which have built up good food reserves in the river for their mammoth journey to the Sargasso Sea. The fully grown fish were caught in wicker baskets, now plastic, like elongated versions of the salmon putchers which can be seen stacked on the salt marshes around the old Severn Bridge. They are very different from the pots used for the incoming elvers.

The 1976 adult eels had slid over the weir to find further passage barred by dry expanses of gravel. They can travel overland by night when conditions are moist, but not in summer sunshine, many dying here in the press of bodies.

Ironically well-meaning would-be rescuers were gathering them up in buckets, no mean task, few things being as slippery as an eel, and emptying them into the water ponded back behind the weir - one step

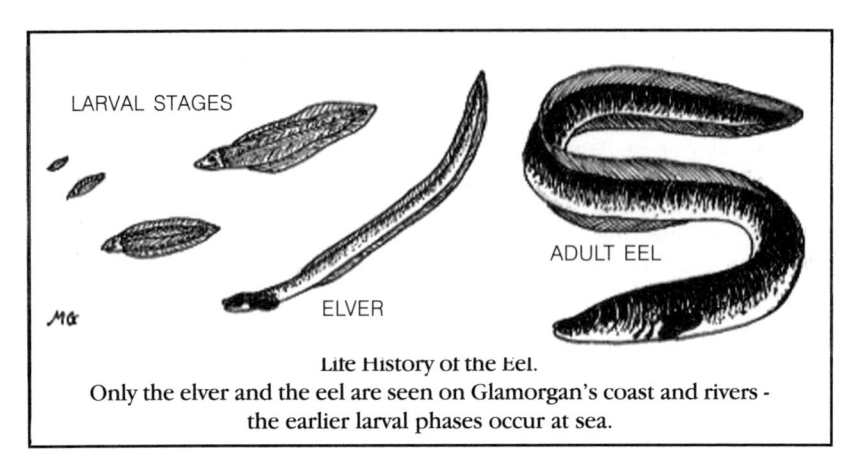

Life History of the Eel.
Only the elver and the eel are seen on Glamorgan's coast and rivers - the earlier larval phases occur at sea.

back in their progress to the sea.

It was reported that their efforts made no impression on the ever growing mound at the foot of the weir, where many were asphyxiated, their white bellies uppermost. It wouldn't. Gulls had a field day, carrying off the quick and the dead to feed their noisily supplicating youngsters, now out of the nest and waiting expectantly on the Sophia Gardens embankment alongside.

When the Boulevard de Nantes canal at Greyfriars was drained a few years earlier it had been found to be seething with massed adult eels attempting a more chancy route to the sea via the feeder channel supplying the docks.

Eels have been the most important fish in the Gwaelod-y-Garth stretch of the Taff over the past few decades - for the unsavoury reason that they can tolerate higher levels of water pollution than any other.

In the bad old days when the Taff was turbid with suspended solids, mostly coal dust, and effluents of domestic, industrial and agricultural origin, a comprehensive fish survey of the entire river was carried out by Mr. A Learner and Ron Williams of the University of Wales Institute of Science and Technology. This was in the early summer of 1971.

They found that trout, present in the upper river, cut out at Pontypridd. Eels were the only fish present in the Taffs Well stretch, which was recorded as being the most polluted of any. Half the fish examined had empty guts, while over 92% of the recognisable remains in the rest were of *Chironomid* larvae, the wriggly, wormlike young of the midges which swarm over the surface of even the most fouled stretches. The significant number of worm bristles was scarcely surprising as worms - *Tubificidae* and *Naididae* - made up 98 to 99% of all the animals found in this stretch.

Other food remains were of the tiny wheat grain or grape pip snail shells *(Potamopyrgis jenkinsi)* and the odd wandering snail *(Lymnaea peregra)*. In less polluted stretches eel guts contained water hog lice *(Asellus aquaticus)*, mayfly nymphs and terrestrial insects.

Suspended solids registered at 230 gms/litre at Taffs Wells, 200 g/l upstream at Upper Boat and 100 g/l at Tongwynlais, rising again to 150 g/l at Llandaff. Coal dust pollution from coal washeries after mining ceased was more of a hazard to life than when mining was in progress. Washeries were reworking waste tips and lagooning the sludge. When the sludge pit banks gave way during heavy rain, finely crushed particles were emptied straight into the river. Thankfully this is a thing of the past.

Coal in suspension is not toxic, but can coat the gills of fish, hindering respiration. Also it cuts down light penetration, making life impossible for submerged green plants, and clogs the digestive tracts of filter feeding invertebrates. The only large plants recorded in the whole river system by Kathryn Benson-Evans were in the upper reaches of the River Cynon.

Green plants at Taffs Well, visible only by virtue of their number, were limited to minute, unicellular *Chlorococcum humicola*, which produced an unsavoury green scum. *Euglena* was also present and seven species of diatoms. *Cladophora glomerata*, larger green algae with branched filaments, were present upstream of Taffs Well.

Sewage fungi dominated our stretch, as they did up river at Merthyr Tydfil. This is a loose terminology for an agglomeration of *Sphaerotilus natans* filaments and *Zooglea*, which consists of bacterial cells embedded in a gelatinous matrix. Filaments predominate in fast flows, jellified growths in quieter, more turbid reaches such as ours.

Things were little better in the spring of 1974 when hundreds of thousands of white worms waved brown-tipped heads back and forth in the gentle current from upright mud tubes and segmented red midge larvae or blood worms, also anchored in mud tubes, thronged along the shore of a slight embayment.

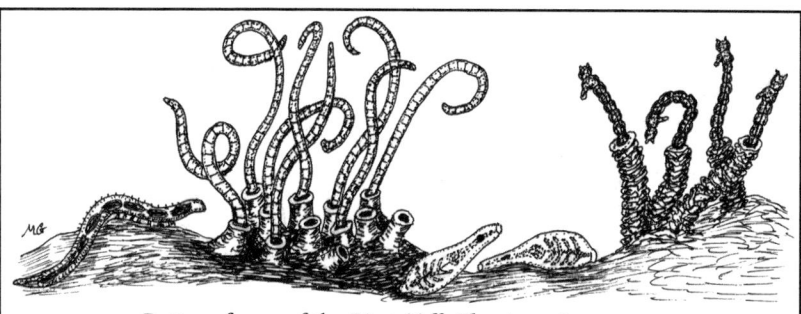

Bottom fauna of the River Taff. *Chaetogaster* worm, *Tubificid* worms in tubes, *Hellobdella* leeches and *Chironomid* midge lavae or blood worms.

The tubificid worms fed on organic detritus among the softly undulating banks of sewage fungi which coated every solid surface, log, boulder or stranded debris. Guts of the midge larvae contained diatoms *(Diatoma vulgare)*. The unsavoury gelatinous mass was impregnated with black coal dust, but the pied and grey wagtails, which seemed to be bending to kiss their reflections in the oily surface, had no complaints. Worms and midge larvae were gastronomic delicacies for insect-eating birds and there was a veritable feast here. Marginal muds were patterned with their footprints, the webbed ones of gulls and unwebbed ones of moorhens. The only other invertebrates spotted in the tangle were a few water hog lice.

Even more unwholesome conditions were reported by Kathryn Benson-Evans immediately above the Portobello Weir in the summer of 1969. Mud and coal dust had built up behind the weir, obscuring the stony river bed, bubbles of gas were rising from the depths and oil patches spread evanescent rainbow hues across the surface.

Only three genera of diatoms were found on the sewage fungus complex of the unstable river silts: *Navicula, Synedra* and *Diatoma*, the last also floating in the plankton with the less common *Suriella*.

This site suffered from the Treforest Trading Estate effluents, the flow too sluggish to carry them away or to re-oxygenate the depleted waters, which were able to sustain only the most meagre animal life. By Tongwynlais, the flow had increased appreciably, with gravel visible after silt-clearing spates. This stretch is now floored with cleanly scoured rock and pebbles. Effluents there were mainly from the flanking farm fields, but the level of sewage was second only to that of the Gwaelod-Taffs Well stretch.

Until this period the monitoring of river pollution had been done by chemical sampling. Since then emphasis has been on the quality of plant and animal life. Spasmodic chemical readings made in between toxic spillages or after a cleansing spate, might show excellent results, although no creatures were able to survive. Sampling of the animal life persisting over a longer term is a much more reliable guide. Insect larvae have widely differing levels of tolerance, so provide a better index of water quality.

Their presence is largely dependent on the availability of oxygen. With an influx of sewage the sewage fungi peak, using up most of the available oxygen in the breakdown process - oxygen which is not replaced by photosynthesising green plants or by turbulence. The first animals to move in while oxygen is still in short supply arc the tube-dwelling *Tubifex* worms, then come the tube-dwelling midge larvae and water hog lice and finally, when oxygen is back to normal levels, freshwater shrimps *(Gammarus pulex)*, mayfly and dragonfly nymphs, bugs, beetles and the rest.

56. Taff Vale Railway bridge over the Taff from the Ffygis frog-spawning pond February 1984

57. TVR bridge over the Taff from Pont Sion Phillips footbridge in the July 1999 drought.

58. The old main Cardiff to Merthyr road winds north from Gwaelod-y-Garth under the east face of the Garth mountain.

THE ROLLING COUNTRY AT THE END MORAINES WHERE THE TAFF GLACIER MELTED AND DUMPED ITS LOAD ON YNYS GAU, UNDER THE GARTH MOUNTAIN,

59. Winter snowfall, January 1982, looking towards Graig-yr-Allt.

60. Summer haytime, July 1999, looking towards the Little Garth.

The principal polluter of our stretch during that period of nearly thirty years ago was the glue and gelatine factory of Leiners - below which great rafts of froth would sometimes build up. One of the most damning features was the wide fluctuation of acidity and alkalinity. All the river water is alkaline, with a pH of around 8.0. On the Gwaelod stretch in 1971 this varied from 6.5 to 9.4 - as against 7.2 to 8.8 at Upper Boat and 7.4 to 9.3 at Tongwynlais (Edwards et al, 1972: *"A Biological Survey of the River Taff Water Pollution Control"*. 2).

The Welsh Water Report of 1984 on *"The Rehabilitation of the River Taff as a Migratory Salmonid Fishery"* showed dramatic recoveries in fish populations and improvements in water quality, although some legacies from the past had not yet been overcome. There were still suspended coal solids and mine water effluents, as well as large abstraction weirs with no fish passes to allow migrating fish free passage, while the creation of reservoirs depleted the spawning and rearing areas.

As the news of the returning fish spread, the anglers gathered and between a hundred to two hundred sewin were caught below Blackweir in 1983. In November an electro-fishing team from the Welsh Water Authority and UWIST waded in, catching a hundred and twenty sewin, four adult and three juvenile salmon and over a dozen brown and rainbow trout, as well as coarse fish. (There had been a thriving roach fishery in the lower river in the 1950s and early 1960s until a major pollution incident wiped this out.)

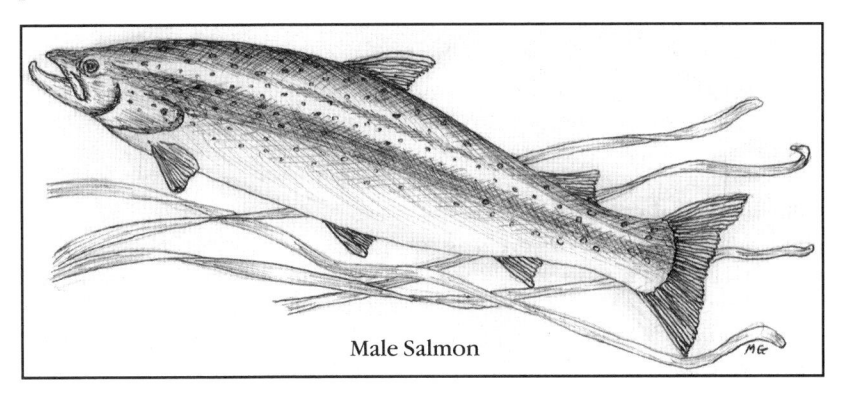

Male Salmon

Fish were transported upstream, past the physical barriers of the weirs and released to find suitable spawning grounds. Renovation of the old masonry salmon trap alongside Radyr Weir was undertaken in 1989, with further improvements in 1993. This eased the passage of fish, but capture and release will have to continue until fish passes are in place at more than just the three lower weirs, as at present. The most formidable barrier is Treforest Weir.

Suspended solids settling on the spawning gravels are lethal to salmonid eggs. The gravels may also be spoiled by sludgy orange patches of ferric hydroxides, where acidic streams from hillside mines enter the alkaline waters of the river and ferric iron is precipitated out. Toxic phenols from the mines can taint fish flesh

While the Fisheries people found that oxygen levels at Taffs Well fell below the minimum necessary value of 3.5 mgm/litre in the first half of the 1980s, my bird notes for that year record heron and kingfisher, both fish eaters, as well as mallard, moorhen, snipe and wagtails along the banks on our side. The herons are quite regular, possibly feeding on fish entering from Gedrys Brook and the water piped under Taffs Well from Graig-yr-Allt. Trout and eels were present to sustain their needs, while there were minnows for the kingfishers.

Monitoring of macro-invertebrates was being carried out twice yearly by this time and showed considerable water improvement, although the more sensitive families were still absent below Treforest.

Edwards et al in 1972 had found trout only above Pontypridd - with bullheads, stone loach, minnows, stickleback and roach, but only eels, minnows and roach below Pontypridd. Winstone (1978) found the Treforest to Radyr Weir stretch to be fishless, due to low oxygen levels, although there was good diversity above and eels and stone loach below.

Local anglers catching brown and rainbow trout just down from the Pont Sion Phillips footbridge reported good 'fly hatches' along this stretch in 1984: *"Sedges and duns, better than ever before."* These (caddis, mayflies &c) showed the river to be in a healthy state at last.

Mawle, Winstone and Brooker in the 1986-87 edition of *"Nature in Wales"* summed up the salmon and sea trout situation to date. They included a reproduction of J.C.Ibbotsen's famous painting of Cardiff in 1789 showing coracle men of the sea trout fishery on and by the Taff. This coracle fishery persisted at least as late as 1828.

Salmon (1936) cites references to valuable fisheries in the lower Taff as far back as Norman times. Rees (1954) quotes a fisheries rent of £24 per year collected by the Lord of Glamorgan in 1596. It is thought that the annual catch from the tidal reaches was of the order of thousands of sea trout and hundreds of salmon. Over one tonne of salmon were sent to Bristol and Gloucester in 1790.

The old fish trap was built into Radyr Weir in 1774-5, when the leat was led off to power the Melin Griffith Works. Apparently the trap operated at weekends, when the water was not required for tinplating.

In 1860 the Commission on Salmon Fisheries in England and Wales reported the destruction of the runs of salmon and sea trout in the Taff, summarising the causes as obstruction, abstraction, pollution and exploitation. The last has always been important, fish massing at the foot of unscalable weirs being sitting targets for legal and illegal takes.

Salmon normally home back to the river in which they were spawned so those recolonising the Taff must have broken the rules to explore new territory. The occasional finding of young smolts heading for the sea in the lower reaches suggests that some of the adults must have found suitable spawning gravels here or in the bigger tributaries. The less fortunate smolts get deflected into feeders - including the docks feeder. The grist mill at Llandaff, which was powered by the leat alongside the cathedral, was said in 1860 to be very destructive to the salmon fry.

While the obstruction, abstraction and exploitation remain, pollution has been largely eliminated. Coal dust has gone, no longer to silt up the filter feeding mechanisms of invertebrate items of fish food or the nets of web-spinning caddis larvae. Children can paddle in the riffles now with smaller expectation of contracting Leptospirosis. In fact few do, because of the plethora of new swimming pools and leisure centres. As with possible inflatable ferries, improvements become redundant before our fast-moving society can catch up with them.

Any who walked by the river in 1992 cannot have failed to see the remarkable flowering of water crowfoot throughout our stretch. The glossy green brushes of finely dissected leaves undulated with the current in water as crystal clear as the best of the Sussex and Dorset chalk streams. Handsome white buttercup flowers formed a veritable sward in places, as they did on the River Cynon at Mountain Ash and elsewhere. The floral display extended up river and down, from Pontypridd to Radyr and beyond.

Floods in July pulled the flowers under water and ripped the flexuous white stems with their elegant foliage from their anchorage. Plants were slow to return, but a few non-flowering tufts 2-3 m long were established again by the autumn of 1998.

The water crowfoots have bewilderingly variable growth forms, depending on depth of water and speed of flow, and hybridise among themselves. They have been subjected to intensive studies and sundry name changes during recent years. While the Taff plants have been diagnosed as *Ranunculus penicillatus ssp. penicillatus*, those persisting in the stretch of Whitchurch Brook running alongside the main road in the south of that suburb were *Ranunculus penicillatus var. calcareus*, the varietal name now changed to *ssp. pseudofluitans*.

The algae associated with the Taff crowfoots are bright green gelatinous strands of blanket weed, neatly combed and streaming with the current like a softer version of the crowfoot. *Spirogyra* is likely to be the main component.

Mimulus or monkey flower, yellow watercress, Himalayan balsam and reed canary grass are coming in along the margins. They can be swept away by floods, but, like the water buttercups, are difficult to erradicate entirely.

Stream Crowfoot

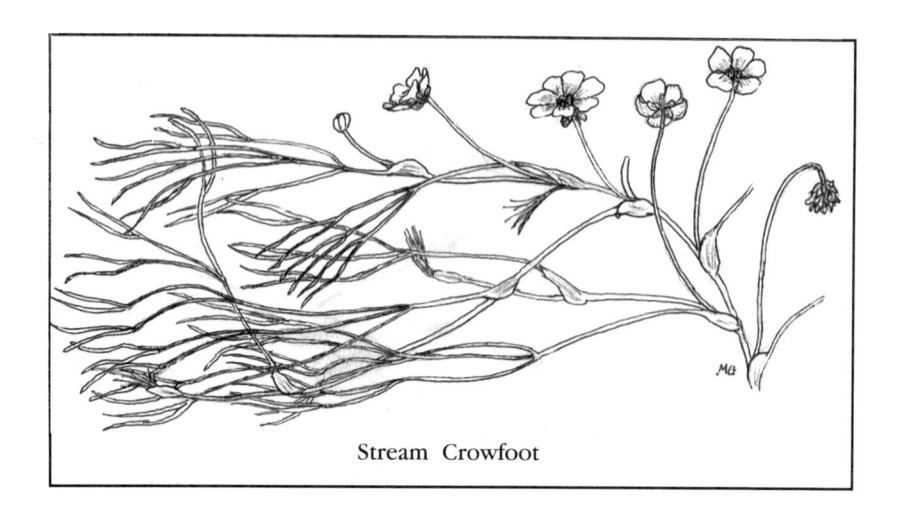

4. Otters, Mink and Riverside Birds

The return of the otter, which is often cited as Britain's best-loved mammal, has set the seal on the post-industrial recovery of the River Taff. Common throughout the country in the 1950s, otters had largely disappeared from most of England and parts of Wales by the late 1970s and from the Taff long before then with the onset of the Industrial Revolution.

The good news for our rivers was officially confirmed at the beginning of the 1990s when Geoffrey Liles of the Otters in Wales Project, functioning under the auspices of the Welsh Wildlife Trusts, reported that otters were crossing the Brecon Beacons from Mid Wales to re-establish themselves in the Taff, Neath, Towy and Usk river systems in significant numbers.

This recovery is important internationally, as otters, still at the end of the century, are absent from seven European countries and in decline in much of the rest of Western Europe.

Otters travel widely and are cannily secretive, so few people are privileged to see them. They have, however, an unquenchable urge to deposit their spraint or 'calling cards' on conspicuous places for the benefit of other otters. These are easily recognised. Sticky when fresh, often slaty grey when older and containing fish scales, they have a fishy yet sweet smell and are easy to spot on offshore boulders, the lower sills of bridges or mounds on the banks.

The Gwaelod stretch of the Taff, once the most polluted of all, is now regarded as one of the most favourable otter habitats. No breeding has been established, but there is good cover along this reach and high steep banks precluding easy access for humans, so hopes are high that some may eventually choose to settle.

Clive Francis, who farms Ynys Gau below the Village Main Road, reports sighting two during the 1992 floods. He had crossed the farm footbridge over the railway to bring the cows in for milking.

"Upstream from the farm I was; the river in flood. I thought it was coming over the bank. Two otters were swimming round and round in the turbulence of the spate. Much bigger than mink, they were."

It pays to get up early!

Their presence here was confirmed by a member of Coed Cymru advising on a new pond. Two boulders just upstream of the railway bridge over the river below the farmhouse are favourite spraining sites.

The Nature Conservancy Council's first records of returning otters at Ynys Gau were for 1986. This section of river had always been good for heron, kingfisher and snipe, yet it was still designated by the Welsh Water Board as the most polluted.

As we have seen, however, eels can withstand considerable pollution, retreating into holes and lying low when oxygen is in short supply. Eels

Otter

are the otters' most sought after food, even when what we regard as choicer fare is available. Also, as air breathers, otters are not deterred by oxygen deficient water.

An otter survey of Wales was undertaken in 1991-2 by the Vincent Wildlife Trust of 10, Lovat Lane, London, published in 1993. The authors (E. Andrews, P. Howell and K. Johnson) covered our stretch in 1992, scrambling along the difficult banks or viewing from a boat on the river. More symbols appear on their map here than anywhere else.

One set of symbols denoted sites where they found spraints or other signs of otter presence, footprints, scrapes and half eaten fish. Another set marked the position of potential holt sites or thickets suitable for lying up in by day.

Suitable cover was thinly scattered along the river as a whole. The next most valuable undergrowth was found between the Tongwynlais Iron Bridge, under the motorway to Radyr Weir. None suitable was found downstream of here and the best stretch upstream of the favoured Ynys Gau habitat was Quakers Yard to Aberfan and again around Troed-y-rhiw.

Eight spraintings sites were identified along the Gwaelod stretch from Ynys Gau to Pont Sion Phillips footbridge and, again on this west bank, five sites along the Gelynis Farm stretch to Radyr, in spite of the close proximity of the railway.

Eight spraining sites occurred downstream of here to the Llandaff road bridge and one further down near Llandaff Weir. Only nine other sites were noted upstream to the northern outskirts of Merthyr Tydfil, three of these near Quakers Yard and three in northern Merthyr.

The notoriously unstoppable Japanese knotweed, which is displacing so much of the native riverside vegetation, is not good news for otters. It dies back in winter, leaving only dead canes, which do not provide adequate lying-up cover. The Himalayan balsam thickets of summer, like the hardy nettles, leave even less in the way of dead stems over winter. The good old fashioned brambles, sallows and gorse are much more welcoming.

The Vincent Wildlife Trust surveyors identified a mink den with scats and tracks where the mini torrent beside the Zig Zag enters upstream of Pont Sion Phillips. There was an otter spraint closeby, suggesting that the two are not mutually exclusive.

I have several times seen mink skittering around the flood debris piled against the stancheons of the footbridge and have received reports of other sightings here. These little creatures are much darker, a rich chocolate-brown, almost black. A freshly dead specimen found on the bank below the River Glade houses on 30th July 1991, afforded opportunity for close examination.

Animals here are American mink escaped from fur farms. Heavier and more thickly furred than European mink, these lack the white muzzle of that species, having just a few white whiskers on the lower lip.

They are not welcome, much as the deluded "do-gooders" of the animal rights movement who release them illegally think they should be. Essentially carnivorous, they are blamed for the present scarcity of water voles, whose local extinction coincided with the spread of feral mink in the early 1960s, and whose burrows may be annexed by the exterminators.

Mink take not only ducklings and moorhens, but adult ducks in moult and unable to fly. Like otters, they swim and dive with great skill, hunting fish, frogs and insects, but they will also eat berries when animal food is in short supply.

Mink

Paul Nelmes, in the BBC Wildlife Magazine of March 1992, 10 3, reports that the arrival of mink on the lower Taff in the early 1980s saw the local extinction of brown rats, but not of the Leptospirosis which these were responsible for spreading. Mink are also carriers. "With 200 cases of Weils Disease in 1990 and human deaths well into double figures, this is a major concern to all partakers in water sports as well as anglers."

Until 1984 a bounty was paid by the Welsh Water Authority for each trapped mink. This was discontinued when it was claimed that mink did not damage fish stocks and that there was a risk of trappers contracting the disease.

Water voles, epitomised for so many of us by "Ratty" of *"Wind in the Willows"*, was once common and easily photographed along the Tongwynlais stretch of the Glamorgan Canal. It is still present in a few sites, but has not been seen on the Taff flood plain for some years now as far as I am aware.

Water shrews do still occur. One was brought in on 6th December 1998 by the family of feral cats which has taken up residence in my garden shed. Like the common and pygmy shrews, whose corpses appear at intervals in the garden, the body was intact.

More distinctively marked than the others, it had thicker fur, black above and white below, with a sharp demarcation between the two, instead of the merging from brown-grey through buff to off-white as in the common shrew. The animal was larger, the snout blunter and there were rows of white hairs along the tail.

Water shrews are known to wander far from water in wooded areas. With so much rain during the preposterously wet summer and autumn of 1998, it had probably not realised it had left the quagmires where water seeps from the base of the scarp below the village street. Maybe it hadn't. That is but a minute's scamper away for a feral cat. I have seen water shrews on the flood plain but not by the main river.

The only bats with a particular affinity for water are the Daubentons. These are not uncommonly seen hunting in summer dusks low over the waters of the Glamorgan Canal to the south, and sightings are also made from the river bridges when there is a fly 'hatch' on.

Noctule bats have been identified over the Radyr Station footbridge, but these fly higher, being less closely dependent on aquatic invertebrates. Hibernation is deferred in mild autumns and I watched a late pipistrelle flying up and down the tree-shaded riverside walk between the Zig Zag and School Lane on the overcast afternoon of 8th November, 1992. Folk who habitually use this route say that the bats commonly hunt there.

Sometimes a mild mid-winter day will tempt them out from their hibernacula, but this is seldom a good idea. The only common flying insects at this time of year are the winter gnats which cleave to patches of sunlight - the very patches that night-flying bats are likely to want to avoid.

Despite mink predation, there is a healthy population of mallard on the Taff, twenty or more birds sometimes congregating upstream of the footbridge to Taffs Well Station or flying in V formation along the river.

There seems to be free commuting between the Taff, the Glamorgan Canal Nature Reserve and Roath Park Lake, but the Taff birds do not expect hand-outs from passers by as the Roath birds do and take off at the least disturbance.

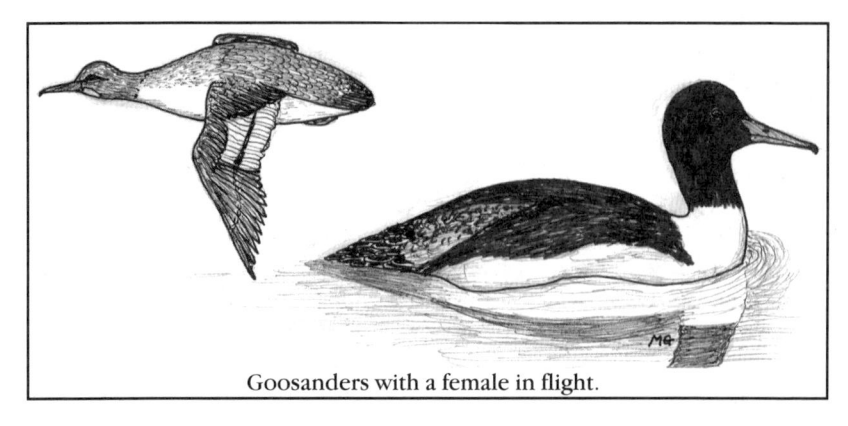

Goosanders with a female in flight.

The presence of a female goosander fishing just above the Iron Bridge on 7th February 1998 was notable, and a sure sign of a healthy river. Fingerling brown trout, 5 cm long, sometimes gather in shoals under the banks, shooting out into the depths at every passing shadow in a flurry of disturbed water. This bird was fishing in mid river and was probably after something more substantial. She was a splendid spectacle when she finally took off, her rufous-red head gleaming in the winter sunshine..

Three more goosanders turned up on the Ynys Bridge stretch of the Taff on 18th April 1998. These birds have been getting increasingly common on Welsh rivers in recent years as they spread down from Scotland. During the early 1990s East Glamorgan boasted gatherings of 25 to 28 birds on ponds and reservoirs in the Merthyr Tydfil area.

In 1996 and 1997 freezing weather in January caused a general movement of goosanders south down river to the Cardiff Roads. They were seen along the Taff from Pontypridd to Cardiff on various occasions, with as many as nine together on 23rd January 1997. A pair spent from 13th April to 17th May on the Taff in Cardiff, during which period a female with an injured wing was seen at Pontypridd. Then they were away, the first autumn return to Cardiff being on 30th August.

Not all leave in summer. In 1996 there were records for eleven of the twelve months in the Taff-Ely Estuary, but only as singles from June to October inclusive. In 1995 a duck frequented the Taff at Radyr from 21st June to 7th July, while two more females were back at Tongwynlais on 6th December. In 1994 another duck spent the summer on this stretch.

Drakes seem not to figure in these sightings, which is a pity, as they are easier to distinguish from merganser drakes than are the two species of duck. Females differ only in the more gradual merging of the red head with the white throat and breast in the merganser, which is a sea-goer rather than a freshwater bird. Compilers of the "East Glamorgan Bird Report" refer to both as 'redheads'.

Moorhens

Other rare visitors in the January 1997 freeze-up were goldeneyes, these ranging up-river to the Tongwynlais-Morganstown stretch with four seen on 1st January, and one on the 2nd here and three in Llandaff on 3rd January, the numbers rising to twelve in Central Cardiff by 13th January.

Paul Wolfle spotted a smew duck on the river just below Ynys Bridge in early January 1997 and a female scaup appeared downstream at Cardiff in early February.

A magnificently plumaged shoveller drake was present below the Zig Zag on 6th January 1996 and tufted duck have appeared occasionally in winter. Small parties of domestic geese have grazed the fields on both sides of the river upstream of Ffygis through the 1980s and 90s. There are always plenty of moorhens, but coot are much less frequent. Little grebes turn up occasionally on our stretch of river, mostly in ones and twos and in the non-breeding season, but up to five have been seen together.

Gulls are mainly black-headed, with a few lesser and greater black-backs and herring gulls, but only a small proportion of the big flocks which commute up and down the valley daily, summer and winter, descend to settle on the river. The gulls are likely to roost at sea or in the Cardiff Roads, or return to the nesting colony on Flatholm Island, travelling up to Merthyr and beyond for feeding sorties by day.

It is a long drawn out process. My windows look out over the valley and I can watch the parties flying up from the piccaninny dawn onwards in small, slowly flapping flocks of ten to thirty birds, returning in similar sized groups for about two hours between sunset and the onset of darkness. Sometimes they are drawn from the sky by some prize and the silent travellers converge on the goodies with much caterwauling and circling before resuming their leisurely journey.

Mid afternoon winter commuters might be picked up by a thermal rising from centrally heated Taffs Well and lifted progressively higher up the flank of the eastern mountain as the sun sinks behind the Garth, plunging the valley into shade and transferring the sun-warmed air uphill.

Other travellers up and down valley on a regular basis are cormorants. A favourite roosting site is on the electricity pylons by the railway bridge where the Melingriffith Tin Mill feeder re-enters the Taff. During the 1960s and 70s there were usually only five or six birds there. By 1998 there were often well over twenty and many more came winging upstream on a daily basis in search of fish. For several decades a midstream boulder by Ynys Gau Farmhouse has been a much used cormorant perch for one or a pair, while in recent years the curved black pipe bridging the river has accommodated as many as fifteen at a time and some are nesting.

At times a heron usurps this site and there are often six or seven of them to be seen along the bank upstream of the railway crossing. Some have nested in the big trees behind the riverside paddocks on our west side since at least the 1980s. This is scarcely a heronry, having seldom more than three or four nests, and Alex Coxhead of the Glamorgan Wildlife Trust recorded only one here in 1991. In the mid 1980s he witnessed an astonishing assemblage of nineteen herons in a field near their riverside haunts on the heights above Gedrys Wood and the Ynys Gau farmer often saw eighteen or more in the heronry by the river, but has made no count of nests. Both cormorants and herons have increased with the return of the fish, The Gelynis farmer has watched a heron standing motionless with dagger-like bill poised over a riverside mole-hill, to be thrust into the mound and bring out a mole. Swallowed whole, that moleskin coat must have been as indigestible as the ostriches glass of Guinness in the popular advertisement.

Desultory heron nesting also occured in big riverside trees on Gelynys Farm near the Iron Bridge. Individual herons have their favourite fishing sites, one of these being the gravel beach immediately below the Radyr Weir on the west bank, opposite the salmon trap.

Dippers

Dippers are other perchers on stones in the Ynys Gau stretch. These walk under water to feed on caddis larvae and the like, so were not seen in the days of suspended solids and organic pollution except occasionally on the lesser tributaries, as at Gedrys. In 1991 a dippers' nest was found under Victoria Bridge in Pontypridd. In 1996, '97 and '98 a pair nested under the railway bridge where the Forge Dyke re-enters the Taff under the Little Garth. Sightings of this attractive bird of mountain streams were not uncommon during the nineties.

Kingfishers are seen more often, a particularly good viewing point being the Iron Bridge, under which they whirr with tantalising speed.

These, too, are increasing and have always nested in the steep, river-cut banks of the Taff, but in the sixties and seventies they were unable to fish in the river. Even if there had been fish to catch, the suspended coal dust would have prevented the birds from spotting them. In those days they relied on the Glamorgan Canal for their victuals. This, unlike the Melingriffith feeder, which was supplied with murky river water, was fed by the clear Nant-y-Fforest bounding down the hill past Castell Coch.

Grey wagtails are more closely tied to the river shoals than are pied wagtails, which range widely over the grassland as well. Traditionally the greys, with their lemon-yellow undersides and long bobbing tails, nest by mountain streams, frequenting lowland rivers more often in winter, but for the last three decades we have had them on our stretch of the Taff both winter and summer. Nesting was suspected by the Nant Llwydrew tributary through the late 1990s. Pied wagtails nest in crevices of stone walls and ruins but not, apparently, in any of the Ynys Gau Farm buildings.

There was a big colony of sand martins just downstream of Ynys Gau in the 3m high west bank until the Water Board moved in to straighten and strengthen with great stone blocks at the start of the 1970s. Another colony of burrows further downstream was washed out by a flood. Mike Wiley and his fellow conservationists in the Glamorgan Canal Nature Reserve made ammends in the early 1990s by erecting a sand-backed 'high rise block' for sand martins by one of the big new ponds adjacent to the canal. Scarcely were the camouflaged drainpipe nest holes in place before the martins started moving in and swooping after flies over the new 'scrapes'.

House martins use the Taff Valley as a flyway during their annual migrations. Martins and swallows, like so many other birds, are suffering dwindling numbers nationwide, but there is no serious shortage of swallows yet hawking insects over the Taff. It is a delightful experience to stand on the various bridges and watch them swooping past below, occasionally dipping to scoop up a beakful of water.

Swallows have always nested in the stone barn at Ynys Gau, as in most old style barns, entering through the great arched door and ever open windows. In 1992 the barn was renovated with a new slate roof, tall timber door and glass windows, but the door facing the river is left open for the swallows and a small pop hole allows them up into the new loft. They had no trouble finding the new way in on their return from South Africa and nested in the same place as in the previous year, continuing to do so to the end of the decade..

Swifts can be much more dramatic in flight. In fine weather they rise to invisible heights in pursuit of ascending prey, but when damp heavy days press their food earthwards the meteoric flights are transposed to our level. So fast are they that it is quite frightening to stand on Pont Sion Phillips Bridge with the sizable birds shooting past the ears like mechanically propelled missiles Their mastery of flight is too skilful for them to make contact, but the rush of air bodes ill for any insect in the path of that advancing gape.

Snipe prefer to probe in the quagmires at the junction of the wooded scarp and flood plain, rather than in such shallows as the river offers, but must needs feed by the river when the still waters get frozen solid. Not only do their beaks fail to penetrate hard frozen soil, but the invertebrates on which they feed move down to unreachable levels when conditions get uncomfortable on top.

1986 produced the coldest February for twenty years when even the beaches and central shoals of the river were iced over. Glassy shelves protruded from the banks and big masses of blue ice built up around piped outlets. Six snipe frequented the frog spawning fields around the end of that month, exploiting the unfrozen margins of the fast flowing stream alongside the railway embankment and wading out to probe the river shallows They were a fine sight, rufous against the sombre background, with longitudinal yellow stripes and long probing bills.

Cold air holds little moisture and this was precipitated out on the grass as hoar frost or frozen dew. So dry was it, that fire warnings were out, as in a summer heatwave, and there was an extensive hill fire on the tinder-dry slopes above Treforest on the night of the 27th February.

Woodcock could be flushed from among the trees and a couple of lapwing winged their way upstream. The cryptically camouflaged woodcock are usually only seen during cold spells, up to four together. Lapwings have never been common in the valley and their absence in recent years reflects the nationwide reduction in these attractive birds.

Common sandpipers are summer migrants frequenting the riverside, bobbing on boulders and whistling as they fly across. They forage particularly under the high banks above the Pont Sion Phillips footbridge, most probably on passage to nest sites by the mountain reservoirs.

Water rails are always secretive and are best seen during heavy frosts when they need to spend more time feeding and the plants which usually hide them are bowed down by the cold. They prefer the springs which bubble from the base of the scarp under the village to replenish the frog spawning ponds.

My best sighting was on 17th February 1985, just after the ditch along the back of this field had been dug out and the frog pools filled in. Where previously the water rail had skulked in private along the overgrown ditch, it was now forced into the open. Only here and in a few of the woodland pools behind was the water unfrozen. It stalked across the barren mud like a scraggy grey moorhen.

As it spotted me and took off, I became aware of a covey of four grey partridges with rufous heads and tails. These merely squatted before continuing their unrelenting quest for food. Like the rails, they are seldom seen here.

5. Plant Colonisation of new Boulder Revetments and Coal Dust Beaches in the 1970s

Removal of the Upper Portobello Weir in April/May 1970 to reduce flooding on the Treforest Trading Estate upstream, lowered the level of the Taff 8 feet (2.5 m) and a further 0.5 m was dredged from the river bed.

Concurrent with weir removal the river was straightened and embanked alongside the football field below the viaduct and a further stretch, where the sand martin colony was destroyed, was similarly treated between the Ffygis or Ynys Gau railway Bridge and Pont Sion Phillips in the latter part of 1971. No longer did bottlenecks and bends hinder the flow. Flood water diverted from Treforest was able to rush down headlong to do its worst in Cardiff.

The inevitable antidote to the erosion caused by the increased rate of flow was the walling of miles of bank with boulder revetments, changing the character of the river to an artificially canalised form. Drapes

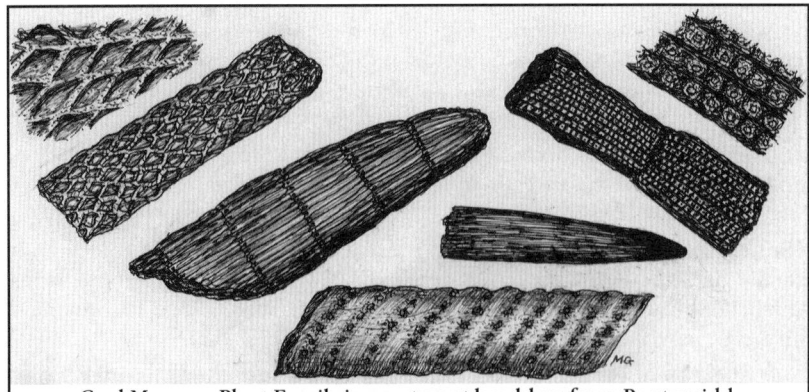

Coal Measure Plant Fossils in revetment boulders from Pontypridd.
(Top corners): *Lepidodendron* and *Sigillaria*, giant club mosses with detail of branch scars.
(centre): *Calamites*, stem of giant horsetail and *Cordaites* leaf are forerunner of conifers.
(lower): *Stigmaria*, underground axis of giant club moss, showing root scars.

of golden saxifrage and brookline which had crept over the moist earth banks were replaced by coarser plants which could root down between the boulders.

Rocks put in place downstream from the Portobello weir under the steep Gwaelod scarp by Cardiff Rural District Council previous to 1960 were from small mine operators at Gwaelod. Those introduced between 1971 and 1974 by the Welsh Water Authority were of two types, from three quarries.

Most interesting from the point of view of fossil content was the blue pennant sandstone from the Craig-yr-Hesg Coalfield quarry at Pontypridd. Cameras worked overtime in 1971 alongside the old Heol Beri pig farm and by the dilapidated swimming pool on the opposite bank recording the magnificent metre long specimens of *Cordaites*, *Calamites*, *Lepidodendron*, *Sigillaria* and *Stigmaria*, but prolonged search revealed no more complex leaf or cone remains.

The other blockstone revetments were dolomitic limestone from the South Crop, some from the Walnut Tree Quarry in the Little Garth and some from Cefn Garw Quarry south of Castell Coch. That in the plant survey area by the field downstream of the Ffygis railway bridge were from Cefn Garw. These calcareous rocks were stained pink or red with haematite and boasted quite splendid crystalline inclusions of calcite, from pale pink through cream to sparkling white, the rhomboidal crystals of diverse sizes, either massed or as veins.

The man-made concrete blocks with limestone inserts known as Dytap Units appearing in the Treforest river section in 1974 and 1975 were not used in our stretch.

The access road for trucks bringing the huge lumps of stone down to river level at the east end of the Pont Sion Phillips footbridge was, and is, periodically under water, despite the drop in river level. Bulldozers worked all that summer on the river bed at low water pushing bottom sediments up to reinforce the artificial banks. For every ten tons of silt and gravel pushed across the river it was reckoned that only about five tons arrived, the rest needing to be re-dredged further down. Both bucket grabs and graders were in use, giving a helping hand to the natural cutting down of the river bed.

Geologists tell us that mean sea level in the Bristol Channel has dropped fifteen feet in relation to the land in the last five thousand years, as South Wales slowly recovers its equilibrium after getting rid of its burden of ice. One of the marginal river terraces left behind during the cutting down process was exploited by the builders of the Taff Vale Railway.

Because the beaches building up behind the revetments were of almost pure coal dust, they provided an excellent opportunity to trace the sequence of vegetation colonising this unusual substrate. This finely pulverised sparkling back powder was very different from the flaky grey clay shales of the waste tips throughout the Coalfield, where many of us were following the sequence of events. Some of those were sown with grass seed or planted with trees. Taff coal dust beaches were colonised naturally by a mixed input of seeds produced locally or brought down by the river.

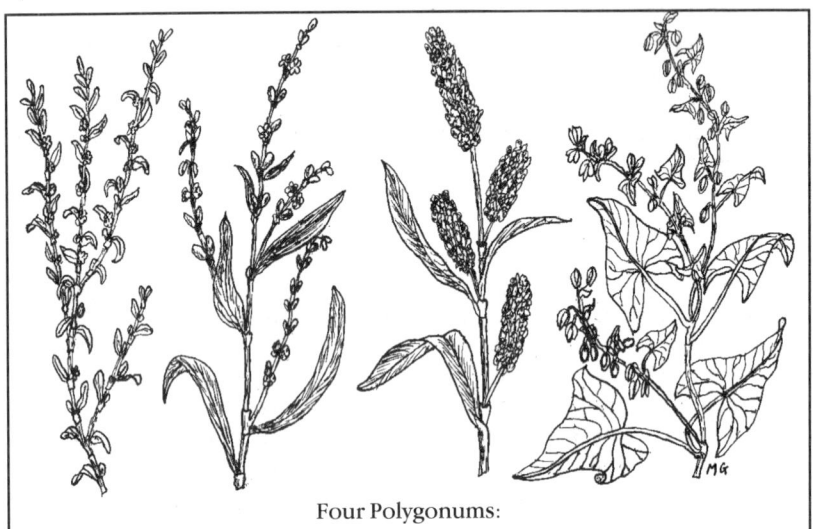

Four Polygonums:
Knot Grass, *P. arenastrum*; Water Pepper, P. *hydropiper*; Pale Persicaria, *P. lapathifolium*, and Black Bindweed, *P. convolvulus*.

Predictably the initial colonisers among the boulders were the two notoriously invasive riverside aliens from the Far East. Undeniably beautiful pink-flowered ranks of Himalayan balsam, first recognised by the Taff in 1910 at Llandaff, shared the sites with Japanese knotweed. This, also beautiful when covered with frothy white blossoms in spring and when the leaves turn yellow in autumn, was introduced to British gardens in 1825, starting its romp across the Welsh countryside from a Maesteg coal tip. In those days it was known as *Polygonum cuspidatum*, but it underwent several name changes to *Reynoutria japonica*.

Featherweight seeds of hemp agrimony and mugwort followed close behind, with field horsetail and tall reed canary grass. By the end of 1973 greater willow herb and nettles had moved in and seedlings of willow and alder were sprouting.

On the coal dust beach, as in most newly establishing plant communities, the great influx of opportunist annuals was soon overwhelmed by a more permanent vegetation of fewer species. Not so among the boulders. By 1973 the number of flowering plants here had risen to twenty one species. By the ninth year (1979) to forty eight and lower plants had begun to colonise the boulders themselves. In February of that year Roy Perry of the National Museum of Wales identified twenty one mosses and eighteen lichens but no liverworts. Many of these have been overwhelmed since, as larger plants join up across the rocks, excluding the light.

The red limestone boulders on the stretch below the railway bridge had weathered to grey and the calcite inclusions no longer sparkled. Orifices between them had disappeared, filled with river-borne silt, the high water levels marked by flood debris on the old beach above.

Reed canary grass formed a more or less continuous band along the river edge at low water, with a few grey and goat sallows anchored in the root mat. Alders 4-5 metres high fringed the top of the zone with Japanese knotweed between the two and increasing downstream towards the junction with the wooded scarp. Many of the rocks were already carpeted with rank, ungrazed grass and creeping buttercups.

About three quarters of the remaining exposed rock surfaces were shrouded in mosses and much of the rest in lichens, the excrement of perching birds boosting their growth in places. This cryptogamic flora was much richer on the calcareous dolomite here than on the more acidic pennant sandstones downstream, where the cover was sparser and the moss species, but not the lichens, fewer.

The Taff returns to rural tranquillity below the Gorge. December 1977

The commonest mosses of the twenty recorded on the dolomite were *Brachythecium rutabulum, Eurhynchium confertum, Tortula muralis* and *Bryum capillare*. Only the first of these was at all common on the pennant, where only six other species were found.

Lichens common on the dolomite were *Physcia orbicularis, Physcia adscendens, Xanthoria parietina* and *Lecanora crenulata*. None were common on the pennant boulders. The only three kinds found on both rock types were *Lecanora muralis* and the two species of *Physcia*. Neither mosses nor lichens featured on the beach above where the competition from higher life forms was too intense.

By the summer of 1979 passage to the riverside was barred altogether by dense seasonal growths of balsam, bramble and greater willow herb below the bridge and 'Japweed' further downstream.

The sequence of pioneering plants on the embanked coal left stranded by the river was very different from that among the boulders. The sources of coal dust on the many beaches beside the Taff from Merthyr Tydfil down were coal washeries and tips that were being reworked by powerful water jets. Analyses in 1968-9 showed suspended solids to be greatest in the Gwaelod stretch where the black beaches were a conspicuous feature.

Erosion faces, often under pipe outlets, showed the sequential accumulations to consist often of alternating bands of black coal dust and yellow sand, like a chocolate and vanilla layer cake. The lighter coloured layers on the Gwaelod stretch at the beginning of the 1970s were sometimes of soil displaced by the building of the A470 trunk road.

The layering was revealed when the western arch of the Ffygis railway bridge was excavated to insert a broad concrete-topped sill of river gravel behind a palisade of iron girders in 1970. This left fragments of the old bank plastered against the pillars of the bridge several metres above the level of the concrete walkway. These clods were of shaggy grass and mounds of liverworts *(Lunularia cruciata* and *Conocephalum conicum)* and fern sporelings, kept moist by limey drips from the mortar, and a very different cryptogamic flora from that withstanding the chancier wet:dry regime on the revetments.

During dry spells in 1970-71 much of the coal surface was bare, blowing in the wind and getting in eyes and nostrils. A decade later, when none was visible, a busy mole had gone along the now unrecognisable beach, throwing up molehills of pure coal dust from below the newly accumulated topsoil. This was obviously an easy medium for burrowing and the mole's presence suggested that coal dust was as earthworm-friendly as the pulverised fuel ash had proved once organic matter became incorporated.

Because of the drop in river level the old beaches studied above the newly installed revetments were subject to inundation only during serious spates, as shown by the little cliff eroded along their upper edges. Short-lived annuals could exploit the drier summer season, but only those perennials able to get their roots well anchored and survive the possible oxygen deficiency of waterlogging could outride the winter floods.

Although seldom more than 6 m wide, a hundred and twenty four species of flowering plants were recorded on the Ynys Gau beach during its first year of 1971. This was proof, if proof was needed, that coal dust in itself is not toxic, although lethal to so much aquatic life. Once sedimented out it behaves like any other soil.

The only problem here was that it was so pure when not affected by washings from the new road, that locals might come to gather it as domestic fuel. In regions where peat is to hand, this is gathered by villagers for like purposes. The Taff product was from the same vegetable source, both more ancient in its formation and more modern in its arrival on site, but just as significant in the recycling of stored energy.

Anthracite dust was collected even more avidly from the Western Valleys, amalgamated at the rate of one part of cement to twenty of coal dust in a concrete mixer and allowed to dry into chunks of easily handled fuel. The lime of the cement was released in the ash on burning. This principle was applied in the commercial production of smokeless fuel nutlets by Larry Ryan and his contemporaries in the 1950s and 60s.

The Ynys Gau beach was not of dredgings but was sifted out from the November 1970 floods. The material impounded behind the old weir was further downstream, where the height of the banks precluded beach formation. With no more significant inputs of silt, it gradually became grassed over and incorporated with the paddock at the top of the stacked boulders. It was reinforced during subsequent years by the planting of more alders to add to those establishing naturally, these now protected from cattle grazing by a wire fence. During the early phases the dairy herd had free access.

Excavations under the railway bridge had exposed the nature of the soil profile. The upper metre of depth was composed of almost homogeneous coal dust, streaked at intervals with wafer-thin flood-borne layers of yellow. Below this was a pale impermeable clay pan up to 30 cm deep holding up water, this an old land surface deposited in an earlier phase of valley infill. Below this again was bouldery gravel from a more turbulent phase.

Of the hundred and twenty four species colonising during the first summer, twenty four were Composites, with easily dispersed, wind-borne seeds, fifteen were grasses, fourteen were Polygonums or persicarias, water peppers, sorrels, docks and 'Japweed', twelve belonged to the campion-chickweed family and nine were cresses. There were four rushes, three willow herbs, three speedwells and two plantains. Normally large families, like the peas and roses were poorly represented. Four tree seedlings already germinated were sycamore, elder, sallow and hawthorn.

There was evidence of quite severe cattle grazing of the beach by May so most of the tree seedlings were chomped off in their infancy. Himalayan balsam, that reprehensible but tenderly palatable invader of riversides, was able to thrive only among unreachable boulders with yellow mimulus, where the cattle did not venture. All within reach were too much of a temptation. Other upstanding species, like evening primrose and soapwort, were able to throw secondary flower shoots just above ground level after being beheaded.

Coal dust clung about the fine roots of Japanese knotweed seedlings in moist black balls. These were true seedlings, not sprouted cuttings, and one of the early indications that these plants, reputed to produce only female flowers in this country, had changed to produce viable seed. This seems like an evolutionary adaption in the aggressor to become even more aggressive, an ability which is surely a hallmark of its roaring success.

Most of the flowers fell unfulfilled but whole banks of plants down river had been fruiting freely, bearing triangular brown winged fruitlets like those of dock or sorrel. These were viable, even when not crossed with Russian vine, although some disputed this, despite the rarity of the vine. Evidently more were fertile upstream to account for arrival of the seed here.

By July of the first summer, perennials from the pasture above had begun to invade, bracken by underground rhizomes and brambles by arching stems rooting at the tips.

Analysis of the longevity of the species arriving during that first summer showed annuals to be in the ascendency in May, but longer-lived plants soon caught up. Lichens and mosses, often quoted as the pioneers of plant successions, were nowhere to be seen on this sort of substrate. As on sand dunes, the grey dune phase dominated by mosses came a long way behind the white dune dominated by larger plants.

By September 1971 57.5% (72 species) were perennials and 42.5% (53 species) annuals, 14 of which can grow on to become biennials. The presence of corn spurrey *(Spergula arvensis)* and sheep's sorrel suggested that the coal dust might be slightly acid although watered by neutral to alkaline river water.

Erosion of the coal dust, whether by wind or water, was neatly shown by undermined plants of cut-leaved cranesbill. Roots radiated from the crown of the plant, now several inches above ground level, like the poles of an Indian tepee, with the leafy branches curved groundwards above them. Yellow rocket or winter cress *(Barbarea vulgaris)* had responded similarly.

Some of the creeping speedwells combated erosion with a stabilising mat of prostrate rooting stems. Black bindweed *(Polygonum convolvulus)* and field bindweed *(Convolvulus arvensis)* spread sideways in the absence of supports up which to climb. White and yellow clovers and birds foot trefoil produced good ground cover later on.

Tomato plants are the traditional evidence of pollution by untreated human sewage, our alimentary systems unable to destroy the viability of all the seeds. The few seedlings germinating on the beach did not persist, but there were some robust 60 cm high plants under the railway bridge bearing ripe edible fruits by September.

While the usual definition of a weed as "A plant out of place" might apply to the tomatoes, a newer proposed definition of a weed as "A plant whose virtues have not yet been discovered" seems to fit many of the others. If that much over-used word of biodiversity is what we are after, we certainly had it here.

Only where the stream from alongside the railway embankment crossed the beach were there any water plants, these mainly fools' watercress, water starwort, water mint, marsh cudweed, brooklime and bulbous rush.

Seedlings and mature plants of white goosefoot *(Chenopodium album)* were affected by roll gall, the rolled leaves concealing *Semiaphis atriplices* greenfly. The plants were also affected by an orange rust fungus, as was the wood soft grass *(Holcus mollis)*.

Among the few marsh plants were cuckoo flower or ladies smock, marsh yellow cress, bog stitchwort, greater chickweed, silverweed, butterbur, marsh foxtail and various rushes and sedges.

Mallard.

Typical of arable land were smooth long-headed poppy *(Papaver dubium)*, a knot-grass of paths and farm gateways *(Polygonum arenastrum)*, pale persicaria *(Polygonum lapathifolium)* and the three daisies, stinking chamomile *(Anthemis cotula)*, corn feverfew *(Chrysanthemum parthenium)* and pineappleweed *(Matricaria matricarioides)*.

By 1973 the riotous growth among the riverward boulders took all the force out of rising flood waters, as it did most of the waterborne debris of polythene and the like. Few of the beach plants got ripped out and seldom did an erosion cliff appear. Gradually but inexorably the whole belt was being absorbed by the pasture, disappearing under a mat of grass, white clover and creeping buttercup. Of the original 114 immigrant species only 36 seemed to have survived. Among these, inevitably, were the Japweed seedlings, now in their third year, and the progeny of the annually distributed explosive Himalayan balsam seeds.

Among newcomers were the woolly white perennial pearly everlasting *(Anaphalis magaritacea)* from North America, with its paper-white 'everlasting' heads, and ground elder, bishopsweed or goutweed *(Aegodpodium podagraria)*, which is such an ineradicable invader of flower beds.

After the early spring exuberance of coltsfoot, summer colour was provided by soapwort, perforated St. John's wort, wild mignonette and silverweed. Bracken, not featuring on the menu of well fed cows, outdid the tree seedlings, which were relished. Incomers from the permanent pasture included mouse-ear chickweed, mouse-ear hawkweed, cat's ear and smooth hawk's beard.

With the erection of the fence in subsequent years, the beach lost its identity altogether between the bouldery alder fringe and the bramble bordered field. More settled shade plants moved in under the trees: marsh woundwort, wood avens, herb Robert, two-flowered cranesbill, hedge garlic or Jack-by-the-hedge and the rare moisture-loving wood horsetail *(Equisetum sylvaticum)*.

New pasture species were creeping cinquefoil, self heal, scorpion grass and lesser stitchwort. Soapwort was still colourfully conspicuous at the end of the first decade, joined by an errant michaelmas daisy. Few of the original ephemeral colonisers persisted, among them hairy bittercress, thyme-leaved sandwort, and broad-leaved willow herb.

Silvery mugwort *(Artemisia absynthium)* had joined the wormwood, while foxglove bells and rosebay willow herb contrasted pleasantly with the yellow of wild parsnip and creeping yellow cress.

Nettles, greater willow herb and marsh woundwort, now growing on the concrete sill under the bridge, were sometimes flattened in spates, as in August 1979. Usually floods reached the old beach only during the dormant period of winter, after filtering through the alders, and had little deleterious effect, but a flood of 27th December 1979 left the whole field with a mantle of black silt.

It also left a long shingle bank downstream of the railway bridge when the spate subsided, due to the checking of current by the bridge piers, causing spillage of the load. In the early 1930s the boys who hired the local rowing boat were likely to run aground on another gravel shoal under the east arch. One of the alders sawn off a metre above ground in the previous winter already had a girth of 10 cm although most were only half this.

Considering the fundamental nature of the vegetation changes, they were very short-lived. In less than a decade they had reached the state of equilibrium decreed by the environment.

On 14th February 1984 bulldozers working on the river bed threw a great new bank of gravel against the revetments and through the alder bases. By the year 2000 there will be good cover here for water birds though not yet enough to form an impregnable haven for otters.

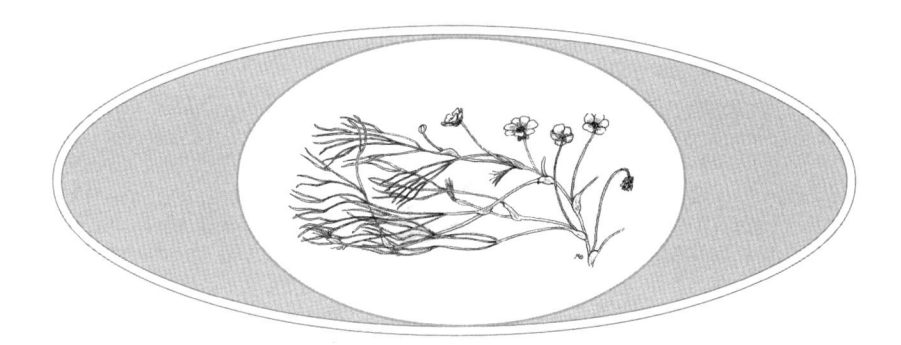

Chapter 11

ANIMAL LIFE AT GWAELOD-Y-GARTH

Introductory

Mammals, being closest to ourselves, are the most popular group, but are difficult to study. Most are secretive, many nocturnal, the exception being the cheeky grey squirrels, which are only too well known to those who put out food for birds. These charmingly pert "tree rats with bushy tails" are notoriously innovative and agile and always one step ahead in gaining any goodies for themselves.

They are aliens, like the too successful mink considered in chapter 10, and are able to exploit the natives, not by preying on them but by out-competing them. Otters, as we have seen, are on the increase, but many others are declining. Stoats, weasels and hares, once fairly common, are now rarely seen.

Rabbit populations wax and wane with recurrences of myxomatosis, as in 1992, or if farmers wage war on them. When present they are very visible. The wily fox, more numerous than is often apparent, wisely keeps a low profile.

Although living in the parish since just before the great freeze-up of 1962-63, roaming its quieter corners at all seasons, I still know very little of the indigenous mammals.

Birds are easier to see and have a big and knowledgeable following. Our encounters with reptiles are haphazard, unless one has a resident population, as I have of slow worms. Amphibians are more dependable, the arrival of each annual increment of frog spawn heralding in another year of activity. Invertebrates are always with us, their population strength depending on vagaries of the seasons, as well as predator:prey relationships.

Although a fair proportion of the detailed nature diaries kept during my thirty seven years of residence relate to vegetation, the animal notes included here can be little more than generalities relating to a complex whole.

1. Mammals

One of our most popular mammals is Brock, the badger, mainly nocturnal but sometimes around at dusk, particularly in summer, when the nights are short. There are no setts in Gwaelod itself, most are on the surrounding hillsides. One, sniffed out by a friendly dog, was in the upper part of an overgrown coal addit. Badgers travel, like otters, particularly young ones, which have outgrown the parental sett and are searching for territories of their own. These are the ones we are likely to see by chance, following the old tramroad tracks through the village outskirts in the absence of well worn paths of their own making.

The four or five known setts, with their large mounds of excavated soil and occasional discarded bedding, are difficult to miss. Other clues are their dung pits which, like otter sprainting sites, are very obvious when we know what to look for, in this case shallow pits near a much used track.

These are often clumped together and are not covered like those of a well brought up cat. The dung is soft and has few recognisable remains if the badgers are feeding on their favourite earthworms, or even bluebell bulbs, but may contain the indigestible remnants of ground beetles and other invertebrates, even blackberry pips. Larger prey or carrion is sometimes taken.

Badgers and moles did well in the wet summers of 1985 and 1998, when there were plenty of earthworms about. Fortunately we are not involved here with the bovine TB controversy and badger culling.

There are few sightings of stoats for recent years. Weasels are seen a little more often, scuttling across a road to disappear into the undergrowth. Males and females are different sizes and so are scarcely in competition with each other. The larger males can take young rabbits, leaving mice and voles for the females, which may be slender enough to enter some of the burrows. They will explore new ones with pleasantly 'lived in' smells, as Mike Wiley, long-term warden of the Forest Farm Country Park and Canal Reserve, discovered when a weasel popped out of the sleeve of a jacket laid in the grass while he worked!

Polecats, although essentially Welsh animals, are rare in our area. There are a few records from the Garth Woods around 1970. One was helped through a hard spell of weather by being fed in gardens near the south of the village, but went its own way in spring. Another enjoyed drinking kitchen sink water swilling along an outside drain.

During the 1980s two cars traversing Pentyrch Hill stopped while a polecat ran round in circles between them, bemused by the headlights. It eventually scampered into the wood. Another, well away from here, was found dead a while later.

The only Mustellid of this ilk that I have encountered personally in the wildwood, was very obviously an escaped ferret. A wild polecat would not have fawned around my gumboots as this one did!

The musty smell of foxes, which is very like that of herb Robert crushed underfoot, can be encountered anywhere. Good views of the animals are uncommon, though one was watched trotting blatantly along village main street during a November rain storm. Another, sauntering along the Garth skyline after a major grass fire on 8th June 1984 was looking for roasted carrion, its silky coat gleaming a golden brown against the all-pervading black.

During the January:February mating period their nocturnal screams and yelps may set the village dogs barking and there are several sites where there is a liklihood of seeing cubs at play. A vixen whelps every year on the overgrown railway embankment through Ynys Gau Farm, but the farmer has never found them to be a problem, maintaining that they forage further afield.

The Pentyrch Hunt is out regularly in winter, but there are so many holes and hideaways on the mountain that the quarry usually eludes the hounds. It is always good to see a fox trotting almost nonchalently through the village when the horns are sounding their menace away on the summit.

Moles live in all the deeper soils and there are few fields or woodland glades where mole hills do not arise, summer or winter, to show where they have been busy underground, finding worms or producing future generations of moles. An occasional animal flooded from its burrow may fall prey to buzzard, crow or gull, but the skins are tough - hence the much-prized moleskin coats of yore - and they are not favoured as prey. The main takers are likely to be tawny owls, as shown by analysis of owl pellets.

Hedgehogs are most often seen as road casualties. They do well during wet summers, fattening up on worms and slugs to carry them through the winter hibernation. Sightings are rare after mid October and likely to be of late youngsters which have failed to gain the necessary weight to carry them through the winter. They have benefitted by the fitting of sloping ramps in the corners of cattle grids on the mountain road, these enabling them to climb out after toppling in.

Hedgehogs

Hedgehogs visiting gardens leave their 'calling cards' on lawns and paths. These are sausage shaped, up to two inches long and tapered at one end like half the twisted scat of a fox. They usually sparkle with the chitinous remains of insects taken as prey. Scraggier dung pellets may contain remnants of small mammals, birds or frogs. Soft black ones found in autumn can be impregnated with blackberry pips, these easily recognised by their kidney shape and reticulated surface.

Shrew numbers were up during the long summer drought of 1995. Plenty of migrant moths and butterflies arrived that year for them to feast on and there was more continuous breeding of others, including Vanessid butterflies. It was in the spring of that year, on 6th April, that I watched six common shrews squeaking in the grass as they chased each other in and out of a hole under a log. Most often they are found dead, dropped in their tracks or brought in by cats which refuse to eat them. Common and pygmy shrews are frequently encountered, the handsome black and white water shrews less often.

Of the bats, our other insectivores, pipistrelles are commonest. They have almost certainly diminished during the past thirty seven years, but there are always some around in summer. For several days between 5 and 6 am in mid August 1983 huge numbers of bats would swarm over my bedroom skylight. The light inside attracted moths and the bats came in to crop them. All came from the east and left to the west, presumably to a roost on the mountain behind - in an old tree, a ruined cottage or a mine addit. This bonus to their night's foraging was afforded only when I woke early to read.

When October temperatures drop below 14^{0}C bats tend to move from summer roosts to snugger winter ones to hibernate. Although normally nocturnal, mild winter days can tempt them out into noon sunshine, when nutriment may be available in the swarms of winter gnats. They emerge in March if the weather is right.

In summer they avoid sunlight. One rescued from indoors in July 1998 and taken outside to the shelter of an ivy-clad wall proceeded to tumble to the ground, plunge through a herbaceous border and scramble across the lawn on all fours, making straight for the dark mass of a lawsons cypress. Once there it was no problem to scramble up the rough bark into the dark recesses where the greenfinch was nesting. It showed no inclination to fly.

Several village dwellings have bat colonies under their eaves, but new houses with double walls offer better sanctuary than the uncompromising rubble-filled sandstone blocks of those in the old village.

Long-eared bats sometimes turn up. About the same size as pipistrelles, they are quite intriguing with those semi-transparent whiffly ears, each three times as big as the entire head. These, too, are associated with houses in summer, often moving to cellars and old mines for a more equable temperature in winter. They are very docile in the hand.

Lesser horseshoe bats, formerly declining, have maintained their numbers over the last five years according to a recent Welsh survey of seventy nine roosts, and whiskered bats have been identified. Larger species are noctules, which fly high over the treetops and Daubentons, which swoop back and forth under the Pont Sion Phillips footbridge, taking the products of aquatic insect larvae.

Short-tailed field voles and gingery-brown bank voles are as common as field mice and more visible because they are less nocturnal. They are everywhere, as shown by the neatly nibbled nuts, acorns, haw stones, yew stones and the like which clutter garden flower beds and get piled up at the entrances to their hideaways.

In thick cover their burrows can be quite superficial, as shown in the wake of a fire or snow melt. A colony of field mice moved into the gap between the ceiling and roof of my kitchen extension one year, the constant pattering of little feet overhead suggesting that they must be wearing Welsh clogs. On two occasions a few took up residence indoors for the winter months, retiring behind skirting boards in cupboards under kitchen sink and bathroom basin. They ate soap, relishing carbolic, and nibbled labels off bottles, but had no access to human food. In the late 1970s a few lived dangerously by helping themselves to cat food at floor level.

In 1980 one nested in the fluff inside the carpet sweeper, entering by one of the corridors between the spiral brushes. After several minute's of carpet sweeping, I sensed that all was not well and tipped the contents into a bucket. The dusty mouse was bemused by the trundling and rumbling but not asphyxiated. Released in the garden, it scuttled off apparently none the worse.

Mice inevitably get brought in by cats, which they easily elude, to make free of any berries in the vases, but few survive for long, even though fed and watered in the hearth. One burrowed into a cushion to die.

Pipistrelle Bats, Stoat, and Weasel

None have come in during the past decade and I have had no problem with house mice. There are no Gwaelod records of yellow-necked mice, dormice or harvest mice. Occasionally brown rats burrow into the compost heap after fruit and vegetable peelings, or tunnel down among rhubarb roots and rose bushes, but none intrude indoors.

For a year from 1st August 1979 I kept notes of 'What the cat brought home', this a fuller record of small mammals than I could have obtained unaided, although remains were scattered around the gardens and many would not have been found.

Long-tailed field or wood mice were the most popular prey at twenty one, plus a nestful of tiny pink ones. Short-tailed field voles were next at thirteen, then bank voles at five. There were one each of brown rat, common shrew and pygmy shrew and eight birds, six of these robins. The catcher was a normal domestic moggie. The three feral cats which moved into the vacant ecological niche early in 1998, although fed twice daily, ate all they caught, except the shrews, so did not assist any census.

Rabbits are always with us, foraging further from cover during the 1995 drought, but have probably diminished in numbers through the late 1990s.

Gwaelod is too steep and wooded to be hare territory and these were never common. It was an event, even back in the 1960s, when one came racing down the mountain, through my garden down a couple of tall walls to the village street and, hopefully, on down the wooded scarp to the more accommodating grass field below.

Red quirrels were present during the 1920s, 30s and 40s, with only one sighting after that. Grey quirrels are everywhere, in and out of gardens and very much acclimatised to the human presence.

This is squirrel country, with every spinney full of hazel bushes. In mast years, such as the scorcher of 1990, hazel nuts were raining down from the late summer on, to be pulverised to a sticky white pulp by traffic using the mountain road. This was despite the fact that squirrels were opening nuts long before they were ripe in a bout of wasteful feeding with many discarded.

Beech, too, had a mast year in 1990 with many pasty white kernels squashed below big roadside trees. Far fewer than usual were the blind, lightweight ones which squirrels do not bother to open. Acorns were also produced in quantity in 1990, scarcely affected by the recently arrived knopper gall, caused by the gall wasp, *Andricus quercuscalicis.*

A puzzling phenomenon of "rain in sunshine" can be experienced during the latter half of July. Apparently sizeable raindrops patter down on ground and vegetation with a very audible sound, while low leaves of hazel and elm rebound to the impact. Careful scrutiny of the sunlit canopy will probably reveal 3 or 4 pendulous grey tails waving gently, as a family of squirrels pluck hard little fruits from the topmost twigs of a tall hawthorn. Holding the tiny marbles in their forepaws, they deftly split them in half with their incisors at incredible speed, severing the hard white shell of the internal stone without bothering to strip away the thin enveloping layer of green flesh and skin. They require only the white kernel which may or may not mature so many weeks before the haws start to swell and turn red. (Squirrels are notorious for eating very unripe green hazel nuts in midsummer.)

If there is not too much ground flora, the discarded debris creates a very visible carpet of neatly halved shells on the soil below. Most fall hollow side up. Those lying green side uppermost appear like whole fruits, but close examination shows they are not. This is an animal-assisted "summer pruning", possibly not depriving fruit eating birds of so much of their autumn harvest as may be surmised.

Large numbers of hazel nuts are buried in my lawns every autumn, many not being harvested until the spring in mild years or when other provender is available. All through April and into May little pits appear with the discarded shells of two or three nuts alongside each.

In 1984 excavation took place regularly between 6 and 7 am each day. No pit was opened where there was no prize, the bewhiskered nose leading unerringly to the right spots. It seemed that smell, not memory, was involved, as youngsters of the year, digging as late as July, were able to locate nuts buried by others the previous autumn.

After each brief scrabble the squirrel would sit back on its haunches to deal with the hand-held prize. The nut was turned rapidly in the forepaws against the incisors, which were inserted in the tip, a half shell falling away on each side. I marvelled at the speed with which this was accomplished until I did a little scrabble myself and found that the hazel had already started to germinate. The shells had split apart, to free the embryonic root and shoot. By leaving this part of its horde until last the squirrel had saved itself a lot of trouble.

I planted some of the germinating nuts to photograph developmental stages. All were tweaked out and taken away, although close to the house door where the squirrel did not normally venture. Was the taker perhaps a jay? By 6th May the visits were more search than find. There were only a few more exploratory calls. Either the supply was exhausted, too much of the nuts' substance had been absorbed into the seedlings or something better had materialised. The following year the horde was almost entirely of acorns.

These had been secreted more superficially in the moss layer. Maybe in the face of such plenty the hoarder had become careless. A rash of oak seedlings germinated on the lawn through April and May between mowing operations. Seedlings beheaded sprouted again, with two or three shoots replacing the original. I even found monozygotic twins, with a little oak tree growing out of each cotyledon of a single seed.

Nature does not supply a surplus to requirements every year. There would have been no hazel copse springing up on my lawn in 1984, but 1985 would certainly have seen the birth of an oakwood if I had not repeatedly cut back the pioneer trees. Swards of beech seedlings were sprouting on the wooded scarps that year - far more than the various furry nibblers could deal with.

All the nuts on my lawn seemed to be viable, either as a source of food or a potential seedling. It is interesting to watch squirrels collecting them. They will pick up and seem to weigh each nut in their forepaws. Subsequent investigation of those discarded shows that all are devoid of contents. Most of the windfall apples are consumed by birds, but some are nibbled by mammals.

Young Grass Snake and Common Toad

2. Reptiles and Amphibians

All reptiles enjoy the sun, warmth being vital to their activity, so are more likely to be found in grassy sites than wooded ones. Most hibernate from November to the end of February.

Adders are uncommon: I can locate only four records, one each in the 1970s and 1990s and two in the 1980s, one of these brought in by a cat.

Grass snakes are seen more often, especially near water, and I have occasionally found them in my garden. A fully grown grass snake had a favourite lying out place throughout the second half of June and first half of July in 1963 and 1964. It had worn a flattened patch in a rockery where it basked, whether the sun was out or not. A while after it disappeared, I found a large tom cat curled up on the same spot.

My next garden record was in the summer of 1996. This was a large female (too big for a male) spread across another rockery near a large compost heap. I hoped she had chosen to lay her eggs there. Sure enough, on June 24th 1997 I came across a baby grass snake, unfortunately dead, on the highway through my garden used by a large proportion of the neighbourhood cats.

It was 18.5 cm (nearly 8 inches) long and 0.7 cm broad. The neck markings were more brilliant and sharply defined than in adults, forming a yellow collar, almost meeting on the underside, instead of side patches, this matching up to its other name of ring snake. Beady black eyes protruded on either side of the flattened head and the lower jaw was tucked well under the upper.

Another youngster, about twice this size, turned up in the other garden on 30th April 1997. I like to think it was a survivor of the same brood. It took refuge under the wheelie bin, just before the refuse collectors were due. Some folk have an unfriendly reaction to snakes, so I had to rescue it and place it in better cover. Grass snakes travel widely, unlike adders, but tend to return to the same site to lay their eggs.

Common lizards appear in the garden occasionally, emerging from cracks in crazy stone paths or crevices in walls. I found one basking in a brief spell of sunshine in the village street in 1998, but they are more often seen on the rough grass heath of the mountain above. The 1995 drought saw more than usual, but they are well able to swim if flooded out.

They are known also as viviparous lizards and bear their young alive, like mammals. Grass snakes are oviparous, laying eggs. Slow worms (legless lizards) are ovoviviparous, the eggs hatching as they emerge from the mother's body. I have hosted a thriving colony of slow worms over thirty five years or so in a pair of compost bins at the opposite end of the premises from the suspected grass snake site. As I empty one bin they move into the other, spending all winter and much of the summer in these.

On the first warm day in March they start emerging from the festering depths of the compost to warm themselves under the black plastic lid of the slatted bin. Numbers gradually build up to six or eight, or sometimes up to a dozen. As the summer advances they move out into the garden. Favourite refuges are dense cushions of mossy saxifrage, stonecrops or other ground cover, including garden debris. Some live dangerously around the lawn edges or among the grass itself, scuttling away in front of the lawn mower with a commendable turn of speed for an animal with such a name.

61. Gwaelod main road winds north past Ynys Gau Farm towards Mynydd Meio. April 1995

62. Young burrs on 430 year old sweet chestnut tree at Gelynys farm. August 1999

63. Yellow Toadflax and Rosebay Willow Herb by TVR line over Ynys Gau Farm. July 1965

64. Toad

65. Harts Tongue Fern anomalously forked.

66. Yew seeds nibbled by small rodent or opened by grey squirrel.

67. Short-tailed Field Vole.

Youngsters are particularly vulnerable on the lawn and sometimes quite numerous, but are faster than adults in their wrigglesome getaway and very conspicuous in their pale gold livery. Newly born ones are like three inch lengths of gold wire, this size being encountered at any time during the summer from late May to September.

The ventral side is of polished black and there is a black diamond on the head, extending down the bright back as a thin line. This disappears in males but persists in females and may be joined by a stripe along each flank. A very new one encountered on 31st May 1983, as small as they come, must have been born early, from a mating in March, this possibly encouraged by the mild winter and not affected by the ensuing cold spell. Yearlings vary from 5.5 to 7 inches long, two year olds from 8 to 9 inches, these still quite slender and often retaining the light golden sheen.

The scheduled mating time is between the end of April and June, the female carrying the eggs in her body for three months or more before giving birth, so that some of the youngsters do not appear until September.

On 10th May 1992 I watched a pair mating. The paler male grasped the bronze female just behind the head, his jaws extended widely, like a snake's. This was going on under the bin lid but continued in the open when this was lifted. The two were 16 and 20 inches (40 and 50 cm) long respectively. A youthful looker-on was bright yellow and the dimensions of a drinking straw. Slow worms have movable eyelids, unlike snakes, where these are fixed as a film across the eyes and are well seen on sloughed skins.

The compost is a living larder of earthworms and woodlice, with slugs when wet and ants' nests when dry, so the slow worms have no cause to forage far afield and make no appreciable inroads on the garden slugs, which are particularly abundant in the adjacent rhubarb clump.

They are preyed upon by most carnivores. I have rescued one from a cat and been too late to rescue one dragged from the compost by a magpie. The occasional rat which burrows into the heap for warmth and vegetable matter would probably eat any which it came across, but, because this is mostly in winter, motionless hibernators might remain unnoticed.

To judge by the number of slow worms showing tail regrowth, there must be a lot that get away from danger by shedding their tails, which continue wriggling for many minutes to confuse the predator. Colonies are scattered throughout the village in dry stone walls and rock piles and casualties are sometimes found on the roads.

Newts are seldom seen and are almost certainly rare here. Toads turn up almost everywhere through the seven months of summer in dry sites and wet. They are aquatic during these for only about a week at breeding time. Almost always encountered singly - except when homing in on the spawning ponds, none of which occur in the village - they return to favourite daytime resting sites.

These are always hidden, often under a stone, but a toad in the summer of 1997 spent several weeks under a thin layer of moss raked from the lawn and spread on concrete. This dried out most days and must have been very hot. The toad remained when I moistened it but objected to being put in water. This was not the aquatic season! Some have to be rescued from empty watering cans and buckets, others appear as pressed specimens on the roads after wet nights.

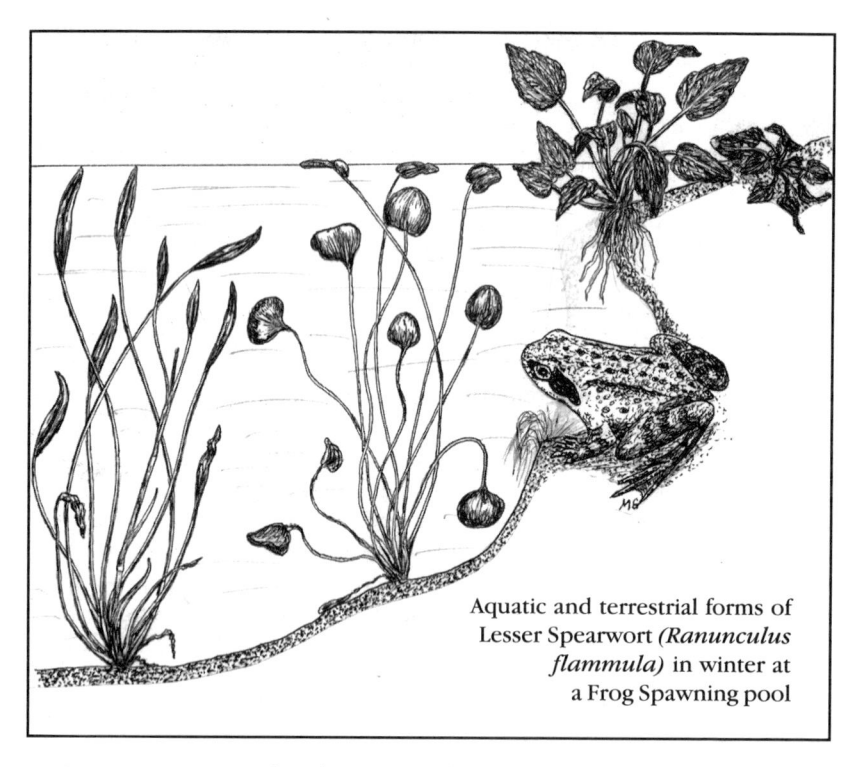

Aquatic and terrestrial forms of Lesser Spearwort *(Ranunculus flammula)* in winter at a Frog Spawning pool

Frogs are seen rather less around the village, preferring mountain quagmires, but a fat fecund female was encountered on my garage drive on 1st January 1984, well away from any muddy pond bed where she might have been hibernating. The garden may be hopping with frogs in wet weather in July and August, sometimes of the same brood, sometimes of quite different sizes, but mostly they are nocturnal, like earthworms.

There are plenty of spawning sites, ranging from large ponds to temporary puddles, old mine entrances or field water troughs, but these do not include the Taff, although many are sited on the river flats. Strings of toad spawn are anchored around plants and can occur in deep or flowing water, where dollops of frogspawn could be washed away. Shallows are preferred by spawning frogs, these often temprorary, so that there is no water for the tadpoles when they hatch.

The most important spawning site is at the junction of the southernmost Ynys Gau pasture and the wooded scarp below the village centre. The nucleus of this locale was an attractive pool at the field edge surrounded by leaning willows and alders. In 1973 a channel was opened out between the pond and a ditch at the foot of the scarp. The terrain was level, providing no fall, and the channel silted up. Natural equilibrium was reinstated until early February 1985, when bulldozers moved in.

The sharp pond edges where cattle had come to drink were levelled, the trees dragged out and sawn up. Orange alder and white willow sawdust became incorporated in the sticky swamp that replaced it. New terra cotta drainpipes opening onto the sides of the new ditch were permanently below water level, with no flow either way.

The intractability of the impermeable soil under the black surface alluvium was shown by the sticky yellow clay clinging to the few deeply penetrating roots of the destroyed alders. Most of the tree roots had been spread through the superficial layers where aeration was better.

Both standing water and frogspawn spread out across the field, the area used by the frogs now six to eight times as large as before but unsatisfactory. During subsequent years a lot of the spawn was left stranded as the widespread water soaked away, while all was more prone to freezing, being unable to submerge to normal levels, iceberg fashion.

The field was ploughed in August 1986 and sown to grass, just in time for the countrywide August floods and "Hurricane Charlie", which struck on 25th August. Water was unable to drain back into the filled and flattened pond, as before, and the field became badly poached, with no longer any transpiring trees to help the water out. Spawn continued to appear in undiminished amounts - several hundred offerings in some years. Frogs seemed as undeterred by silt in suspension as by the ginger ferric hydroxide that makes some of the mountain spawn look like rice pudding with an overdose of nutmeg.

Laying dates for spawn, collected over thirty years and more, brings the average to around 12th to 14th February. In the mild, wild, hurricane spring of 1990 it was as early as 21st January; earlier in other parts of Glamorgan. One year it was not seen until March. Early to mid February is well ahead of the projected dates for the Home Counties and is a lot earlier than it used to be here in South Wales.

"The Natural History of Glamorgan", published in 1930, states the earliest frog spawning date to that time to be 13th April - in 1905 - a full two months later! Can this be put down to changing climate?

Toads at present lay a month later than frogs on average, but the 1930 tome gives the earliest date for these as 5th April - in 1906! It seems that only the frogs are responding and seldom a January passes without some records coming into the Glamorgan Wildlife Trusts's "Frog hop line" of the arrival of spawn, from the Gower to the Rhondda.

Not all lay at once. By 11th March 1991 I estimated 300 clutches at different stages of development spread across an area six times the size of the original pond, although school children had been down with their buckets, carrying a lot up to the village. Some of the earliest is likely to be where springs emerge from underground at constant temperature, sometimes from an old mine. Sites are traditional, with similar sites never used.

It seems that those little froggy brains are programmed to a precise spot but not to a precise date. When the temperature is right the sexual urge takes over - en masse - with no thought for the lethal frosts that may overtake their progeny in the months to come or the droughts that may deprive their 'pollywogs' of vital water.

3. Garden Birds

Thirty seven years of bird recording is sufficient to show changes in population levels. These have been widespread and sometimes catastrophic nationally, as the western world races headlong into the new millennium, but changes in Gwaelod-y-Garth have not always followed the general trend.

With so many topographical irregularities, quagmires too soggy and slopes too steep for development, the terrain has remained largely unchanged over the last half century. Reaching further back, to our industrial past, it has improved immeasurably as Nature has reclaimed and healed borrowed acres that seemed devastated beyond repair.

On our southern outskirts big new housing estates have mushroomed but, as domestic gardens have taken shape, birds have filtered back, some to a semblance of their old habitat, some to make free of bird tables and nut containers, half domesticated and yet retaining the free spirit of their forebears.

Because this is dry stone wall country, with ample crevices, from river revetments to rocks pulled apart by the expanding roots of great beeches, the hole-nesters have not needed so many of the pre-fab living quarters that are, commendably, so popular. Where these have been provided, as in the Coed-y-bedw Nature Reserve, they have been well used; indeed, there has been competition for them, with new arrivals of the same or different species sometimes turfing out the original arrivals and boosting the numbers of shy species near the edge of their range, the pied flycatchers and redstarts.

Some of the Gwaelod trends have been opposite to the national U K ones. Thus song thrushes are recorded here more often now than in the 1960s. Could this have something to do with the recurring plagues of slugs and snails during recent mild, wet years? Some may appear more numerous because they have become bolder in moving into gardens.

Greenfinches and goldfinches are seen more often, being now as abundant in gardens as chaffinches, although those greatly outnumber them still in the woods. This trend on a countrywide basis has been put down to the fact that they used to be farm birds, eating spilled grain and gleaning stubbles, but this can scarcely be the reason in a non-arable district such as this.

Each region has its own characteristic inhabitants. Thus siskins have flocked into gardens after peanuts in the nearby suburb of Whitchurch, but here they have stuck more faithfully to the riverside and wetland alders, whose seed-stuffed cones remain on the twigs from one year's crop to the next.

Surburban gardens are inhabited by house sparrows, but the last of these town style birds that I saw in mine was in November 1981, although dwindling numbers have chirruped around the village main road into the late 1990s.

Starlings, another expected garden bird, made desultory visits in the 1980s, nesting under house eaves in the village street, but I have seen very few during the 1990s. Yet in Whitchurch in 1998 these irrepressible opportunists were strutting among shoppers' feet on the pavements harvesting spilled potato crisps and converging in the evenings on a communal roost.

Collared doves, too, are townees, since their arrival here from Southeast Europe, to largely replace the diminishing turtle doves. On a dozen occasions at most a pair has visited to bill and coo outside my window in spring, but none have stayed.

Magpies have always outnumbered jays, but jays have seemed commoner since the eighties because they are visiting gardens more. Nothing outnumbers the mobs of jackdaws for noise and nuisance value These birds are the prerogative of the Valley towns with their welcoming regiments of chimneys above coal-burning fires, fewer resorting to the smoke-free suburbs.

Many of the birds which I watch from my windows are not garden birds in the true sense in that they never alight. These are the buzzards and ravens that come sailing out from the mountain, the hirundines and other migrants that use the Taff Valley as a flyway and the daily commuting gulls, greater and lesser black-backs, herring gulls and black-headeds. Improved water quality has led to an increase of mallard, cormorants and herons winging past, high or low, depending on atmospheric pressure.

Tawny owls and kestrels are a little more intimate, the owl sometimes perching on my chimney stack or apple tree and the kestrel peering in from vibrating pinions close above.

From November 1981 to April 1982 I kept a day to day record of my garden visitors. Of almost daily occurrence throughout the winter were robin, blackbird, blue tit, great tit, chaffinch, magpie, carrion crow and, of course, the inevitable jackdaws. This still holds at the end of the nineties, with rather fewer tits and crows.

Sunbathing Blackbird and Hop Trefoil

Jay was recorded on 93 of the 140 days (67%) with dunnock and starling next, each on 50 days (36%), although starlings no longer visit. Wrens were present on 30 days (22%), 24 of these in the first six weeks to 14th December and then none until after the snows, with the first records on 15th and 16th March. Mistle thrush, at 25 days (18%), appeared more regularly than song thrush at 17 days (12%), with more after 10th February, a trend which has since been reversed. The only house sparrow recorded was a single bird on 17th November.

These figures have no bearing on population numbers, records sometimes referring to the daily appearance of a single individual or pair, as with wren or robin, and sometimes to sizeable flocks, as with tits, chaffinches and jackdaws.

Long-tailed tits flocked through on eight days up to the first week of December, but only once thereafter, these, like the wrens, possibly suffering from the cold snap. The other small enough to be particularly vulnerable was the goldcrest, with only one record, this in mid February. Both are more frequent now, as are coal tits, marsh tits and green woodpeckers.

The total number of garden birds proper in that winter was thirty, this including the chiff chaff which turned up on 24th March. Others arrived later, willow warbler on 13th April, whitethroat and blackcap soon after. Early on 2nd November 1982 both whitethroat and blackcap were preening in my now leafless ash, a tail-over of summer visitors, probably lagging because of the mild October.

The last blackcap in 1983 was on 17th September but one was in full song in February 1998, when the temperature climbed to 18^0 C. This was an overwintering bird, likely to be an immigrant from the North, our summer birds moving south. Blackcaps are the first of the warblers able to adapt their diet to fit our ameliorated winters and they are staying over in a lot of gardens now.

My 1981-82 figures are likely to be modest by average standards because of the presence of cats and absence of bird table or nut feeder. Hanging seed containers are available but tits are hard to tempt and finches not interested. The only regular takers during 1997-98 were, surprisingly, the supposedly insectivorous robins. As I write in January 1999 a fine crop of green wheat seedlings is sprouting from the feeder and the desultory hovering of a single blue tit, obviously put off by the lush greensward, has been the only visitor observed.

Wrens and robins are particularly partial to spiders lurking in wall crevices and ivy, sometimes creeping mouse-like round the garage interior tweaking these from the copious cobwebs. Particular robins have sometimes ventured indoors.

Nesting sites are readily taken up. Blue tits and great tits post themselves into slots in stone walls, their broods unwisely advertising the sites by their irrepressible squeaking. The robin always finds a corner somewhere. In 1998 this was a tool box on a shelf in the garden shed, which has since been taken over by a trio of feral cats. Chaffinch and greenfinch regularly built in the dark interiors of the lawson's cypresses, lately removed, the young emerging early in June. Bullfinches build in the Japanese honeysuckle *(Leycesteria formosa)*, always moving about in pairs, summer and winter alike, unless one is on duty at the nest.

Wood pigeons and magpies build in overhanging trees and blackbirds in thick cover lower down. Nothing has nested under my house eaves, although in the seventies and eighties house martins, pied wagtails and starlings did so regularly on cottages in the village street.

Blue Tit family and Dog Rose Hips

Like everyone else, I have been plagued by jackdaws nesting in chimneys, making fire lighting a no go area. With no suitable ledges on which to lodge them, the birds empty quantities of sticks down any orifice, to pile up in the hearths below.

Wire netting failed to deter them, even when rolled up and rammed in hard. I have watched four birds together tugging at such impediments for days until they finally freed them and tossed them to the ground. Presumably the helpers were birds of the previous year's brood.

They collected most of their material from the ash tree outside my window, always standing on the safe side of the twig which they were breaking off, but dropping many, these never retrieved. One year all the material came from a rubbish dump. My bin bag filled from two indoor hearths contained flattened tins, bottles, wires, cardboard packs, polythene and debris of every description. At this juncture the human builders were called in and my roof is finally jackdaw-proof, at great cost. I now watch the birds popping in and out of other peoples' chimneys, from which smoke emerges only in the non-nesting season.

Feeding opportunities are used by various species, but the regular broadcasting of crumbs and kitchen scraps has been discontinued. Passerines, the intended recipients, arrived immediately, but three or four pecks later the jackdaw mob descended and cleared the lot in record time.

Daws are instrumental in pushing most of the apples off the bramley tree, pecking wedges out of all the best specimens. The red and yellow tints of mellow maturity prove irresistable, the only specimens left intact, as keepers, being the wizened or green ones. The fact that in thirty seven years the tree has never produced a maggoty apple is small compensation.

Jays help in the apple destruction, but usually visit only in ones and twos and are more decorative. Once a way is made through the waxy peel blackbirds and song thrushes move in, sometimes other thrushes if windfalls linger into the cold months. Unbruised flesh is pecked cleanly from the peel, leaving the emptied green cups, often unsullied. Wasps and red admirals appreciate the sweet juices in autumn, the butterflies seeming to prefer these after fermentation has set in.

On 24th November one year a jay commuted repeatedly across the garden in both directions, with an acorn in its beak on alternate flights, carrying this to bury on the mountain above. This was a case of 'coals to Newcastle', but at least the disseminules were being transported uphill, a direction they could not have achieved unaided.

All the visiting Corvids, including magpies, chisel holes in the lawns in search of invertebrates, green woodpeckers joining them in summer, to winkle out the yellow and black ants. I watched one of these feeding on the lawn in early August for twenty minutes. Except for the initial monosyllabic squawk, which drew my attention, it remained silent throughout. Although on the ground, it fed in true woodpecker style, leaning back on its stiffened tail. When on the alert the body was erect, the tail bent at a right angle, like a seasick green guillemot. At rest it sank flat, almost submerged in the grass, its body merging, with only the obliquely held head and beak clearly visible, like a red-headed diver, low in the water.

The bird would chisel repeatedly at the same hole, sometimes wandering away, only to return to it. Presumably the continued disturbance caused more and more ants to emerge. Before leaving, it deposited its characteristic 'calling card', shaped like a two inch long, curve-topped walking stick, impregnated with the chitinpous skeletons of earlier meals. This was a young bird, more speckled than adults.

A neighbour's bird table was visited regularly by a greater spotted woodpecker, which habitually chiselled away at the supporting post until the whole contraption collapsed. The lure, for both woodpecker and a couple of nuthatches, was chunks of suet impaled on spikes.

Nuthatches feeding on my rockeries or upstanding rock borders are a constant source of amusement in preferring to feed inverted, reaching down from the rock summit instead of upwards from the ground.

Blackbirds and chaffinches come in unisexual flocks in winter, males invariably commoner than females. Members of the thrush tribe take their quota of raspberries and blackcurrants in season and are joined by jays and wood pigeons when they start on the gooseberries. More often the passerines go for berries which I regard as inedible.

Trees of the same species must produce fruits of different flavours. Thus my garden holly is stripped of fruits by November while one across the road retains its berries far into the following summer, where they persist alongside the May time flowers and new fruits swelling through July.

Of the Cotoneasters, *Cotoneaster conspicua*, a species sometimes planted as pheasant fodder, is much the most popular. Blackbirds, thrushes and robins come for the fruit, greenfinches and chaffinches for the seeds. Sometimes the finches are the first takers, the others following to clear the mangled flesh which they leave behind. At other times the thrushes arrive first, the finches picking the undigested seeds from the crop pellets which they cough up on the paths round about.

When food is in ample supply there may be plenty of these, as well as guano splodges impregnated with unprocessed pips. Blackbirds have been watched spitting out Cotoneaster pellets immediately after imbibing the fruit, if something tastier appears through the back door and can be grabbed before the jackdaws descend. If nothing better is on offer, the reject may be re-imbibed by the same or another.

Cotoneaster bullata comes second in order of preference, but birds feeds wastefully on this, reaching up and tweaking off many fruits which fall to succour the ground-feeding dunnocks and small rodents. Equally attractive looking berries of *C. simondsii* and *C. horizontalis* are seldom touched: nor are my firethorn *(Pyracantha)* fruits, although these are relished elsewhere. During the third week of August in 1983 a pair of blackcaps brought their seven youngsters to feed on *Leycesteria formosa* berries three days running.

Bullfinches are the only birds that help to reduce the plethora of ash seeds that spin earthwards to germinate all over the garden. They, too, feed wastefully, the ground becoming littered with dropped seeds nipped in half. The many other birds feeding on the ash are after minuteae adhering to the twigs. At other seasons bullfinches make themselves unpopular by harvesting the unopened Forscythia buds.

Particularly welcome garden visitors, summer and winter, are goldfinches, which come in charms of up to around a dozen to feed on the seed heads of evening primrose, teasel and elecampane. The first, with its secondary crop of flowers in late autumn, is a particular draw, the four valves of the elongated capsules spreading progressively wider to expose the many small seeds in sequence over several weeks. Teasel seeds may last into February. Any spillage is cleared up by dunnocks and wrens, both of which can be year-long songsters with rather similar songs, the dunnocks' muted, the wrens' strident.

From early July to well into winter big family parties of long-tailed tits move through, chattering among themselves like children let out of school, sometimes with other tits, goldcrests and dunnocks. They seem to have regular rounds, arriving at the same time each day and staying for about twenty minutes. In some seasons the flocks number as many as a hundred birds, but more often there are about twenty.

Song thrushes seem to favour a certain section of crazy paving for smashing snails, although this is on the main cat thoroughfare and there are hard rock surfaces throughout the premises. Seldom do they tackle the more rampant slugs. When they do, more time is spent wiping the slime off the bodies than eating, this exuded as a deterrent to predators and effective with most others.

My garden 'pond' is a mere dustbin lid, but is much used by birds for bathing as well as drinking. It is particularly important for them to wash their downy 'thermal underwear' in freezing weather when these ablutions seem most inappropriate. Shaken dry and meticulously preened, robins can fluff themselves into a veritable sphere after the bath, the trapped air affording vital insulation. Blackbirds and thrushes are great bathers, starlings too, in the old days when they visited.

Robins and blackbirds also spend a lot of time sun-bathing, flattening themselves on a particular stretch of sun-warmed path, again on the feline highway, and conveniently near my deckchair. Here they relax, with body, wings and tail spread to the sun. Year after year this same spot is preferred and, if disturbed, they invariably return to it.

Both species practise 'anting', pushing ants into the fluffed-up feathers - another activity concerned with their physical well-being and apparent enjoyment. The presence of the ants dictates where this shall take place.

We are not blessed with nightingales this far west, although the odd bird has turned up in Radyr and Whitchurch, and my best garden songsters are other members of the thrush tribe. Robins take pride of place for their sheer persistence, summer and winter. It takes very little to stimulate them into song. A light switched on indoors for a few minutes at dead of night will provoke the one roosting in the ivy outside into a non-stop sub-song, which continues for five minutes or so after the light is switched off, this occurring in January as well as the 'proper' singing season.

Song thrushes run them a close second for persistence. These sing their unmistakable, repetitive song well before daylight and well after dark, as a regular ploy and seem seldom to let up by day when at singing peak. One is at it as I write in January 1999. I wonder when it takes time off to feed.

It is the larger mistle thrush which has been dubbed the storm cock for its habit of defying strong winds and heavy rain with its defiant song. A rattling call, like a harsher version of the repetitive chur of the greenfinch, is characteristic. The full song is rather like a blackbird's, but lacks the variety and mellifluous tones, the thrush repeating shorter, less interesting phrases. The blackbird's chacking alarm call and hysterical chortling indulged in particularly at dusk, increase its fluty repertoire. The spring dawn chorus is always rewarding and there is no better place to listen to it than tucked up among the sheets.

Baled Hay on the glacial mounds north of Gwaelod village.
August 1999

4. Other Birds

As a non-arable area with a wealth of pools on the river flats and streams bubbling from aquifers, Gwaelod-y-Garth has been spared some of the nation-wide decline of bird specias arising from over-use of agro-chemicals and loss of wetlands.

Numbers are certainly less than they were, but not all is gloom and doom. We have already considered the recent diversification of birds along our stretch of the River Taff. A brief look at the non-aquatic species, in chronological order, shows that others, like the raptors, are also on the increase, since the too random use of DDT and related poisons contaminating their prey fell into disrepute.

Buzzards must always take pride of place for numbers, motorways, the accepted domain of the kestrel, excepted. They are spreading from their Welsh strongholds across the Cotswolds to the Chilterns, where they share the hillsides with newly introduced red kites from the continent, those formerly the prerogative of Wales and our national bird. Buzzards nest in tall trees and quarries, one pair well out on a high limb near the old pheasant rearing pens in open grassland. Few days pass when some are not circling over the village.

Sometimes four are soaring together, at the height of the breeding season when one feels they should be otherwise engaged. On 3rd October 1982 no less than ten circled leisurely across the valley from east to west, moving ahead of a bad weather front. Only a single mew drew my attention from the bonfire I was tending, for the rest they were unusually silent, and left alone by the self-assured rapscallions of jackdaws that usually harry them.

Generally they harness thermals pushed eastward across the valley by the prevailing westerlies. On reaching their neighbours' territory on the other side, they swoop back west to pick up another thermal and repeat the spiral climb. On one occasion I watched four from each side circling amicably together over the river, like vultures converging on a kill. Nine were present on the Garth side of the valley on 16th March 1997.

While rabbits are preferred as food, they will take small rodents, lizards, slow worms and even beetles, with frogs and moles flooded from their burrows in wet weather. Occasionally one perches on the tall ashes at the end of my garden or blunders away low among the trunks of the neighbouring wood.

Kestrels appear less regularly north of the M4 intersection at Coryton, and usually singly. Heading into the wind to hover motionless, they seldom use the thermals rising over Taffs Well, although one was seen turning in tight circles when being mobbed by carrion crows. When pestered by disruptive jackdaws, they tend to lurch sideways from the bullying and indulge in rapid fluttering before resuming the minimal wing vibration that keeps them airborne. They are less molested than the patient buzzards, whose imperturbable circling seems to goad the grey-naped riff-raff into action.

Kestrels nested in one of the Ynys Gau farm barns until the early 1990s. The chicks were ringed by George Wood and Alex Coxhead in 1990, 1991 and 1992. Two of the 1990 youngsters were recovered within a few days of each other, one in Hampshire and one in Dorset. They must have flown south together, but, unfortunately, both were dead when found. In 1991 one of the three chicks fell out of the nest and was demolished by cat or rat. In 1992 three ringed fledgelings left the nest around 8th July. None have bred in the barn since.

Their nearest neighbours were in the Tyn-y-darren quarry above the farm on the steep eastern flank of the Garth, on the cliff from which pennant slabs were hewn to build village houses. Others nest in working and disused quarries round about and the pair returned to the cliff under Castell Coch in 1997. This is a traditional site but nesters sometimes get put off by climbers. One was knocked down by a peregrine in the Walnut Tree Quarry.

These magnificent peregrine falcons have made a spectacular recovery from near extinction over the past few decades in Glamorgan, although pairs in this vicinity can still be counted on the fingers of one hand. The odd bird comes winging across Lan Farm from the direction of Creigiau and on one memorable occasion I witnessed food passing in flight.

Sparrow hawks seem to be increasing too and are now thought to outnumber kestrels. They have learned about gatherings of small birds at bird tables and swoop in to benefit from the largesse at second hand.

The larger hen bird can take larger prey and one is thought to be responsible for the disappearance of two collared doves from a Pentyrch garden. Smaller tiercels have been watched flying low along a concealing hedge, then flipping over the top to pounce on an unsuspecting tit or finch. During their erratic hunting flights between obstacles they have been known to crash into greenhouses. One swooped dangerously close to my oncoming car on the lane north from the village to scoop up a road casualty.

Goshawks, formerly rare, are apparently well on the way to becoming established, having appeared in woodlands throughout our parish, particularly in Spring. One pair raised young in 1997 and another one or two pairs are suspected to have done so in East Glamorgan. Birds were seen flying over the Garth in 1998. Grey squirrels figure in their diet and Cliff Woodhead of the Coed-y-Bedw Nature Reserve wonders if one may be responsible for two squirrel corpses found recently.

He saw a hobby over the Garth on 30th May 1998, pitching into a small woodland, and John Llewellyn saw one the next day. Another watched by Paul Wolfle on 30th August that year seemed interested in the swallows and martins lined up on wires prior to migration and was not seen again after the hirundines departed. Paul had seen another near Radyr on 1st June 1997.

Hobbies are uncommon summer visitors and passage migrants. Merlins are even less common winter visitors and passage migrants. It is some years since one was spotted over the Garth and the nearest 1997 report was of a bird at Nant Garw opposite Gedrys.

Ospreys are rare passage migrants, sometimes using the Taff Valley as a flyway to the north. Singles were seen in 1997 at Tongwynlais on 10th April and at Radyr on 8th August.

Game birds are thin on the ground since the rearing of pheasants and partridges ceased in the valley between the Great and Little Garths. Grey partridges are diminishing countrywide and most Glamorgan birds are now coastal.

It was good news, therefore, to learn of the presence of the rarest of them all, a quail. Paul Wolfle's dog flushed one on the Graig-yr-Allt side of the Taff on 31st May 1997 and there was another on the Garth side in 1998. Both continued to call after disappearing, this usually the only indication one has, the notes issuing from the depths of a cereal crop.

These both took refuge in purple moor grass. Quail are uncommon summer visitors and have been known to breed here.

Moorhens are as at home on tiny ponds and seepages as on the Taff. Nests may be fairly close together, a group sometimes built by the same pair and protected from human intrusion by sticky mud. One which incorporated the stems of surrounding rushes into its fabric also included a slab of wet cardboard and some crumpled wrapping paper. Another, of more orthodox materials, couched among greater water plantain overtopped by reedmace, was in orange, iron-stained water, but this seemed not to sully the birds' plumage.

Early nests can be quite conspicuous among the small heart-shaped winter leaves of lesser spearwort and the even smaller ones of mud crowfoot before the onset of the growing season. Later ones can be equally vulnerable when the water recedes, leaving them balanced on a sodden log or tuft that was formerly islanded. The surrounding swamps are busy places as youngsters of early broods mingle with those of later ones.

Curlew have nested in the purple moor grass of the mountains, one confirmed in the early 1960s on the north of the Garth, but they probably no longer do so. Their haunting calls were sometimes to be heard in the breeding season, as during the thundrous afternoon of 14th July 1986, when a ground mist lay over the sultry hills, with slanting shafts of sunlight radiating from billowing black cumulus.

Ynys Gau haybarn with Mynydd Meio behind.

Lapwings nested on fields at the back of the Garth when these were ploughed, dive-bombing passing dogs. From 1979 the farm buildings became derelict, the land was turned over to sheep and the lapwings left.

Woodcock, as already indicated, are commonest in hard weather, but have been seen roding along woodland rides in summer. The maximum 1997 count in "East Glamorgan Bird Report" was of twelve at Coed-y-Bedw on 13th December.

There is no roof-nesting by gulls in the village, as in Cardiff and some of its suburbs. The daily commuters seldom land except when ants are abroad on their nuptial flights on humid summer days. In the confined space of gardens they usually leave this winged bounty to the smaller passerines, but will share it with Corvids in the fields, as they do with goodies turned up by the Ynys Gau plough.

Ant feeding is ground-based but may involve brief vertical flights to catch the slow-flying insects, as well as random sideways darts. On 12th September thirty herring and lesser black-backed gulls were fluttering up 10-15 m with rapid wing beats and snatching beaks, then gliding back in wide circles for another flutter.

Wood pigeons are everywhere and on 28th February 1985 a flock of forty was feeding on the winter kale crop on the Ynys Gau toboggan field. Stock doves are rare but were breeding at both Creigiau and Morganstown in 1997 and probably at Draethen further along the Caerphilly Mountain Project area. In 1991 a pair nested in the derelict barn below the ruins of the Colliers Arms on the Mountain Road.

Collared doves, too, bred in Creigiau in 1997, but are not a familiar part of the Gwaelod scene. My first here was on 19th March 1992. They arrived in Britain (Norfolk) in 1955, in Glamorgan in 1962 and in Cardiff by 1974, radiating out through the suburbs to cash in on garden feeding stations. An elegant flock of domesticated white doves circled daily over the Gwaelod during the 1990s.

Cuckoos visit every year, but their evocative calls are no longer an everyday occurrence through early summer, as hitherto. The first in 1997 was heard on 5th April, but there was little sign of others until well into May. Their dwindling numbers may be related to the dwindling of meadow pipits, their principal hosts, on the hills.

Tawny owls are always about, heard rather than seen, particularly when their reciprocated calls echo through the still winter air, and when the youngsters are sent packing to fend for themselves. Holes in ancient oaks are favoured as nest sites.

One flew past my window just after dark on 28th January 1999, another continued calling from my apple tree after I had switched on a garden

68. Greater Bird's-foot Trefoil.

69. Soapwort on the Taff revetments.

70. Tall Centaury in long grass.

71. Tormentil in acid grassland.

72. The walk to Ynys Gau cow byre for milk when Gwaelod was 'cut off' in January 1982.

73. Near the bottom of Mountain Road, December 1967.

Grey Wagtail and Moorland Water Crowfoot

light and gone outside. It was gratifying, and a little awesome, to be so close to the nocturnal hunter. Even better was the occasion when I lay in bed watching one perched in the ash tree outside. It was tempting to think that it was responsible for dropping the parrot leg ring found under the perch next day, but a garbage-scavenging jackdaw or magpie seems a more likely culprit.

Barn owls formerly nested in one of the Ynys Gau barns but have not done so since 1983. Although much scarcer now, a pair nested in Caerphilly town centre in 1997 and one was picked up as a road casualty on the Coryton roundabout on 20th October of that year. In 1991 a barn owl nested in Walnut Tree Quarry, in a safe area where blasting had ceased.

Little owls nest in holes, one confirmed in Church Village north of the Garth in 1997. Their call is a shriller cheeping than that used by the commoner tawnies and a sharp, terrier-like yap. The utterances of either may overlap with the dawn chorus as birds of the day proclaim territory while waiting for their prey to warm into action. Owls probably swallow shrews whole, the exudation from glands along the mammals' flanks not worrying them as it does other predators. Skeletal remains can be teased from the pellets accumulating under their perches.

Nightjars breed no closer than the Wern Ddu Claypits under Caerphilly Mountain, but a male was heard churring across the valley at Graig-yr-Allt on 26th April, 1997. Clear-felling of the conifers on the steep eastern flank of the Great Garth in 1998 may perhaps entice a pair over this side.

Swifts, like nightjars, are tardy migrants, not usually arriving until May, although one was seen up-river on 17th April, 1997. In fine weather they rise to heights beyond our ken, sinking to our level under heavy skies. Numbers were spectacular in the rainstorm of 12th August, 1985, when the Gedrys Brook overflowed, blocking the road with sizable rocks and gravel at its crossing and halting traffic on the northern route to the village.

In the late afternoon of 23rd July, 1986, a typical year, a hundred or so swifts were screaming over my cottage in company with the usual house martins. Big flocks continue to appear until well into August, with only strays thereafter.

The cheerful yaffling of green woodpeckers can be heard throughout the year, from woodland and pasture alike, one pair nesting in a tree-hole only 1 metre above ground! Almost as common in the woods are greater spotted woodpeckers, which indulge in a similar looping flight. Cliff Woodhead tells of their depredations to nest boxes in the Coed-y-Bedw Nature Reserve, where two pairs bred in 1997.

One had ripped a box open and demolished the contents, then started work on another, which was repaired with plywood. A few days later, the warden found a pair of wings, the sole remains of a woodpecker, draped over the hand rail of a footbridge in a sparrow hawk's territory: the hunter hunted.

Twenty five years earlier a nest hole bored by a greater spotted woodpecker in a telegraph pole was taken over by starlings, a not uncommon situation with holes in beech trees. New nest excavations can be located by the pile of fresh wood chippings underneath. The much rarer sparrow-sized lesser spotted woodpeckers have nested both in and out of the reserve in recent years

Nuts or scraps from a bird table wedged into holes in tree bark may be the work of either woodpecker or nuthatch. Bread taken from a neighbour's feeding station one year was usually wedged into a cracked telegraph pole for future consumption.

House martins are always more in evidence than swallows. The first to appear in March move on up-river and there may be a gap of several weeks before the resident flock builds up. Inclement springs set them back. In 1985 the bitter north-east winds that dried the soil to powder during April and created a fire hazard on the hills, held the hirundines in check. Reports came through of swallows being blown back to North Africa when trying to battle across the Straits of Gibraltar.

Our drought broke on 7th June and house martins had arrived in force with swifts by the third week of June, almost three months behind the first comers, which had forestalled the headwinds; one swallow on 9th March and a house martin on 14th March. By mid August that year the Gwaelod martin flock numbered well over a hundred.

Through mid June I watched four birds repeatedly trying to enter one nest, some having to veer away at the last moment to make room. Were these birds of an earlier brood helping or a disorientated pair hindering?

Youngsters are on the wing from mid July in a normal year with flocks building up to two hundred and more by mid September and continuing into October, with laggards around until the start of November. The autumn passage south down the Taff flyway is always more spectacular and long drawn out than the more direct spring passage north. Rain does not stop them during the fall, suggesting that these are not feeding flights, despite continuous rapid circling.

Carrion crows are present all year and sometimes gather in flocks, but do not assume the overwhelming presence of jackdaws. Rooks, traditionally birds of arable land, are seldom seen, although a rookery of thirty four pairs was thriving at Nant Garw in the late 1990s. A hundred and fifty were feeding on the north of the Garth on 8th June, 1984, this unusual.

Ravens have bred three years running (1996,97 and 98) in tall trees in the Ty Nant Quarry. The nest is occupied early and can be viewed from the Ynys Bridge, but a telescope was needed to observe the progress of the young in the nest in March and April. It was feared that they might be put off by the tree felling in February 1999 near the track opposite the building development between the Little Garth and the Taff. Not a bit of it! When the contractor's backs were turned they collected some of their scarlet fencing material and incorporated it in their tree-top nest, a dangerous advertising exercise inappropriate to any less formidable home-builders.

A pair bred on the steep eastern face of the Garth below the new Forstry Commission track to Gedrys in the early 1980s.

Magpies eat anything and everything and are everywhere, singly or in small groups. Seven were fussing round the Ynys Gau farmyard in January 1999, but as many as ten may turn up together. These birds have been seen 'anting', pushing ants under their wings, but not so frequently as members of the thrush family.

Jay flocking is similarly sporadic, with an unusual six appearing together every day during the first week of April in 1983. This was a year when an inordinate number came flocking into Britain, driven west by a dearth of acorns in their native Europe. These gatherings are invariably noisy, the raucous shrieks filling the woods more insistently than the chuckling and piping of the equally excitable magpies.

Jackdaws, traditionally nesters in holes in trees and cliffs, are inevitably drawn to chimneys of the regimented terraced houses through the South Wales Coalfield, but may have to return to more natural sites as coal fires give way to cleaner forms of heating. A few already have, a nest of squawling youngsters being found in a sawn-off, ivy-clad stump in 1991.

When gathering nest material in April, they hold twigs under one foot, parrot-fashion, while breaking off others, and are very likely to lose the lot. The spillage is not retrieved and serves me well for kindling, as they collect only dead material. Thirteen ounces of sheer self-assurance, they are great scavengers and eaters of carrion and do well when others are dying in hard weather.

They were already regarded as a pest in the sixteenth century and Henry VIII passed an act ordering their control, but "Jack", the knave and the rogue, continued to thrive. Up to eight eggs are laid in a clutch, mottled blue-green, like oversized blackbirds' eggs, and the adults, which are monogamous, pairing for life, stuff the chicks with caterpillars, insects and a motley of other goodies.

Jackdaws outshine their equally intelligent Corvid relatives, cashing in on human activities, and they tame easily when the bribes are suitably large. Having few natural enemies, they can live into their teens, long enough to learn new mischief, including that of pilfering useful knick knacks and playing tricks on other birds, some of these well documented.

The various tits are familiar everywhere. They are omnivorous, concentrating on proteinaceous morsels when they have young to rear. The blue tits pecking open oriental and opium poppy heads, may be after the oily seeds, the milky opiates or insect parasites, and they will shell ash seeds.

Small they may be by crow standards, but they are bright enough to learn new tricks, like opening the bottles containing the creamiest milk on the window sill of the Gwaelod-y-Garth Inn in 1963. Modern packaging defeats them but local milk still comes in those tempting foil-topped glass bottles.

They are partial to blackfly on elder but will abandon the useful task of ridding plants of aphids to peck at the putty round window frames and the sticky adhesive under waterproofing strips on greenhouses.

Blue tits tend to dominate the mixed flocks in oak, beech and alder woods, with more coal tits and goldcrests among conifers. Great tits prefer deciduous woods. In the denser plantations small birds favour the edges and rides,leaving the darker interiors to owls and Corvids.

I have watched a blue and great tit locked claw to claw in combat, falling repeatedly to the ground and rolling over and over before breaking free to re-engage. A wren and another blue tit joined the fray before it finally broke up. This was 14th November so was not to do with nesting territory.

Tits generally have been fewer during the 1998-99 winter, possibly as a result of the disastrously wet summer. The really soggy weather started in June, as the first broods were leaving the nests to fend for themselves. Few probably survived and late broods would have had an even harder time.

All but long-tailed tits are hole-nesters, coal tits unusual in sometimes nesting in the ground among tree roots or rotting logs, the entrance simulating a mouse hole.

Seldom does a quiet walk through the local woods not yield sight or sound of nuthatch, tree creeper, dunnock, wren, goldcrest, greenfinch or chaffinch, the last the most numerous of these. Commonest encounters, however, are with robins.

Ash Keys and Autumn influx of Fieldfares

These are innovative feeders and have learned to hover, humming bird fashion, to pluck elderberries or tweak seeds from garden feeders. I have watched them picking grounded clouds of winter gnats from snow patches, to be thwarted when the sun came out and warmed the gnats into flight. Unlike snow fleas, these gangling, evanescent creatures are unable to hop abut on the snow surface at temperatures near freezing.

The best known feeding ploy of robins is to follow large mammals such as gardeners and ramblers for the insects which they disturb. This behaviour is instinctive and is indulged in by speckled youngsters fresh from the nest in May and June, endearing morsels that will hop from spade handle to toe as one scratches among the plants. From early August these lightweight opportunists are being driven from the home patch by possessive parents.

Crop pellets produced by robins are soft, black and not much bigger than peas, as opposed to the scraggier ones of blackbirds, which can reach 3-4 cm long. There is no prior retching as with the larger birds, the rejected material just pops out.

Blackbird pellets are not always of seeds but can contain small snail shells and the tough skins of leather jackets. Until May they often include the unmistakably large pips of ivy berries, which are also a favourite with wood pigeons. This fare is abandoned in favour of small animal life when they start feeding youngsters. The locals habitually probe my lawn for these, taking care to avoid the tunnels of the mining bees. Cocks become sufficiently aggressive at this time to drive off passing cats.

Although better camouflaged than blackbirds, which sway dangerously on the outsides of berry-bearing bushes when feeding, families of song thrushes will gather in the centre of these, making little upward jumps to pull the fruit down within reach. Guelder rose berries are bitter but are relished. Blackcaps are partial to the scarlet berries of lily-of-the-valley.

Redwings are generally more numerous than fieldfares. In 1997 some lingered well into March and others were back by 6th September. The first fieldfares seen that autumn were on 18th October. The cold snap of early February in 1999 brought redwings here in force. Blackbird numbers are always boosted in winter by immigrants from Northern Europe. Wheatears may be seen in late March, hurrying north over the Garth to nesting sites in the mountains.

Chiff chaffs, like blackcaps, are beginning to over-winter in the woods, but don't usually come to bird tables. They arrive early, often in March.

Redstarts are thinning out here, at the southern edge of their Welsh range, and are best known in Coed-y-Bedw, where they take to nest boxes less readily than pied flycatchers, which prefer them to natural holes. Nevertheless, a pair of pieds nested recently in a hole in a woodland oak at the riverward toe of Graig-yr-allt. It was their presence here, again near their southern limits, that inspired Dr. John Edington to suggest putting up nest boxes in the Nature Reserve. The birds did not take long to find these. Old oaks are favoured by redstarts and a good place to spot them is the hedge bordering the mountain road.

Meadow pipits were part and parcel of the Garth scene, but are decreasing, along with the skylarks. Grey wagtails by the river below are thriving. One, in Georgetown, emulated the more cosmopolitan pied wagtails in becoming a garden bird and pottering on a glass roof, demonstrating the beauty of the yellow under-belly to the occupants below. Pied wagtails are among those to be seen sun bathing in summer. In winter they are joined by continental white wagtails.

It was 1984 when I last watched a starling in the village, collecting moss to line a nest under the eaves of the village inn. My chief memory of these birds is of the one which indulged in mimicry and became expert in copying a green woodpecker. It was a definite learning process, the sound of rattling peas changing through gutteral chirrups to a trilling giggle and finally to the characteristic yaffle.

By February 1999 the urban starlings in Whitchurch were blatantly helping themselves to grapes from the greengrocers' pavement displays. These cheeky customers are among the many that negate the pundits' outdated idea that birds live by instinct alone.

Goldfinches in the wild are partial to willow herb seed as well as the usual thistles, sow thistles and dandelions. Feeding is accompanied by a tinkling song, which seems not to hinder their dexterous tweaking of the seeds from the accompanying fluff. Linnets and marsh tits may join them, the tits nipping off the thistle down and taking the seed to a branch to hold under a foot for shelling.

Linnets join siskins, redpolls and greenfinches on birch seed catkins, but also feed on the ground with chaffinches. A big flock will quarter a field with a rolling motion, birds at the back constantly flying over the others to get a turn at the front. Linnets were building in gorse in March 1999; the redpolls prefering conifer plantations.

A misguided chaffinch spent part of a cold March day pecking vainly at the outside of a window trying to get at the aphids on the pot plants within. Two bullfinches watched with interest, but did not join in. The frequency with which wagtails will fight their own image in car wing mirrors is well known.

Hawfinches are birds of the treetops and seldom seen, but twelve were noted at Taffs Well in 1991. Three appeared at Castell Coch on 29th March 1997, two on 12th July and a juvenile on 7th July, suggesting successful breeding. One was seen in the south of the village under the Little Garth in the breeding season that year.

Bramblings appear most winters, five hundred at Castell Coch a few years ago, but I know of no waxwings in this area.

Crossbills are exciting visitors to the valley. Paul Wolfle saw fifty near Castell Coch on 27th June 1997 and twelve there just before Christmas in 1998. Another dozen were feeding among larches by the upper ride on 28th January 1999.

Reed buntings are rare hereabouts, although they are no longer confined to reeds, yellowhammers even rarer. In 1963 when house sparrows were present, I noticed a constant trek of birds to a water butt to drink in dry weather. That was the year that I saw a kestrel dive into a flock of sparrows in the village street, levelling up only a foot or so from the ground. The sparrows scattered and none were caught.

5. Invertebrates

In a general interest book it would be tedious to enumerate too many of the wealth of insects and other small animals recorded over the last decades. This rather random selection tries to indicate the biodiversity that is with us still, although the numbers of both species and individuals are poorer than they were in foregoing years - except for a few of the unwanted, like slugs! Many have already been referred to in the habitat chapters.

Butterflies have been flitting in and out of the more general sections, but reference should be made to the commonest of them all, the meadow browns, which flutter in veritable swarms over the more flowery grasslands on sunny midsummer days. There are others which turn up quite rarely.

Fritillaries are less common than twenty years ago, although there is no shortage of violets, in and out of gardens, for egg laying. Small pearl bordereds are the most often seen, with the handsome silver washed fritillaries flying regally along woodland rides during the height of summer. A dark green fritillary turned up in my garden on 6th July 1992, unfortunately drowned, and John Edington has recorded the much rarer high brown fritillary just across the Taff on Graig-yr-Allt.

29th June that year saw my first ringlets in the garden, these the only species on the wing during the dull spell which followed. Graylings are most likely to be seen on the mountain. There were more about in the early days because they have a special affinity for partially vegetated industrial waste tips. They are particularly prone to infestation by scarlet mites.

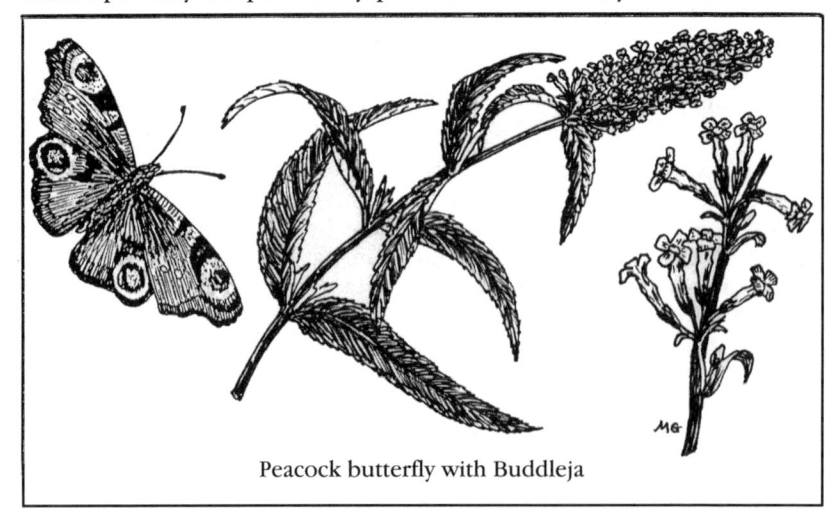

Peacock butterfly with Buddleja

Purple hairstreaks lead secluded lives in oak trees and are seldom seen. Those which do appear in full daylight exhibit a subtle iridescence, changing from navy blue through regal purple to sparkling silver according to the incidence of the sun's rays. The flattened brown caterpillars can be located by tapping them off the lower oak boughs into a collecting tray or sheet.

Other hairstreaks are rare, the white-lettered having suffered a setback with the onset of Dutch elm disease. Even green hairstreaks are seldom seen here, although quite common in the moorland country of North Glamorgan and Brecon, where they favour bilberry, gorse and scattered hill shrubs.

A few decades ago certain years went down in the annals as "clouded yellow years". 1983 was one such, producing the largest number of these migrants for thirty five years. Few years have passed since when some have not reached our shores, the ameliorating climate evidently beckoning them northwards.

When the weather is auspicious for clouded yellows, it is likely to be right for painted ladies and other southern visitors. These leave the Mediterranean as the spring flowers start to wither in the heightening May sunshine. The journey is said to take about two weeks, with a following wind and stops to feed. 1996 was a bumper year, with the winged flotillas arriving around mid June.

Each group of butterflies is associated with particular food plants. The whites, large, small and green-veined, and orange tips, are attracted by the mustard oils of the cabbage family. Favourite nectar plants with the adults are lady's smock, Jack-by-the-hedge and the various yellow mustards in the wild, honesty, wallflowers and stocks in gardens. This

Red Admiral and Comma butterflies on Gwaelod Strawberry Tree in October

cress family is also chosen for egg laying and caterpillar nosh. The mustard oils which they absorb from their food plants make them distasteful to birds.

Hemp agrimony, ice plant and michaelmas daisies are sure lures for many in late summer, when smaller nectar feeders are swarming round golden rod. Small coppers enjoy butter if it comes to their notice and the catholic tastes of red admirals embrace anything sugary or alcoholic, from sweet chutney and jam accompanying al fresco meals to fermenting fruit.

These and other vanessids remain on the wing into November some years, when one of the dwindling sources of nectar is the Gwaelod village strawberry tree, which bears its white bell flowers and knobbly red fruits at the same time. Speckled woods may join them there, even in squally autumns like that of 1981.

The vanessids finally adjourn to houses and outhouses to hibernate. Brimstones prefer to settle among ivy, but also use evergreen Japanese spindle. They match the yellowing leaves of both perfectly, needing only camouflage, not shelter from cold, as they are provided with their own internal anti-freeze. Brimstones are often the last to retire in Autumn and the first to appear in Spring.

Large whites are particularly decorative during their mating flights, fluttering round each other like wind-blown shuttlecocks, but are a serious pest. Home bred ones are augmented some years by incomers from abroad, with a reciprocal emigration in Autumn, after the damage is done.

They produce two broods of speckled caterpillars, munching their way through the brassicas in July and September, with a partial third brood in October during warm summers. These pass the winter as straw-coloured pupae cemented to a wall or tree trunk, but do not keep strictly to timetable.

Two half grown caterpillars were feeding sluggishly on the Ynys Gau kale crop as late as 3rd December in 1985. To judge by the collection of cast skins from earlier instars, they were the sole survivors of a much larger brood. I took them indoors to follow their progress.

One drowned and the other continued feeding for twelve days before escaping from confinement and obeying the urge to set off ceilingwards with a view to pupating. Although still puny, it accomplished an astonishing distance up and down walls and over obstacles before settling, head down, to construct a little pad of silk on the kitchen wall, then right itself to spin an attachment girdle, the head and first three body segments swaying rhythmically from side to side as it worked.

Comatose from 18th December, it responded by wriggling when touched throughout the next seven months, finally emerging as a butterfly on the 2nd June 1986. As it vacated the transparent chrysalid it left a trail of dark red body fluids on the wall, then pumped up the wings, but it was a very stunted specimen that I released into the garden for its maiden flight.

Being 'out of season', it had escaped the dreaded *Apanteles glomeratus* wasps which lay their eggs in so many others, producing clusters of creamy larvae or yellow pupae on the outside of the deceased victim. Nevertheless, it had accomplished a miracle of survival after such a bad start in life. It is this capacity to survive that has made its kind such a serious pest.

Large white caterpillars also have strong homing instincts. When I moved a group a considerable distance and headed them towards my boundary, they all turned round and marched solemnly back to their point of origin, passing enticing cabbage smells en route! Some breed on my Tropaeolum plants, where I have seen them being molested by biting ants.

Most spectacular of our other Lepidoptera are the hawk moths, headed by large elephant hawks *(Deilephila elpenor)*, which are on the wing in June. The fat caterpillars feed on rosebay, greater willow herb and Himalayan balsam on the river flats and I have found the rarer green form on bedstraw. In gardens they favour Fuchsia and evening primrose, both of the willow herb family. Balsam is a new departure from a different family developed since the introduction of the plant to Glamorgan in the early 1900s. By withdrawing the head into the thorax when disturbed, the mottled, usually brown, caterpillar expands the four eyespots with a view to frightening off predators.

Small elephant hawks *(Deilephila porcellus)* have a similar pink and khaki colour scheme to the larger one. Their larvae feed on purple loosestrife as well as willow herbs.

Humming bird hawks *(Macroglossum stellatarum)* are among our more interesting immigrants, arriving in early summer rather more frequently than in the past. They produce a British generation on bedstraws, but this fails to survive our winters.

Poplar hawk moths *(Laothoe populi)* breed occasionally on willow, poplar or aspen. These are residents. Another immigrant which I have come across here only once is the convolvulus hawk moth *(Agrius convolvuli)*, which seldom breeds in Britain's short summers.

Equally spectacular are our representatives of the silk moths, the emperors *(Saturnia pavonia)*. These are based on the mountain, where their big stripy caterpillars feed on bilberry, heather, bramble and hawthorn. The odd females settled in my garden never fail to attract a mate with their powerful emission of pheromones.

Willow Beauty
Peribatodes rhomboidaria
& Little Emerald, *Jodis Lactearia*
Geometer caterpillars emulating twigs,

Solomon's Seal
Sawfly caterpillars

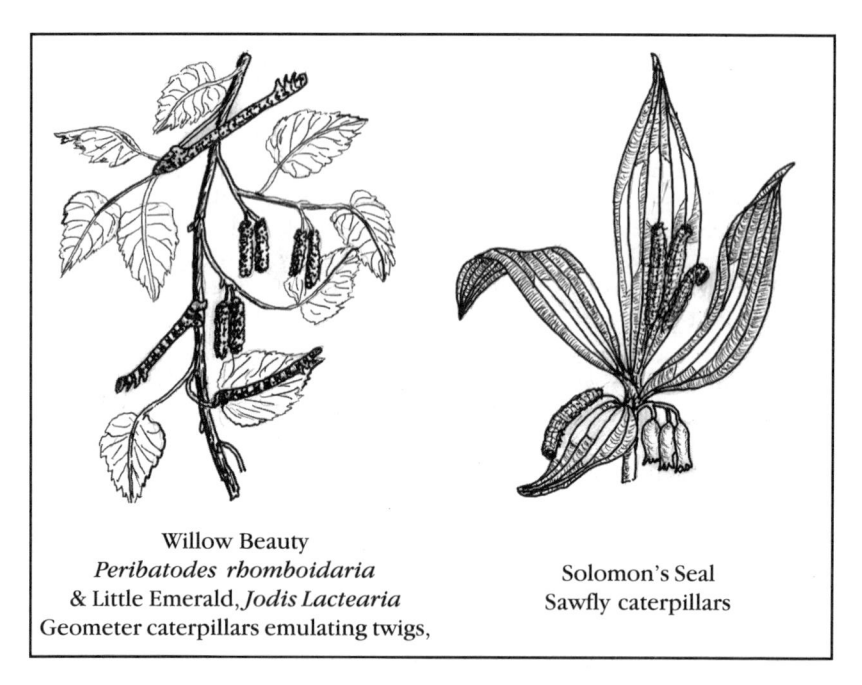

Most are less gaudy, many of the more conspicuous are noctuids. One of the commonest, leaping up from the grass or found as gingery brown chrysalids when digging in the flower beds, are large yellow underwings *(Noctua pronuba)*, Larvae are fairly omnivorous, hiding in the soil by day, and the moths, too, tend to disappear when they alight and fold the upper wings over the spectacular apricot coloured hind ones.

Lesser yellow underwings *(Noctua comes)* and red underwings *(Catocala nupta)* appear regularly in gardens. Copper underwings *(Amphipyra pyramidea)* have been dying in droves in my garden shed ever since it was erected in the late seventies, but it is not clear why they go in. I can only think it is to lay their overwintering eggs in dry crevices, the caterpillars having to find their way out to the nearby ash tree.

Other noctuids are chestnut moths *(Conistra vaccinii)*, which feed on ivy flowers in autumn and sallows in spring, the larvae not necessarily on the bilberry suggested by their specific name. Red line quaker moths *(Agrochola lota)*, fly late into November, so are other customers on the prolific ivy flowers. Small quakers *(Orthosia cruda)* emerge early enough to take nectar from pussy willow catkins in March, their caterpillars thriving on these or on oak.

The rather attractive angleshades *(Phlogophora meticulosa)* are around all the year, the caterpillars chomping away at my indoor Pelargoniums when it gets too chilly outside and pupating among spare blankets. The second brood is likely to be supplemented by immigrants and outdoor caterpillars may hibernate, but I find moths emerging on window sills at any time during the winter, their normal cycle upset by the warmth. (This is a thought to bear in mind in relation to global warming. What next, we ask?!)

White ermines *(Spilosoma lubricipeda)* are among many attracted to lights in midsummer, the 'woolly bear' caterpillars munching dandelion, dock and other weeds through the late summer. They have a remarkable turn of speed when gliding across the lawn in autumn seeking a site to pupate.

Best known of all, because they are poisonous and fly blatantly in broad daylight, are the black and red cinnabars *(Tyria jacobaea)*, bred on ragwort and the five spot and six spot burnets *(Zygaena trifoliae* and *Zygaena filipendulae)* reared on small legumes. Prettily fringed white plume moths *(Alucita pentadactyla)* are conspicuous both day and night.

This is by no means true for the geometer caterpillars (the Americans' 'inch worms') that mimic twigs. Two that live on birch, the willow beauty *(Peribatodes rhomboidaria)* and light emerald *(Jodis lactaeria)* are illustrated. Others, more decorative in the adult stage, are the primrose coloured swallow tailed moths *(Ouropteryx sambucaria)*, riband waves *(Sterrha aversata)* and the red-flecked yellow brimstone moths *(Opisthograptis luteolata)*.

Sawflies are related to bees and wasps, which they resemble as adults, but the larvae are easily mistaken for caterpillars. The crucial difference is that they have a larger number of stumpy pro-legs at their back end. They have equally voracious appetites, as is only too apparent with the regiments of gooseberry sawflies *(Nematum ribes)*, rose sawflies *(Arge ochropus)* and birch sawflies *(Cimbex femorata)*.

All leaves on some branches of my gooseberries are stripped to the veins each year, while others remain intact. Rose sawfly caterpillars range themselves round the leaf edges and elevate their tails in unison when disturbed, a corporate display sufficiently intimidating to send most predators packing.

A relatively new arrival in Britain is the solomons seal sawfly *(Phymatocera aterrima)* and this indulges in no such reaction, the hordes of speckled grey caterpillars ranged side by side as they feed their way up the long leaves until only the parallel veins remain.

Because they do not strike until late June, when flowering is well past, the persistent hordes present no problem. The massed pendant bell flowers appear unabashed every spring. Most leaf eaters prefer young leaves. By taking old ones these have with-held the hands that might have been ranged against them. Probably because of the phenomenally rapid growth of the spring shoots the leaves are for ever young.

Black and green adult *Rhogogaster viridis* sawflies lap nectar and pollen from hogweed and other umbellifers on the river flats. One of the many sawflies producing galls is *Pontania proxima*, which is responsible for red bean galls on willow leaves. Less common among those affecting willow is *Cryptocampus saliceti*, the sawfly causing the frilling of leaves to produce gherkin galls.

Wood wasps are others of this group, one of the most striking the greater horntail *(Sirex gigas)*. The 'horn tail' appears only on the female, being the ovipositor, with which she lays up to a hundred eggs in a hundred different punctures in felled or diseased coniferous trees.

Ironically, there are other wasps, members of the vast concourse of ichneumons, which come along later and lay eggs which hatch to devour the developing horntail larvae. *Pimpla rufa* is one of the biggest of the ichneumons, all black except for the long red legs and the red ovipositor in its split black sheath. This is 2 cm long, with gauzy wings. Many ichneumons impose important checks on their prey species and can be used in biological pest control. These attack animals.

Those attacking plants include the many cynipid wasps, a number of which are responsible for most of the common galls on oak trees. Another, *Diplolepis rosae*, creates the familiar fuzzy red robin's pincushions on wild roses. Unusually coloured solitary wasps are the sheeny green and red ruby tails *(Chrysis ignita)*, which commonly appear in our gardens, where they parasitise solitary bees.

Discs the size of 5P pieces cut from the leaves of roses or the stouter ones of Japanese spindle are the work of leaf-cutter bees *(Megachile centuncularis)*. They use these to line their nest holes, sometimes oval pieces for the walls and circular ones for the lid. Favourite nesting sites in my garden are narrow iron pipes protruding from walls and spaces under a flat roof. They work by day and can be watched carving the discs and pushing them into the holes which they will furnish with nectar and pollen for their offspring. This is the traditional food of young bees: the young of burrow-forming wasps are nourished on paralysed caterpillars or similar animal life.

Other solitary bees, *Halictus*, took up residence in my lawn for a few years. These are mining bees and I first noticed them on 14th April 1984, throwing up neatly conical 'volcanoes' of finely granulated soil, bigger than average, possibly to get clear of the choking moss. During mid morning, in bright sunlight, all had a pencil sized hole in the top. By mid afternoon, when it had turned dull, all but one hole had been sealed, the plug of soil still damp.

I was wrong in thinking they had been stocked with food and new laid eggs and sealed for good, as all the holes were open next morning, with a bee sitting in each tunnel facing outwards, but popping back inside when I got too close. Later, when sufficiently warmed up, they started bringing in nectar and pollen for the 'marzipan balls' that would sustain the hatchlings.

There were thirty nine holes on one lawn, two on the other and three in the cracks of the crazy stone path between the two. The little 'volcanoes' appeared in the next few years in exactly the same place and on dates no more than three days away from that of their initial discovery in 1984. In 1985 bees were stoking up from summer snowflake flowers, their pollen baskets packed with orange pollen.

Like the similar *Andraena* bees seen on sandy sections of riverside, they are colonial as well as solitary, each home burrow a few inches from those around. This must facilitate getting together sexually on emergence.

Occasionally common wasps *(Vespa vulgaris)*, which are far from solitary hang one of their radially constructed paper nests from the roof of my garden shed. Their nuisance value when they develop a taste for jam tarts in autumn is offset by the number of pests they destroy when feeding their grubs on animal proteins.

In several consecutive years a swarm of honey bees moved in under my balcony floor, with devastating results and unreachable honey stores leaking through the ceiling and trickling down inside walls. Even though the queen and her subjects were eventually winkled out of the sticky mess and all likely entrances blocked, the evocative honey scent attracted roving swarms in subsequent years.

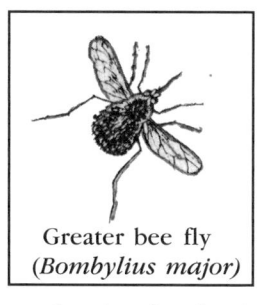

Greater bee fly
(Bombylius major)

Bee-like in appearance is the fat, furry greater bee fly *(Bombylius major)*, which is one of the most dependable of my garden flies in spring. I first recorded it on 6th April in 1978 and it has not missed a year since, although sometimes not arriving until early May.

It is a sun-lover, so much so that on sunny spring days every year one or two spend their non-feeding time hovering motionless a foot away from the shiny reflective leaves on the south side of a closely trimmed Japanese spindle bush. I cannot fail to notice them as, on that sort of day, my deckchair is usually positioned closeby. Always on the sunny side, although headed, tern-like, into any slight breeze, they are patently enjoying the reflected warmth.

The wings persist in their rapid beating when the insect pushes its long non-retractable proboscis in for nectar, although the front feet are grasping the flower. With the exception of primroses, the flowers they patronise seem always to be blue. Garden favourites are forget-me-nots, Aubretia, honesty, grape hyacinths and periwinkles. The food plants may be anywhere, but each generation is faithful to that one piece of empty air on the sunny side of my bush. I have not seen them hanging motionless for so long anywhere else.

Female bee flies drop their eggs haphazardly close to the nests of solitary bees and the larvae which hatch crawl inside to feed on the bee grubs and pupae. My *Halictus* bee colony was only a few feet away, perhaps the bee flies were responsible for its eventual destruction.

Other distinctive springtime Diptera are St. Marks flies *(Bibio marci)*. Swarms of males, hang in the air, trailing hairy black legs obliquely and maintaining position almost as faithfully as the bee flies. They are a little later, emerging around St. Marks day, 25th April. In bad weather they lie low, reappearing through May, when starlings attempting to catch them in the air may be led a pretty dance.

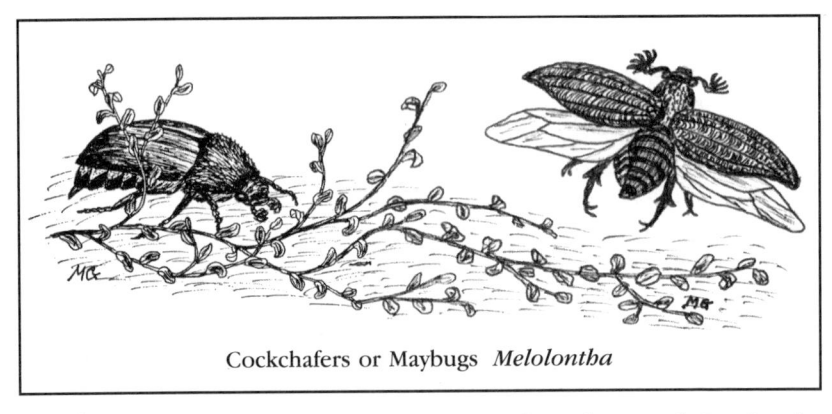

Cockchafers or Maybugs *Melolontha*

Summer is full of hover flies, such as *Syrphus ribesii* and *Catabomba pyrastri*, most of them disguised in black and yellow stripes, like wasps, as a precaution against predators. The young are aphid eaters, the adults flower feeders, choosing open blooms like candytuft, where their short tongues can reach the sweets. Misguided ones may search the double flowers of Kerria, which are infertile and devoid of lures, in an effort to find the few small single flowers which might come up with the goods.

Larger related flower feeders concentrating on the daisy family are drone flies *(Eristalis tenax)* and the similar *Scaeva pyrastri*. Biggest of the familiar dipterons are marsh and common craneflies *(Tipula paludosa* and *Tipula oleracea)*, which sometimes build up to plague proportions by the end of summer. These lay hundreds of eggs among grass, the grubs hatching from these being the notorious leather jackets, munching away at roots and stems.

On one occasion I watched a prolonged battle between a leather jacket and a Geophilomorph centipede, which pursued it doggedly across a flower bed, sometimes out of sight, sometimes erupting at the surface in a tangle of bodies.

Tiny fruit flies *(Drosophila)* and hairy owl midges *(Psychoda)* are nourished, along with soldier flies *(Chloromyia)*, on compost heaps. Various kinds of flies found dead in a cobwebby fuzz on autumn plants are likely to be victims of *Entomophora* fungus.

The more magnificent and unrelated dragonflies may wander far from the ponds and streams of their nymphal phase. Most frequent garden visitors are the red and khaki common darters *(Sympetrum striolatum)*. Once a golden ringed dragonfly *(Cordulegaster boltoni)* shot past my nose at a rate of knots and grabbed a gatekeeper butterfly in flight. The smaller damselflies are adept at hovering to pick small flies off vegetation, as well as catching them in flight in their 'basket' of legs.

Water Cricket, *Velia*, and Mayfly, *Cloëon*

Freshwater insects are legion. Those illustrated are the mayfly *(Cloëon)*, during its brief adulthood, which is by no means seen only in May, and a *Velia* water cricket, which lives on the surface film, with water boatmen, water measurers, whirligig beetles and dangling hordes of mosquito larvae.

In view of the fact that beetles are the largest group of insects, with something like a quarter of a million species, we see relatively few these days. The shiny bloody-nosed beetle *(Timarcha tenebricosa)*, largest of the leaf beetles, is one of the earliest abroad in spring, distasteful and hence bold. Perhaps most striking is the minotaur beetle *(Typhaeus typhoeus)*, so-called for the paired processes from the sturdy thorax, which resemble a bull's horns. This can appear from the last week of March, associated with rabbit and sheep droppings, but was more likely to be seen in the 1970s than the 1990s. When disturbed or upside down it emits an agitated whirring noise.

Another of these chunky ground beetles or Carabids is the bumble dor *(Geotrupes stercorarius)*, which is still common on the Garth. This is known also as the lousy watchman, for the load of tiny fawn mites with which many are burdened. Maybugs or cockchafers *(Melolontha melolontha)* and the much commoner garden chafers *(Phyllopertha horticola)* are related to these.

One of our most decorative is the black and yellow wasp beetle *(Clytus arietus)* which, like the devils coach horse *(Ocypus olens)*, sometimes ventures indoors. Cardinals *(Pyrochroa coccinea)* are pillar box red,as are the scarlet lily beetles *(Lilioceris lillii)* which first struck my Pyrenean lilies in 1999, making lace of the whorled leaves. Tortoise beetles *(Cassida rubiginosa)* are a startling pea green, like some of the shield bugs and capsid bugs and oak bush crickets *(Meconema varium)*. Rather commoner than the last are dark bush crickets *(Pholidoptera griseoaptera)*. Crickets can be distinguished from grasshoppers in having much longer antennae.

The funnel shaped webs of *Agalena labyrinthica* spiders can be found in tussock and gorse on the mountain, where infant money spiders balloon across the sward on autumn nights. Other spiders spin webs far into December, the strands holding water droplets, which can have the most beautiful prismatic effect in sunlight. Change the angle of viewing ever so little and all the colours of the rainbow appear in sequence.

Harvestmen or daddy longlegs come in various guises. One, with the smallest body and longest legs, often found spreadeagled symmetrically on whitewashed walls, is *Leiobunum rotundum*. Legs are flattened to the wall when at rest, the 'knees' raised high when striding over plants, by day or night.

Cattle by the Ynys Gau farm bridge over the Taff Vale railway.

Renovations in the Ynys Gau farmyard, July 1999

Chapter 12

SEASONAL WILDSCAPE VIEWING

1. Winter Wildlife

Winter is the slack season in the great out-of-doors but has many redeeming features. Gwaelod is poised between the windy summit of the Garth and the frosty valley bottom. On still winter nights air cooled on the heights rolls down through the village to settle in the frost pocket below. We wake to gleaming white hoar frost coating the riverside fields when our lawns are innocent of ice crystals and half-hardy garden plants remain unblemished.

The surest source of these rimy carpets are freezing fogs. As night temperatures drop below zero the air can no longer hold its moisture, which is jettisoned as frozen dew. Upstanding plants of the valley bottom may be encrusted like the grass, into a veritable winter wonderland. Leaves are fringed with sparkling crystals, like Christmas decorations. Only in the harder frosts does rime spread across their surfaces. I wonder why. Is this a feature of leaf temperature or moisture retention?

As the ice melts the warming air is able to take up moisture again to give morning ground mists spread along the valley bottom. Steam rises over moving water and white mist billows up from the river as from the nostrils of a cavalcade of gallopping horses. Those viewing from the village, at its 'lofty' elevation of two hundred feet, are above the clouds, which may rise to envelope them before dissipating into the sun-warmed air.

On slopes which remain all day in shadow the frost does not melt. In dry weather when the air holds little moisture,the cold is manifested as black frost, which can prove lethal to both plants and animals.

Snow lies longest on hilltops and bottomlands. At such times the low winter sun may pick out patterns of old ridge and furrow ploughlands on the Ynys Gau riverside fields: a reminder of the days of fixed ploughshares when it was necessary to work round and round each land to allow the horses room to turn on the headlands.

The slice of topsoil was overturned towards the centre of each strip, leaving deeper furrows between successive series of circuits, these not normally visible under the cloaking grass. Snow, lying longest in the furrows, reveals the hidden story in the ground as aerial photographs reveal lost archeological remains.

The sculpted lands lie at right angles to the river bank upstream of the Ffygis:Ynys Gau railway bridge and parallel to it on the downstream side. The two sets converge on the railway line, at right angles to each other and oblique to the track. The lower field was ploughed again in

1986, after the unsuccessful attempt to drain the frog spawning pools, only the part against the scarp being too wet to support the heavy tractor necessary to draw today's multi-furrow turnabout plough.

Longer-lying snow protects both plants and animals from biting winds and traps insulating air pockets. Protruding leaf tips may be blackened by frost while the heart of the plant remains ready to sprout at the appropriate time. The metabolism of spring growth may release heat energy manifested by snow-free pockets above precocious celandine or primrose flowers.

Snow melts to reveal runs worn through the sole of the turf where mice and voles have been leading a normal life, nibbling at the plant bases, and even breeding, away from the prying eyes and noses of foraging fox and prowling puss. There is no need to burrow into frozen ground with that protective blanket above.

Shrews, too, are active under the snow, needing to eat half to three quarters of their body weight every day. Their diet of invertebrates and fresh carrion may be supplemented by oily seeds in winter, when they have to work harder to combat heat loss, to which they are very susceptible with such a large surface:volume ratio to their tiny bodies. Wood lice are known to figure on their menu and there is no shortage of these. All these small mammals grow thicker fur in winter.

Mole hills can appear overnight through snow or ground frost, but not when the surface soil defies the gardener's spade. Moles must work harder and burrow deeper to find the worms and beetles that have burrowed down before them to avoid the immobilising chill, so molehills may be larger. After a night of frost a whole molehill can be lifted as a solid slab until frozen to the soil which it protects below.

With so many of our mammals nocturnal, a walk in the snow can reveal more of their activities than can be gleaned in the summer. Only then do we realise how common foxes and rabbits are , their tracks criss crossing everywhere from mountain top to river flats, but particularly along the protective lines of the old field hedgerows.

It is possible to see where an animal changed from a run to a walk, where it paused to preen, scuffled with another of its own kind, leapt on prey or was leapt upon. A fox's tracks are neatly registered until it makes a long leap at the junction with a one-way rabbit track. Where the marks of a small rodent come to a halt in a flurry of snow, the predator is likely to be one of the local tawny owls which call through the long winter nights.

Passerines taking off from the snow crouch before they leap into the air, leaving a pretty pattern of splayed wing and tail feathers in the snow. The deeper the snow the deeper the feather prints, as the bird draws the body lower to get sufficient power for the launch.

Larger birds may need a short run before taking off or after alighting. Their footprints are further apart as they leave or approach the ruffled snow at the point of take-off or landfall, the bigger strides necessary to promote or absorb the impetus of travel. Moorhen and coot usually have short mincing steps: pheasants trail a central toe which leaves a track like a lizard's tail: but no lizard is likely to be out in the snow.

Bud scales scattered across pristine snow show where bullfinches have been feeding on buds, very likely of garden Forscythia or flowering cherry. Other finches leave a debris of seed husks or flesh ripped from rose hips or Cotoneaster berries to get at the seeds within. Particularly vivid are the orange arils stripped from white seeds taken from the pink capsules of spindle bushes. Seeding catkins of birch are very brittle and the little winged seeds get spilled across the snow when siskins or long-tailed tits are feeding on them.

In hard conditions old enmities are forgotten and suspicious neighbours feed side by side. The night of 12th December 1981 was said to be the coldest on record for thirty years and three of the usually belligerent robins fed ammicably together, the survivors ignoring the one which died breast uppermost, although experiment has shown that movement is not necessary to trigger aggression.

The Ynys Gau toboggan slope in the late 70s.

Wrens, with their propensity for diving into snow-covered tussocks for spiders and other goodies get by rather well despite their large surface:volume ratio. Heat loss is minimised by communal roosting.

The big freeze-up starting around 6th January in 1982 was said to be the worst since 1947. The sea froze at Aberystwyth for the first time in living memory. The sea had frozen at Penarth in 1963, with big ice floes crowded along the driftline and the docks iron-hard, but water is not so salty there, probably less than two thirds full sea strength in winter when the rivers are running full, so its freezing point will be higher.

A small flock of grey geese flew over in the late afternoon of 7th January, with between nine hundred and a thousand flying in V formation around midday on the 8th. These took a full three minutes to pass, skein after skein, flapping on a broad front. This was a day of icy blue skies and sunshine, with a buzzard sailing high over the valley.

At this time, in 1982, Gwaelod village was cut off for several days, with no deliveries of milk or bread. People at the south end walked out to meet the milk van on the Pentyrch road. Those of us at the north walked to Ynys Gau Farm, where there was no means of getting the milk away by vehicle and Clive Francis was as pleased to sell it as we were to buy.

A little flock of free range Welsh mountain sheep commuted up and down the lane in front of every walker. They had escaped the bitter regime on the Garth, where starlings had been warming their naked feet in the woolly fleeces, but were barred entry to the fields and found only the winter-bare hedges to nibble.

Unlike the birds, whose numbers had built up in gardens, their shyness remained. There was no way to get past them and we felt guilty making them expend so much precious energy to get away from us. They did not belong this side of the mountain, so could not be claimed, even if they had been missed. Sheep often take refuge in the woods under these conditions, where at least the bramble leaves and a few ferns remain winter-green.

Such harsh conditions are rare and usually short-lived. The progression of the seasons is becoming continually more disrupted with higher temperatures sometimes occurring in winter than summer. An unseasonal overlap of winter and spring wildlife occurred in the early part of 1985. Seldom do we see butterflies in flight over persistent snowfields and even less often do we see these symbols of summer in the same glance as a flock of bramblings, which epitomise winter for us, in this mild oceanic land to which they flee from continental freeze-ups. February 24th 1985 yielded such an overlap.

Four strongly flying male brimstones were about, but the small tortoiseshell was flying weakly, its hunger unslaked. Energy reserves must have been at an all time low after a winter of hibernation but there was no

Frozen Aquifers in the Taff Gorge. February 1998

Winter Heliotrope in December, and March.

sugary solution for a butterfly's proboscis to suck up among the residual snow patches; no coltsfoot, celandine or even a nectar-laden willow catkin.

The vanilla-scented sweets of winter heliotrope produced back in January, when there were no insects around to benefit, had all been crisped to a frazzle by recent frosts. A few red admirals over-wintered that year, one had ventured out into my living room a fortnight earlier but was not tempted out of doors.

The comparative mildness of the previous November and December had come to an abrupt halt with the dawning of 1985. The hard weather came in three spells, so that wild creatures had a chance to feed up after each set-back in preparation for the next. The thaw at the end of January came just in time to save many birds suffering critical weight losses, which can be as much as half the total.

Redwings were particularly vulnerable. Berries had been stripped by the New Year, plentiful though they had been, and berry eaters were out on the Ynys Gau fields trying to haul invertebrates from the frozen soil. Many villagers hosted redwings in their gardens during this period.

Blackbirds were the most successful, indulging in litter scratching, like barnyard fowls, and uncovering goodies hidden from others. They are inveterate fruit eaters, even spurning calorie-rich offerings of bread and cheese in favour of windfall apples, frozen solid and probably at least 95% water at best.

Seed-eaters were less affected by the cold, the outstanding mast year of 1984 ensuring an adequate supply of the more durable foodstuffs of their choice. Some householders complained that they had fewer tits in their gardens than usual. These diminutive opportunists often seek our assistance only when driven to it. While food stocks last they are content to stay in the woods.

On January days, when iced Japanese knotweed leaves crunched and shattered underfoot, the local kingfishers and grey wagtails had to close up a bit to make way for an overspill from colder lands up-river. They shared the cleaner riffles with snipe, heron and moorhen.

Wrens crept among the riverside revetments, seeking out other troglodytes hiding from the cold; flocks of goldfinches swung on frost-rimed birch twigs and tattered teasel heads; siskins and redpolls poked at the myriad alder cones, seeking the last of the unshed nutlets.

During the respite of late January and early February queen bumble bees were on the wing and honey bees came to sip from the tubular petal nectaries of hellebores and to gather pollen from the winter-flowering heathers. For a brief spell the pink daisy heads of winter heliotrope, which usually waste their heavy fragrance on the empty air, were visited by pollinating insects. Then we plunged into the second cold spell and were able to walk dry shod over iron-hard woodland quagmires again until that sunny day of 24th February.

The mild spell lasted until 11th March, with the first bat sighted on the 9th and honey bees scrambling around inside the crocusses, gorging themselves on the orange pollen. Ice and intermittent blizzards clamped down again between the 12th and the 22nd, but the dawn chorus was building up and formerly complacent wood pigeons were indulging in their insistent cooing, impatient for the coming of spring.

February 1986 saw similar frosts. Unusual visitors on the 12th were seven redpolls, which descended onto my frozen lawn to gather seeds drifted into the holes left by squirrels digging for buried nuts. Apples pushed off the trees by jackdaws and jays were being attacked by blackbirds and song thrushes, fieldfares and redwings. The boldy patterned fieldfares emerged at the top of the peck order except during the rare visits of a mistle thrush.

During mid February birds flocked to the supply of fresh water alongside as many as a fortnight's unthawed ice moulds. The green woodpeckers, which laugh the winter away with their yaffling, had to forego their favourite food of ants and return to the traditional woodpecker fare found under loose bark.

Flowers of christmas rose bowed groundwards, their petals frozen rigid, like fine porcelain. Early crocus flowers also froze overnight, but their self-generated heat caused a little dimple in the snow as they strove to push up by day.

Stinkhorn and 'egg', Norway Spruce cones nibbled by squirrels.

Winter-green ferns went flaccid in the physiological drought, with water water everywhere but not a drop liquid enough to drink. Even the evergreen leaves of the cherry laurel began to drop as the frost persisted.

But the inevitability of spring, fortunately, is something we can always rely on. By 22nd February the black-headed gulls on the river already wore the dark chocolate heads of their summer plumage. Soon after that alder catkins were loosening up and pussy willows were pussying.

The Ynys Gau dairy cows might be turned out in the frozen home paddock for a few hours between milkings. Steam rises from their nostrils and body heat radiates from their ample flanks, tempting birds to come and warm their feet. There are welcome gleanings from the seeding hay fed in the field and possible meatier titbits in the silage.

Even better, there are steaming cow pats offering a second hand bounty of undigested seeds to wood pigeons, jackdaws, crows, starlings and finches, before these freeze solid when the donors are tucked up indoors.

By 1998 Clive Francis had given up milking, due to other commitments, falling prices and increasing tagging and paper work. He purchased a Limousin bull, so progeny of the former milkers were now destined to be sold as beef calves or kept on for the meat market, the cows used as sucklers. Young store cattle were out on the fly ash field - the only suitably unpoachable substrate - for longer stretches, so more birds benefitted.

Now, a decade on, the winters are generally gentler and only the weakest of the wildlife fall by the wayside.

2. The Flavour of Winters in the Nineteen Nineties

Gentle winters do not necessarily emerge into balmy springs and that of 1990 was wild as well as mild. A bare three months after 1998's butterflies had made their final exit, spring appeared over the Christmassy landscape. From early January the Gwaelod-y-Garth village street was bright with yellow and white johnquills and winter pansies. No frosts came to lay these low and it was only during the briefest of cold snaps that our lawns sparkled with early morning frosts.

Purple irises flowered bravely from December to March, their tender petals chewed by slugs and woodlice - even caterpillars, which had dispensed with any semblance of hibernation. Winter gnats and winter moths enjoyed extra time on the wing and over active queen wasps buzzed impatiently at the windows to be out and away. Golden-eyed lacewings displayed their gauzy wings on the panes and the odd tortoiseshell butterfly emerged from uneasy slumber to flaunt its colours.

There were no hard weather movements of birds, no winter influx of bramblings, fieldfares or redwings, no snipe or water rail feeding boldly in the open on the frozen river flats. The unruly jackdaws were collecting sticks throughout February and song birds were in full voice. None were moved to collect the fallen crabapples but many enjoyed the sweeter windfalls in the gardens.

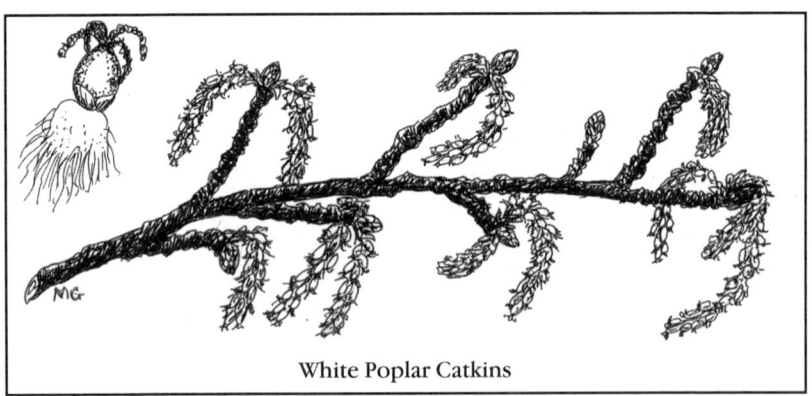

White Poplar Catkins

Half the hazel catkins were at full stretch by the first week of January, including those on a branch which had been broken off before autumn leaf fall but had retained sufficient resources to expand the yellow lambs' tails well ahead of schedule. No corky abscission layers had formed at the leaf bases to squeeze the leaves off and prevent water loss from the scars, so the leaves withered on the bough.

Ground Ivy, Coltsfoot, and Wild Arum

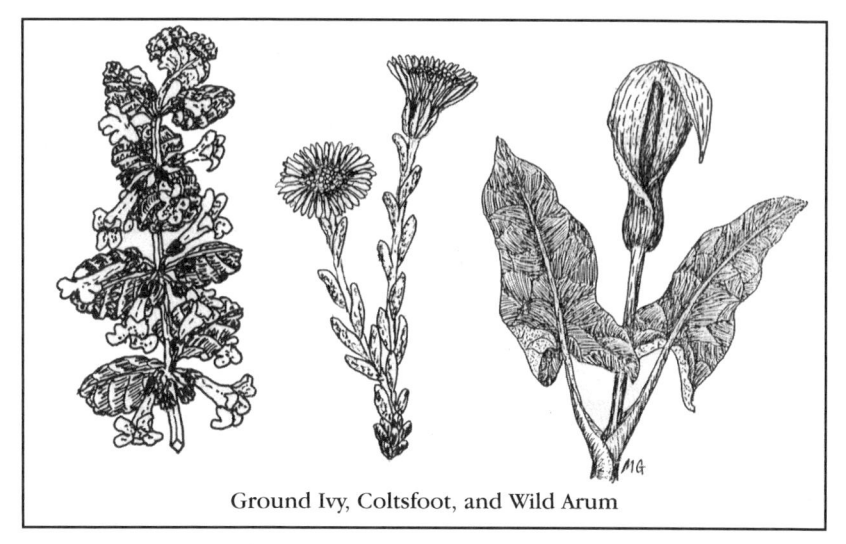

Pussy willows bulldozed beside the Forestry Commission track from Gwaelod to Gedrys did even better. Stimulated into a last ditch attempt to perennate their kind before succumbing to the damage, these had produced terminal rosettes of undersized leaves and mature fruiting catkins by 7th January. Willows cling more tenaciously to life than most and the maltreated parent plants were already putting out new roots and shoots to correct their upended stance.

Dandelions, groundsel and daisies, red dead-nettle and ivy-leaved toadflax flowered throughout the winter on roadsides; polyanthus, candytuft, Bergenia and jasmin in gardens. Alpine crocusses and Daphne were out by mid January, celandines and snowdrops not far behind.

So much for the mildness, what of the wildness? While our neighbours on the heights of Pentyrch were having panes torn from their greenhouses, roof slates ripped off and paling fences laid low, we in Gwaelod were tucked snugly away in the lee of the mountain. Not all went unscathed, however, and a flowering cherry on our approach road fell victim to gusts sneaking down Heol Goch from the heights.

March came in like the proverbial lion, but hairy catkins had already opened on the white poplars and daffodils were showing yellow. Among the first of the woodland flowers were ground ivy, coltsfoot, wood anemones and wild arum. (Ground ivy was predecessor of the hop in old English brewing, its hoof-shaped leaves bitterly aromatic and its vernacular name 'ale hoof'.)

In 1994 the first celandines opened on the lane verge on 6th February. Yellow-green hellebore and spurge smiled above a few shy primroses and blushing Bergenia lightened dark corners. We woke to the repetitive notes of song thrush and mellifluous tones of blackbirds revving up for the summer's labours.

The thirteenth of February revealed the usual masses of frogspawn on the river flats, upstanding clusters frosted with ice. The exquisitely patterned feathers of a snipe had been wind wafted across the thin ice film, where one life had been sacrificed to sustain another. Supper for a fox, perhaps, or a mink. A sparrow hawk would have taken its prey to a plucking post to de-feather. There was no sign of the carcase, nor that of the owner of a wood pigeon's feathered remains held by the ice.

We had been awash for most of the winter, but spring was on its way. One of the first of the roadside flowers to open was the humble shepherds purse, but the mediaeval shepherd with purse the shape of its flattened fruits would have been rich if it had held as many pennies as those heart-shaped capsules held seeds. With it were hairy bitter cress and barren strawberry with a spattering of pale bue speedwells. Brighter by far were the yellows of the apricot-scented gorse and the coltsfoot and dandelion among golden saxifrage and dogs mercury.

Spring Hares and Daffodils

Wood anemones were out by the first week of March with violets in sequestered corners, the white or richly red-purple sweet violets ahead of the common wood violets. Two tiny plants of industrial waste on the site of the old forge were lesser cudweed and wall speedwell. These are easily overlooked and a hand lens is needed to appreciate their finer points. They survive on powdery coal waste and slag which is liable to dry out by getting through their diminished life cycle in record time. In damp summers they can achieve several generations in a single year.

A mayfly was on the wing on 6th March and by the 12th brimstone, small tortoiseshell and peacock butterflies had emerged from hibernation, with red admirals not far behind. The first greater bee-fly was hovering over the blue flowers of ground ivy by the 26th and by the end of the month white blossoms had appeared on blackthorn and wild cherry in the hedges.

Two brief sorties made in early February 1996 depict the characteristic winter scene in the Gwaelod woods.

The frosty grass was crisp underfoot and the ridged soil iron-hard, but sunshine had transformed a precocious hazel into a shower of gold. This was not the only one to unfurl its catkins prematurely and a silvery sheen was already peeping from pussy willow buds. It was, after all, 3rd February, but the land had been in the grip of ice through much of the month logged as 'the dullest January since 1909'.

A brighter speck of gold gleamed from the head of the little bird fossicking among the yellow tassels - a goldcrest, unperturbed by my presence as it dawdled between hazel and larch. Working up the trunk of a nearby scots pine was a nuthatch and the noise of an argument between two jays rang through the treetops.

A buzzard broke from the woodland edge to circle low over the cocksfoot meadow before returning to cover. It was another two hours before a thermal developed to carry it, mewing, over the mountainside. Fresh pigeon remains marked the sparrow hawk's plucking post, no carcase, just neat grey feathers and white guano. A survivor closeby mustered its full springtime call of "You two fools, you two" among more indeterminate utterances.

Seven carrion crows cawed their way riverwards, a change from the ever-present, chattering jackdaws that terrorised the village and pillaged food put out for smaller birds. Moss carpets were pocked with mouse-sized holes where their chisel beaks had probed. There were mice about, or bank voles, leaving roundly nibbled hazel nut shells. Most of the neatly split husks were elevated on rocks or stumps - squirrels' dining tables. I was almost back to the village when I spotted the siskins, neatly patterned in green, yellow and black. So that was what I had been hearing!

On Saturday I walked up valley: on Sunday I walked down. Both ways I encountered song thrushes - regular denizens of our village gardens, which is gratifying as they are said to be getting rare on a national front.

I turned into the south wood along the ancient track, deeply recessed by years of wear, so that only my head reached above the bank. Village elders tell how men speeded the deepening by digging out mud that hindered the horse-drawn wagons bringing coal down from the levels on the Garth Mountain. The wren was down there with me, darting into every hole under the dangling curtains of moss, as unperturbed as yesterday's goldcrest. The tree creeper was working up from the head-high bases of conifers alongside.

The 'wait and see' technique of bird watching holds greater attractions as the bones stiffen up. It paid off today, not least with the sprucely dressed coal tit that dropped almost at my feet to sip iron-stained water filtering through a trellis of icicles from one of the old mines. But why, when one is trying to simulate part of a tree trunk, are the birds always directly overhead? Shall I ever get the crick out of my neck?

The nuthatch moved into the picture as I watched great tits and chaffinches. The sun's rays highlighted the slaty blue and apricot pink, providing a superb spectacle. Fresh chippings under an elderly birch, killed by razor strop brackets, told where the greater spotted woodpecker had been at work.

Nine blackbirds, all cocks, were flipping over the crunchy beech litter, but there were none of the hoped for bramblings which had descended on the beech nuts two years before. The pair of ravens from the mountain added their harsh voices to those of jay and magpie. These would soon be nesting.

I was enjoying the blue tits cavorting in an oak when the two grey squirrels scampered into view. They seemed inseparable, usually within touching distance, jumping over each other and riding pick-a-back. Were these shinannikins significant? Consulting the books on my return I learned that mating takes place in Dec:Jan and again in May:June. It seemed that this must be loitering with intent, their January ardour cooled by the weeks of frost.

A regular in my garden is the plump cock blackcap, which shares the halved bramley apples with blackbird and thrush. Blackcaps are with me in summer, too, but recent ringing suggests that our nesters have the good sense to go to the Mediterranean in winter. My present bird is likely to have homed in on the apples from Northern Europe.

No birds eat apple peel. When restaurateurs serve the lazy option of a fresh fruit salad with apples unpeeled, I feel like presenting them with some of the waxy cups of peel pecked clean but undamaged, which pile up on my flower beds. If pointy-beaked birds can't cope under the duress of frost and hunger, I don't see why I should be expected to in the luxury of plenty! (Thrushes also leave the well-cleaned skins of jacket potatoes.)

On Sunday night the frost clamped down again. On Monday night it snowed, the calls of the local tawny owls penetrating sharp and clear across the muffled world. I woke to a depth of 8-9 inches of snow. Hebe, Escallonia and Euonymus were bowed to the ground with its weight and a big cherry-laurel torn from its roothold effectively blocked the mountain road beside my garage. Of the evergreens, only the conifers and holly were in any sort of shape. Deciduous twigs bore 2 inch columns of snow, but were still offering edible minuteae to a passing flock of tits and finches.

The school was closed, the lane serving as a toboggan run, and the row of snow-mounded cars remained unbroken. The village had ground to a halt.

People were out with shovels and grit, enjoying the sort of camaradie engendered only by natural disasters or wars and the indispensable village shop was doing a roaring trade.

The bramblings were back, up among branches laden with beech mast and down on the snow, which was thickly strewn with newly fallen husks. Back in the garden the blackcap was hopping jauntily over the snow to the cleared patch of apples and biscuit crumbs. It savoured of the best of both worlds, summer and winter.

In 1998 winter came in April, mostly over the Easter weekend, bringing us down from cloud nine, where we had been wafted by the unseasonably warm months before. Fortunately the night frosts were insufficient to nip the apple blossom. Unfortunately they were also insufficient to curb the slugs, which went their way rejoicing throughout the twelve months of that designated "Year of the slug".

During February temperatures hovered for days around 13^0 C, rising to 19^0 C (68^0 F), the long shadows incompatible with the warmth of the midday sun which shed them. The 1997 winter had not been very different but that summer was a vast improvement on the lamentable washout of 1998.

The haphazard weather regime was exemplified in 1999 when January 6th was dubbed the warmest January day since records began. Even the birds mistook the sunlit 3rd January for the first day of spring. The Taff was roaring down, as through much of the winter, with only just room for the two low-flying cormorants to get under the arches of the Ffygis railway bridge. Mallard and moorhen were safely tucked up on the banks, watching the flood debris being swept past.

I turned up School Lane, to find myself surrounded by bird song, as the avian world made whoopee after days of skulking out of drenching rain. The initial cafuffle arose from the concerted efforts of blackbird, song thrush, dunnock and robin to rout a chattering grey squirrel. When they desisted a pair of magpies took up the cudgels, with even more vocals.

The tree creeper, winkling hibernating insects from the rough bark of an old ash, ignored the squirrel, even when it settled on a branch only 2 metres below. A goldcrest, working up and down some holly twigs at my elbow, took as little notice of me and I had close views of nuthatches searching the beech trunks on both sides of the lane.

When a sparrow hawk swooped between the widely spaced trunks the loose flock of blue, great and cole tits scattered, cheeping and scolding, but the chaffinches foraging among the leaf mould held their ground, unruffled. The wren creeping round a mossy oak trunk was too cryptic to be a potential target.

Two wood pigeons flapping and fluttering in a tangle of arboreal ivy were not after the berries but were displaying to each other. Standing beak to beak they bowed low, splaying the ample tail feathers above their backs to give their partner a good view of the black and white banding above and me of the jet black below. The breeding season is a long one and they may raise several broods, but this seemed a little premature, with January scarcely begun.

To press the point that spring was in the air, a magpie flew in carrying two hefty twigs to add to its domed nest a couple of months ahead of schedule. Even the prolific jackdaws had not yet started building. Two flocks of these had amalgamated in the rollicking breeze over the swaying beech tops, ignoring the soaring buzzard above.

Seventeen species in rather fewer minutes spent in the sloping half acre of beechwood below the school would not be a bad tally at any time of year, let alone its bleakest month. And birds were not the only interest.

A single fallen beech trunk supported six species of fungi. Crusty black *Hypoxylon fragiforme* pustules shared the grey flanks of the fallen giant with jelly blobs of *Tremella encephala*, twiggy candle snuff *(Xylaria polymorpha)* the broken end with tiny toadstools. Delicate *Pleurotus* 'oyster-of-the-woods' splayed out alongside chunkier shelves of *Ganoderma applanatum*.

Other brackets, *Stereum hirsutum* and *Coriolus versicolor*, sprouted from a decaying oak log and razor strop from a fallen birch. All these were beavering away to return the might of the forest monarchs to the soil, to be incorporated into more fruit and nuts, bugs and worms to succour more birds and squirrels. Long may the cycle continue.

Orange Fairy Club,
Clavaria helvola

Yellow Waxcaps, *Hygrocybe chlorophanus*

3. From Verdant Spring to Summer Drought

In 1984 a cold wet spring was followed by fierce northerly gales in April, blowing petals prematurely from the fruit trees. The black death of hill fires commonly occurs in February or March, but this year a broad swathe of the Garth above Gwaelod was devastated by fire as late as 29th May, with the inevitable destruction of skylark, wren and dunnock nests.

Bluebell flowers pushed up among leaves charred by earlier fires along the fringes of Garth Wood and bracken sprouted from undamaged underground stems, while that all that might have helped to check the fronds lay in incinerated ruins. But June is the month of 'green peace', good to look upon, even when mismanagement has reduced the green to an impoverished bracken cover - victuals for neither man nor beast.

'Flaming June' lived up to its name, if a little hesitantly at times, and it was difficult to recall what had gone before. Early migrants were delayed, later ones on time, so all was suddenly hustle and bustle in the bird world as well as the plant world, where spring and summer flowers broke bud together.

Lesser Cudweed

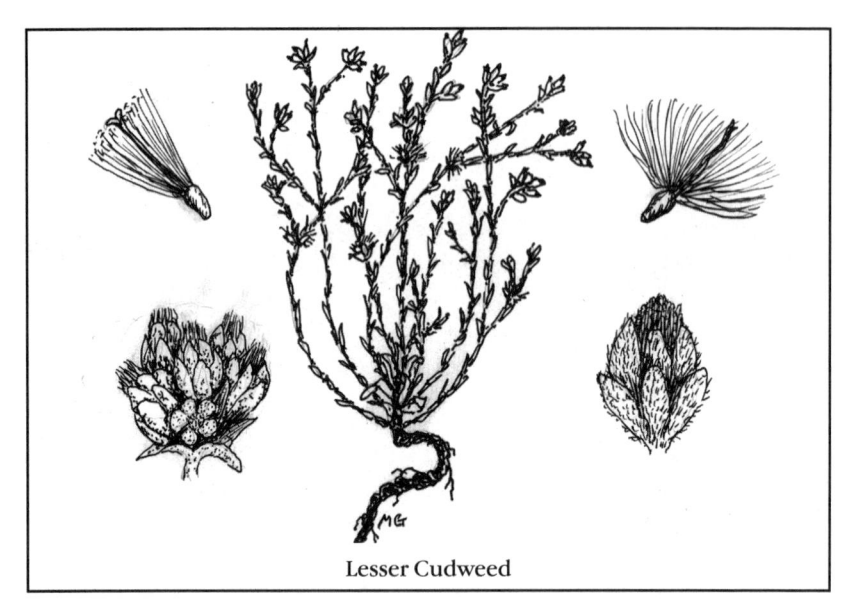

Normally first comers get the best choice of nest sites, but can be clobbered by bad weather and have to start all over again, so that latecomers score. Where cocks arrive a week or ten days before the hens, to stake out their plot, some of the travelling cohorts decimated by storms may leave a languishing population of unfulfilled bachelors or spinsters. This year most were competing on equal terms.

Chiffchaffs were among the few to beat the 1984 storms and had launched into their monotonous bisyllabic chanting by 20th March, a full six and a half weeks before we heard the fluting couplet of the cuckoo on 4th May. 31st March saw the first house martin, 23rd April, St. George's day, the first swift.

The ability to be where it is always summer is surely an idyllic way of life, but it has to be worked for and costs can be high. Once again there had been an earth-cracking drought in the Sahel Region of the Sahara, where our whitethroats, sedge warblers and sand martins swap our winter for prolonged sunshine. Only time and nest census figures would tell how badly they had suffered.

Willow warblers winter in secondary forest further south, so have only to cross the desert - a formidable enough undertaking when one considers their fragility. Clever Clogs man would fare a great deal worse in an unmechanised desert crossing with no water bottle or tucker bag.

Many of our swallows now migrate to the Cape of Good Hope or Namibia. In March when the aloes and red hot pokers are bursting into bloom at the beginning of the southern winter, they set off on a leisurely six week journey north, feeding along the way. Some were back in Gwaelod by 14th April: Southern Scandinavia had to wait until the end of April: Northern Norway until mid May. Some British-bred house martins have given up the unequal struggle and started nesting under house eaves in Capetown and who could blame them?

Those few butterflies that survived our winter as adults were lothe to leave their hibernating quarters that spring and were beaten by the bats, one of which was seen flitting through the dusk on 22nd March. Not until 27th March was the first small tortoiseshell on the wing. There were peacocks, commas and brimstones by 9th April, with various whites and orange tips during the ensuing week. Speckled woods were out by the first week of May, common blues by the second, small heaths by the third and wall browns by the fourth.

There was a glut of pussy willow seeds during the months of drought and wind. The flying fluff got everywhere, indoors and out, caught in spiders' webs, floating on pools and drifted into crannies - an efficient dispersal mechanism if ever there was one. No wonder these water-loving saplings appear in such unlikely places as wall tops.

The summer of 1984 proved hot and dry, like that of the previous year. Foliage wilted, the weak died, but many of the survivors flowered and fruited as never before. It is not only man who vegetates when pampered and well fed, but fights for racial survival when denied an adequate living. The starved lettuce does not wax fat as an individual, but remains lean and 'bolts' to ensure a plenteous supply of seed for the perennation of its kind. 1984 proved to be a spectacular mast year.

Beeches, which are shallow-rooted and particularly prone to damage by drought, were weighed down by mast. Sturdy oaks were labouring under an unaccustomed burden of acorns (as during the even more severe 1976 drought) and apple boughs were bending beneath their load. Hazel nuts, sloes, rowan and blackberries, hips and haws, all were booming. Grasses failed to tiller to feed the livestock, throwing instead copious wispy seed heads, reducing the value of the hay but good news for seed-eaters.

Tits tapping the beech mast should have received fewer hollow echoes from blind nuts than usual. Jays flocking in from the continent that autumn, as they had done in such prodigious numbers the previous year, would have found plenty of acorns, but it seemed most found enough in Europe to save them the journey. There was an acorn mountain in the Common Market in 1984 as well as a wheat mountain.

Most insects revelled in the warmth and some would be over-wintering in sheltered nooks, so not only the vegetarians would feed well during the lean months. Grasshoppers and crickets chirruped their way through the torrid days with Mediterranean verve, ants emerged from sun-baked cracks to swarm everywhere and the muggy nights were full of moths.

Moisture, laboriously extracted by plants from an unwilling soil, was being eagerly tapped by the aphid hordes. To get enough protein for their phenomenal rate of growth and reproduction, these plant bugs had to imbibe far more of the weak sugar solutions than their portly little bodies could hold. The excess oozed out at the back as honeydew. Ants which 'milked' them for their sweet fluid were helping the process along. Hover flies which preyed on aphids had a bonanza and there were local plagues of aphid-eating ladybirds, as experienced in the 1976 drought.

In 1990, another scorcher, aphids sucked their way through many generations for a full nine months, while the ladybirds were decimated by April frosts before they could get to grips with the juicy hordes.

Everything in the plant world was speeded up. We could have been in Mediterranean climes. Lawns were straw-coloured by May, blackberries ripe by July, bracken bronzed by August and the purple sheen of heather across the valley on Graig-yr-Allt faded by mid September. Fungi came late, unable to push through hard-baked soil, but burst forth in profusion as the sun-warmed ground softened in October rains.

This exceptional summer will be remembered for the swarms of butterflies and the glut of fruit and nuts. Brimstones brightened the gloom of March and October, like floating primroses, joining the riot of others in between. Hedge browns, speckled woods and small coppers had a particularly good year, as did tortoiseshells and red admirals, but few peacocks turned up in the autumn brood. Silver Y moths moved in from the south in hordes, patronising the phlox flowers, but were confused by the gaudy trumpets of the petunias, losing their way across the expanse of colour to the source of the goodies. The plant breeders had taken no account of the helpful 'honey guides'.

By 19th October fieldfares and redwings had already arrived to feed on the succulent fruits of guelder rose, rowan, hips and haws. This year was among the forerunners of those milder winters through the nineties that are taking us inexorably into the globally warmed third millennium.

4. The Last of the Summer Wine

The seering droughts of those introductory summers, which baked our land to the crispness of fresh shortbread, seemed long ago and far away as we leapt over temporary torrents and splashed through persistent puddles in the ensuing autumns. On 4th December 1984, the weather men announced that we had reached the normal rainfall quota for the year. Our fundamentally equable climate had compensated again. Then, as in September 1976, the Brecon reservoirs were brimming over with generous increments from the mountain catchment, the dried out bridges and walls of their beds once more drowned in chilly depths.

The sodden autumn was mild, but not mild enough to tempt the butteflies to linger. My last sighting of Vanessids was on 28th October. Small wonder that they lay low. A drop of rain is the size of a butterfly's head, half a bucket at a time! I, too, would wish to go into hibernation after much of such treatment.

Red, white and black knot grass caterpillars, protected by their spreading bristles, were still cavorting among persicaria leaves on 10th October. On still wintry nights, when the spine-chilling calls of hunting tawny owls came echoing up from the riverside wood, sombre-hued December moths were doggedly banging their furry noses on uncurtained window panes. Unseasonally summery December days, when buzzards were out in force, saw ladybirds still spreading gauzy wings from beneath the pillar box wing cases to "fly away home". Ants were flying as late as 5th December, when the fly hordes were sipping the last of the summer wine from nectar-laden ivy flowers.

House martins were flocking south along the Taff flyway in their hundreds daily until 30th September, when numbers dropped abruptly. My biggest counts thereafter were 20 on 9th October and 30 on 13th. A limited number of winter thrushes moved in from Northern Europe to

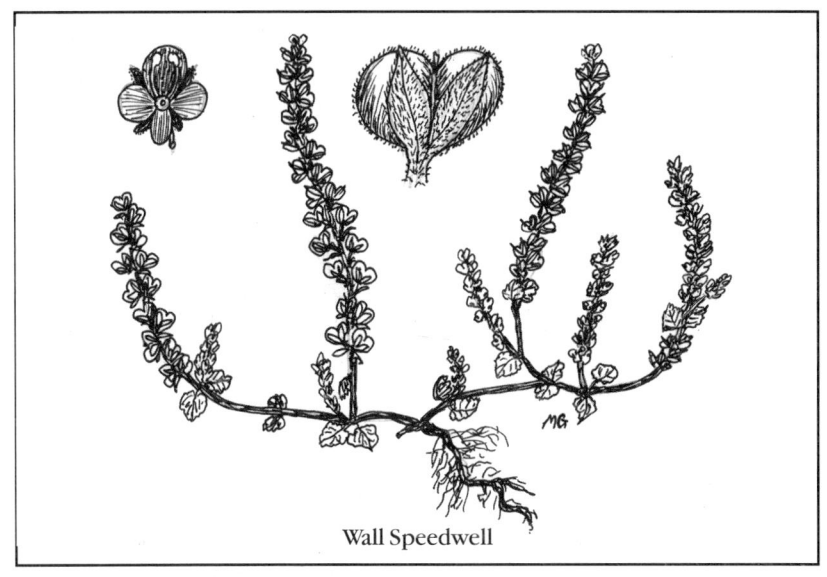

Wall Speedwell

replace them. It took these a while to work their way across from Southeast England, but flocks of fifty to a hundred were flying over Gwaelod with increasing frequency during early December and there must have been close on four hundred passing over Pentyrch from the mountain in the rain of 2nd December.

Nuthatches visited the garden more frequently, sometimes in company with roving bands of coal tits and marsh tits. Goldcrssts, too, were present with wren and dunnock among the ubiquitous blue and great tits. Out in the woods greater spotted woodpeckers were busy hammering away at wedged hazel nuts.

On the Little Garth plump acorns strewn under isolated oaks in the beechwood were germinating prematurely on 7th December, even when more than half their substance had gone to feed the local jays. Their single white roots sprouted into empty air, reddening in the diffuse light. On the sunlit rim of Walnut Tree Quarry wild strawberry and autumnal hawkbit were still flowering. It would not be long before wood spurge, wood sanicle and sweet woodruff would be doing likewise.

The environs of our other limestone quarry at Creigiau were beautified during early December by scarlet fruits of semi-evergreen Himalayan tree Cotoneaster among red, yellow and green leaves. Pink spindle fruits, crimson haws and scarlet berries of black bryony and woody nightshade added further colour among the last mauve flowers of cushion calamint and herb Robert.

Chaffinches and greenfinches had been attacking the rounded hips of field rose more avidly than the flask-shaped ones of dog rose, ripping out the seeds to leave a tattered red rim lined with cheesy yellow flesh - the wherewithal for a our wartime, vitamin-rich rosehip syrup. Pheasants sratched languidly among the fallen leaves, helping the more spritely grey squirrels to deal with the Christmas fruit and nut harvest.

Brightest of all among the sodden browns and greens were the fungi. Some twenty were identified in a Gwaelod field, from elegant 'fairy clubs' to spreading 'parasols', and no less than fifteen on a single old beech at the top of the Little Garth. Two-toothed door snails and netted slugs perambulated among the moss on this same beech, uncaring that Decmeber was the time for lying low.

1989 produced another magnificent summer, rising to a crescendo of brillance as the leaves took on their autumn tints, undiluted by too much rain. Ivy clawed its way up walls and tree trunks, to splay out in spreading clusters of yellow flowers, peppered with pollen and brimming with nectar.

Countless insects had got the message and homed in on the sugary riches, to stock up for the long hibernation ahead or as a last spree before lowering temperatures snuffed out their little lives. A congregation of six species of butterflies in mid October in this era of pesticides and pollution, must surely spell hope for our erring world.

The red admirals were present in droves, dashingly handsome with their orange-scarlet wing bands. 1996 was another peak year for these. Not all went unscathed. Neat, beak-shaped sections removed from the hind wings showed where some had been caught napping by a bird but had managed to slip away, marred but still functional.

Speckled woods were as abundant as during the August heatwave, where the dappled shade of their woodland habitat had proved a lure to some of the more committed sun-lovers. Large whites and the odd comma had joined the throng, while a few small coppers and a couple of wall browns basked on stones, absorbing heat energy to help them on their way.

The wall browns must have been from a small third brood, which is only produced in warm summers such as this. Flight times for the two main broods are June and August, the insects overwintering as caterpillars. This species had done particularly well throughout the year.

Holly blues, too, had a good year. Although never seen in flocks like the common blue, their numbers fluctuate widely, increasing markedly in hot summers. Nevertheless, they were the only butterflies to do particularly well in the washout summer of 1998. It is not unknown to see them in October, but there were none with the ivy haunting throng that I observed. They are as dependent as the others on the late flowering of the ivy, but in a different way.

The adults are uninterested in nectar, being more likely to sip from puddles, carrion, fermenting fruits or leaking tree sap, but the caterpillars are flower and fruit eaters. In May and June they feed mainly on persitent holly berries and 1989 produced a phenomenally good holly crop. In August and September they feed on ivy buds and flowers. Those so doing would have disappeared to pupate in some obscure crevice by now, to emerge as butterflies at the beginning of April, before any other blues are on the wing. The second brood flies from July through to September.

Hover flies and drone flies shared the ivy's bounty, greenbottles and bluebottles, dung flies and flesh flies, common wasps and gall wasps, bumble bees and honey bees. Ivy flowers and the so much showier Himalayan balsam down by the river were instrumental in keeping the apiarists' charges in food for as much as a month after other sources of nectar had dried up.

More red admirals flocked in to suck the fermenting juices of bruised, daw-pecked apples or settle on the stewed fruit and custard of my garden lunches, along with the odd wasp. The butterflies sipped elegantly through unfurled drinking straws, wings held proudly erect: the wasps chomped greedily with sideways working jaws, their bottoms waggling ecstatically, like the tails of sucking lambs.

All were celebrating the bounty of the sun god in his final fling of the summer. For the red admirals this was a farewell party. Begat from the offspring of butterflies winging their way north from the Mediterranean in spring, they were unable to withstand the rigours of our winter. This no longer holds for all, however. Like the blackcaps and chiff chaffs, a few have been experimenting with the idea of staying over during the nineteen nineties.

Only the queens among the wasps and bumble bees would survive the cold months, but the honey bees, sustained by a winter ration of sugar, were headed for a long drowsy spell in the dimness of their stuffy hives until tempted out by spring sunshine.

The bounty of the ivy flowers might outlive the warmth necessary to keep the insect hordes buzzing. Late flowering implies late fruiting and fleshy ivy berries are a godsend to fruit eaters in spring. The world seems at peak in April and May, but not for the frugivorous. The frequency of expectorated and defaecated ivy pips on fence posts and walls in late spring speaks eloquently of the berries' popularity.

November gales strips the last of the red and yellow leaves from maple, cherry, oak and sycamore. The twisted skeletons of ash and haw along old stone-faced field boundaries are already bared to the brutality of the winter to come. In the subsequent months the steep slope below Gwaelod village is as thickly carpeted with bronze beech leaf pennies as the gentler slopes of the Little Garth.

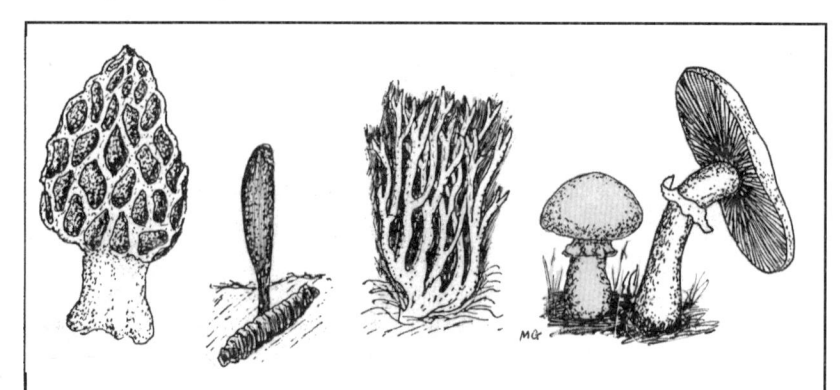

Edible Morel, *Morchella esculenta,* Caterpillar Club, *Cordyceps militaris,* White Coral fungus, *Ramaria stricta,* and Field Mushroom, *Agaricus campestris*

Pushing through the flexible coinage are the paler gold of puffballs, distorted shapes of yellow toadstools and more elegant branches of white coral fungi and orange fairy clubs. Their spreading mycelia slept unseen through the arid summer, being brought to fruition only as the sun which sustained the others abated its impact.

Slabby chunks of *Clitocybe nebularis* come bursting through the leaf mould and more elegant *Galerina rubiginosa* and *Mycena galericulata* from sodden logs. Edible morels sprout from my rhubarb clump and join the field mushrooms and elf cups among the grass. Caterpillar clubs of military scarlet *(Cordyceps militaris)* emerge from doomed chrysalids of moths which burrowed into the soil to pupate.

More permanent are the charcoal-textured dead man's fingers and candle snuff fungus on old tree boles, among firm jelly clusters of gum drops *(Leotia lubrica)*. While only these may survive in the open to show their whereabouts, all will be working quietly away through the winter achieving their destiny as recyclers of Nature's bounty.

Clitocybe nebularis, Galerina rubiginosa, and *Mycena galericulata*

5.Weather Patterns for the new Millennium

"Bio-diversity" has become the 'in' word in this last decade of the twentieth century, but "weather diversity" would be just as applicable. We have ricocheted between seering droughts and spreading floods, sultry thunderstorms and howling gales. The dreary monotony of the torrid Tropics is not something we suffer from.

Temperature-wise the maxima and minima have diverged less widely than in past decades, but more haphazardly. No longer do we roast oxen on the Thames in winter, nor ourselves on U K beaches in summer, but we are repeatedly being told that we are having 'the warmest January' or 'the coldest July' since records began.

December 1993 held the distinction of being Cardiff's 'wettest ever' month, with 11.76 inches (295 mm) of rain. This was half an inch more than the exceptional December 1934 total recorded in The Transactions of the Cardiff Naturalists' Society nearly sixty years before.

Since 1993 Stan Jones of the Cardiff Naturalists' has been keeping weather records for publication in the society's News Letter. He found the most notable feature of 1993 was the persistent rainfall towards the end of the year: 44 rain days in November:December, with 26 of these consecutive and Christmas and Boxing days the only ones in December with no measurable rainfall. The total for the year was 52.76 inches.

Once again, in 1994, the rainfall in November:December proved to be the dominant feature, with 10.52 inches in December and 17.09 inches in the two months, totalling 67.16 inches for the year. Rhondda suffered over 8 inches in the last week!

1995 produced a less horrific annual total of 49.92 inches, but gave us the second wettest January since rainfall records began in 1727. That month saw 9.12 inches - not a lot more than the 8.58 and 8.14 inches in the two previous years. The record breaking figures for 1995 related to temperature, this year producing the warmest twelve months and the hottest August since temperature recording began in 1659, the sunniest year since 1909 and the mildest autumn of the century.

In 1996 rainfall climbed a little, to 50.77 inches, with October:November the wettest months (8.65 and 8.04 inches). The record breaking trends continued temperature-wise, but in the wrong direction, with the lowest amount of sunshine in January since that otherwise sunny year of 1909. 5th February brought the most significant fall of snow for some years, but this was one of only five days when snow fell.

In 1997 rainfall was back up to 57.65 inches, with February and August the wettest months, producing 9.63 and 9.54 inches of these, with over 7 inches in both November and December. In this we were out of step with the rest of the U K, which registered the driest two year period (May 1995 to April 1997) since records began, this counteracted by the wettest June for 130 years, the wettest August for twenty years and the sunniest October for forty years. Our June rainfall was only 4.2 inches and January was the driest since 1796, with 0.71 inches in Cardiff.

We had the feeling that it rained through most of the 1998 summer. In fact the annual total was 65.45 inches, or 1.71 inches less than in 1994. Nearly 13 inches of this was in October. On January 9th the temperature reached 14^0 C (58^0 F), the mildest January day on record. (The same was claimed for January 6th in 1999, when thermometers crept up to 15^0 C.).

February 1998 was the mildest February on record, with maximum temperatures in double figures on each day between the 9th and 27th and as high as 16⁰ C on the 11th and 12th, the unseasonable mildness rousing some of our butterflies from hibernation.

Alas, the 1998 February sunshine dissolved into 7 inches of rain in the first seven days of March. Sleet fell on the 4th and 11th April and light snow on the 14th. This was the only snow of the year, saved up for the Easter holiday week, but temperatures rose to 18⁰ C before the end of that so-called spring month. May improved, thermometers registering over 20⁰ C (70⁰ F) on sixteen days and up to 25⁰ C on one, this scarcely bettered in August.

This year of 1998 saw the wettest June in Wales since records began (7.73 inches), or three times the average, this setting the pattern for the rest of the year, but there were twenty seven July days when the temperature exceeded 20⁰ C.

The 8th February snow fall in 1999 that caused school closure and road disruption as close as Pontypridd, scarcely affected our community. Snow lay on the grass for a day but barely at all on the roads, although traces remained on the high ground for nearly a week. I am indebted to Stan Jones for the foregoing weather data.

Individual efforts to curb global warming can have little impact, but our conservationists hatched up a plan to mitigate its effects as the twentieth century drew to its close. This major project was in one of our prime sites, the Coed-y-Bedw Nature Reserve, to improve accessibilty and make the area more people-friendly without disadvantaging the wildlife.

Over the years the hard-working Glamorgan Wildlife Trust wardens have done most of the maintenance work here, with bands of volunteers. During the second week of February in 1999 they were joined by a businesslike squad of men from the Royal Regiment of Wales. These were based at Maindy Barracks in Cardiff, the helicopter which transported materials from the Taffside football field to the nature reserve came from Netheravon in Wiltshire.

The regiment was just back from the "Exercise Dead Moon" tour of South Africa, where it had been helping to commemorate the 120th anniversary of the battles of Rorke's Drift and Isandhlwana. It was the height of summer there. The day they started work at Gwaelod-y-Garth was that of the year's first snowfall. Fortunately the sun shone for most of the rest of the week and they had to battle with mud rather than hard-frozen ground. On completion they were returning to their base in Germany which, in common with much of Europe, would probably be under more permanent snow, in weather unmitigated by our benevolent Gulf Stream.

The project on which the army laboured was the completion of a circular path round the steep valley woodland. Much was already in place, but the most difficult part, across the quagmire occupying the lower eastern end of Cwm Llwydrew, had been impossible to achieve with the available man power.

An approximate length of 100 metres of timber structures was necessary to span the swamp and scale the formidable slope on the south side. It started with a 5 m span of timber bridge across the brook, joining a 30 m length of board walk over wet peat and then a 5 m length of stairway up a steep gradient, culminating in a 60 m zig-zag line of steps joining up with the southern path.

Board Walk constructed by the Welsh Guards in the Coed-y-Bedw reserve, in February 1999.

All the timber used was Welsh oak. Generous grant aid came from the Forstry Commission, former owners of the site, and the Cardiff County Council, new administrators since our community was annexed in the latest shuffling of boundaries.

The official viewing day on Thursday 13th February was a public relations exercise for the army, in the hope of drawing new recruits. A rash of camouflaged tents and trucks appeared on the football field downstream of the new South Glade housing estate, with some of the army personnel in full camouflage gear, the goat handlers in scarlet.

Local dogs were most intrigued by the magnificent white regimental mascot with his fine spread of silver-tipped horns. They had to be forcibly restrained from making his closer acquaintance!

Local bird watchers (and there were plenty there as stalwarts from the county Wildlife Trust converged from further west) were most intrigued by the four buzzards which came winging out from the Little Garth beechwood, to suss out the repeated passing of the helicopter.

Such a noisy military intrusion should have precipitated a strategic retreat, but not a bit of it. The raptors were used to helicopters in the main Taff flyway, but not so intimately in their own side valley. A deep prru-prruk croaking heralded the arrival of a wedge-tailed raven. The peregrines did not emerge to investigate and the tawny owl seen by the warden just before the first helicopter touchdown, wisely chose to stay out of sight for the rest of the day..

The photographers and other media men had to cope with more mud on site than they were used to, but the walkway was already well advanced and looking most impressive. Three months hence the whole slope around the zig zag stairway would be white with the flowers of wild garlic, smiling down on kingcups in the fen peat below.

The prophets of global warming predict more rain in the future. We are starting to prepare. Locals and visitors alike will be able to circumnavigate our show piece virtually dry-shod.

So what of the future? As nuthatches extend their range northwards, more blackcaps and chiffchaffs risk spending winters here, cettis warblers and little egrets move into South Wales from Southern Europe and frogspawn appearing as early as 15th January in 1998, shall we be far-seeing enough to deal with less pleasing changes?

The commemorative beech tree planted by Sir David Attenborough in Coed-y-Bedw on a wintry 12th November day in 1985 will be an upstanding youngster of fifteen years at the end of this century. By the turn of the next it could be catching up with its more venerable neighbours in this haven of ever-changing permanence. Conservationists, in preserving the status quo, must be in the vanguard of our forward thinking to enhance it.

Candle Snuff. *Xylosphaera hypoxylon*, Gum Drops, *Leotia lubrica* and Dead Man's Fingers or Wood Club fungus, *Xylosphaera polymorpha*.

APPENDIX 1: FLOWERING PLANTS AND FERNS mentioned in the text.

Alphabetically under vernacular names

Vernacular	Qualifier	Scientific
Agrimony		Agrimonia eupatoria
Alder,	common	Alnus glutinosa
	grey	A. incana
Alder buckthorn		Frangula alnus
Anemone,	wood	Anemone nemorosa
Angelica		Angelica sylvestris
Arum, wild		Arum maculatum
Ash		Fraxinus excelsior
Aspen		Populus tremula
Balsam,	Himalayan or Indian	Impatiens glandulifera
Barren strawberry		Potentilla sterilis
Bartsia, red		Odontites verna
Basil		Clinopodium vulgare
Bedstraw,	heath	Gallum saxatile
	hedge	G. mollugo
	lady's	G. verum,
	marsh	G. palustre
Bee Orchid		Ophrys apifera
Beech		Fagus sylvatica
Bell flower,	ivy-leaved	Wahlenbergia hederacea
Bent grass		Agrostis tenuis
Barberry		Berberis spp.
Betony		Stachys officinalis
Bilberry		Vaccinium myrtilus
Birch,	downy	Betula pubescens
	silver	B. pendula (verrucosa)
Birds nest	orchid	Neottia nidus-avis
	yellow	Monotropa hypopitys
Bindweed,	black	Polygonum convolvulus
	field	Convolvulus arvensis
	great	Calystegia sylvestris
	hedge,	C. sepium
Birds-foot trefoil,	common	Lotus corniculatus
	greater	L. uliginosus
Bishopsweed		Aegopodium podagraria
Bistort		Polygonum bistorta
Bittercress,	hairy	Cardamine hirsuta
	wavy	C. flexuosa
Bitter-sweet		Solanum dulcamara
Blackberry		Rubus fruticosus agg.
Black bindweed		Polygonum convolvulus
Black bryony		Tamus communis
Black medick		Medicago lupulina
Black nightshade		Solanum nigrum
Blackthorn		Prunus spinosa
Bluebell		Hyacinthoides non-scripta
Bogbean		Menyanthes trifoliata
Brier rose		Rosa spp,
Broad-leaved pandweed		Potamogeton natans
Brome,	sterile	Bromus sterilis
	wood false	Brachypodium sylvaticum
Brooklime		Veronica beccabunga
Brookweed		Samolus valerandi
Broom,	common	Cytisus scoparius
	Spanish	Spartium junceum
Buckthorn,	alder	Frangula, alnus
	purging or common	Rhamnus catharticus

Common name	Variety	Scientific name
Buddleja		Buddleja davidii
Bugle		Ajuga reptans
Bullace		Prunus, institia
Burdock		Arctium minus
Bur marigold,	nodding	Bidens cernua
	tripartite	B. tripartita
Burnet,	salad	Sanguisorba minor (Poterium)
	saxifrage,	Pimpinella saxifraga
Bur-reed,	branched,	Sparganium erectum
Butterbur		Petasites hybridus
Buttercup,	bulbous	Ranunculus bulbosus
	creeping	R. repens
	meadow or upright	R. acris
Butterfly bush		Buddleja davidii
Calamint,	common	Calamintha sylvatica (ascendens)
	cushion	Clinopodium vulgare
Campion,	red	Silene dioica (Melandrium rubrum)
	white	Silene alba
Canadian pondweed		Elodea canadensis
Carrot,	wild	Daucus carota
Castor oil,		Ricinus communis
Cats-ear		Hypochoeris radicata
Cats-tail		Typha latifolia
Celandine,	greater	Chelidonium majus
	lesser	Ranunculus ficaria
Centaury		Erythraea centaurium
Cherry	laurel	Prunus lauro-cerasus
	wild	P. cerasus
Chestnut,	horse	Aesculus hippocastanum
	sweet or Spanish	Castanea sativa,
Chickweed,	cammon	Stellaria media
	greater	S. neglecta
	mouse-ear	Cerastium glomeratum & spp.
Cinquefoil,	creeping	Potentilla reptans
Cleavers		Galium aperine
Clematis,	wild	Clematis vitalba
Clover,	hares-foot	Trifolium arvense
	red	T. pratense
	white	T. repens
	yellow	T. dubium
Club rush		Eleocharis palustris
Cocksfoot grass		Dactylis glomerata
Coltsfoot		Tussilago farfara
Columbine		Aquilegia vulgaris
Comfrey		Symphytum X uplandicum
Corn feverfew		Chrysanthemum parthenium
Cornish moneywart		Sibthorpia eurapaea
Corn spurrey		Spergula arvensis
Cotton-grass,	many headed	Eriophorum angustifolium
Cow parsley		Anthriscus sylvestris
Cowslip		Primula veris
Cow wheat		Melampyrum pratense
Crabapple		Mallus sylvestris
Cranesbill,	out-leaved	Geranium dissectum
	doves-foot	G. molle
	meadow	G. pratense
	two-flowered	G. columbinum

Creeping yellow-cress	Rorippa sylvestris
Crested dogstail grass	Cynosurus cristatus
Crosswart.	Cruciata laevipes (Galium)
Crown vetch	Coronilla varia
Cuckoo flower	Cardamine pratensis
Cuckoo pint	Arum maculatum
Cudweed, lesser	Filago minima
marsh	Gnaphalium uliginosum
Currant	Ribes sylvatica and spp.
Cypress, lawsons	Chamaecyparis lawsoniana
Daffodil	Narcissus pseudo-narcissus
Dandelion	Taraxacum officinale agg.
Deer sedge	Scirpus caespitosue (Trichophorum)
Devils-bit scabious	Succisa pratensis
Dogs mercury	Mercurialis perennis
Dogwood	Cornus sanguinea (Thelycrania)
Duckweed, ivy-leaved	Lemna trisulca
lesser	L. minor
Early purple orchid	Orchis mascula
Elder	Sambucus nigra
Elecampane	Inula helenium
Elm, English	Ulmus procera
wych	U. glabra
Enchanters nightshade	Circaea lutetiana
Evening primrose, large-flowered	Oenothera erythrosepala
Welsh	O. cambrica
Everlasting pea, broad	Lathyrus latifolius
Eyebright	Euphrasia spp.
Fairy flax	Linum catharticum
False oxlip	Primula veris X vulgaris
Ferns: Bracken	Pteridium aquilinum
Broad buckler	Dryopteris dilatata
Hard	Blechnum spicant
Harts-tongue	Scolopendrium vulgare (Phyllites)
Lady	Athyrium filix-femina
Maidenhair spleenwort	Asplenium trichomanes
Male	Dryopteris filix-mas
Polypody, common	Polypodium vulgare
greater	P. interjectum
Rusty-back	Ceterach officinarum
Soft shield	Polystichum setiferum
Wall rue	Asplenium ruta-muraria
Fescue, red	Festuca rubra
sheeps	F. ovina
Field cranesbill	Geranium pratense
Field daisy	Bellis perennis
Field madder	Sherardia arvensis
Field maple	Acer campestre
Fig	Ficus carica
Figwort, knotted	Scrophularia nodosa
water	S. aquatica
Fleabane	Pulicaria dysenterica
Flote grass	Glyceria fluitans
Fools watercress	Apium. nodiflorum
Forget-me-not	Myosotis spp.
Foxglove	Digitalis purpurea
Fuchsia	Fuchsia magellanica

Garlic,	hedge	Alliaria petiolata
	wild	Allium ursinum
Germander speedwell		Veronica chamaedrys
Giant fir		Abies grandis
Gipsywort		Lycopus europaeus
Goatsbeard		Tragopogon pratensis
Globe thistle		Echinops Sp.
Golden rod,	wild	Solidago virgaurea
Golden saxifrage		Chrysosplenium oppositifolium
Goldilocks		Ranunculus auricomus
Gooseberry		Ribes uva-crispa
Gorse,	European	Ulex europaea
	western	U. gallii
Goutweed,		Aegopodium podagraria
Grannies nightcap		Aquilegia vulgaris
Greater stitchwort		Stellaria holostea
Greater water plantain		Alisma plantago-aquatica
Green alkanet		Pentaglottis sempervirens
Ground elder		Aegopodlux podagraria
Ground ivy		Glechoma hederacea
Guelder rose		Viburnum opulus
Harebell		Campanula rotundifolia
Haresfoot clover		Trifolium arvense
Hawksbeard,	smooth	Crepis capillaris
Hawkbit,	rough	Leontodon hispidus
	autumnal	L. autumalis
Hawkweed,	mouse-ear	Pilosella officinarum (Hieracium)
	(a rare sp)	Hieracium exotericum f. grandidens
Hawthorn		Crataegus monogyna
Hazel		Corylus avellana
Heartsease		Viola arvensis
Heath	cross-leaved	Erica tetralix
	fine~leaved	E. cinerea
Heather,	ling	Calluna vulgaris
Hedge garlic		Alliaria petiolata
Hedge woundwort		Stachys sylvestris
Helleborine,	broad	Epipactis helleborine
Hemlock,	common	Conium maculatum
	western	Tsuga heterophylla
	water dropwort	Oenanthe crocata.
Hemp agrimony		Eupatorlun cannabinum
Hemp nettle		Galeopsis tetrahit
Herb Paris		Paris quadrifolia
Himalayan balsam		Impatiens glandulifera
Hogweed		Heracleum sphondylium
Holly		Ilex aquifolium
Honeysuckle		Lonicera periclymenum
Hop		Humulus lupulus
Hop trefoil		Trifolium. campestre
Hornbeam		Carpinus betulus
Horsetail,	field	Equisetum arvense
	giant	E. telmateia
	marsh	E. palustre
	shade	E. pratense
	water	E, fluviatile
	wood	E, sylvaticum
Ice plant		Sedum spectabile
Iris, yellow		Iris pseudacorus

Ivy		Hedera helix
Ivy-leaved bellflower		Wahlenbergia hederacea
Ivy-leaved toadflax		Cymbalaria muralis
Jack-by-the-hedge		Aliaria petiolata
Japanese honeysuckle		Leycesteria formosa
		Lonicera nitida
Japanese knotweed		Reynoutria japonica (Polygonum cuspidatum)
Japanese spindle		Euonymus japonicus
Kerria		Kerria Japonica
Kidney vetch		Anthyllis vulneraria
Kingcup		Caltha palustris
Knapweed,	common	Centaurea nigra
	greater	C. scabiosa
Knot grass		Polygonum aviculare
		F. arenastrum
Lady's finger		Anthyllis vulneraria
Lady's smock		Cardamine pratensis
Larch,	European	Larix decidua (europaea)
	hybrid	L. X eurolepis
	Japanese	L. kaempferi (leptolepis)
Lesser spearwort		Ranunculus flammula
Lesser stitchwort		Stellaria graminea
Lime,	large-leaved	Tilia platyphylla
Lousewort,	common	Pedicularis palustris
	marsh	P. sylvatica
Madder,	field	Sherardia arvensis
Mahonia		Mahonia aquifolium
Mallow.	common	Malva sylvestris
	musk	M. moschata
	tree	Lavatera arborea
Marestail		Hippuris vulgaris
Marjoram		Origanum vulgare
Marsh bedstraw		Galium palustre
Marsh cudweed		Gnaphalium uliginosum
Marsh foxtail grass		Alopecurus geniculatus
Marsh yellow-cress		Rorippa islandica
Mat grass		Nardus stricta
Meadow plume thistle		Cirsium dissectum
Meadowsweet		Filipendula ulmaria
Meadow vetchling		Lathyrus pratensis
Melilot		Melilotus spp.
Michaelmas daisy		Aster sp,
Mignonette,	wild	Reseda lutea
Milkmaid		Cardamine pratensis
Milkwort,	heath	Polygala serpyllifolia
Mimulus		Mimulus guttatus
Mint,	corn	Mentha arvensis
	peppermint	M. X piperata
	round-leaved or apple	M. rotundifolia
	verticillata	M. X verticillata
	water	M. aquatica
Monkey flower		Mimulus guttatus
Moon daisy		Leucanthemum vulgare (Chysanthemum)
Montbretia		Crocosmia X crocosmiifolia
Moschatel		Adoxa moschatellina
Mossy saxifrage		Saxifraga hypnoides
Mouse-ear chickweed		Cerastium holostioides & spp.
Mouse-ear hawkweed		Pilosella officinarum

Mud crowfoot		Ranunculus omiophyllus
Mugwort		Artemisia absynthium
Mullein, great		Verbascum thapsus
Nettle		Urtica dioica
Nipplewort		Lapsana communis
Oak,	durmast or sessile	Quercus petraea (sessiliflora)
	lowland or pedunculate	Q. robur (pedunculata)
Old man's beard		Clematis vitalba
Onion couch		Arrhenatherum eliatius
Orchid,	bee	Ophrys apifera
	bird's nest	Neottia nidus-avis
	broad helleborine	Epipactis helleborine,
	common spotted	Dactylorhiza fuchsii
	early purple	Orchis mascula
	heath spotted	Dactylorhiza ericetorum
	pyramidal	Anacamptis pyramidalis
Ox-eye daisy		Leucanthemum vulgare
Pampas grass		Cortaderia selloana
Parsnip,	yellow	Pastinaca sativa
Pearly everlasting		Anaphalis margaritacea
Periwinkle,	greater	Vinca major
	lesser	V. minor
Persicaria,	amphibious	Polygonum amphibium
	common redshanks	P. persicaria
	noded	P. nodosum
	pale	P. lapathifolium
Petty whin		Genista anglica
Pignut		Conopodium majus
Pine,	lodgepole	Pinus contorta
	scots	P. sylvestris
Pineappleweed		Matricaria matricarioides
Plantain,	greater	Plantago major
	ribwort	P. lanceolata
Ploughman's spikenard		Inula conyza
Primrose		Primula vulgaris
Poplar,	balsam	Populus trichocarpa
	Italian black	P. serotina
	white	P. alba
Poppy,	long smooth-headed	Papaver dubium
	opium	P. somniferum
	oriental	P. orientale
Purple loosestrife		Lythrum salicaria
Purple moor grass		Molinia caerulea.
Pussy willow		Salix caprea, S. cinerea
Quaking grass		Briza media
Queen Anne's lace		Anthriscus sylvestris
Ragged robin		Lychnis flos-cuculi
Ragwort,	common	Senecio jacobaea
	marsh	S. aquaticus
R a m s o n s		Allium ursinum
Ra s p b e r r y		Rubus idaeus
Red bartsia		Odontites verna
Red campion		Silene dioica
Red rattle		Pedicularis sylvatica
Reed		Phragmites australis.
Reed canary grass		Phalaris arundinacea
Reedmace		Typha latifolia
Reed sweet grass		Glyceria maxima
Rhododendron		Rhododendron ponticum

Rhubarb		Rheum rhabarbarum
Ribwort plantain		Plantago lanceolata
Rock rose		Helianthemum spp.
Rose,	burnet	Rosa pimpinellifolia
	dog	R. canina
	field	R. arvensis
Rosebay willow-herb		Epilobium angustifoliam
Rose-of-sharon		Hypericum calycinum
Rowan or mountain ash		Sorbus aucuparia
Rue-leaved saxifrage		Saxifraga tridactylita
Rush,	hard	Juncus inflexus
	jointed	J. articulatus
	pathfinder	J. tenuifolius
	soft	J. effusus
	toad	J. bufonius
Russian vine		Polygonum balschuanicum
Saint John's wort,	hairy	Hypericum hirsutum
	perforated	H. perforatum
	slender	H. pulchrum
	spotted	H. maculatum
Salad burnet		Sanguisorba minor (Poterium)
Sallow,	goat	Salix caprea
	grey	S. cinerea
Sanicle		Sanicula europaea
Saxifrage,	golden	Chrysosplenium oppositifolium
	mossy	Saxifraga hypnoides
	rue-leaved	S. tridactylita
Scabious,	greater	Knautia arvensis
	lesser	Scabiosa columbaria
Scarlet Pimpernel		Anagallis arvensis
Scorpion grass		smaller Myosotis spp.
Sedge,	oval	Carex ovalis
	remote	C. remota
	smooth-stalked	C. laevigata
	star	C. echinata
	wood	C. sylvatica.
	yellow	C. demissa
Self heal		Prunella vulgaris
Sheep's bit		Jasione montana
Sheep's fescue		Festuca ovina
Sheep's sorrel		Rumex acetosella
Shepherd's purse		Capsella bursa-pastoris
Silverweed		Potentilla anserina
Skullcap,	lesser	Scutellaria minor
Sloe		Prunus spinosus
Smooth hawksbeard		Crepis capillaris
Snake root		Polygonum bistorta
Snowberry		Symphoricarpos rivularis
Snowdrop		Galanthus nivalis
Soapwort		Saponaria officinalis
Solomon's Seal		Polygonatum multiflorum
Sorrel,	common	Rumex acetosa
	sheep's	R. acetosella.
Spearwort,	greater	Ranunculus lingua
	lesser	R. flammula
Speedwell,	field	Veronica agrestis
	germander	V. chamaedrys
	heath or common	V. officinalis
	ivy-leaved	V. hederacea

Spindle,	European	Euonymus europaeus
	Japanese	E. japonica
Spring whitlow-grass		Erophila verna
Spruce,	Norway	Picea abies
	sitka	Picea stitchensis
Spurge, wood		Euphorbia amygdaloides
Stitchwort,	greater	Stellaria holostea
	lesser	S. graminea
Stonecrop,	white	Sedum album
	yellow	S. acre
Strawberry,	barren	Potentilla sterilis
	wild	Fragaria vesca
Strawberry tree		Arbutus unedo
Stream crowfoot		Ranunculus penicillatus
Summer snowflake		Leucojum aestivum
Sweet vernal Srass		Anthoxanthum odoratum
Sweet violet		Viola odorata
Sweet woodruff		Asperula odorata
Sycamore		Acer pseudoplatanus
Tall oat grass		Arrhenatherum elatius
Tare		Vicia sativa
Teasel		Dipsacus fullonum
Thale cress		Arabidopsis thaliana
Thistle,	creeping	Cirsium repens
	marsh	C. palustre
	meadow plume	C. dissectum
	nodding	Carduus nutans
	spear	Cirsium vulgare
Thyme		Thymus drucei
Timothy grass		Phleum pratense
Toadflax,	ivy-leaved	Cymbalaria muralis
	lesser	Chaenorhinum minus
	pale	Linaria repens
	yellow	L vulgaris
Tomato		Lycopersicum esculentum
Toothwort		Lathraea squamaria
Tormentil		Potentilla erecta
Totter grass		Briza media
Traveller's joy		Clematis vitalba
Tufted hair grass		Deschampsia caespitosa
Tufted vetch		Vicia cracca
Tutsan		Hypericum androsaemum
Valerian,	cats or common	Valeriana officinalis
	marsh	V. dioica
Vetch,	bush	Vicia sepium
	common	V. sativa
	hairy	V. hirsuta
	tufted	V. cracca
Violet,	dog	Viola riviniana
	early wood	V. reichenbachiana
	marsh	V. palustre
	sweet	V. odorata
Viper's bugloss		Echium vulgare
Wall lettuce		Mycelis muralis
Walnut		Juglans regia
Water blinks		Montia verna

Water cress,	creeping	Rorippa sylvestris
	yellow fool's	Apium nodosum
	common	Nasturtium officinale
Water forget-me-not		Myosotis scorpioides
Water mint		Mentha aquatica
Water pepper		Polygonum hydropiper
Water plantain,	greater	Alisma plantago-aquatica
Water purslane		Lythrum portula (Peplis)
Water starwort,	common	Callitriche stagnalis
Wavy bittercress		Cardamine flexuosa
Wavy hair grass		Deschampsia flexuosa
Wayfaring tree		Viburnum lantana
Weld		Reseda luteola
Western hemlock		Tsuga heterophylla
Whimberry		Vaccinium myrtilus
White goosefoot		Chenopodium album
Whitethorn		Crataegus monogyna
Willow		Salix spp,
Willow herb,	broad-leaved	Epilobium montanum
	greater	E. hirsutum
	hairy	E. parviflorum
	New Zealand	E. nerterioldes
	rosebay	E. angustifolium
Winter cress		Barbarea vulgaris
Winter heliotrope		Petasites fragrans
Wood anemone		Anemone nemorosa
Wood avens		Geum urbanum
Woodland. loosestrife		Lysimachia nemorum
Wood melick		Melica uniflora.
Woodruff		Asperula odorata
Wood sage		Teucrium scorodonia
Wood sedge		Carex sylvatica
Wood sorrel		Oxalis acetosella
Wood soft grass		Holcus mollis
Wood speedwell		Veronica montana.
Wood spurge		Euphorbia amygdaloides
Woody nightshade		Solanum dulcamara
Wormwood		Artemisia vulgaris
Yarrow		Achillea millefolium
Yellow archangel		Lamiastrum galeobdolon (G.luteum)
Yellow bird's nest		Monotropa hypopitys
Yellow pea		Lathyrus pratensis
Yellow pimpernel		Lysimachia nemorum
Yellow rattle.		Rhinanthus minor
Yellow rocket		Barbarea vulgaris
Yellow watercress		Rorippa sylvestris
Yew,	English	Taxus baccata
	Irish	T. baccata fastigiata
Yorkshire fog grass		Holcus lanatus

Suggestions for further reading

Adams, John, 1986. Ogof Ffynnon Taf; new find under quarrying threat. Descent, The Cavers' Magazine. 70

Anderson, J.C.G., 1972. Buried channels and the South Wales Valleys Proc. S. Wales Inst. of Engineers; Vol. LXXXVIII, Cardiff.

Andrews, E., Howell, P. and Johnson, K. 1993, Otter survey of Wales,1991 The Vincent Wildlife Trust.

Benson-Evans, K.,1969. Botanical report on the Taff catchment. Cardiff.

Brown, the Rev. Lee, 1983. Ffynnon Taff, Cardiff,

Chapman, Phil, 1982. Caves and caving: spiders and flies. Bull., British Cave Research Association.
1983. Caves and caving: Beetles, millipedes and springtails. Bull., British Cave Research Association.

Chappell, Edgar L., 1940. Historic Melingriffith. Cardiff.

Cooke, T.C. 1977. Wenvoe and Walnut Tree Quarries. BSc. thesis, unpublished Cardiff.

Edwards, R.W., 1969. Fish Survey of the Taff Catchment and survey of aquatic invertebrates. UWIST, Cardiff

Edwards, R,W., Benson-Evans, K., Williams, P. and Williams, R. 1971. A biological survey of the River Taff. UWIST, Cardiff.

Evans, F.G., 1872. The Garth Iron Mines in 1872, Trans. Cardiff Nats. III.

Glamorgan Bird Club, 1994 - 1997, Mid & South Glam. Bird Reps. 1994 & 95. Eastern Glam. Bird Reps. 1996 & 97.

Hussey, X.S, 1967, Little Garth Caves. Trans. Cardiff Nats. XCIII,

Jefferson, T., 1982. Caves and Caving. Life in the twilight zone. Bull. British Cave Research Association.
1989. Species recorded in Lesser Garth Cave.
Limestone and caves in Wales: E.T.Ford.

John, Roger, 1990. Little Garth Underground Lake. Community Link; July.

Jones, Stanley, 1993-98. Annual weather reports. Cardiff Nats. Newsletters.

Llewellyn, Don, 1989. Rediscovering the furnaces of the old Pentyrch Iron works. Community Link.22,

Lewis, T,E. 1912 Finds in the Little Garth Cave. Unpublished. Cardiff.

Manly, G., 1902, An historic and picturesque guide through the counties of Monmouthshire, Glamorgan and Brecknock.

Mawle, G.W., Winstone, A. and Brooker, M.P. 1986. Salmon & sea trout in the Taff. Past, present and future. Nature in Wales. V. 4. 1. & 2,

Mid-Glam. Co. Council, 1971-72. The Taff Valley Project. Internal documents,

Nicholson, 1840, The Cambrian Travellers' guide of 1840,

Oldham, Tony, 1985. The caves of the southern outcrop, Limestone caves of South Wales, no. 5.

Pentyrch History Society, 1997. Pentyrch, Creiglau and Gwaelod-y-Garth, Archives photographs series, Glos.

Riden, Phillip, 1992. Early ironworks in the Lower Taff Valley. Jour. Glam. Hist. Soc,

Thomas, J.W., 1877. On the waters of Taffs Well. Trans, Cardiff Nats. Soc. IX,

Tyler, John, 1988, Iron in the Soul. Iron mines in the Little Garth, Cardiff.

Wheeler, R.E.M., 1960. Excavations in the Little Garth Cave. Unpublished.

Acknowledgements

I am indebted to local residents who have helped with information and reminiscences. Jack and Clive Francis of Ynys Gau allowed access to their land and gave information on the farming. Andy Kendall, Rhian Hicks and Geoff Watkins put me in the picture regarding the Little Garth caves and quarrying.

The three wardens of the Coed-y-Bedw Nature Reserve, Brian Stiles, Alan Lock and Cliff Woodhead, kept me informed about management operations and, along with the bird ringers George Wood and Alex Coxhead, supplied data on recoveries of ringed birds. Other ornithological information came from Paul Wolfle, Dave Palmer and Richard Smith. Critical plant and invertebrate specimens were identified by Roy Perry, George Hutchinson, June Chatfield and Cynthia Merrett of the National Museum of Wales.

Octogenarians, the late Willie Charles Thomas of Gwaelod and Mr. Bale of Gelynis Farm, shared interesting recollections on the industrial history, Derek Thomas and the late David Jenkins provided useful discussion an surviving relics.

Gordon Atkins and the late Valerie Miles recalled facets of past life in the villages and Stan Jones supplied meteorological data.

My thanks go to all of these and others who have helped in various ways.

About the Author

Born in Ealing in 1921, Mary Gillham left her London office job at the outbreak of the second world war to join the Womens' Land Army, some of the experiences of those early years recounted in her "Town Bred: Country Nurtured".

In the post war years sbe attended the University of Wales as an agricultural student, gaining a first class honours in botany at Aberystwyth and a doctorate in Island Ecology at Bangor. In later life she spent thirty six years on the lecturing staff of the University in Cardiff, involved in adult education and the conducting of field courses in Britain and overseas, from the Caribbean to the Seychelles.

In between she lectured in the universities of Exeter (Devon), Massey (New Zealand), Melbourne (Australia) and Kano (Nigeria), the Antipodes posts held in conjunction with ecological research on Southern Hemisphere sea-bird islands, Other research projects were undertaken around South Africa, in the Indian Ocean and the Bahamas and on Macquarrie Island, as one of the first contingent of four women to travel South with the Australian Antarctic Division in 1959-60. Some of these experiences have been written about in scientific journals and anecdotal travel books.

The present work follows a series of seven natural history books on the South Wales coast and several with other authors in the upper Taff Valley around Merthyr and the Brecon Beacons.